# REVOLUTIONARY TIME

# REVOLUTIONARY TIME

On Time and Difference in Kristeva and Irigaray

Fanny Söderbäck

Cover art: Anne Thulin, *Swerve*, pigment, acrylic, and wax on paper, 2018

Published by State University of New York Press, Albany

For information, contact State University of New York Press, Albany, NY www.sunypress.edu

**Library of Congress Cataloging-in-Publication Data**

Names: Söderbäck, Fanny, 1978– author.
Title: Revolutionary time : on time and difference in Kristeva and Irigaray / Fanny Söderbäck.
Description: Albany : State University of New York, 2019. | Includes bibliographical references and index.
Identifiers: LCCN 2018059958 | ISBN 9781438476995 (hardcover : alk. paper) | ISBN 9781438477008 (pbk. : alk. paper) | ISBN 9781438477015 (ebook)
Subjects: LCSH: Time. | Sex differences. | Feminist theory. | Kristeva, Julia, 1941– | Irigaray, Luce.
Classification: LCC B638 .S63 2019 | DDC 115—dc23
LC record available at https://lccn.loc.gov/2018059958

10 9 8 7 6 5 4 3 2 1

*For James, who taught me how to ride the swerves.*

# Contents

Acknowledgments                                                      xi

Abbreviations                                                        xv

## PART I. WHY TIME?

Introduction: Time for Change                                        3
　　French Feminism and the Problem of Time                          5
　　On Time and Change                                               10
　　Decolonial and Queer Critiques of Time                           15
　　A Note on Language                                                20

## PART II. REVOLUTIONARY TIME

1　Linear Time, Cyclical Time, Revolutionary Time                    29
　　From Beauvoir's Sexual Division of Temporal Labor
　　　　to Revolutionary Time                                         33
　　Three Temporal Models, Three Feminist Waves                      38
　　Kristeva and Irigaray on Time and Difference                     45
　　Conclusion                                                       50

2　Alterity and Alteration                                           53
　　Time, Change, and Sexuate Difference                             55
　　Remaking Immanence and Transcendence                             59
　　Mimesis, Imitation, and Strategic Displacement                   73
　　Conclusion                                                       82

3   Revolutionizing Time                                        85
      Returning to the Body . . . and the Soul                  88
      Intimate Revolt: The Time of Psychoanalysis               94
      Re-Membering the Past: Memorial Art                      101
      Conclusion                                               109

PART III. THE PRESENT

4   The Problem of the Present                                 113
      Metaphysical Presence                                    116
      Metaphysical Absence                                     119
      To Be Finite Is to Have Been Born                        123
      Conclusion                                               131

5   Temporalizing the Present                                  135
      Breathing Life into Presence: The Praxis of Yoga
        and Pranayama                                          136
      (Re)presenting Becoming: Poetry as a Practice of
        Presencing                                             141
      Time for Love: Presence as Co-presence                   147
      Conclusion                                               156

6   An Ethics of Temporal Difference                           159
      On the Propriety of Self and Other                       160
      Becoming Two: Encountering the Stranger Within           163
      (Un)Timely Revolutions: The Timelessness of the
        Unconscious                                            170
      Conclusion                                               179

PART IV. THE PAST

7   Returning to the Maternal Body                             185
      Feminism and Motherhood                                  186
      Mothers Lost: Matricide                                  192
      Other Mothers: A Colonial Maternal Continent             196
      Conclusion                                               199

8   Motherhood According to Kristeva                           201
      Plato's Chōra Revisited: Receptacle or Revolutionary?    202
      Flesh Flash: On Time and Motherhood                      214

Temporalizing Mat(t)er: On the Interdependence
   Between Semiotic and Symbolic 218
Conclusion 230

9  Motherhood According to Irigaray 233
   Plato's Cave Revisited: An Impossible Metaphor 236
   The Substitution of Origins for Beginnings 246
   Mother Lost, Time Lost 254
   Conclusion 260

## PART V. THE FUTURE

A Non-Conclusive Conclusion: New Beginnings 265
   Suspended Time, Foreclosed Futures 266
   Arendt and the Unpredictability of the Future 269
   New Beginnings 273

Notes 277

Bibliography 362

Index 381

# Acknowledgments

This book has taken me a decade to write, and there is no way that my remarks here can do justice to the incredible community of people who have supported me along the way. It was conceived as a dissertation project at The New School for Social Research, underwent revisions during my years at Siena College, then final changes in my time at DePaul University. Ten years, three institutional contexts, countless revisions, and an amazing community of interlocutors.

From my time at The New School, I owe special thanks to Jay Bernstein, whose thesis supervision and mentoring were invaluable; Claudia Baracchi, in whose seminar on French Feminism the idea to examine the question of time in the work of Kristeva and Irigaray was born; and Tina Chanter, my external reader, whose work has been, and continues to be, a source of inspiration for my own thought. The folks in *People in Support of Women in Philosophy*, among others Grayson Hunt, Marianne LeNabat, Karen Ng, and Francey Russell, provided a vital and nourishing social context for what can otherwise be a lonely endeavor. Ella Brians, Kristin Gissberg, and Rocío Zambrana were there from the very start, and have offered helpful feedback along the way. Rocío was, and continues to be, the philosophical sister that carried me through, and for that I am forever grateful.

At Siena College I was blessed with supportive colleagues in and beyond my department. Special thanks to Karen Ng for postpartum soup, to Laurie Naranch for keeping the feminist conversations going, to Vera Eccarius-Kelly for being a force of nature, to Marcela Garcés for reminding me of what matters in life, and to Jennifer McErlean for making life-changing introductions.

I completed this book at DePaul University, where I am lucky to have first-rate colleagues and students. My wholehearted thanks go out to the students in my graduate seminar on Luce Irigaray, where I fine-tuned many of the ideas running through this book, and to the fantastic group of philosophers who make up my academic home and who inspire me in my daily work. I especially want to thank María del Rosario Acosta López, whose intellectual energy and loving friendship is one of a kind.

Importantly, I would like to thank Julia Kristeva and Luce Irigaray. It is as daunting as it is exciting to write a book on two thinkers who are not only alive, but who still lead very active intellectual lives. My work owes a great deal to the conversations I had with Luce Irigaray at the doctoral seminar she taught at Liverpool Hope University in the summer of 2007, as well as the tightknit community of scholars who partook in that course. Similarly, the three seminars I took with Julia Kristeva at The New School for Social Research in 2004, 2006, and 2008 provided important insights into her work, and marked the beginning of a lasting intellectual friendship for which I am immensely grateful. My reading of both of these thinkers' work has, in other words, been informed by their teaching in the present and by questions that they themselves have raised in response to my work. This has brought the texts with which I engage to life—a fact that seems especially apt given the importance that I ascribe to life and aliveness in my examination of time.

I want to extend thanks to the participants of the many conferences and workshops where I have presented bits and pieces of this book, and who have asked all the right questions along the way. I am particularly indebted to members of the Irigaray Circle and the Kristeva Circle. I want to also express my gratitude to the many individuals beyond my institutional affiliations, who, at different stages of the process, have read drafts, provided invaluable comments, and stubbornly challenged and engaged me in conversation about the matters treated here: Sara Beardsworth, Emanuela Bianchi, Matt Congdon, Ben Goldfarb, Lisa Guenther, Matt Hackett, Sarah Hansen, Sabrina Hom, Martin Hägglund, Rachel Jones, Thomas Khurana, Sina Kramer, Lisa Folkmarson Käll, Anne van Leeuwen, Mary Beth Mader, Lori Marso, Danae McLeod, Sara McNamara, Elaine Miller, Holly Moore, Johanna Oksala, Kelly Oliver, and Adam Rosen-Carole. Thanks to the mentorship of Cecilia Sjöholm, Marcia Sá Cavalcante Schuback, and Fredrika Spindler, who believed in me in my very earliest days of philosophizing, and who continue to inspire. I also want to thank the two anonymous readers who offered productive feedback, and who pushed me to make crucial improvements to the manuscript. The book is far better thanks to their careful reading. And Andrew Kenyon at SUNY Press, whose trust and support made it all possible.

I am grateful to Anne Thulin for making the beautiful art work for the cover—a red revolutionary swerve that only Anne could have made—and to Tana Ross for providing the abode in which much of this book was written. I am indebted to Eileen Nizer for her editorial work, and to Eliza Little for making the index. My Swedish community—Karin Andersson, Stina Bergman, Hanna Larsson, Marcus Lindeen, Annika Malmborg, and Julia Marko-Nord among others—have sustained me through summer research and much needed breaks. My lifelong friendship with Stina keeps me grounded. I also owe thanks to Shayna Silverstein for helping me navigate new beginnings. I am blessed by the presence in my life of Shiri Levinas, who provides orientation, and Nikki Byrd, with whom important foundations were laid. And, of course, my parents—Yvonne Rock and Björn Söderbäck—and my siblings—Jonna Rock and Joel Söderbäck—for their unfaltering support and encouragement on this decade-long journey.

It is hard not to notice that my intellectual support system is mostly female. It is women who have nourished me, kept me sane, let conversations spill into the night, and who have provided the attentive care that I depended on to write and think. This book would have never been without the women in my life—mentors, friends, colleagues, students, and the women whose work I read and learn from every day—and I feel immense gratitude for each of you.

Last, but not least, I want to thank James Walker, my love, to whom this book is dedicated. His patience, aptitude for true dialogue, and insistence on cherishing the present are gifts I could have never dreamt of having. His ongoing engagement with my work keeps it exciting and new. And he gave me the greatest gifts of all, Olana and Amina, whose presence in the world gives me hope for the future.

∽

Earlier versions of parts of chapters 1 and 3 have been published as "Revolutionary Time: Revolt as Temporal Return," *Signs: Journal of Women in Culture and Society* 37, no. 2 (2012): 301–24; an earlier version of parts of chapter 3 has been published as "Forging A Head and Forging Ahead—Miller's *Head Cases*," review of Elaine P. Miller's *Head Cases: Julia Kristeva on Philosophy and Art in Depressed Times, Theory &*

*Event* 20, no. 1 (2017): 274–79; an earlier version of parts of chapter 4 has been published as "Being in the Present: Derrida and Irigaray on the Metaphysics of Presence," *Journal of Speculative Philosophy* 27, no. 3 (2013): 253–64; an earlier version of parts of chapter 5 has been published as "Time for Love: Plato and Irigaray on Erotic Relations," in *Thinking Life with Luce Irigaray: Language, Origin, Art, Love*, edited by Gail Schwab (Albany: State University of New York Press, forthcoming); an earlier version of parts of chapter 6 has been published as "Timely Revolutions: On the Timelessness of the Unconscious," *Journal of French and Francophone Philosophy* 22, no. 2 (2014): 46–55; an earlier version of parts of chapter 7 has been published as "Birth," in *The Bloomsbury Handbook of 21st-Century Feminist Theory*, edited by Robin Truth Goodman (London: Bloomsbury Academic, 2019); an earlier version of parts of chapter 8 has been published as "Motherhood According to Kristeva: On Time and Matter in Plato and Kristeva," *philoSOPHIA: A Journal of Continental Feminism* 1, no. 1 (2011): 65–87; and an earlier version of parts of chapter 9 has been published as "In Search for the Mother Through the Looking-Glass: On Time, Origins and Beginnings in Plato and Irigaray," in *Engaging the World: Thinking after Irigaray*, edited by Mary C. Rawlinson, 11–37 (Albany: State University of New York Press, 2016).

∽

Generous financial support has been provided by the DePaul University Research Council, DePaul Faculty Recognition Grant, Fredrika Bremer-stiftelsen, Gertrude och Ivar Philipsons Stiftelse, Helge Ax:son Johnsons Stiftelse, Hermelestiftelsen, Israelitiska Ynglingaföreningen, the New School Holocaust Memorial Dissertation Fellowship, Petrus Hedlunds Stiftelse, Siena College Summer Research Fellowship, and the Thanks to Scandinavia Scholarship.

# Abbreviations

Hannah Arendt
**HC** The Human Condition

Simone de Beauvoir
**EoA** The Ethics of Ambiguity
**SS** The Second Sex

Judith Butler
**GT** Gender Trouble

Jacques Derrida
**Df** "Différance"
**OG** "Ousia and Grammē: Note on a Note from Being and Time"

Luce Irigaray
**BAB** "Body Against Body: In Relation to the Mother"
**BEW** Between East and West: From Singularity to Community
**FAMH** The Forgetting of Air in Martin Heidegger
**FG** "The Female Gender"
**PH** "Plato's Hystera"
**SD** "Sexual Difference"
**WOL** The Way of Love

Julia Kristeva
**IR** Intimate Revolt
**RPL** Revolution in Poetic Language
**SM** "Stabat Mater"

**SNS** The Sense and Non-Sense of Revolt
**SO** Strangers to Ourselves
**WL** "What's Left of 1968?"
**WT** "Women's Time"

Cecilia Sjöholm
   **KP** Kristeva and the Political

# PART I

# WHY TIME?

Every human problem cries out to be considered on the basis of time.

—Frantz Fanon

Let us talk about time, fine. But whose time will it be and for what?

—Nicolas Abraham

# Introduction

## Time for Change

Around noontime on October 15, 2017, American actress Alyssa Milano took to Twitter and encouraged people to use the hashtag #MeToo in an effort to raise awareness about the magnitude of sexual assault and harassment experienced by girls and women around the world, and to let others know they are not alone in what can otherwise be an extremely isolating experience. To say that it "went viral" is an understatement. Within twenty-four hours, the phrase had been tweeted by half a million people and had appeared in twelve million Facebook posts. Since then, it has been used in at least eighty-five countries, and has instigated heated public debate about the experiences that have surfaced, the power dynamics they reveal, and the pervasive nature of sexual offenses that they attest to—cross-culturally, cross-generationally, and across social and professional strata.

But this was not the first time these words had been used for the purpose of empowering survivors of sexual violence. Over a decade earlier, in 2006, the activist and community organizer Tarana Burke had begun using the phrase on MySpace, following a conversation she had had with a thirteen-year-old girl at a summer camp confiding to her about having been sexually assaulted. At the time, Burke had not felt ready to offer advice or support to the girl, and later, she recounts, the guilt she felt became a refrain, a repeated question: "Why couldn't you just say 'me too?'"[1] A movement was born, and since then Burke has been hard at work to help women and girls—particularly women and girls of color—who, like her, had endured sexual abuse.

Why do I begin here, in the bifurcated birth of the MeToo Movement, as I set out to examine the role of time in the work of two French feminist thinkers? On the one hand, because it is a story about a moment in very recent feminist history that mirrors just about every story about feminist moments and movements. As Abby Ohlheiser puts it, "a viral hashtag that was largely spread and amplified by white women actually has its origins in a decade of work by a woman of color."[2] It serves as a reminder that each and every feminist beginning (and of course not only feminist beginnings but, as I will argue in this book, all beginnings) points to yet another beginning—sometimes through an act of erasure or appropriation, other times through acknowledgment or mutual exchange. Feminist work is always already in some sense feminist historiography, and feminists have had a lot to say about history, beginnings, and birth.

But much more specifically, the MeToo Movement brings attention to the complex ways in which feminist concerns tend to be embedded in temporal questions and considerations, even when these are not explicit. Burke's inability to say "me too" to the young teenage girl who came to her for advice, and her subsequent ability to do so loudly and publicly in a heroic effort to support women and girls throughout her community and eventually across the world, each speaks of different temporal modes of existence and response, and of the gendered nature of temporal experience. "Me too" are words meant to communicate identification, solidarity, affinity, and support—what Burke calls "empowerment through empathy."[3] As such, they signal a relational temporality of sorts—the "too" is pronounced with reference to a claim made by an other (or others)—but through its current usage it has also come to function as an assertion that opens up the possibility for certain forms of relationality and solidarity ("me too" not as a response to what another confides to me, but rather as a statement that invites for collective action and public conversation). As such, these two words reverse a linear temporal order requiring that "this happened to me" comes before "it happened to me too," and open up for an alternative temporal and relational order.

At the same time, "me too" inevitably tells the story of a past to which the speaker must return in order to utter those words, most likely not without pain, and at the risk of having traumatic memories from that past resurface. Pronounced here and now, in a present marked by a flood-wave of Hollywood scandals and everyday abuse, the words "me too" open up a passage to a past that is singular and collective both at once (it tells of my story, but also of a story shared by many, and this juncture between the singular and the globally shared is what gives it its power). By pronouncing those words we partake in the act of acknowledging and giving voice to past events (and those that are still ongoing) that by and large have remained silenced and suppressed through the pressures of social taboos and mechanisms of shame. This has happened. To you. To me. To us. And once a movement is born, there is a sense that things could be different. That healing is to come. That there can be change.

∽

While this book is not about the MeToo Movement, it is about change. *Time* And it tries to lay bare the temporal structure that allows for change: a *Change* temporal movement of return, from the present of our here-and-now, to a past that by and large has been silenced and repressed, into a future that might be otherwise.

## French Feminism and the Problem of Time

In her essay "Women's Time," Julia Kristeva defines the different waves of the feminist movement in terms of their respective relationship to time.[4] My own task, in this book, is to continue the trajectory of that essay, and to focus specifically on two of the most important feminist thinkers of our time—Julia Kristeva and Luce Irigaray—as I offer the first extended reading of their work that systematically unearths the role of time in their corpus. While I acknowledge profound differences between these two thinkers, I argue that the particular issue of time is one that brings their respective work together in ways that should shed new light on the particularities of each of their thinking.[5] The objectives of my project are twofold: On the one hand, I trace a dialogical relationship between Kristeva and Irigaray, suggesting that their respective projects are structured around and driven by a common interest in questions of time and temporality. On the other hand, I look at the broader political implications of this re-articulation of time—most importantly its capacity to formulate a useful critique of patriarchal presuppositions about sexual difference.

My ambition is thus to show that by bringing the issue of time to the forefront, we can highlight some hitherto neglected aspects of the thought of these two thinkers—aspects that connect them in perhaps unexpected ways. Despite the fact that temporal questions are present throughout their texts—from the earliest to the most recent ones—few serious engagements with this aspect of their thought have emerged, and no book-length reading of this kind exists.[6] This might in part be due to the fact that neither Kristeva nor Irigaray has published a comprehensive text where their own "theory of time" is spelled out: there is nothing like Aristotle's examination of time in the *Physics*; no engagement as sustained as the one Saint Augustine presents in his *Confessions*; nor do we find in Kristeva or Irigaray any claim to a radical reinterpretation of time like we see in Immanuel Kant, Edmund Husserl, Henri Bergson, Martin Heidegger, Walter Benjamin, Gilles Deleuze, or Jacques Derrida.[7] The question of time is, instead, raised throughout their texts: it appears in almost all of them, at times explicitly, more often as an implicit subtheme.[8]

While Kristeva's and Irigaray's works differ significantly, I argue that the question of time stands at the heart of both of their writing, and that it functions as that which organizes and motivates their respective feminist projects.[9] I claim, moreover, that a feminist critique of identity thinking relies on a re-articulation of time as it has been conceived in the Western tradition. Feminist scholarship has up until recently tended to focus on issues of spatiality and embodiment—both of which are typically associated with femininity—but I argue that a philosophical critique of time and temporality is essential for an adequate discussion of questions of sexual difference and female embodiment and subjectivity.[10]

Time has, of course, been a central philosophical concern for millennia. The early ancients and Plato associated it with the movement of the celestial bodies, thus framing it in cyclical terms and modeling it upon the cycles of nature. Aristotle conceptualized time as an infinite series of now-points that constantly are coming in and going out of presence. We then see a trajectory from Augustine to G. W. F. Hegel, where time becomes conceptualized as an "extension of the soul" (Augustine) or "the form of inner sense" (Kant); a tradition, in other words, that associates time with the internal, non-corporeal mind and that, since René Descartes, posits a transcendental subject or ego capable of temporal synthesis.[11] Heidegger famously suggested that temporality should be seen as the fundamental structure of the existential analysis of Dasein, and in so doing he transformed our very conception of time and the inquiry into our own temporal experience, and set the stage for a revitalization of the question of time within the framework of phenomenological, existentialist, and poststructuralist critiques of Western metaphysics.[12]

But if to exist, as Heidegger claims, is to project oneself toward the future and to resolutely seize hold of ecstatic temporality, what, Elaine P. Miller asks, happens if there is a fundamental, historically determined structural difference in the ways in which the sexes are able to carry out this existential project? What if, for certain subjects, the possibility of taking hold of the present, releasing the past, and anticipating the future were from the outset prevented or brought to a halt?[13] It is this structural foreclosure of the possibility of embracing existential temporality that feminists, queer theorists, and decolonial thinkers alike have subjected to critical analysis. I will introduce this problem by turning to the account provided by Simone de Beauvoir in *The Second Sex*. I will proceed, however, to point to some problematic aspects of her analysis, as I argue that the works of Kristeva and Irigaray allow us to better address the question of time with this set of problems in mind. I will then go on to elaborate an analysis of temporal experience that acknowledges and sheds light on the relation between the question of time and that of sexual difference.

What do I mean when I say that there is a relation between the question of time and that of sexual difference? Let me address this question by making a rather general claim about the way in which time and temporal movement have been perceived. By and large, two models of time have been made available: cyclical time, and linear time.[14] Each of these has been associated with its own particular mode of subjectivity. Women, so often relegated to the natural realm and to embodiment, have become the bearers of cyclical time, while men, who have taken upon themselves the task of subordinating nature and the body in the name of culture and reason, have come to lay claim on linear time and the progress associated with it. Historically speaking, the two models thus correspond to the conception of woman as an embodied creature and man as a rational subject not bound to his body.[15]

On this view, female (cyclical) time is associated with temporal stasis, while male (linear) time reaches forward into the transcendent future. Man becomes associated with time (with progress, futurity, and forward-thrusting movement), while woman is reduced to spatiality and repetition (the eternal recurrence of nature and the docile receptive materiality that regenerates life without itself being capable of creativity or agency). Woman, as Beauvoir has noted, gives life, while man tran-

scends or risks it.[16] Western patriarchal society, we might say, depends
on a sexual division of temporal labor. The question of time—even as
it has been treated in the Western philosophical canon—is in other
words intimately linked to the question of sexual difference. But this
link has remained unacknowledged, and my task in this book is not
only to draw attention to this link as such but also to show that the
covering over of this relation has led to a disfiguring of both time (and
the relationship between the different modes of time: past, present, and
future) and sexual difference.

To deconstruct the Western patriarchal distinction between
nature-woman-immanence and culture-man-transcendence, we must therefore undertake to deconstruct the temporal division between cyclicality
and linearity, offering instead a temporal model that moves beyond such
dichotomies. While some feminist scholars have attempted to recuperate
and valorize cyclical time, and while others have attempted to grant
women access to linear time, I argue in this book that neither cyclical
nor linear time carries true potential for liberation and change. Building
on the work of Kristeva and Irigaray, I seek to develop my own concept
of revolutionary time, which is modeled upon the perpetual movement
of return that is meant to retrieve the very body that was repressed in
order to construct the linear-cyclical dichotomy and paradigm. When
Kristeva and Irigaray urge us to return to the body, what is at stake, I
argue, is not an essentialist tendency to imprison us in our bodies. Rather,
we can trace in their work the effort to construct a model of time and
transcendence that neither represses the body nor confines women and
other oppressed groups to the realm of embodiment, but which recognizes
embodiment as the condition of possibility for futurity. In developing
the concept of revolutionary time, I aim to make this implicit effort
explicit, and to lay the groundwork for a politics of futurity and change.

My concern with time is threefold: First, I am interested in looking
at the ways in which Kristeva and Irigaray seek to establish a view of
presence that remains grounded in the past and open towards the future
(what I call a living present or co-presence). Second, I want to look
at the past by examining what it would mean to retrieve what they
see as forgotten histories, and critically think through the relationship
between what they call maternal beginnings and what has traditionally
been articulated in terms of a single paternal origin. Third, I wish to
address very briefly a set of questions about the future—briefly precisely
because the future remains elusive. I argue that both Kristeva and Iri-

garay are devoted to the possibility of the not-yet, the new, and the unforeseen, but that such an unpredictable future fundamentally depends on an initial return into the past and a vitalization of the present. The future is, in other words, not a break with the past, but rather a result of our perpetual and active return to and tarrying with the past, and this movement of return can only take as its point of departure a living present. I am thus attempting to establish a dynamic link between the three modes of time (much like Heidegger did when developing his notion of ecstatic temporality), while (and here, to be sure, I depart from Heidegger) bringing life back to each of them by linking them to the question of sexual difference.

॰ఞ౧

My discussion of time in this book evolves over five parts. The present one introduces the question of time, its relationship to change, and its place not only in French feminism, but also in recent scholarship in decolonial and queer theory. The next one treats the question of time as it appears in Kristeva and Irigaray, respectively, and sketches their critique of both linear and cyclical time and teleological-progressive models of development. My discussion in this part draws from the analysis provided by Beauvoir in *The Second Sex*. Turning to the work of Kristeva and Irigaray, I trace a view of time as a perpetual movement of return, articulated in terms of revolution and revolt. On my account, it is only through this movement of return into the past that futurity and change become possible. The attempt to develop a theory of time as perpetual return is thus meant to make possible a feminist politics of transformation and change. In the remaining three parts, I examine the aforementioned three moments in this movement of return and renewal: the present, the past, and the future. Part 3 focuses on the tradition that we have come to call the metaphysics of presence, and offers a series of alternative ways of treating the question of presence in intersubjective terms (through phenomena such as yoga, poetry, and love; and through the psychoanalytical view of the subject as inherently divided, not only by the unconscious but also by time). Through an engagement with Derrida's deconstructive project, I depart from him by arguing that the metaphysical tradition is one concerned with absence rather than with presence, and through a discussion of Sigmund Freud's work on the timelessness of the unconscious, I begin to develop an ethics grounded in co-presence and temporal difference. Part 4 examines the past, more specifically articulated in terms of maternal beginnings. This part offers an examination of the role of the maternal in Kristeva and Irigaray, respectively, with reference to central passages from Plato's *Timaeus* and *Republic*, as well as a critical engagement with Judith Butler's work. In the final part, which also serves as a conclusion, I turn to the future, and to a set of issues connected to novelty and change, by putting Kristeva and Irigaray's work into conversation with that of Hannah Arendt.

While the overarching argument of the book is that the concern with time is a common feature of the work of Kristeva and Irigaray alike, and while I argue throughout that an analysis of the role of time in their œuvre allows us to explore the similarities of their respective projects, I would, as I have mentioned already, not want to uncritically bundle them together, nor suggest that they are in full agreement about matters of time and difference. I hope to be able to treat them in their differences, and to remain sensitive to the singularity of each of their works. That said, however, the reader will notice that the core ideas and the central tropes of my analysis appear in my reading of both thinkers, and my comparative study is meant to show that these two thinkers complement each other in fruitful ways. It will thus often be the case that I turn to Irigaray in order to develop an argument that my reading of Kristeva fails to fully articulate, or that I address gaps in the work of Irigaray by turning to Kristeva. In this way, I hope to show that the differences between their respective bodies of work are productive ones, and that taken together they allow us to treat the question of time in its relation to difference in rich and profound ways.

## On Time and Change

Before fleshing out the notion of revolutionary time and its relation to sexual difference in further detail, allow me to say a few words about what motivated me to treat the issue of time in the first place. My own work has always been concerned with the possibility of change, and more specifically with the prospect of challenging patriarchal assumptions about sex and gender. With this book, I hope to lay bare the conceptual structure that we assume every time that we speak of the possibility for such change to occur. Time has always provided the framework through which we are able to articulate both continuity and change, yet the progressive temporal paradigm that is taken for granted in Western modernity (linear time, which, I will argue, functions through a repression of cyclical time and the material conditions of our existence) is one that runs the risk both of *forgetfulness* (it does not allow for the "return" into the past that would ground us in history and materiality) and, at the same time, of *repetition* (it simultaneously and paradoxically traps us in the past, foreclosing the production of "new" horizons).[17] As Tina Chanter has noted before me, we "need an understanding of processes of social change that accommodates both a sense of continuity with the past and the possibility of and need for discontinuity."[18]

The temporal model that I elaborate here is meant to provide exactly that. It seems to me that any feminist politics depends on the belief that things can change, that we need not repeat a history that has tended to exclude and silence women and other oppressed groups. Feminism is the vision that things can be otherwise, that the future holds unprecedented opportunities and the potential for emancipatory change—that we can "break" with a past that has excluded women and other minorities to protect white male privileges. As Elizabeth Grosz has pointed out: "One of the most challenging issues facing any future feminism is precisely how to articulate a future in which futurity itself has a feminine form, in which the female subject can see itself projected beyond its present positions as other to the one."[19]

Women, people of color, and queer folk (among others) have a particularly strong investment in moving beyond a past that has locked them in their bodies and in positions of subordination. As Frantz Fanon puts it, the Black man "is a slave to the past," so to refuse alienation is to refuse to "be locked in the substantialized 'tower of the past,'" which is to say that he must reclaim time in his own terms: "I do not want to sing the past to the detriment of my present and my future."[20] Yet at the same time, it seems to me, feminism must also be an antidote to the future-oriented *forgetfulness* that characterizes Western culture: the covering over of our maternal beginnings, bodily registers of experience, and our place in the cosmos, as well as our tendencies to conceal and silence the lived realities of marginalized groups. In this sense, it is colonial patriarchy instead that marks a "break" with certain aspects of history, and our task would be a work of recovery, of anamnesis, of unearthing a forgotten history and silenced stories.

The task for feminism is thus both to uncover forgotten aspects of history, and to change structures and patterns that have been repeated for generations. To be sure, woman, like the Black man in Fanon's work, should no longer be locked in the past. But to claim the present and the future—to engage in what Fanon calls "disalienation"—requires that she revisit and reclaim the past too.[21] Recalling a Nietzschean trope, we must both remember and actively forget. The latter, in fact, depends on the former. This dual task can be achieved through a view of time as a movement of perpetual return and renewal—what I call revolutionary time.[22] If both traditional accounts of time have failed to establish future horizons (cyclical time allegedly repeats itself indefinitely, and linear-progressive time is driven by a teleological desire to produce a future according to already established ideals and norms, which means that it too is bound by repetition), what I call revolutionary time is meant not only to put an end to the dichotomy between these two models (a dichotomy that on my reading structures the very regime of colonial patriarchy), but more importantly to achieve what these models of time have failed to do, namely to set in motion a temporal movement that neither forgets nor repeats the past; a model of time that allows us to redeem the past and the present without instrumentalizing them in the name of a future always already defined in the present.

I want, in other words, to suggest that our current conceptions of time foreclose the very possibility of change, since time in Western modernity has become reduced to a copying of sorts, a recurring movement of repetition. The founding principles of this tradition—the belief in a singular origin and in linear progress alike—set into motion a repetitive reproduction of sameness, hence thwarting variation and difference and the heterogeneity of life itself. It is first and foremost this heterogeneity and the production of irreducible difference that is at stake as we try to re-conceptualize time as a movement of return. If Western metaphysics most commonly has been the study of things that do not change—the nature of Being and the first cause of things—I want to develop something like an ontology of the living, of becoming, and of change. And if philosophers have placed their discussion of time in their treatises on nature (think only of Plato, Aristotle, or Hegel), most modern accounts of time tend to nevertheless overshadow or foreclose the rhythms and oscillations of nature. I want to reclaim the cyclical movement of time without reducing it to monotonous repetition.

The model of time that I articulate here can thus not be equated with the kind of cyclicality that so often has been ascribed to women and to the female body (as well as to the "primitive" cultures of colonized and indigenous people). I am, rather, interested in the ways in which both Kristeva and Irigaray think cyclicality (the "revolutionary" nature of time) in terms of difference, differentiation, displacement, and change. For both, I argue, it is through a temporal model of return only—through revolutionary time—that we can think and live beginnings as that which makes politics and political change possible and revitalizable. As Irigaray puts it: "To return means to make possible a new beginning."[23]

To be sure, such a feminist appeal to a temporality of change is also an appeal to a more dynamic understanding of the relationship between corporeality and social construction. As Chanter puts it:

> It has become increasingly evident that the notion of social construction, and the view of historical change that informs it, is in need of conceptual clarification, if we are to move beyond the impasses that have appeared in many areas of cultural studies, feminist theory, and race theory, and indeed in any political debate, insofar as the possibility of change is central to its concerns. Inherent in the notion of historical change are preconceptions about time.[24]

The notion of social construction—and the manifold feminist and queer theories that have attempted to conceptualize the relationship between sex and gender—has in the last few decades revolutionized our understanding of identity, subject formation, and the relationship between nature and culture. But while these new concepts have provided hope for the possibility of change and a sense of liberation from historical structures that previously had seemed "natural" or "essential" (and hence presumably unalterable), the constructivist and "anti-essentialist" rhetoric has also brought to us a set of pressing concerns and questions regarding the status of materiality, embodiment, and sexual difference.

It is my contention that an analysis of time and temporal matters, and a reconfiguration of the relationship between "nature" and "culture" and the temporal terms that we have been prone to use to articulate the complex entanglement between them, might offer some of the "conceptual clarification" that Chanter calls for. In the wake of Beauvoir, much feminist discourse has been grounded in the view that "nature" (and hence the body, or our sex) is static, while "culture" (and hence language, or our gender) is dynamic and subject to change. It has thus inherited and reproduced the assumption that cyclical time (insofar as it is associated with the life of the body) should be understood as repetition (stasis) while linear time (associated instead with the life of the mind) must be linked to progress. By disrupting this division, and by paying attention to the dynamic character of the realm that we call "nature" (the body, our sex) we might begin to articulate a more complex account of the relationship between sex and gender (although it should be clear that this also will involve critical analysis of the very concept of nature, such that it can be freed from the moors of essentialism).[25] As Grosz points out:

> Culture produces the nature it needs to justify itself, but nature is also that which resists by operating according to its own logic or procedures. A reconfiguration of nature as dynamic, of matter as culturally productive, of time as a force of proliferation, is thus central to the ways feminism itself may be able to move beyond the politics of equalization to more actively embrace a politics affirmative of difference elaborated in the most dynamic forms of feminist theory today.[26]

While I am unable here to devote sufficient attention to extremely complex categories such as "nature" and "culture," or "sex" and "gender," this book is nevertheless meant to contribute to feminist theories that seek to avoid reducing sexual difference either to static essence or to mere discursive construction. My ambition is to provide additional concepts to contribute to those projects that seek to complicate the relationship between embodiment/materiality and social change, exactly by providing a critique of the temporal structure that hitherto has organized our discourse on these matters. Thinking the body in relation to revolutionary time will allow us to get beyond the impasse of essentialism and anti-essentialism, and to productively intervene in debates about the relation of sex, gender, and the body.

To be sure, many twentieth-century thinkers within the so-called continental tradition have articulated interesting critiques of linear time and progress. The reason that I turn to Kristeva and Irigaray, specifically, to articulate my own views on political change, is precisely that their insistence on the relation between time and sexual difference allows us to think through the question of time as inherently linked to questions of embodiment and materiality.[27] If the body most commonly is seen as that which limits our freedom and transcendence, I see it instead as the condition of possibility for transcendence (I will say more about how I use this term in what follows). It is only insofar as we are embodied, I argue, that we have access to time and to temporal change.

## Decolonial and Queer Critiques of Time

Before we look more carefully in the chapters that follow at how it is that Kristeva and Irigaray, respectively, tie the question of time to that of sexual difference, it is worth noting that questions of time (and those related to it, such as history, memory, revolution, and change) are at the heart of much contemporary discourse on coloniality and race, as well as recent work in queer theory. Time is an issue of power, and normative temporal regimes are, arguably, not only patriarchal in nature, but also colonial, heteronormative, and cisnormative, and they have served to ostracize all those who fail to conform to Western modern conventions about time, progress, and development. What Dana Luciano in Foucauldian fashion has termed chronobiopolitics,[28] what Daniel Innerarity simply describes as the social rhythm of chronopolitics,[29] and what Elizabeth Freeman in turn refers to as chrononormativity,[30] are all concepts that name the temporal regimes "by which institutional forces come to seem like somatic facts," or "forms of temporal experience that seem natural to those whom they privilege."[31]

Clearly, if time is a feminist issue, it cannot be framed as an issue of sexual difference alone, but must be understood at the intersection between sexual, racial, and colonial difference, among others. If women have been made to bear the burden of embodiment such that men could be liberated from their bodies as they embarked on their project of progress, so have indigenous and subaltern people (male and female alike), from the cotton fields in times of slavery to contemporary sweatshops and mines. And black and brown women are constantly made to bear an especially heavy burden of embodiment such that white women are able to join their male counterparts on that linear trajectory forward. From domestic work (housekeepers) to childcare (nannies) and reproductive labor (surrogate mothers), these women put their bodies on the line so that their white "sisters" can enter linear time.

Let me be clear that Kristeva and Irigaray's work is limited in this respect, and that it is marked by European whiteness in ways that should trouble us from the start. Important work has been done to address this limitation of their work, such as Penelope Deutscher's A *Politics of Impossible Difference*, and Gayatri Chakravorty Spivak's now classic essay "French Feminism in an International Frame."[32] We should also add that their work by and large engages questions of sexual difference in cis- and heteronormative fashion. With this in mind, I want to speak briefly to the ways in which the concept of time is tied up with coloniality, heteronormativity, and cisnormativity, respectively, so as to highlight the need for cross-fertilization between feminist, decolonial, and queer work on these issues, despite the blind spots that haunt much French feminist thought in this regard. It is my hope that these initial remarks will reverberate throughout the book, such that conversations can be opened up between French feminist thought on time and the important body of work wherein temporal matters are tackled more explicitly from decolonial and queer perspectives.

❧

While we tend to associate colonization with space—the imperialist "discovery" and annexation of "far away lands"—it was and remains just as much about annexing time. In *The Darker Side of Western Modernity*, Walter Mignolo, for example, argues that "the Western concept of 'time' became the essential 'connector' of colonial and imperial differences throughout the globe," and that time as we know it today, "is a result and a consequence of the colonial matrix of power."[33] The colonial logic entails that "the planet was all of a sudden living in different temporalities, with Europe in the present and the rest in the past."[34] Or, as Aníbal Quijano puts it, Eurocentric modernity basically relied (and continues to rely) on the foundational myth of "a linear, one-directional evolutionism from some state of nature to modern European society," as well as "the distorted-temporal relocation" of cultural differences through the displacement of non-Europeans into the past.[35] The rendering of racialized and indigenous people as inferior ultimately depended on rendering them as anterior, as "belonging to the past in the progress of the species."[36]

It is worth noting that such temporal division between a colonized past and a European present (the latter of which, we should add, simultaneously lays claim to the future) depends through-and-through on the very distinction between nature-cyclicality and culture-linearity that we have examined above. Mignolo speaks of "an imaginary chronological line going from nature to culture," and ties this very construction to the colonial division between modernity and tradition, such that time becomes a colonizing device that turns geography into chronology in a move that reduces non-European others to "primitives" who are seen as "closer to nature" (rather than at the peak of culture) and "traditional" (rather than modern).[37] Mignolo elaborates: "At the inception of the colonial matrix of power, 'barbarians' were located in space. By the eighteenth century, when 'time' came into the picture and the colonial difference was redefined, 'barbarians' were translated into 'primitives' and located in time rather than in space. 'Primitives' were on the lower scale of a chronological order driving toward 'civilization.'"[38] María Lugones has also written about this moment as one whereby Europeans came to justify the colonial project with reference to a temporal-hierarchical distinction between primitive and civilized, such that "other human inhabitants of the planet came to be mythically conceived not as dominated through conquest, nor as inferior in terms of wealth or political power, but as an anterior stage in the history of the species, in this unidirectional path."[39]

A linear-progressive temporal regime was thus installed at the heart of Western modernity, one that figured—and that continues to figure—"uncivilized" others as relentlessly stuck in the past, in the cyclicality of nature and mythology. As Mignolo goes on to note, "'Modern man' built his sense of superiority and his pride in the process of cutting the umbilical cord with 'nature,' while 'primitive man' was still too close to it; and being too close to nature meant (from the perspective of 'modern man') being far from civilization."[40] It also of course meant being figured as "inert and fixed," as incapable of progressive movement forward and obstinately tied down by "slow time" in a world propelled by the survival of the fastest.[41] Linear time's embeddedness in notions such as "progress" and "development" is, in other words, far from innocent from the point of view of the colonized. And just like there can be no linear time without an underpinning repression of cyclical time (a notion that I will develop at length in this book), there can be no "development" without the complementary notion of "underdevelopment," nor any modernity without its hidden side, namely coloniality.[42]

Quijano frames his analysis of the temporal regimes of European modernity by attending to the link imposed on racialized subjects to the state (and stasis?) of nature: "According to . . . the chain of the civilizing process that culminates in European civilization, some races—blacks, American Indians, or yellows—are closer to nature than whites."[43] Importantly, he goes on to stress that this "new and radical dualism affected not only the racial relations of domination, but the older sexual relations of domination as well."[44] His analysis in this context relies heavily on a critical examination of the (Cartesian) mind-body dualism that organizes the Western modern project, and the association of man (as in "the human" but also the male gender) with the mind and of women—especially women of color—with the body. Quijano's analysis is a reminder that these things cannot be thought apart—that the examination of the sexual division of temporal labor that I offer in this book is inextricably tangled up with these important discussions of racial, cultural, and colonial difference.[45]

Chandra Talpade Mohanty has proposed that transnational feminist coalition building depends on "a temporality of struggle, which disrupts and challenges the logic of linearity, development, and progress that are the hallmarks of European modernity," adding that such temporality of struggle "suggests an insistent, simultaneous, nonsynchronous, process characterized by multiple locations, rather than a search for origins and endings."[46] I will return at length to this idea that we have to disrupt any and all logics that appeal to "origins" and "endings" as I insist, in my discussion of revolutionary time, that we upend the colonial-patriarchal annexing of time, and the hierarchical model of difference it perpetuates. To be sure, if time as we know it "continues to nourish the imaginary that reproduces colonial and imperial difference,"[47] then new temporal imaginaries are desperately needed. It is my hope that the concept of revolutionary time developed in this book can offer some resources on the path to further exploring such imaginaries.

❦

If time has come to be viewed as a pressing feminist issue in the last few decades, some of the most important attempts to challenge stereotypical conceptions of time and change have come from queer theorists thinking about these issues.[48] The editors of a special issue on trans temporalities bring attention to the link between the coloniality of time and the heteronormative cis-masculinity of time: "Western queer and trans subjects were temporalized in ways that mimicked the temporalization of colonial subjects," they note, such that "norms concerning race and colonization have formed the basis for measuring gender nonnormativity as 'out of time.'"[49] Queer time offers an obvious alternative to the normative straightness of linear time, and queer and trans theorists have "opened up a number of ways of exploring the limitations of progressive and generational modes of time."[50] Queer and trans temporalities swerve and interrupt, stretch and bend, wrinkle and fold, halt and diverge, redeploy and twist, are "out of joint" and uncanny while attending to gaps, failures, and slippages in the seemingly smooth texture of heterolinear time. The task—like my own in this book—has been to reenvision time so as to put critical pressure on normative assumptions about past, present, and future alike.

Just as in feminist and decolonial engagements with time and history, the past in queer thinking about time is broached as an ongoing site of contestation. As Freeman puts it, "one of the most obvious ways that sex meets temporality is in the persistent description of queers as temporally backward, though paradoxically dislocated from any specific historical moment."[51] Queer folk, like women and racialized subjects, are simultaneously seen as relentlessly stuck in the past and as lacking a past of their own. "Gays and lesbians have been figured as having no past: no childhood, no origin or precedent in nature, no family traditions or legends, and, crucially, no history as a distinct people."[52] The challenge has thus been to establish alternative historiographies and archives, ones that return to and reclaim the past in queer terms, ones that defy linear-generational narratives and that disrupt the very notion that the past can be located in the "before" of our present—that the "now" follows in linear fashion from a "then" that is no longer.

That queerness has a temporal dimension, indeed one with a particularly complex relation to the present, should be evident, Carolyn Dinshaw notes, to anyone "whose desire has been branded as 'arrested development' or dismissed as 'just a phase.'"[53] Similar to feminist and decolonial critiques of the so called "metaphysics of presence" (a tradition that I will examine in chapter 4), queer theorists have insisted that time in general, and presence in particular, is lived rather than hollow: "it is full of attachments and desires, histories and futures," which is to say that it is neither empty nor neutral, and that we need "a fuller, denser, more crowded now" than that we tend to encounter in heterolinear accounts of time and presence.[54] We need, in other words, to examine the present in its intimate relation to desire, pleasure, embodiment, and affective attachments, as I will in part 3 of this book.

The status and value of the future is also contested in queer theory. Sometimes queer time is future-oriented, such as in José Esteban Muñoz's *Cruising Utopia*, where queerness is envisioned as "not yet here," as a "rejection of the here and now" and the "quagmire of the present," indeed, as an "ideality that can be distilled from the past and used to imagine a future."[55] Others conceptualize queer time as precisely refusing any and all futural logics, insofar as such logics allegedly depend on heteronormative assumptions about the value of reproduction and child rearing. In Lee Edelman's *No Future*, for example, queerness comes to name "the side outside the consensus by which all politics confirms the absolute value of reproductive futurism."[56] Others still navigate the precarious reality of a seemingly foreclosed future—in the context of looming death during the AIDS crisis—while at the same time trying to articulate a futural vision "unscripted by the conventions of family, inheritance, and child rearing," such as in the work of Jack Halberstam.[57]

In her introduction to a special issue of GLQ on queer temporalities, Freeman insists that what makes time a distinctly queer question is its embeddedness in issues of embodiment and eroticism. Time, she notes, not only has, but is a body.[58] Yet, as I argue throughout this book, the embodied nature of time has by and large been ignored in a cultural context wedded to abstract-universal models of time that link temporal experience to the mind alone. "We are still in the process of creating," Freeman notes, "a historiographic method that would admit the flesh, that would avow that history is written on and felt with the body, and that would let eroticism into the notion of historical thought itself."[59] In the chapters that follow, I hope to contribute to the making of such historiographic method admitting of the flesh, giving time its body back, as it were, while attending to the heterogeneity that marks bodies as sexed and singular.

## A Note on Language

Let me conclude this introduction by drawing attention to some of the vocabulary that I will use in what follows. Both Kristeva and Irigaray have focused on the significance of language and the weight that words carry as we go about describing—and shaping—the world in which we live. Their political thought is, from the outset, motivated by a commitment to the idea that any transformation of our views on subjectivity and identity depends on a thoroughgoing revolution in language. In other words, words matter, and I hope in what follows to use them with care and precision.

*Time vs temporality*

In the wake of Heidegger and subsequent phenomenological thought on time, contemporary philosophers tend to distinguish between time and temporality. I should flag that I myself use these terms interchangeably. While revolutionary time is meant to express temporal experience, or lived time, rather than some abstract objective notion of time (and in this sense temporality might have been a better term to use throughout), I nevertheless have chosen to speak of it in terms of time, since this is *Temporality* the term most often used by Kristeva and Irigaray in their texts. That said, I ask the reader to bear in mind that the time of which I speak is, *experience* precisely, lived and experienced time, and I am just as much concerned *subjectivity* with questions of subjectivity as I am with the question of time. To be sure, while I view my project as pushing a set of ontological questions, it does not do so in any traditional sense. I am thus not, for example, concerned with whether or not time is "real." I view it as an irreducible aspect of human experience, and it is as such that I want to examine it.

Revolutionary time can be reduced neither to linear nor to cyclical time, but it nevertheless includes certain aspects of both temporal models. My aim is thus not to simply discard these two models once and for all. Such revision would neither be possible nor is it desirable. As we shall see in my discussion of her critique of the symbolic order in chapter 8, Kristeva's strategy is not to erase or destroy the symbolic law altogether, but rather to shed light on the interdependence between symbolic and semiotic (categories to which I will return) in an attempt to thereby transform and revitalize a symbolic order all too driven by disembodied abstraction. Both Kristeva and Irigaray are thinkers of the in-between—a category that links dual opposites while simultaneously exceeding them altogether. Revolutionary time similarly both bridges cyclical and linear time (by showing that one cannot exist without the other) while introducing entirely new aspects of time that neither of those two models was able to embody (precisely because of their one-sided character). As the term as such implies, revolutionary time is indeed repetitive (like the revolutions of the planets around the sun or those of the moon around the earth), yet it brings about novelty and change (like political, cultural, or scientific revolutions aim to do). It is this tension and oscillation between repetition and change that I want to explore, and I will argue that it is intimately linked to a critical analysis of sexual difference.

This is not to say, however, that revolutionary time is equivalent to women's time or feminine time. The latter are terms often used both by Kristeva and Irigaray (as well as other feminist thinkers), but I deliberately do not use them in my own account. At the heart of my elaboration of revolutionary time stands the conviction that time only can be experienced in the singular (which is not to say individual—nor does it assume any clear-cut distinction from relational or collective), and I will emphasize this precisely by stressing that revolutionary time is a movement of perpetual return to the body. My model of time is, in other words, grounded in the singularity of the body, and as such it can be reduced neither to ideal form nor to an expression of experience in any general(ized) sense. I will pay close attention to—and provide a critical analysis of—the fact that each temporal model hitherto available to us has been associated with one of the two normative sexes (male or female), and with that sex alone. But my own model of time is precisely meant to disrupt that division, and to articulate temporal experience in singular rather than gendered terms. To say that time depends on sexual relations does not amount to saying that time is feminine, or that all women (or all men) experience time in the same way. Nor does it assume a binary model of sexuate identity. It allows us, rather, to think time in embodied and singular terms, which is to say that the very concept of revolutionary time is one that avoids (even refuses) abstraction and universalization, as well as sexual dimorphism.

As I read their work, both Kristeva and Irigaray aim at establishing a new beginning for woman, where she can enter into history on her own terms, projecting herself into the future and not just securing the projection of man. We might add, in light of what we have said above, that such new beginnings are at stake not only for women, but for all those who have been excluded from and erased by the modern project of history and progress, and also that an interruption of that project involves a fundamental re-articulation of what it means to be a "woman" (or any such marginalized subject) in the first place. The language of "woman," in what follows, will therefore often be used in reference to a subject position as of yet unthought, rather than as an already defined identity category that serves as a (complementary) counterpart to "man." In light of this, it may well be that we should get rid of terms such as "woman" and "man" altogether, so as to not reproduce their current meaning and normative force. I have nevertheless decided to keep them in what follows (again, in part because both Kristeva and Irigaray do), but would ask the reader to engage the text with these claims in mind.

This brings me to another term that needs some elaboration: I will from now on use the term sexuate difference, rather than sexual difference, whenever I speak of difference understood beyond the logic of the same; a difference that Irigaray famously claims is covered over in Western patriarchal culture. "Sexuate" is a term that Irigaray herself has begun to deploy in some of her later works (although not systematically), and I make use of it here in order to clearly distinguish the sexual relation that revolutionary time is meant to make possible and express from the disfigured model born from the cyclical-linear paradigm (one where woman is reduced to the negative mirror image of man).[60] If our culture is pervaded by the latter (sexual difference, which is to say our current stereotypical-dichotomous gender roles), the former (sexuate difference) has yet to be elaborated and experienced.

Following Irigaray, I argue that a cultivation of sexuate difference depends on an initial and thoroughgoing critical analysis of the concept of time, a claim that will be developed at length in chapter 2. This leads to a seemingly paradoxical claim, one that is at the very heart of my argument: If sexual difference as we know it (stereotypical-hierarchical gender roles) has resulted in the disfiguring of time and the foreclosure of true change, careful attention to and cultivation of sexuate difference is instead what frees temporal experience from being over-determined by gender (such as the sexual division of temporal labor that organizes the cyclical-linear paradigm). When I argue in chapter 2 that revolutionary time and sexuate difference need to be thought together, what I have in mind is thus not a need to reinforce or embrace current gender norms, but rather the urgency of articulating a temporal model that allows for (open-ended) singularity and heterogeneity.[61]

Another term that is worth mentioning is one that is often used in discussions of time and temporality, namely transcendence. There are, roughly speaking, four ways in which I use this term, and I hope that the context in each instance will reveal the specific meaning that I attribute to it: First, and perhaps most traditionally, transcendence is understood as an escape from the sensible realm and from finitude. I address this kind of transcendence most explicitly in my chapters on the present, where I articulate a critique of the metaphysics of presence. Here, transcendence is seen as a way of overcoming time and temporal existence, and it implies a projection into a realm beyond the natural and intersubjective (literally a meta-physical realm). Transcendence understood in this sense represents the most extreme form of ideality—a complete denial of and escape from finite embodied existence.

Second, I use transcendence as it appears in the work of existentialist thinkers like Beauvoir and Jean-Paul Sartre. They speak of transcendence not so much as an escape into a metaphysical realm of selfsame ideas but rather as projection forward within this world. Transcendence is in this case equivalent to freedom—if by the latter we understand a project of self-realization. It is, in other words, not an escape from time and temporal life but rather a taking-upon-oneself one's temporal existence and futurity in the sense of pursuing projects, thrusting oneself into the future, and making actual what was given to us as a potential.[62] If the former model of transcendence sought to escape time altogether, the latter, as we will see in the opening chapters of this book, depends on a repression not of time in general but of cyclical time in particular. It represents a less extreme form of ideality but nevertheless establishes ideality as an internal aspect of our existence—to be achieved precisely by a subject who surpasses their past and their embodiment (what the existentialists refer to as "facticity"). Albeit in very different fashion, both models thus depend on an escape from the body. If the former model achieves such a repression through oppression (transcendence is attained by placing the burden of embodiment on women and other marginalized groups), the latter seeks to overcome such oppression but it does so by demanding that these marginalized subjects enter the patriarchal-disembodied time of progress and projection, and thus at least to some extent give up her own specificity.

These two forms of transcendence both appear within a linear temporal paradigm. One is an attempt to escape linear time, the other is an attempt to inhabit it, but both ultimately depend on the linear model of time and on an initial repression of cyclical time. Both, similarly, depend on a binary model of sexual difference, which is another way of saying that they both depend on a mono-sexual model, or a logic of identity.[63] The remaining two instances in which I use the term transcendence are meant, in contrast, to challenge such rigid binaries, and to accompany my own model of revolutionary time and an asymmetrical and non-hierarchical notion of sexuate difference. Third, then, Irigaray speaks of transcendence when she describes the irreducible distance that unfolds between sexed subjects. The kind of "immanent transcendence" of which she speaks is neither meant to describe the vertical relation between a human self and a divine Other, nor the (also vertical) relation between our freedom (our capacity to realize our projects) and the body that we inhabit (or, for that matter, the past which we drag along as we move through life). She seeks, instead, to elaborate horizontal transcendence between sexed subjects, and I will explore this notion in detail in my reading of Irigaray in chapter 2.

Finally, I speak of transcendence as that which my own model of time (revolutionary time) seeks to achieve: a thrust into the future (a future within this world, not in a world beyond) that rather than repressing the body or the past instead depends on a perpetual return to the body and to the past. Such a notion of transcendence cannot be reduced to teleological progress or movement forward toward a future already established by us. It is marked by undecidability and unpredictability, and as such it challenges the ideological aspects of transcendence that I criticize in the opening chapters of this book. My own notion of transcendence does, importantly, not stand in opposition to immanence, the past, or to embodiment, but is rather an integral aspect of our embodied existence, insofar as the latter is sexed and marked by the incessantly revolutionizing movement of time. On my account, the first two models of transcendence turn out to be quite similar to our current notion of immanence (in the sense of repetition). As I will try to show, they can achieve no change at all but rather produce perpetual reproduction of the same (while they are posited as offering a framework for change). The latter two forms of transcendence do, on the contrary, carry potential for change in the true sense of the term, since they seek to overcome the very distinction between immanence and transcendence that makes our freedom depend on the repression-oppression of the body, of nature, of woman, and of the other. In this sense, I seek to elaborate a notion of transcendence that need not be seen as an escape from the realm of embodiment and immanence, but that rather entails a cultivation of those spheres as conditions of possibility for change.

The time has come to make change—both with regards to our views on time and our understanding of sexual difference (and the relationship between the two). We must, in other words, develop a notion of revolutionary time, which is nothing other than, precisely, a time capable of transformation in difference—a time for change.

# PART II

# REVOLUTIONARY TIME

A woman is shut up in a kitchen or a boudoir,
and one is surprised her horizon is limited;
her wings are cut, and then she is blamed for not knowing how
    to fly.
Let a future be open to her
and she will no longer be obliged to settle in the present.

—Simone de Beauvoir


Perhaps the shared culture-making projects we call 'movements'
might do well to feel the tug backwards
as a potentially transformative part of movement itself.

—Elizabeth Freeman

# 1

# Linear Time, Cyclical Time, Revolutionary Time

In *The Second Sex*, Beauvoir famously examines the process through which woman has become viewed as Other in Western patriarchal culture. One of the central distinctions that she uses to structure her account is that between immanence and transcendence: she argues that women have been confined to the reproductive natural realm while men, in having women bear the burden of embodiment for them, have transcended nature and laid claim on spirituality, agency, and creativity. In short, women have been made the bearers of necessity while men have taken as their own the realm of freedom. Men, therefore, have been characterized as active, while women have been described as passive—a distinction that survives to this day and that provides the foundation for one of the central claims of Beauvoir's analysis, namely that subjectivity, historically, has been articulated along masculine parameters, while women have been reduced to objects: objects to be owned and exchanged; objects to be looked at, studied, and scrutinized; objects to be sexually possessed and penetrated.

The dichotomies that structure Beauvoir's account—dichotomies that arguably are mere constructs serving to uphold male supremacy and power—have been made to look like natural distinctions rooted in biology, or worse yet, metaphysical unchangeable truths above and beyond our reach. As Beauvoir notes in *The Ethics of Ambiguity*, "one of the ruses of oppression is to camouflage itself behind a natural situation since, after all, one can not revolt against nature" (83). Man, within such a regime, comes to be seen as the norm, while woman is viewed as a deviation from this norm: she is a lacking being and a negative pole, while he upholds neutrality and positivity both at once.

Beauvoir's existentialist study is meant to disrupt this division: to reveal it, precisely, as a patriarchal construction; to liberate women from the role they have hitherto been forced to play; and hence to elevate them to subjects in their own right. From the outset of what must be described as the founding text for contemporary feminist theory, Beauvoir, interestingly, frames the problem in temporal terms: As birth-givers, she explains, women have become imprisoned in "repetition and immanence," they have produced "nothing new" (SS 73). Because women are expected to secure the survival of the species, they have lost their place in the time of history and development: "She must ensure the monotonous repetition of life in its contingence and facticity: it is natural for her to repeat herself, to begin again, without ever inventing, to feel that time seems to be going around in circles without going anywhere" (SS 644). Think only of Julianne Moore's character in Stephen Daldry's film *The Hours* (based on Michael Cunningham's novel of the same name): suffocated and confined by the repetitive patterns of suburban housewife life, where each day looks just like the previous one and like that which will follow, she is driven by the desire to put an end to a life that was doomed to dead ends from the outset.[1]

If Moore's character is cursed by boredom and repetition (having too much time on her hands), women have also lost a place in history by being trapped in the unending cycles of physical labor (not having any time to spare). Saidiya Hartman reflects on this temporal destiny of woman as she journeys along a slave route in Ghana in an attempt to trace the history of the Atlantic slave trade:

> The men had appointed themselves the official custodians of history. Besides, the women never had an afternoon to waste ruminating about history. They didn't have an hour to spare; they were selling goods in the market or laboring in the fields or carrying pails of water or hauling a load of firewood or washing laundry, the very chores that made the labor of slave women so highly prized. Who could stop to talk when there were children to be tended, food to be cooked, rooms to be swept, and a husband to be maintained? When later I asked the women in town about slavery, they joked, "The wife is the true slave."[2]

Both of these conditions create a situation wherein women have lost both past and future, toiling away in the present. On Beauvoir's account, woman is both destined to repeat the past and is unable to thrust herself into the future: "it is easy to understand why she is ruled by routine; time has no dimension of novelty for her, it is not a creative spring; because she is doomed to repetition, she does not see in the future anything but a duplication of the past" (SS 640). Man, on the other hand, "has been an inventor since the beginning of time," by transcending his animal nature, he "spills over the present and opens the future" (SS 73).[3]

Beauvoir concedes that this is "the key to the whole mystery" (SS 74). Her thesis might be stated as follows: *The subjugation of women in patriarchal society depends on a sexual division of temporal labor.* As upholders of reproduction, embodiment and the survival of the species, women are confined to the cyclical time of nature—a temporal model that is said to merely repeat itself indefinitely: "Her misfortune," as Beauvoir puts it, "is to have been biologically destined to repeat Life" (SS 74). As inventors of a world that transcends our natural conditions, men are instead bearers of linear time—and thus capable of change and progress: "man's project is not to repeat himself in time: it is to reign the instant and to forge the future" (SS 75). Freeman makes a similar claim: "History . . . emerges as textual, humanmade, and linear only in contradistinction to a mute female body laboring 'naturally' and recurrently in childbirth."[4]

We must add that this division, in turn, robs women of temporal existence altogether. Within a paradigm that understands time as linear movement forward, cyclicality loses its temporal status and becomes articulated in spatial terms: woman is seen as the space in which man reproduces himself; she provides the ground from which he can thrust himself forward.[5] This is perhaps most concretely exemplified by the way in which reproduction was viewed until fairly recently: the docile egg awaiting the active sperm during conception; the female body providing a container for the life that grows within her—a passive receiver of the life created by man alone.[6] An example with more obvious sociopolitical implications is the expectation upon women, as representatives of the private realm, to provide the abode and the necessary conditions for men to achieve transcendence and enter into the public realm: the burden upon women to do the tasks of the household, so that men (having been fed, cleaned, ironed, loved, and provided with heirs) can build and enter into a world of spirituality, culture, innovation, and art. We should note that woman quite literally has been seen as incapable of entering into the time of development and progress: she has been confined to what we might call an "infantile" world—she is said to suffer from constitutive immaturity and is thus viewed as unable to project herself forward into the "adult" realm of reason and freedom.[7] Beauvoir attempts to show that woman has been enslaved by man precisely by being reduced to a childish creature who knows not how to take upon herself the task of freedom, the task of thrusting herself into the unknowns of adult enlightened life.[8] She is thus bound to repeat the time of childhood and fails to move forward into the future.[9] As Butler puts it: "existence as a woman becomes what Hegel termed 'a motionless tautology.' "[10]

Subjectivity and (mature) agency have, in other words, been elaborated primarily in masculine terms and, moreover, in terms of time: "cut off from his transcendence, reduced to the facticity of his presence, an individual is nothing," Beauvoir asserts (EoA 115). The active subject projects himself forward (I use the male pronoun intentionally here), he transcends his biological-immanent existence, goes through a process of development and growth, produces objects and creates art, thrusts himself beyond the here and now, leaves permanent traces behind, plans for the future and realizes dreams and projects while reminiscing over events past. All this takes place through a repression of the corporeal dimensions of our existence. Man rids himself of his body by ascribing embodiment to woman. He thus becomes a creature of time while she is reduced to mere body.

Women, in Butler's terms, "are defined by a masculine perspective that seeks to safeguard its own disembodied status through identifying women generally with the bodily sphere. Masculine disembodiment is only possible on the condition that women occupy their bodies as their essential and enslaving identities."[11] To associate woman with cyclical time is thus to associate her with embodiment and with a natural realm that is said to be static. Man, on the other hand, enters linear time by refuting his own bodily existence: transcendence and temporal existence come to depend upon the subjugation of women and of the body, and change is said to reside within a discursive realm over and above the body (time departs from space, and woman becomes confined to the latter). Women have, as a consequence, become associated with passivity, immanence, and the (allegedly) repetitive process of biological rhythms and reproduction. Man has cut her off from the future, and has therefore turned her into a thing (EoA 82).[12] And in making woman the bearer of embodied life, man could leave his body behind as he thrust himself forward in the projective stream of time.

This male *repression* of the body entails an *oppression* of women and women's bodies.[13] As discussed already in the introduction to this book, however, this argument is in no way limited to gender alone. Fanon brilliantly describes the predicament of the Black man vis-à-vis his white oppressor in similar terms: if the "present always serves to build the future,"[14] he notes, we should not forget that certain subjects—such as colonized and racialized people—have been reduced to immanence and presence in the service of building the future for those who have laid claim to transcendence and freedom—their white colonizers. As Deutscher notes:

> This point can be extended beyond discussions of gender oppression. The same phenomenon occurs in the embodiment of poverty and race. One does not only live a devalued embodiment. One lives an inhibited embodiment marked by one's sense that a more diverse range of possibilities is prohibited in advance. In class, race, gender, and age oppression, one does not know the ways in which one might be otherwise, but one knows that one anticipates them and one knows they have been rejected in advance by the social forces inhabiting one.[15]

As we have seen, important work has been done to illuminate this predicament for a range of marginalized and oppressed subjects—most prominently in recent decolonial and queer theory. I would thus remind the reader to understand my discussion of time in what follows as inviting dialogue with those who have theorized time more explicitly in decolonial and queer terms, and I hope to show how these axes of analysis are bound to intersect and overlap around issues of time and temporal labor.

## From Beauvoir's Sexual Division of Temporal Labor to Revolutionary Time

If this is an accurate (albeit schematically recounted) diagnosis of the temporal regimes that uphold what bell hooks has called "imperialist white-supremacist capitalist patriarchy,"[16] then the questions that feminist thinkers must ask themselves are: How can we be liberated from these narrow definitions? How might we provide a temporal model that avoids the rigid dualism between immanent-cyclical spatiality, on the one hand, and transcendent-linear temporality, on the other? What kind of temporal account will give women and other oppressed groups access to freedom and to future horizons hitherto gained by white men alone? How can we, as it were, give women their wings back, so that they too can fly into the future?[17]

Most feminists would agree with the portrayal of patriarchy that Beauvoir offers in *The Second Sex*. Where feminist thinkers tend to differ, however, is in their assessment of how we might overcome these conditions and change the situation. To put it in the most schematic terms possible, some (following Beauvoir) have argued that women just need to claim a place on the "male side" of the schema; that they need to prove the system wrong by achieving the many characteristics and positions that have been withheld from them through the vocabulary of natural destiny and various strategies of subjugation. Women, in other words, can become men's *equals* only by becoming *like* them.[18] Others have instead claimed that such a strategy merely would reproduce the logic of identity or sameness that gave the system legitimacy in the first place; that women, instead of aspiring to a place on the "male side" of the schema, should question the very values that have been attached to the different sides of the dualist structure to begin with, and attribute value to the characteristics hitherto ascribed to women. The point, then, would not be for women to become "like men" but rather that they should take pride and worth in the tasks and positions upheld by members of their own sex. Framing these responses in temporal terms, we might say that the first group of feminists have laid claim to linear time, while the second group has wanted to revalue cyclical time.[19]

This is precisely how Kristeva has characterized the difference between the feminist "waves" or "generations" of the last century. Her essay "Women's Time," published in English in *New Maladies of the Soul*, provides her most explicit and nuanced discussion of feminism to date. Her description of the feminist "waves" and their respective stumbling blocks is, interestingly, marked by a reflection on the nature of time, and on each feminist generation's particular response to the division of temporal labor and the privilege granted to the masculine-linear temporal model that dominates our culture. The first wave, on her account, seeks "to stake out its place in the linear time of planning and history," and it functions according to the *"logic of identification* with . . . the dominant rationality of the nation and the state," that wants women to gain access to the privileges and positions hitherto granted to men alone (WT 207). Put simply, representatives of this liberal-egalitarian (read Beauvoirean) model want to change the position of and opportunities for women without necessarily challenging the very values that excluded and failed to recognize them in the first place.[20] Cyclical time, within this tradition, is that which women must overcome and transcend in order to gain freedom and equality, since freedom is defined as (linear) projection forward.

The second wave of feminism is, according to Kristeva, "characterized by a quasi-universal rejection of linear temporality" (WT 208). This more radical movement emphasizes differences between the sexes, explores the specificities of the female psyche and feminine writing, and rejects linear temporality as a construct that fails to recognize the particular nature of female subjectivity, desire, and discourse. For these feminists, "female subjectivity poses a problem only with respect to a certain conception of time, that of time as planning, as teleology, as linear and prospective development—the time of departure, of transport and arrival, that is, the time of history" (WT 205). Rather than demanding access to positions and privileges from which women had been excluded up until that point, feminists since May '68 have attempted to question the very values that earlier feminists had aspired to. Instead of repressing cyclical time in order to gain access to linear time, these feminists revalued the cyclicality that the old system had devalued, and sought to return to and reclaim archaic cyclicality as a locus for liberation from the shackles of paternal law.

Kristeva herself, however, identifies with neither of these movements. She posits a "third generation" of feminism, and describes it as one that offers a profound challenge to the very notion of "identity" hitherto assumed in feminist and non-feminist discourses alike, and that focuses instead on singularity and difference—both articulated in temporal terms. We will return to this third form of feminism in what follows, but let me first articulate what I take to be the main stakes in this discussion, and how I want to position myself within the set of issues that I have elaborated so far. This will then allow me to express more clearly why I turn to the work of Kristeva and Irigaray in order to develop what I see as the temporal model that best addresses the challenges with which we are faced.

While I think that Beauvoir offers an accurate *descriptive* account of the regime of patriarchy in its various historical guises, I have two major concerns about her *prescriptive* conclusion and the critical analysis that she provides of the situation that she so brilliantly has unearthed. Both have to do, incidentally, with her temporal analysis, but they have profound implications for (a) her view on how liberation can be achieved; and (b) her views on female subjectivity within and beyond the Western patriarchal system. First—and in this sense I belong to the second wave of feminists as described by Kristeva—I do not believe that emancipation can or should be achieved by granting continued privilege to linear time. I agree with those critics who have noted that Beauvoir's egalitarian feminism fails to properly account for female specificity (although she does begin to gesture toward what we might call a politics of difference in the closing pages of her book[21]), as well as those who worry that her account privileges certain (read: white, European) female experiences at the expense of others.[22] I also find it troubling that she never explicitly and seriously questions the linear paradigm as the only model that would allow for transcendence, futurity, and liberation, especially given its colonial-patriarchal legacy.[23]

This brings me to my second concern: Not only do I think that Beauvoir idealizes the linear model of time, thus failing to properly acknowledge that it, in fact, is made possible through a repetition of the same (read: colonial-masculine subjectivity) and thus by no means allows us to transcend into futures as of yet unknown to us; I also think that, while I take her account of cyclical time to be accurate insofar as it is *descriptive* of how cyclicality has been perceived within the Western patriarchal tradition, she does not sufficiently attempt to provide an account of how we might conceptualize cyclicality *otherwise*. Her analysis is, for the most part, limited to the view that nature is a repetitive-immanent realm, and hence that woman's creativity and agency (her capacity to transcend) will depend on her overcoming her "natural" conditions, as man has done before her (and at the expense of her capacity to do so). This view is, in my mind, a reflection of a patriarchal culture that represses embodiment in order to achieve ideality—not an objective truth that we should reproduce beyond it.

I want to suggest the following: Neither linear nor cyclical time, as they have been conceived within the Western patriarchal tradition, carry true potential for transcendence, freedom, and change. If we—both women and men, and those who identify beyond such binaries—want

*[handwritten margin note: Critique of Beauvoir]*

to liberate ourselves from the regime that these two models of time constitute (a colonial-patriarchal regime indeed), we must articulate a model of time (and a set of practices accompanying it) that rejects those two forms that have hitherto been available. As we take on this task, however, we must bear in mind an important fact that remains unthematized not only by Beauvoir and the first generation of feminists that Kristeva associates her with, but also at least to some extent by that second generation who wants to retrieve cyclicality as a challenge to the linear temporal paradigm. The very cyclical model of time that Beauvoir urges women to overcome, and that Kristeva's second wave of feminists conversely wants to reclaim, is in itself an imaginary construct created by a society organized around a linear model of time. Just as the female subject has been constructed as a negative mirror image of the male one (woman as lack, woman as deviation), cyclicality is the "non-time" that patriarchy needs in order to raise linear time and development over and above it (it is a time that, precisely, has been reduced to space, to a docile ground that silently dictates man's linear journey upward and forward).

Recall Mignolo's claim, discussed in the introduction, that Western modernity framed indigenous populations as "uncivilized" or "primitive" in order to construct itself as a project of invention and progress. A similar logic is at work here. The view of nature as a realm that immanently reproduces itself in an eternal mime (and the concomitant association of woman with such a repetitive realm) provides a contrast against which man can raise what he sees as a culture of innovation, creativity, and change. By returning to and recovering this model of time, we remain within the patriarchal regime that produced it in the first place. What is covered over, in the process, is the fact that nature in truth is full of variation and change; that the cycles of nature never quite repeat themselves identically; and that generation is a movement of alteration and differentiation, not an act of repetition or mimicry. We might even say that it is linear culture that repeats and reproduces "the same" in an eternal and immanent mime (insofar as it is one that functions according to a logic of identity and sameness, as I will discuss further when turning to Irigaray). While the linear model gives priority to the future, I will thus argue that it—paradoxically—yields not novelty but repetition, and that it does so because it is governed by an abstract ideal that delegitimizes present and past practices.

In order to move beyond the impasse of such rigid dualism (and the paralysis that it generates), I will try to articulate a model of time that overcomes the distinction between "static nature" (cyclical time, immanence) and "dynamic culture" (linear time, transcendence). I want to provide a temporal model that shares much in common with the cyclical time so often associated with women and other minorities, but one that explicitly conceptualizes cyclicality not as a repetition of the same but, rather, as a dynamic process of displacement and alteration. Cyclical time, on this account, is never without variation and change (it is, in other words, not *merely* cyclical). In order to mark the difference between my model of time and the cyclical-repetitive model described by Beauvoir, I have chosen the term *revolutionary time.* The choice of term signals a set of aspects that carry weight for me: first, that I view time as in some sense cyclical in character—think of the revolutions of the heavenly bodies around the sun; second, that time on my account is a movement of perpetual return—a set of restorations or re-authorizations of the past (restorations, as we shall see, that simultaneously seek to *de-authorize* certain notions of the past and of history); third, that it has much in common with the notion of time inherent in modern revolutionary movements (although, as will become evident, it is not reducible to it); and last, that the articulation of this temporal model has political implications and that it is meant to provide a framework for a feminist revolution that puts an end to, or at least forcefully challenges, the systematic oppression and objectification of women so poignantly assessed by Beauvoir. I will provide a detailed etymological analysis of the term when I discuss Kristeva's treatment of the concept of revolt. For now, let me return in more detail to the essay "Women's Time," as I begin to situate Kristeva and Irigaray as thinkers who might help us examine the revolutionary potential of this alternative temporal model.

## Three Temporal Models, Three Feminist Waves

Kristeva begins her essay by taking up some of the issues that this book seeks to address. She notes that much of our contemporary "progressive" political discourse is driven by what seems like a teleological structure that is bound to repeat itself, thus foreclosing change in any true sense of the term. The Enlightenment idea of progress—with all the landmark inventions and major developments that doubtless have emerged in its wake—nevertheless carries with it a mode of thought and action that has let itself be hypnotized by the appeal of a future that (and this is the promise of the model) is shapeable by us. A culture that sees itself as "progressive" seeks "to implement the program set out by its founding members," Kristeva notes (WT 208). Within such a tradition, the present (its practices, its subjects, its bodies, its modes of existence) becomes a mere means to guarantee a better and more desirable (idealized) future. An extreme example of this is the emergence of totalitarian regimes in the twentieth century—which led to events that would pervert completely the Kantian kingdom of ends, as human beings were reduced to disposable means in the name of achieving "higher" political ideals and goals (an "equal" society, a "free" society, a racially "pure" society, and so on).[24]

Born and raised behind the iron curtain, Kristeva has had firsthand experience of the "side effects" of the socialist dream of freedom and equality. Women in the Eastern bloc had undeniably achieved equal positions in society and in the state—they had, to put it in the terms that I have used hitherto, gained their place in linear time. But at what cost? Had this really allowed them to "fly" (as Beauvoir put it)? Besides the many lives that had been lost, the very specificity and particularity of their experience was also under threat: "In the spirit of the egalitarian and universalist context of Enlightenment humanism," Kristeva contends, "the only idea that socialism has held to is the notion that identity between the sexes is the only way to liberate the 'second sex'" (WT 209). The socialist ideology (one that Kristeva describes as totalizing, indeed totalitarian in spirit) is founded on the idea that "the specific nature of women is unimportant, if not nonexistent" (WT 209). As we will see when we turn to Irigaray, this erasure of sexuate difference inevitably leads to a culture that (re)produces the same in its own image. If man had been the model in a society where he himself ruled, man remained the model even as woman became his equal.

The same can, of course, be said about multiple forms of oppression. Immigrants are welcome as long as they behave, speak, and try to look "like us." Homosexuality is more readily accepted if it just adapts to the norms of a heterosexual lifestyle (marriage, monogamy, and the desire to reproduce). And trans folk are able to receive the medical treatment they want if and only if they inhabit and perform their gender in line with binary gender norms. Ambiguity, difference, and transgressive modes of being are strictly regulated and prohibited. And, as Dean Spade puts it: "this establishes the requirement that gender transgressive people be even more 'normal' than 'normal people' when it comes to gender presentation, thereby discouraging gender disruptive behavior."[25]

The annihilation of ambiguity and differences neatly situates everyone on the linear path that we call progress and that supposedly is to be pursued in the interest of a neutral and abstract "all" that nevertheless hierarchizes identities by distinguishing center from margin. Immigrants are made to make sense of their lives in terms of a "before" and "after" the move, where it is assumed that what was left behind is unequivocally undesirable, whereas the place to which one has arrived is where one wants to be—a place with which one wholly identifies, and in which one can envision a viable future.[26] Assimilation involves rejecting the specificity of one's past (in all of its complexity) such that one can identify with the "shared" (read: white, Western, colonial, patriarchal) past of a linear History that depicts "lesser" histories as a source of disgrace or shame. In *Strangers to Ourselves*, Kristeva describes such assimilation in terms of a "leveling and forgetting" that annihilates difference, and she describes the foreigner as no longer belonging to "any place" or "any time," stuck in a "rummaging memory, the present in abeyance."[27] Albert Memmi also resorts to a language of temporal displacement in his discussion of colonialism: "the colonized in the throes of assimilation hides his past, his traditions, in fact all his origins which have become ignominious."[28]

Similarly again, trans folk are expected to narrate their lives according to a predefined linear trajectory, beginning in a troubled childhood marked by cross-dressing and dis-identification, and culminating in the unambiguously liberatory correction-completion of one's identity through gender affirming procedures.[29] This narrative requires a chasm between the past self (and body) and the future self (and body).[30] The state's policing of identity is, in other words, deeply embedded in regulatory temporal norms, ones that require that identity be stable and that such stability be accomplished through linear development alone. As Marie Draz has argued in an article that speaks specifically to the state-sanctioned temporality of "born this way" narratives, these temporal norms come to determine the legal terms of sex designation on documents such as birth certificates. "Through its focus on permanence," she notes, "the state says: We will grant you a new origin, but only if you agree that the same logic of a stable and knowable linear temporal organization of identity grounded in a fixed origin applies."[31] We should thus be wary of any and all such state-regulated appeals to assimilation and normalization, even when they are couched in equal rights discourse. As the editors of a special issue on trans temporalities point out, "the hegemonic trans life-story as linear (tortured past, liminal present, hopeful future)" ultimately fails to capture the complexity of trans experience: "As we listen to trans stories, autobiographies, poems, prose and narratives out-side the clinic we notice that they are irreducible to the presupposed chronological progression from a 'terrible-present-in-the-wrong-body' to a 'better-future-in-the-right-body.' Trans lives are more complicated and nuanced than this temporal sequence indicates."[32]

The second generation's feminists were, according to Kristeva, much better equipped to sustain the differences upon which a culture of change would depend. Their mistake, however, was to maintain an oppositional conception of difference. If the first generation aspired to linear time, the second saw as their task to reclaim and revalue the cyclical temporality that had been devalued by a male Western subject seeking to subordinate women and female characteristics. But the very notion of cyclicality to which they sought to return was a product of the masculine-linear paradigm they were trying to subvert. A castling of the positions within a dualist and hierarchical system is nothing more than, precisely, a shift in positions. The system as such remains intact: "If we take this logic at face value," Kristeva wonders, "does feminism not become a sort of reverse sexism?" (WT 216).

Kristeva's worry is that these feminists, by putting Woman on a pedestal and celebrating cyclical time, repeated the mistake committed by their forerunners: the feminism of difference became a religion of sorts, just like egalitarian feminism (or socialism) had been, and the problem with religions is that they are so mesmerized by future ideals that they forget about the past and the present (or, rather, they instrumentalize these latter modes of time in order to, at all cost, achieve their ideal).[33] Such feminism thus comes to follow the very linear-teleological logic that it was meant to challenge: for both feminist waves the past and the present become mere means to achieve an already defined future—with the consequence that the future becomes closed off, and that past and present modes of existence lose their dynamic and singular character.

Kristeva does acknowledge the power that can be attained from the marginal position of the second wave of feminists. She sees it emerge in the activist groups so often supported by women—the Palestinian commandos, the Baader-Meinhoff Gang, and the Red Brigades—but she laments that the terrorist violence perpetuated by such groups is "even more repressive and sacrificial than the one it is fighting" (WT 217). Cyclicality thus takes on the very form that Western patriarchy assigned to it in the first place: it perpetuates vicious cycles of the same (violence is countered by more violence), and it serves to repeat an archaic image of Woman that leaves little or no room for the singularity of each and every woman: "we may remember Lacan's scandalous pronouncement that 'There is no such thing as Woman,'" Kristeva asserts. "Indeed, she does not exist with a capital 'W,' as a holder of a mythical plenitude, a supreme power upon which the terror of power as well as terrorism as the desire for power base themselves" (WT 218).

Political projects that follow the linear model of time end up replicating the past through a repression of sorts (the past is overshadowed by an idealized notion of futurity). Those that, instead, follow the cyclical model repeat the very same past by idealizing it. In both cases, both past and present are emptied of authority, and the future becomes predictable and reduced to ideological slogans and agendas. For Kristeva, feminism as ideology is no exception to this rule, which is why she herself has been wary of this label. In an essay on the work of Beauvoir, she laments what she sees as a tendency in feminism to close off the future:

> Feminists share the totalizing ambitions of the libertarian movements that came out of Enlightenment philosophy and, further upstream, the dissolution of the religious continent, in its vow to bring happiness to the whole world. We are only too familiar today with the impasses of this paradisiacal teleology, with these totalitarian promises. Feminism itself, in all of the diverse paths it has taken in Europe and America, has not escaped these aims, and with this tendency it has become ossified in a militantism without tomorrow, which, leaving aside the singularity of its subjects, thinks itself capable of enclosing all women, including all the proletarians or the whole third world, in a demand that is as absolute as it is desperate.[34]

Political transformation in Western society (a society which, according to Kristeva, in a certain sense is *incapable* of revolt—and I will examine her notion of revolt in more detail in what follows), can only occur "within a paradoxical temporal structure, a sort of 'future perfect' in which the most deeply repressed and transnational past gives a distinctive character to programmed uniformity" (WT 202). In this sense it can never quite be a transformation, but is bound to repeat what we already know. *Both* our failure to revisit the past, *and* our tendencies to idealize it, leads to a repetition of this past, and a future always already conditioned by past and present agendas—the result being that we lose both present, past, and future.

To put all this differently, we might say that the three tenses of time become instrumentalized and deprived of their living dynamism. What we are lacking is a living past and a living present, and, consequently, a living future.[35] A future that is detached from the other temporal modalities is all too abstract and becomes frozen in an idealized form. As I hope to show in the course of this book, a successful revolution—one that opens new doors into a future not already destined by the past—depends on a non-idealizing and continuously interrogative movement of return into the past, and a chance to experience the dynamic and active processes of the present as they unfold. Both of these, in turn, depend on a thoroughgoing return to the repressed of our current linear temporal model: the body. It is precisely the acknowledgment of (hitherto repressed) bodily processes and drives that most effectively can provide the dynamic ("living") layer that the temporal modes as we have known them hitherto have been lacking.

Kristeva herself therefore identifies with neither of the two feminist movements discussed so far. She posits a third generation of feminism, describing it as one that offers a profound challenge to the very notion of identity assumed in much feminist and nonfeminist discourse alike, and that focuses instead on singularity (not to be confused with individuality) and difference, both of which are articulated in temporal and embodied terms. The third wave of feminism, on Kristeva's account, is one in which time and space can no longer be so easily distinguished, in which time must be understood as inherently linked to embodiment: "The meaning that I am attributing to the word 'generation' suggests less a chronology than a *signifying space*, a mental space that is at once corporeal and desirous" (WT 222).

That signification depends on a breakdown of the traditional distinction between mental and corporeal is one of the great insights of Kristeva's thought—one to which I will return at length. She consistently argues that the distinction between the cultural-linguistic and the natural-somatic cannot be demarcated: "The drive is a pivot between 'soma' and 'psyche,' between biology and representation . . . For what we understand by biology is—drives and energy, if you wish, but always already a 'carrier of meaning' and a 'relation' to another person, even though this person may be yourself."[36] Put in temporal terms, we might say that she refuses to accept the dichotomy between "natural" cyclical time on the one hand, and "cultural" linear time on the other. By collapsing the separation of these two rigid models, we are able to articulate a model of time that inscribes women and men, as well as those who identify with neither of these terms, in a signifying space in which we all can be understood as signifying embodied beings (the term Kristeva uses is *sujet en procès*, a subject-in-process or a subject-on-trial).

As I have noted already, in the Western patriarchal tradition men have been associated with time and women with space or embodiment. In "Women's Time," Kristeva draws our attention to this female confinement to "the *space* that *generates* the human species more than it does *time*, destiny, or history" (204). She alludes to James Joyce's maxim "father's time, mother's species" (204), and notes that this division has come to shape Western modern conceptions of subjectivity. Kristeva has suggested elsewhere that the philosophy of the twentieth century first and foremost has been preoccupied with questions of time and subjectivity, questions that are coextensive and must be thought together.[37] On the one hand, we cannot deconstruct male subjectivity without deconstructing the temporal paradigm that accompanies it. And on the other hand, we cannot construct female subjectivity without constructing an accompanying temporal model.[38]

As givers of life, women provide the silent conditions by virtue of which men can be the takers of life, and it is the latter that has been granted value in a culture marked by a sacrificial logic. Western history is depicted as a series of deaths—wars, heroic sacrifices, battles—rather than a string of births: one wonders how all these men who were willing to sacrifice themselves came into the world in the first place. To say that a dynamic account of time depends on a return to the body amounts to framing the question of time not only in terms of death and mortality but also as an issue of birth and natality (a theme that will be developed at length in this book). Only then, in my mind, does renewal become possible in any real sense.

∽

Let me, finally, offer a brief meditation on the notion of feminist "waves," since this might help us more clearly illuminate the movement of revolutionary time or a time of return. One might well object that the very metaphor of waves that has been used to describe the different generations

of feminists for quite some time now in itself signals the linear-progressive idea that each feminist generation rejects the former in the name
of newer and better ideas (feminism as a kind of matricide performed by
the daughters of each new wave). Or, conversely, that the wave metaphor
is cyclical in that it implies a certain repetition of the same, that new
generations of feminists would be under the illusion that they think new
thoughts or provide fresh critical analysis, while in reality each generation
replicates the former and invents the wheel time and again.

But if we think more carefully about the nature of waves we will
find that this metaphor captures cyclicality understood in terms of displacement, variation, and change quite well. Waves follow a rhythmic
movement of ebbs and flows, of crosscurrents and whirlpools. Their
movement is both regular and marked by variation. They are distinct and
singular while always already being part of a larger body of water. Each
wave brings with it something new and unexpected as it moves toward
the shore, while singing old songs from the depths of the sea. Waves
are carriers of continuity without stability or permanence. They follow a
movement of return yet thrust themselves freely and unpredictably into
a future as of yet unknown. Their sound can be a soothing lullaby or a
roaring symphony, their rhythm regular or erratic.

This rhythmic dimension distinguishes Kristeva and Irigaray's
writing from much philosophical discourse. From Kristeva's semiotic and
the oscillation of abjection to Irigaray's mimetic-poetic language and her
fascination with fluids, breath, and the element of water, the rhythmic
movement of the wave possesses a central position in their work as a
whole. And this rhythmic movement that unfolds through their work
is, I want to suggest, a movement of time, of wave-like temporal flow, a
time of return and simultaneous renewal. The wave provides continuity
and alteration, a past and a future, materialized movement, and perhaps
more than anything a present marked by continuous flow and incessant
becoming and change.

## Kristeva and Irigaray on Time and Difference

So, why turn to Kristeva and Irigaray as we search for a time capable
of sustaining the aliveness of present, past, and future—the time that I
call revolutionary time? It should be clear from what I have said so far
that Kristeva is a philosopher who has thought extensively about these
matters, and who sees them as organizing any feminist project concerned

with change. She invites us to revisit the theme of subjectivity and the question of time in the context of imagining political change: "Let us not be afraid to examine meticulously these explorations of subjective space, these complexities, these impasses; let us not be afraid to raise the debate concerning the experience of time," she urges in *The Sense and Non-Sense of Revolt* (9). On my reading, her essay "Women's Time" epitomizes not only the set of issues that my own project aims to address, but also the very project that Kristeva herself has been pursuing for about half a century now. This quite early text sketches what I take to be the core problem of Kristeva's thinking: It sets up—in temporal terms—the problematic separation of nature/drive/semiotic from culture/signification/symbolic, and shows how such a division brings about political ideologies that, per definition, fail to maintain the unpredictability, openness, and aliveness of the future.[39] That she frames the problem in temporal terms, and situates herself as someone who wants to deconstruct such distinctions exactly by articulating a temporal model that bridges the gap and overcomes the division between two ostensibly separate realms should give us a clue as to how to read her work as a whole.

Irigaray, too, is manifestly concerned with the question of time and with the way in which the openness of the future is under threat in our culture. As we will see in what follows, she views the linear temporal paradigm as one that forecloses change, futurity, and novelty, and just like Kristeva she sees this foreclosure of variation and change as an immediate consequence of the abstraction of and escape from the body in our culture. For Irigaray, the split between soma and psyche is more explicitly characterized as a consequence of the erasure of sexuate difference. She describes our culture as mono-sexual (woman, on her account, has been reduced to a negative mirror-image of man), and she mourns the fact that such a culture is bound to repeat itself indefinitely. Throughout her work, she argues that the Western models of time (linear and cyclical time) ultimately collapse into one and the same figure. Linear time, she notes in *The Forgetting of Air in Martin Heidegger*, is nothing but a circle in which "beginning and end coincide," since it repeatedly brings us back to the same.[40] Within a linear paradigm of progress, the "course is measured and, therefore, closed" (FAMH 151). Echoing Kristeva's comment on the future perfect of progress, she suggests that the "not-yet" has been reduced to an "always-already" (FAMH 53). We might add that the traditional notion of cyclical time similarly coincides with linear time, insofar as it, too, moves through repetition.

Time as we know it—time as repetitive cyclicality or as linear progression forward—fails to disrupt the logic of the same.

If Kristeva calls for a return to the semiotic and to somatic affects and drives, Irigaray emphasizes the need to cultivate sexuate difference. This cultivation would, on my reading, depend on a model of time that gives appropriate weight and significance to each of the temporal modalities (present, past, and future), and that does so by bringing the body to the forefront of our conception of time. Just as the regime of Western patriarchy is an ideology that disfigures the two sexes by reducing the relationship between them into a rigid dichotomy, so the temporal ideology that underpins patriarchal culture is one that posits a duality between linear and cyclical time, disfiguring both through a reification and idealization (read: de-sexualization) of the body.[41] Time as we know it, in other words, is nothing but an ideology—and by ideology I mean not only the desire to attain an established and self-proclaimed ideal, but also the escape from the body that such ideal(ity) implies.

Woman—understood as something other than the negative of man—strictly speaking does not exist in our culture. This is why, in Irigaray's work, she is so often referred to as a *not-yet*: she is placed on a horizon of future possibilities.[42] Sexuate difference, on Irigaray's account, is primordial but it requires cultivation. It is thus *not* (at least not yet) a lived reality, but it remains a future possibility. In *An Ethics of Sexual Difference*, for instance, she notes that sexuate difference "has not had its chance to develop, either empirically or transcendentally" (15). We must, in other words, be careful not to understand sexuate difference as in any way similar to or reducible to the complementary difference between the sexes that we know from our current culture. Sexuate difference has yet to come (*à-venir*); yet to be experienced. And it will, moreover, never *be* (in the sense of being definable once and for all), but is and must always remain in an open-ended state of *becoming*. As Deutscher puts it: "one would never be confronted with the presence of sexual difference. Sexual difference could only be that which is to come."[43] To "become woman" (or man, or something beyond the binary of these two), does not merely imply the Beauvoirean notion that we are not sexually determined at birth. For Irigaray, it moreover signifies that our becoming is a matter of cultivating our sexuate identity, and that such cultivation is a process without end (this is one of many reasons that the accusation that Irigaray would be an essentialist is implausible).

Sexuate difference, therefore, carries a promise for change without establishing beforehand what such a change might amount to: it is, I argue, the condition of possibility for novelty. And as such it is already marked by a time different from the one we know, a time irreducible to the teleological line advancing irrevocably from the past to an already defined future. As Grosz has noted: "The only time of sexual difference is that of the future . . . it is an event yet to occur, an event strangely out of time, for it does not yet have a time; and it is clear that its time may never come."[44] We will see that such future horizons can only be achieved if we view time as a perpetual movement of return (revolutionary time) rather than as linear progression forward. Men, in Irigaray's words, "forget that they are obliged to go back down to their roots [the sexed body, their material conditions of possibility] if they are to grow."[45]

Irigaray consistently emphasizes that cyclicality, for her, by no means represents a repetitive or immanent movement. She grounds her account very firmly in nature but, as we will see once we turn to her work in further detail, she does so first and foremost to show that nature is a realm that in fact is marked by change and variation. This is a view that challenges the Western patriarchal division between static-immanent nature and dynamic-transcendent culture—a division that, in turn, has served to construct the very dichotomy between cyclical and linear time, and that has been put to use not only to oppress women but other minorities too. Irigaray explicitly questions the traditional association of women with a natural realm construed as repetitive: "I know that this relation to natural temporality has meant that women have sometimes been considered a brake on culture, as 'reactionaries,' and that women see themselves in this way. I am not personally in agreement with this interpretation."[46] She views cyclical time as interrupting the morbid return of the same. Each cycle, precisely because it is similar to the cycles of nature, involves displacement: it alters the previous one, because nature, in fact, never repeats itself—it is always marked by difference, heterogeneity, and change.

If the liberation of women for Beauvoir amounted to giving them access to linear time—to grant them the transcendence that has been the privilege of (some) men for millennia already, and that is seen as achievable only through linear time—Irigaray seems to suggest that what is at stake, instead, is to make clear once and for all that the cyclicality of nature by no means is "immanent" or "repetitive" in character. She suggests, instead, that "we need to cultivate this affiliation with nature and not destroy it in order to impose a double nature that has been split off from our bodies and their elementary environment."[47] Cyclicality, importantly, never achieves closure: it must not be confused with the kind of repetition that Irigaray accuses Western philosophy of imposing on human life. It is marked, instead, by new beginnings. And this makes it a fruitful locus to turn to as we embark on a journey to install a culture of difference and a world where change is both possible and realizable.

As has been carefully explained, Kristeva expresses skepticism toward the two initial movements of feminism, positing instead a third alternative with which she herself identifies. As I have noted, however (and as will become increasingly clear as we proceed through the chapters of this book), her own account of time—while being different from the Western depiction of cyclical time—is nevertheless quite similar to that offered by the second wave of feminists. What I have called revolutionary time is in fact profoundly grounded in a cyclical account of time, with one important qualification: If cyclicality typically has been viewed as inherently repetitive in character, the cyclicality of revolt is marked instead by differentiation, alteration, and displacement. Each return provides an opening into the future—it displaces rather than repeats the past and it is thus an engine for change.

Kristeva's primary worry is that the second generation of feminists put too much emphasis on the difference between the sexes—thus reaffirming the very dichotomy that her own work is meant to challenge—and she is concerned that this emphasis on sexual difference forecloses futurity as an open horizon of possibilities in that it overshadows the singularity of each human individual (it would, we might say, establish yet another ideology or teleology). The third generation of which she speaks acknowledges that "the dichotomy between man and woman as an opposition of two rival entities is a *problem for metaphysics*" (WT 222). She goes on to state that difference must be seen as residing *within* us rather than *between* us (an idea to which I will return at length in chapter 6).

It is certainly the case that Irigaray strongly emphasizes sexuate difference while Kristeva puts more emphasis on singularity and on the differences that reside within us. This is a central contrast between our two thinkers—one that under no circumstances must be glossed over. That said, however, it is important to note that Irigaray also rejects the oppositional dichotomy between the sexes (she too sees it as a central aspect of metaphysics) and her philosophy of sexuate difference is marked throughout by the conviction that sexuate difference is asymmetrical and non-hierarchical; that it cannot be reduced to a simple dichotomy of rivaling entities. Irigaray rarely speaks of a "war between the sexes," but rather seeks to elaborate the contours of a world where we can be *with* one another without erasing or annihilating our differences (the logic of oppositional difference is, on her account, in fact a product of a culture of sameness, a culture that has failed to conceptualize difference in non-oppositional terms). I take her to claim that sexuate difference is the condition of possibility for singular differences to appear, and I hope that this will become apparent in my discussion of sexuate difference in what follows.[48]

If early readers of Irigaray tended to accuse her of essentialism—and the debate continues to this day—most readers of her work have come to acknowledge that her philosophy of sexuate difference is far more complex, and by no means can be reduced to an account that freezes woman in some eternal image or essence. In the dozens of books that Irigaray has published, there is, to my knowledge, no precise definition of woman. While I will not engage in an explicit discussion of her alleged essentialism here—many have already provided convincing arguments of this kind before me—I hope that the temporal account that I offer here might serve as a rigorous challenge to any such views.[49] If what I argue is correct—namely that time is the underpinning question that Irigaray seeks to address, and that she sees subjectivity (be it male or female—or, we should add, neither of those two) as irreducibly temporal and processual—then the very notion of essence would be inadequate to describe her work and her views. As I hope to make clear, thinking the body in relation to revolutionary time will allow us to move beyond the impasse of essentialism and anti-essentialism, and to productively (yet for the most part implicitly) intervene in debates about the relation between sex and gender.

## Conclusion

In this opening chapter I have offered a reading of Beauvoir's *The Second Sex* and *The Ethics of Ambiguity* in an attempt to show that the subjugation of woman in Western patriarchal society depends on a sexual division of temporal labor. As upholders of reproduction, embodiment, and the survival of the species, women have been confined to the cyclical time of nature. As inventors of a world that transcends our natural conditions, men have instead been the bearers of linear time. Drawing from Beauvoir's historical-existential analysis, I examined this sexual division of temporal labor to show why a critical analysis of time is essential for the articulation of a feminist politics of change. Contra Beauvoir, however, I suggested that while the linear model of time gives priority to the future, it paradoxically yields not novelty but repetition, and this is so because it is governed by an abstract ideal that delegitimizes present and past practices.

In order to move beyond the impasse of this rigid dichotomy (and the paralysis that it generates), I have therefore begun to articulate a model of time that overcomes the distinction between "static nature" (cyclical time, immanence) and "dynamic culture" (linear time, transcendence)—what I call *revolutionary time*. This temporal model shares much in common with the cyclical time so often associated with women and women's bodies, but it explicitly conceptualizes cyclicality not as a repetition of the same but, rather, as a dynamic process of displacement and alteration.

Both Kristeva and Irigaray view linear, teleological, and disembodied notions of time as being patriarchal in nature. On their account—and with this I wholly agree—any feminist project that aims at rejecting Western patriarchal structures must tackle the very notion of time that supports these structures. In the simplest terms, we might say that their work amounts to establishing a place for female subjectivity and to give women access to time. Both take as their point of departure a re-articulation of time in order to move away both from the linear temporal model that has excluded women (and other minorities) from the position of agency and subjectivity, and from cyclicality as it has been construed within the regime of linear time—cyclicality as repetition, as immanence, as the silent ground and condition for colonial-masculine time. In their work, we will find the conceptual toolbox and interpretive ground that we need in order to develop a theory of time that rejects these two traditional modes—linear and cyclical time—and instead offer a model of time that depends neither on a sexual or colonial division of temporal labor, nor on the reduction of women and other minorities to timeless objects, and that moreover makes possible a revolutionary politics of change.

# 2

# Alterity and Alteration

The most systematic aspect of Irigaray's thinking is her view that Western patriarchal society and thought is marked by sameness, that it is a culture of men for men, and that this paradigm deprives us of the means to articulate the specificity and irreducibility of female experience. The result, in her view, is that our culture repeats itself indefinitely: we have lost our capacity to create and engender, to begin anew. A culture of sameness is a static one—one that reproduces itself in its own frozen image. In this sense it is a culture emptied of life and aliveness. It is, we might say, a culture of the past: it repeats the already-known, the already-said, the always-already-dead. Without sexuate difference, we lose the prospect of a different future, a yet-to-come, horizons as of yet unknown. Irigaray speaks of an "almost fatal repetition at the cultural level," and complains that women within such a culture "are brought up (whether consciously or not) to be trained in repetition, to adapt to a society's systems, and educated to do *like*, to be *like*, without any decisive innovations or discoveries of [their] own."[1]

The worries expressed here might help us understand the urgency that Irigaray ascribes to the establishment of a culture of sexuate difference, and her famous claim that such difference "is one of the major philosophical issues, if not *the* issue, of our age" (SD 5, emphasis mine). If we fail to take on this task we will, quite simply, be deprived of a livable future.[2] We will continue repeating the same tropes over and over again, articulating subjectivity in the same reductive terms. As Irigaray puts it in the opening chapter of *An Ethics of Sexual Difference*, "Sexual difference is probably the issue in our time which could be our 'salvation' if we thought it through" (SD 5). Sexuate difference carries a promise of fecundity, not only on the level of biology but—I think much more importantly for Irigaray—on a cultural, spiritual, and aesthetic level. It has the potential to disrupt the logic of sameness that marks our current culture. If patriarchal culture is bound to repeat the same, a culture of sexuate difference would provide the variation and fecundity that we need in order to imagine and live in times different from our own. A culture of the same lacks imagination. It follows established paths and patterns and repeats them in its own selfsame image.

For Irigaray, the transition from a culture of sameness to one of sexuate difference depends on a reassessment of the most fundamental categories of human experience: "In order to make it possible to think through, and live, this difference, we must reconsider the whole problematic of *space* and *time*," she asserts (SD 7). Without a model of time different from the ones we have known hitherto, we would not be able to cultivate or even articulate difference beyond the dichotomous form that we ascribe to it today. Irigaray's critique of our current culture of sameness in other words runs parallel to her critique of the sexual division of temporal labor and the dichotomous models of time that accompany it (cyclical repetition and linear progress). Just as sexuate difference has been covered over, so has the model of time that would allow for its cultivation.

To reconsider space and time so as to make possible a culture of sexuate difference would be the "revolution in thought and ethics" that Irigaray herself calls for (SD 6); the transformative work that her own philosophical thought is meant to inaugurate. "In order for an ethics of sexual difference to come into being, we must constitute a possible place for each sex, body and flesh to inhabit. Which presupposes a memory of the past, a hope for the future, memory bridging the present and disconcerting the mirror symmetry that annihilates the difference of identity" (SD 17–18). The spatiotemporal model that she seeks to establish—one that would provide a dwelling for irreducibly different sexuate subjects in the present—thus hinges upon the work of memory. Our hope for the future, and our chances of living in a present no longer marked by mirror symmetry (in other words, a present where sexed subjects can be defined in their own terms, not merely as positive-neutral or negative poles in a static system of values), depends on a "memory of the past." But what does this mean? Why this emphasis on the past, when what is at stake is the future? In what follows, I hope to elucidate these questions. We will, however, initially have to retrace our steps, in order to illuminate what is at stake in all this for Irigaray.

## Time, Change, and Sexuate Difference

As we have seen, Irigaray believes that the possibility of a different future hinges on the establishment of a new relation to space and time: "The transition to a new age requires a change in our perception and conception of *space-time*" (SD 7). Regretting the sublation of time from cyclical rhythm to line, she argues that linear time unfolds according to a "patriarchal genealogical order, substituting itself for natural engender-ing, either cosmic or maternal," forgetful of the "cyclical character of feminine sexuality" or "the cycles of the moon and even of the earth."[3] Time as we know it in Western modernity—time as line—is thus put in place through an act of repression (a repression, more precisely, of our maternal-material conditions of possibility). It is through this model of time that male subjectivity becomes construed as disembodied rationality, and it is through linear time that man repeats himself in an eternal mime.

Echoing both Beauvoir and Kristeva, Irigaray emphasizes that wom-en's role as (passive) objects rather than (active) subjects follows from the sexual division of temporal labor and the reduction of woman from a temporal creature of transcendence to the non-temporal immanent and material ground that man needed in order to achieve his own transcen-dence. If man's entry into linear time gave him the potency to project himself above and beyond nature, woman, meanwhile, has been reduced to lack or absence; to a timeless envelope or container in which man can fulfill his own growth (just like colonized populations were reduced to "primitives" so as to make possible the birth of the modern, "civilized" man). Woman, Irigaray notes in critical dialogue with Heidegger, "provides material for the ek-stasis of time. Though not therein herself existing as a subject" (FAMH 103). Ewa Płonowska Ziarek has suggested that "Irigaray's emphasis on temporality displaces the concept of femininity from the negation of essence, expressed in Lacan's famous statement that Woman does not exist."[4] Irigaray's engagement with the question of time would thus amount to attributing subjectivity to woman, thus freeing her from her captivity in and as a passive-receptive space or object—but it would do so without positing a female essence.

Irigaray speaks of a tradition where time has become "the *interiority* of the subject itself, and space, its *exteriority*," and this has, in turn, resulted in the feminine being "experienced as space while the masculine is experienced as time" (SD 7).[5] If the male subject is "the master of time" (SD 7), woman, instead, "finds herself delineated as thing" (SD 10). More specifically, she has been delineated as a timeless thing. The objectification of women is, as I have already noted, at least in part to be blamed on the fact that they have been denied access to time, or that the current Western temporal models fail to capture the specificity of female experience. Time, subjectivity, and masculinity have become viewed as synonymous. As I have elucidated already by examining Beauvoir's analysis in *The Second Sex*, man's entry into the time of history and transcendence depends on a repression of sorts: he lets woman bear the burden of embodiment so as to free himself from it. His transcendence depends on her immanence. He achieves the status of subject by turning her into an object. He enters into time by reducing her to a receptive space.

Irigaray agrees with Beauvoir's diagnosis: "If traditionally, and as a mother, woman represents *place* for man, such a limit means that she becomes a *thing* . . . Moreover, the maternal-feminine also serves as an *envelope*, a *container*, the starting point from which man limits his things" (SD 10). The woman-mother has thus become a silent ground from which man can project himself into a paternal-ideal world.[6] Irigaray calls for a fundamental "remaking of immanence and transcendence" (SD 18), but while Beauvoir wanted to grant women transcendence by giving them access to linear time, Irigaray urges us to critically assess these notions as such, to unveil the very mechanisms that established a dichotomy between (repetitive) immanence-nature-cyclicality and (progressive) transcendence-culture-linearity in the first place.

What is at stake in this chapter—and in my project as a whole—is the possibility to make change. In an interview from 1985, Irigaray again stresses the urgency of establishing a culture of sexuate difference, and ties the possibility of change to it: "The world can't afford the luxury of this repression anymore. It needs sexual difference not just in order to reproduce, but to be revived and produce a new culture."[7] It is, according to Irigaray, only within a framework of difference—and more specifically sexuate difference—that we can avoid the perpetual repetition of the same. Sexuate difference, on her account, is the condition of possibility for novelty. It is creative, it generates new and unforeseen horizons, and it is therefore needed for the renewal of human life and culture: "*Sexual difference is necessary for the continuation of our species*, not only because it constitutes the locus for procreation, but also because it's here that life is regenerated," Irigaray writes.[8]

I want to emphasize the qualification that she makes here between sexuate difference as a locus for biological procreation, on the one hand, and its simultaneous capacity to regenerate or rejuvenate life understood more broadly, on the other. Elsewhere, Irigaray has noted that it "is a source of fecundity, not only physical but also cultural, spiritual,"[9] and she consistently stresses that sex is linked to a "specific imaginary creation as well as to regeneration, procreation, and more generally, life."[10] Whenever she speaks of sexuate difference—the central theme of her corpus—we must thus assume that both of these aspects are in play: on the one hand, the biological role of sexuate difference as that which guarantees the survival of the species, and, on the other hand, its cultural and spiritual significance and its capacity not only to keep us alive (in the literal sense of the term) but, perhaps more importantly, to inject life and vitality into our culture, to make it a dynamic and imaginative culture of renewal and change.[11]

Irigaray stresses this duality throughout her work: "Sexual difference would constitute the horizon of worlds more fecund than any known to date—at least in the West—and without reducing fecundity to the reproduction of bodies and flesh. For loving partners this would be a fecundity of birth and regeneration, but also the production of a new age of thought, art, poetry, and language: the creation of a new *poetics*" (SD 5).[12] I stress this because, ultimately, I am more interested in the social ramifications of our cultivation of sexuate difference than biological ones. While thinkers like Grosz have used Irigaray as a resource to argue for the importance of sexuate difference in the biological realm, I am consciously leaving questions of biology aside, in part because they are not really relevant for my project, in part because I worry about the heteronormative implications of pursuing such a path, and in part because I do not have the appropriate expertise to speak to issues of biological evolution. While I will offer a tentative analysis of nature as a realm marked by diversity and variation, my remarks on this topic by and large lack specific references to the natural sciences.[13] Sexuate difference, as Irigaray conceives it, is a crucial factor for *any* form of renewal and change, not only, or even primarily, evolutionary or reproductive change. And if it is true that it has been forgotten or covered over in

Western culture, we begin to see the stakes involved in returning to it in order to save the present and the future from repeating the past. If sexuate difference indeed is a necessary condition for variation and change, then it should be clear why it is inseparable from a discussion of time and temporal experience.

In the course of this book, the role and status of sexuate difference will be elucidated in several steps. The present chapter seeks to sketch the contours of its relationship to the question of time. While my discussion here is framed by an assessment of the dynamics of the two ostensibly separate realms that we call "nature" and "culture" (typically linked to cyclical and linear time, respectively), it remains rather abstract in this initial attempt at elucidation. My ambition is first and foremost to argue for the irreducible status of both time and difference. In my chapters treating the present, I deepen this argument by adding to it a more explicit discussion of the relationship between sexed subjects, and the temporal status of such a relation. Sexuate difference is thus given some more concretion there, in that it is viewed in light of intersub-jective relations and, hence, a set of ethical and political concerns. In the chapters on the past I revisit the interdependence between time and sexuate difference, and while the discussion there serves to elaborate what we might call the ontological stakes of my argument (through an analysis of our relationship to "origins"), I focus more specifically on the ontogenetic aspects of temporal succession and sexuate difference. If the present chapter seeks to argue that revolutionary time hinges on a return to the sexed body, I point more specifically in those chapters to the maternal body as the lost continent that revolutionary time is meant to reclaim, through a movement of return.

The conceptual work that sexuate difference is intended to do in all chapters of this book is to undermine one of the central claims of a Western tradition that views time as a line: in positing linear time, or the time of history, we assume an ultimate beginning or origin (*archē*) and an ultimate end or goal (*telos*). On this model, time would flow forward between these end-points, from the past into the future, from the beginning to the end of time. As I will argue in what follows, the primacy of sexuate difference makes impossible any notion of a singular origin; and the irreducibility of sexuate difference similarly undermines the notion of a final end. With sexuate difference we inscribe variation and differentiation—heterogeneity—into the very process of becoming, with the result that any notion of an absolute beginning or a final end is rendered obsolete. It is precisely insofar as becoming depends on sexuate difference that it remains unpredictable, open-ended, and irreducible to a singular and selfsame origin (an origin that, precisely, would escape the alterity of difference and, moreover, the movement of time).[14]

My argument, in what follows, will proceed in two steps. First, I will unpack the two assumptions inherent in the traditional temporal division between (female-natural) cyclical and (male-cultural) linear time, namely (a) that the cyclical time of nature repeats itself indefinitely (hence its association with immanence); and (b) that linear time is a time of progress and change (hence its association with transcendence). I will attempt to show that both of these assumptions, on Irigaray's account, are false. If it is true, as Irigaray claims, that change depends on sexuate difference, then it would be *nature* (cyclical time) that was capable of change, since nature, arguably, is thoroughly marked by difference and differentiation, while our current culture, at least according to Irigaray, is a culture of sameness. Second, I want to offer some preliminary remarks about the temporality that would accompany the culture of difference that Irigaray seeks to establish. To this end, I will examine her efforts to redefine the very categories of immanence and transcendence, and then go on to discuss the strategies used by Irigaray herself in her attempt to introduce an alternative temporal model as she elaborates the making of a world inhabited by sexed subjects irreducible to one another.

## Remaking Immanence and Transcendence

My reading of Beauvoir's *The Second Sex* led me to conclude that life in Western modernity has been organized according to a sexual division of temporal labor: women carrying the burden of embodiment and reproduction; men being the carriers instead of spirituality and production. While I argued that her analysis is accurate on a descriptive level, I suggested that she nevertheless fails to acknowledge that the very conception of cyclical time as repetitive and linear time as progressive in itself is a colonial-patriarchal construction in need of critical analysis—one that she fails to offer.

Beauvoir is by no means alone in characterizing the cycles of nature and life as repetitive and driven by mere necessity. This is a common and paradigmatically persistent portrayal of nature. Arendt, for instance, speaks of the "gigantic circle of nature herself" as one "where no beginning and no end exist and where all natural things swing in changeless, deathless repetition."[15] She contrasts brute nature—a sphere that, on her account, forces all living beings into cyclical movement and where "neither birth nor death as we understand them" exist (HC 96)—with a specifically human space or home that provides worldliness and the durability or permanence that "makes appearance and disappearance possible" (HC 97). "Without a world into which men are born and from which they die, there would be nothing but changeless eternal recurrence, the deathless everlastingness of the human as of all other animal species" (HC 97). Nature, on this account, is characterized as incapable of change and variation, and is quite simply described as an eternal return of the same, an everlasting repetitive movement of cycles where beginning and end coincide.

Arendt describes the specifically human life (*bios*, as distinguished from *zoē*) as "the time interval between birth and death" (HC 97), and while this interval by no means can escape the cyclical time of nature, it nevertheless is described first and foremost as linear development: "Limited by a beginning and an end, that is, by the two supreme events of appearance and disappearance within the world," she notes, human life "follows a strictly linear movement whose very motion nevertheless is driven by the motor of biological life which man shares with other living things and which forever retains the cyclical movement of nature" (HC 97). We see, again, that linear time is raised above and against the cyclicality of our natural condition, and that it is what makes us "human" in the sense of providing us with a means to escape the brute materiality of our existence (it is, precisely, what allows us to maintain the illusion that we can transcend our bodies). Linear time becomes equated with freedom and human projects (both understood as largely disembodied), while cyclical time remains associated with necessity, embodiment, and brute nature. And the very dichotomy between "nature" and "culture" relies on the assumption that the former is static while the latter is prone to change. As historian of science Barbara Duden notes, "the body and its environment have been consigned to opposing realms: on the one side are the body, nature, and biology, stable and unchanging phenomena; on the other side are the social environment and history, realms of constant change."[16]

In her essay "The Female Gender," Irigaray endeavors to challenge this common view of nature as static, repetitive, and "timeless." She makes a clear distinction between the cyclical time of nature and the linear time of culture but, contrary to the common view, she characterizes the former (nature) as capable of variation and change while the latter (culture) is described as repeating the same. Why, we must ask, does culture, on Irigaray's account, repeat itself, while the cycles of nature do not? Irigaray characterizes culture as a kind of mechanical existence, due to its inability to acknowledge sexuate difference and the differentiation that such a difference would be capable of instigating. Insofar as Western modernity is a culture of sexuate sameness, it is bound to reproduce the same subject positions in an eternal mime. "A machine has no sex," Irigaray notes in the opening paragraph of the essay (FG 107). "Nature, on the other hand, always has a sex" (FG 107). What is lost in mechanical reproduction (and, I should add, in Western modernity as a whole, if we accept Irigaray's diagnosis) is sexuate difference. And whereas the work of the machine "is always the same" insofar as it "works by repetition," nature follows rhythms and "respects the differences in rhythms" (FG 108). Nature does not repeat. "It is in continuous becoming. Even when similarities in her cycles occur, nature never repeats herself identically," because nature has a sex, "always and everywhere" (FG 108).

The problem, however, is that we "are out of tune with our natural rhythms."[17] We are, in other words, trapped in a technocratic time of repetition, disconnected from the heterogeneity that our natural belonging would provide. Linear time, on Irigaray's account, is blind to difference and reproduces sameness. While nature is marked by variation and heterogeneity, it is culture (the world that men have erected as their home on earth) that is bound by mimetic repetition and the eternal return of the same. This view runs as a mantra through Irigaray's work: "The same . . . Same . . . Always the same."[18] We are culturally and linearly imprisoned by sameness and repetition. The "natural elements" have been "forced to bow to man's affect and will," and as a consequence our universe has been closed up "into a circle," a line biting its own tail and therefore foreclosing the possibility of indeterminacy and undecidability.[19]

Nature, Irigaray insists, engenders rather than repeats. It follows what we might call a time of generation, and each generation is unique and different from the former and that which follows. It is linear time that, on Irigaray's account, crops up in a circle where beginning and end coincide. In her reading of Aristotle in *Speculum of the Other Woman*, she turns straight to his conception of time in order to show that it forecloses renewal and change. The fact that Aristotle (on her account) posits an absolute beginning (the prime mover), and an already established end (a *telos*), means that he posits and assumes a linear-temporal paradigm that, according to Irigaray, cuts us off from our maternal-material beginnings (note the plural) and from future possibilities of becoming: "Everyone, in effect, is pulled up by the roots, deprived of the 'body's' first resources, of the endless possibilities of being in space. . . . All that remains is for each person to realize his essence as perfectly as he can, to give full expression to his *telos*, within the limits ascribed to him."[20] Irigaray highlights that "this philosophical construct reduces the potential for generation, growth, change, and expansion for all beings."[21] Within the paradigm of linear time, she argues, nothing new ever appears. We simply follow the course already outlined for us from the start. Her claims are, here as elsewhere, hyperbolic in character. Let me therefore pause for a moment to consider them more carefully.

It may seem strange to argue that nothing new has been produced over the past several centuries. Western modernity is of course an age of incessant proliferation of new ideas, new inventions, new identities, new medicines, and new political structures. It is an age of revolutions, of redrawn maps, of scientific discoveries, of new spiritual landscapes. But, as we saw in the opening chapter, it is also a time driven by ideologies, by technocratic goals and agendas, and by a tendency to erase the past in order to install an already defined future. It is, moreover, a time of colonial violence and genocides. And it is a time marked by sexual sameness. Irigaray often suggests that what we view as "plurality" in fact is nothing of the sort—exactly because it is thought and achieved within a world that remains driven by a logic of sameness. True proliferation and variation could only be attained if this logic was thoroughly challenged, if we established a culture of (at least) two, even a metaphysics of (at least) two. She obviously does not deny the reality of modern revolutions and inventions, but she consistently emphasizes that they are made possible through a sacrifice of sorts: a sacrifice of the body, of nature, and of the specificity of female subjectivity (and, we should add, despite Irigaray's troubling silence on these issues: of black and brown bodies, queer and trans lives, indigenous cultures, and so on). Progress, in other words, is violent, and her own task (and my task here) is to think futurity and change in non-sacrificial terms. Insofar as progress proceeds violently—insofar as it is based on a sacrificial logic it repeats a common trope, and it depends on a repression of sorts. What is at stake is thus not merely to replace violent progress with nonviolent change, but to acknowledge that our violent-progressive culture in fact undermines change altogether; that it leads to repetition.

To put all this differently, we might say that our culture produces all kinds of new things and events, but that human relations remain largely the same—and will continue to do so—as long as we fail to cultivate sexuate difference. Even as women and LGBTQ folk have gained social liberties and political rights, we continue to lack a rich account of sexed subjectivity understood as irreducibly different from the straight cis-male model upon which it has hitherto been crafted. Our projects and products will thus irrevocably bring us back to the same normative framework, albeit in seemingly novel form. We have yet to see what kind of changes and inventions a culture of sexuate difference would bring about—if ever it will be realized.

Cyclical time, if viewed not in the traditional way but as Irigaray depicts it here (which, using my own vocabulary instead, would be revolutionary time), is unpredictable and renewable because it starts from difference and engenders difference. If Arendt suggested that nature is "endlessly repetitive" and "always moves in the same circle" (HC 98), Irigaray time and again insists that it is linear time and culture that "always comes back to the same thing."[22] Linear time, and its counterpart notion of cyclical time, are only flip sides of the same coin: they converge in that they both amount to little more than repetition. What the present discussion is meant to show, then, is that Irigaray's analysis of sexuate difference (understood first and foremost as that which must be cultivated to establish a living and livable culture) provides the conceptual framework that we need in order to develop a working model of time that can replace the linear-cyclical paradigm, and that reveals the fact that linear time is bound to close itself up in a selfsame circle. If the linear-cyclical paradigm (which, as I have argued, is one of the founding features of our colonial-patriarchal culture) is premised on an escape from the body and on an abstract idealism that reduces material processes to dead repetition, Irigaray offers instead a model of time that allows us to see the transformative character of a body that, on her account, necessarily is sexed and temporal at once (and it is precisely by virtue of it being sexed and temporal that it is capable of transformation and change).

On my reading—and here I clearly move beyond Irigaray's own explicit account and agenda—this not only has the potential of transforming the meaning of identity categories such as "man" and "woman," but makes possible an account of sexed embodiment that would be more flexible in terms of the relationship between sex and gender than what was implied by Beauvoir's famous "one is not born a woman." As

Anne Fausto-Sterling has pointed out, "the sex/gender dualism limits feminist analysis," insofar as gender "necessarily excludes biology," which makes "a sociocultural analysis of the body seem impossible."[23] Troubling more fundamentally the long-held assumption that nature (and sex) is *unchanging*, while culture (and gender), is *constructed*[24] would shed new light on the current inhumane practice of imposing non-consensual surgeries on intersex infants to assure that their sex unambiguously matches their gender identity, since we would be better equipped to recognize as "natural" the malleability and heterogeneity of sexed bodies (not just intersexed bodies, but *all* bodies).

And if trans embodiment, as we saw in the previous chapter, has tended to be locked into a narrowly scripted temporal regime that requires that we experience and narrate our embodied lives linearly from past via present to the future (the demand that trans folk exhibit a "troubled queer childhood" in order to access procedures that will guarantee a static and unambiguous body for the future, one that fits neatly into binary norms about the sex-gender-relation, and passes as such),[25] the temporal model explored here has the potential of broadening the horizon of possibilities such that, as Spade puts it, "some birth-assigned 'women' [who] might want to take hormones and become sexy 'bearded ladies' who are interpreted in a variety of ways but feel great about how they look" can do so without being seen as betraying an otherwise unambiguous "natural" embodied reality.[26] The standards that the gatekeepers demand that trans folk measure up to—what Talia Mae Bettcher has called "reality enforcement"[27]—are not only ones that produce "a fiction of natural gender in which normal, non-transsexual people grow up with minimal to no gender trouble or exploration,"[28] but also a fiction of nature (or "reality") itself as unchanging, unambiguous, and productive of bodies that neatly abide by a binary model of sex. Again, these are not the implications Irigaray herself imagined as she examined the relationship between sexuate difference and change. But, if put into conversation with more recent work on intersex issues as well as with trans studies, her work in fact offers interesting resources for exploring these matters.[29]

Given what I have already said about the potential of a culture of sexuate difference to generate renewal both on the biological and on the cultural-spiritual level, we might say that sexuate difference, as it is elaborated by Irigaray, offers a horizon that cuts across the division between nature and culture (as well as sex and gender). Revolutionary time, similarly, undermines the rigid division between two temporal models corresponding to these ostensibly separate realms, and thus provides a model of time that renders implausible any simplistic division between repetitive nature and a culture of progress and change. Both sexuate difference and revolutionary time thus challenge such dualist accounts, and refuse the standard distinction between (static) sex and (flexible) gender—a distinction that all-too-often has colored our conception of categories such as time, freedom, and subjectivity, and that serves to police "gender deviants" and folk whose bodily experiences do not match cis-gendered expectations and norms.

In "The Female Gender," Irigaray addresses an issue that often recurs in her work and that is equally central for Kristeva. The mechanical and technological culture described there—a culture based on an eternal mime of the same—is articulated not only in terms of repetition, but also in terms of death. It is a predictable culture where everything is already said and—hence—always already dead, finished, finalized. I will discuss this further both in my discussion of Kristeva in the next chapter, and in the section on the present, where I look at Irigaray's attempt to artic-ulate what I call a living present. What we need to establish, according to Irigaray, is "proof that we are living men and living women and not individuals in the abstract, impersonal, rather like robots or strange beings beyond the reach of death."[30] As I have already noted, the linear model of time coincides with a form of idealism. The modern progressive subject is a disembodied subject.[31] This loss of the body (a loss more commonly described as a *liberation* from the body) is a loss of heterogeneity, and the consequence is that "something of the manner in which physical beings grow is lost. Things, cut from their natural enrootedness, float about, wandering the propositional landscape. The *phuein* of physical beings is forgotten in the *physis* of the *logos*. The physical constitution of beings is forgotten in the metaphysics of Being" (FAMH 86–87). The ideality of linear time generates a path away from our material conditions. The becoming of human life is, therefore, reduced to an abstract notion of futurity, with the result that the future is cut off altogether, since renewal depends on heterogeneity.

For Irigaray, both life and the renewal of life depend on sexuate difference. She asserts that "as long as we are still living, we are sexually differentiated. Otherwise, we are dead" (FG 107). Time and again, she emphasizes that in order to live and to be alive, we must "have a sex" and be "born of sexedness" (FG 118). Sexuate difference, in other words, is what gives us access to time. It is as embodied (and sexed) beings that we are finite. It is as embodied (and sexed) beings that we have (and sometimes lack) time. The machine "does at times protect and assist life," but insofar as it has no sex, "it never creates or engenders life" (FG 107).

While I will not have time to discuss this problem at length, we must at least acknowledge, at this juncture, that this line of argument in Irigaray's work sounds alarmingly heteronormative. It is obviously not the case that homosexual relations promote a "culture of death," nor that they would lack a fecundity of their own. Any such claims would have to be rejected in the strongest terms. But when Irigaray speaks of a homosexual or mono-sexual culture of death, I take her to have a male-dominated, misogynist, and patriarchal culture of sameness—not same-sex desire—in mind. As we have seen, such a patriarchal culture is one that discriminates not only against women but also against the LGBTQ community. So, while it seems clear that Irigaray all-too-often slips into heteronormative language, I ultimately do not think that her discussion of sexuate difference *need* to be heteronormative, and I am interested here in pursuing such a generous reading so as to unveil the conceptual potential of her work for feminist interrogations into questions of time and difference.[32]

Because Western culture has failed to develop in difference and to embrace the specificity of both (or rather all) genders, it has lost its capacity for renewal: "A nontraditional, fecund encounter between the sexes barely exists," Irigaray explains (SD 6). And if sexuate difference might exist on a biological level, it has unfortunately been reduced to this level alone, and has thus lost its capacities for cultural and spiritual renewal: "Sexual difference has always served procreation. For some time now, sexual difference has not played a part in the *creation of culture*, except in a division of roles and functions that does not allow both [indeed all] sexes to be subjects."[33] We are reminded that Irigaray is wary of our tendency to confine sexuate difference to the realm of procreation—a wariness that she shares with queer theorists working on issues of time.

For Irigaray, sexuate difference and temporal differentiation are thus integral to the possibility for novelty and change. This is exactly why life does not repeat itself, why it is marked by alteration from the start. Life is fundamentally marked by variation and differentiation: a life that remains the same is no life. This challenges the idea that transcendence occurs in culture alone while nature would be confined to repetitive immanence. The distinction that we tend to draw between (repetitive) reproduction and (creative) production is thus, again, a problematic one: it implies that the former would be stuck in sheer replication while the latter carries a promise for change.

What is at stake as we try to elaborate sexed subjectivity is, among other things, to acknowledge the potential for transcendence in both nature and culture (which in turn would lead to a collapse of the very demarcation that we tend to assume between the two realms—as if they were opposites or even distinct from one another). This task not only amounts to recognizing the capacity for transcendence in what we call nature. It also involves bringing awareness to the fact that a culture marked by sameness is one *incapable* of transcendence and thus one that is bound to repeat itself indefinitely (an a-temporal culture, a culture unable to invent anew).[34] By highlighting the central position of time in Irigaray's corpus, and by pointing out the inseparability of her discussion of time and her treatment of the question of sexuate difference, I hope to have shown that this dual task is integral to her project as a whole and that it depends on an elaboration of time in nonlinear terms. I wish now to examine questions of freedom, transcendence, and relationality in light of what I have said about time and its relation to sexuate difference.

Let us revisit a remark that was made earlier in this chapter: Irigaray, I noted, calls for a fundamental "remaking of immanence and transcendence" (SD 18). How, we must ask, is she using these terms, and what would it mean to "remake" them? How, moreover, might her usage of them elucidate her views on time, on the one hand, and sexuate difference, on the other? In an attempt to respond to these questions, I want to look at the opening two paragraphs of *Sharing the World*. The book as a whole is an implicit engagement with Heidegger, as Irigaray is fleshing out some of the central themes of her own work: that the sexes are irreducibly different and that the encounter between them depends on the establishment of different worlds, or horizons of experience. It should come as no surprise that Irigaray approaches these themes through a discussion of the categories of space and time. But here, more than elsewhere, she broaches the question of time by raising the issue of transcendence. Let me turn to the passage in question, as I begin to examine the relationship between time and transcendence, and the concomitant relationship between these categories and that of sexuate difference:

When the world corresponds to the transcendence projected by a single subject as the horizon of the totality of all that exists, this world converts time into space. Although such a transcendence represents a temporal project on the part of the subject, the fact that this subject ensures, from a unique standpoint, the gathering or the closure of the whole of finite things results in the world closing up, even in advance, in a circle. The intuition of the infinite can remain, but the dynamic, indeed the dialectical, relations between time and space somehow or other freeze. Passing from one horizon to another, from one epoch of history to another, will thus not happen without some harm: for example, without war according to Hegel, without destruction or deconstruction according to Heidegger.

In contrast, if the transcendental also has its origin in a respect for the irreducible difference of the other really considered as other, in the fact that their otherness is thus never knowable nor appropriable by myself—although it appears limited to my perceptions and even my intuitions—then transcendence no longer amounts to merely making objective a projection of my own subjectivity. So long as the other subject remains alive and free with respect to another world, especially to my world, time and space are kept in a dialectical process between us in an always indefinite and open way.[35]

This passage will need careful unpacking. First, we should note that Irigaray wants to free transcendence from its metaphysical connotations. When she speaks of transcendence—here and elsewhere—she is not referring to a projection beyond this world or beyond nature. Transcendence is also not meant as a way of overcoming temporal existence—it is rather a necessary feature of temporalization. The transcendent, for Irigaray, is the other of sexuate difference. While she doubtlessly is a thinker of immanence in that she refuses to posit a realm beyond the sensible realm (*phusis*), or a world beyond temporal experience, she could be described as a transcendental thinker in that she consistently stresses that this world of ours, this world that we (finite human beings) inhabit, always and irreducibly must be thought in heterogeneous terms—not as one.[36] On her account, there is no world *beyond* the natural-human world, but there are (at least) *two human worlds*—each inhabited by different (indeed irreducible) sexuate experiences. The ethical challenge that follows from this view of transcendence is, in Irigaray's view, that the sharing of the world—our ability to encounter the other, respect the other, come close to the other, even love the other—depends on our cultivating separate and irreducibly different worlds. The task that an ethics of sexuate difference amounts to is, in other words, to resist the temptation to overcome the difference between these worlds (to reduce one to the other, to bridge the gap, to deny their separation through an act of appropriation), but to do so without turning our back on the other and their world. The challenge is precisely to cultivate dialogue and intimacy in difference.

What does it mean that the sexually other is transcendent to me? It means that they remain—and must remain—a mystery to me. I will return to this aspect of Irigaray's thought in detail in the section on presence (and say more about its ethical implications then), but let me already now stress the importance of this statement. When Irigaray, in the quote above, says that the other is irreducible because their otherness never is "knowable or appropriable by myself," she is not positing a Levinasian absolute Other whose ethical call I have a responsibility to answer. As I understand her, she is simply saying that there will always be a certain distance between myself and the other. This distance implies no hierarchy, yet it cannot be overcome (we should add that it would not be desirable to overcome it—I will say more about this later). This distance, I want to suggest, is temporal. Let me develop this further.

*Sharing the World* opens with the following statement: "When the world corresponds to the transcendence projected by a single subject as the horizon of the totality of all that exists, this world converts time into space." What does this mean? Given what I have just said, I take Irigaray to mean that in a world of one—in a world dominated by a male subject who reduces women (and, we should add, any and all subjects who transgress the gender binary) to mute objects deprived of a world of their own—transcendence becomes impossible. The selfsame subject (man) is under the impression that he transcends, while in fact his world has become a world of immanence: he merely repeats himself in his own selfsame image. That a world of sameness is bound by repetition we have already seen, but we should now be better equipped to examine this idea in further detail.

Recall Beauvoir's contention that man's transcendence, in a patriarchal world, sprang out of his letting woman carry the burden of his embodiment. Beauvoir wanted to give woman her cut wings back, so that she too could fly into the sky and no longer be burdened with the weight not only of her own body, but also of the body that man had put on her in order to escape his own material conditions. Remember, also, that Beauvoir's analysis helped me draw the conclusion that man's escaping his embodiment robbed woman of time. We might say, following Irigaray's statement above, that woman's time was converted into space: she was deprived of her ability to "fly" (transcend), and was imprisoned in a body that doomed her to immanence—reducing her thus to the immobile and passive space from which man could begin his own flight. Irigaray would indeed agree with this analysis, but when she states that time is converted into space, I take her to mean not only that woman has been reduced from a temporal to a merely spatial being, but that time in general, temporal change, has disappeared and been converted into static space.

In a world where transcendence is defined from the point of view of one subject alone (the male subject who transcends linearly and forwardly through his various projects and projections), transcendence is no longer a question of time but rather a repetitive movement within a confined space: the space of one single subject. In such a world we are incapable of renewal and creative production since all it can do is produce selfsame images of the one that inhabits it alone. The world, and time, close up "in a circle." And such transcendence—which in fact is no transcendence at all—can only proceed violently: the dynamic dialectic of time becomes reduced to a historical dialectic that, as Irigaray puts it, assures progress only at the cost of "some harm."[37] When sexuate difference is reduced to sexual difference (when woman, in other words, is seen as other to same rather than as other to other, irreducibly different), we lose time and temporal difference. And we become trapped in a hall of mirrors where the same images are reflected and reflected again, with no difference or differentiation in sight.

Transcendence, for Irigaray, depends on the establishment of (at least) two worlds, which is to say that it depends on a culture of sexuate difference. To put it in the Heideggerian terminology that pervades Irigaray's analysis in this book, we might say that Heidegger impossibly could sustain the ecstatic character of Dasein as long as he maintains that Dasein is sexually neutral. This is where his analysis of time fails, on Irigaray's account. Without sexuate difference, there can be no transcendence (or ek-stasis), and without transcendence, we cannot even really speak about time. If sexuate difference is the condition of possibility for transcendence (the latter here understood not metaphysically, but as the thrusting beyond a selfsame subject—the "being-there" or "Dasein" of human existence), sexuate difference is needed if we are to think time as transcendence (ek-stasis). To again put this in terms that echo my discussion of Beauvoir, if woman seeks freedom and transcendence by attempting to enter the linear time of man—a time the very existence of which depends on the erasure of sexuate difference—she would foreclose freedom and transcendence altogether, and we would all have lost our wings, in that we would be deprived of a livable future.

If the existentialist model for self-realization follows a linear model of time—project forward, projection into the future—Irigaray instead situates the very possibility for transcendence in a time that unfolds *between* human subjects, in a sexuate relation: a time that is shared and embodied rather than interior and abstract. My relation to the sexuate other (which, at least on my reading, need not be *heterosexually* other, as in "of the opposite sex," but rather an incarnate singular other who is irreducibly different from me and from any and all notions of a sexually neutral "hu/man") is, on Irigaray's account, what enables my transcendence and self-realization. While Beauvoir grants that my freedom and transcendence depend on the freedom of others rather than being threatened by it (this is indeed one of the founding ideas of any existentialist ethics), she remains within a paradigm of sameness in that she seeks to overcome the irreducible difference between sexuate subjects. Following Irigaray, we must conclude that such ethics, despite its intention to give a rigorously intersubjective account of freedom, nevertheless runs the risk of positing a model of freedom and transcendence that reduces the other to a mirror image of the same. As we will see in my discussion of presence and co-presence in the next part of this book, such a model of ethics cannot be understood as addressing questions of intersubjectivity at all, since it is operating within a paradigm incapable of thinking irreducibly different subjects. Despite its own intentions, it therefore remains within a subject-object-paradigm, and the other is, as a consequence, reduced to a thing.

In addition, I should note that if transcendence for the existentialist is a surpassing of the in-itself that is our past and our body (transcendence is, precisely, an escape from immanence), Irigaray elaborates a model of transcendence that need not surpass the past (nor the body) at all. Beauvoir's definition of ethics as a "triumph of freedom over facticity" (EoA

44) clearly posits freedom not only in opposition to facticity (our past and our body) but also as an active repression of it. Insofar as Irigaray views freedom and transcendence not as a repression of facticity but rather as an active cultivation of it, she not only differs from Beauvoir but she challenges some of the most fundamental aspects of the existentialist view on subjectivity. If Sartre in *Being and Nothingness* saw facticity as a paralyzing contingency that we attempt to flee and modify, but that we nevertheless have to drag along (since we cannot completely suppress or change it), Irigaray instead views it as the actual locus for change and transcendence.[38] What is radical about Irigaray's thinking is that it allows us to think the past, the body, and our relation to the other as the very horizons upon which transcendence—and temporal transformation and change—can take place. Rather than being burdens that we must escape in order to transcend into the future, they are the conditions of possibility for transcendence and futurity.

So, to ask the question again: What would it mean to remake immanence and transcendence? First, transcendence would no longer mean the projection of one subject onto the other, nor would it mean the escape from this world into some otherworldly realm (the latter, in fact, is no different from the former, in that such escape always has depended on the projection of man's embodiment onto woman). To "remake" transcendence would mean to think it as the rift that opens up between two subjects irreducibly different from one another. We would thus make a shift from a paradigm in which woman was an enigma (the ever-lacking dark continent and mystery for a male knowledge-seeking subject), to a paradigm where any "other" is, and must remain, an enigmatic figure for any "self." This would allow us to stop using the labels "time" and "space" to describe male and female subjectivity, respectively, and instead place those categories in and as the distance that always and irreducibly unfolds between us.

And immanence? It should be clear by now that immanence, as we have traditionally understood this term, is a product of the "false" transcendence that I hope to have just unpacked by way of reading Irigaray. Just as woman (and others who have been subjugated) carried the burden of the embodiment that man was seeking to escape (and therefore was reduced to lack); and just as this turned the cycles of nature into the "non-time" that man needed in order to construct linear time; immanence is the negative that was put in place in order to assure the projective capacities of transcendence (we saw in the introduction that the same holds true for colonized or "primitive" cultures who linger in the shadow of modern progress). To live in a world of at least two (or rather, to inhabit one out of at least two coexisting worlds) would mean to live in a world where transcendence is immanent, where every encounter with the other entails a thrust beyond my world without reducing the world of the other to my own. And where each such thrust entails a return, a return to my own world, an immanently transcendent world, a world where immanence and transcendence no longer can be defined along oppositional lines, and where man can no longer confine woman to the realm of immanence alone.

If feminist scholars in recent years have emphasized and returned to immanence (this is a trend that has emerged primarily in the wake of Deleuze's philosophy of immanence—one that in turn draws from the work of Baruch Spinoza), I want to instead elaborate the idea that the very distinction between immanence and transcendence is a false one, and that it is a result of the sexual division of temporal labor that I have outlined above (where immanence is marked as feminine and associated with cyclical time, whereas transcendence is marked as masculine and associated with linear time). To overcome such a false distinction, we must neither resort to cyclicality nor to immanence (as these have been traditionally conceived), but instead emphasize that these two (cyclicality and immanence) always already are marked by transcendence and, similarly, that transcendence always already in a certain sense is immanent and embodied. Only then could we truly "remake" immanence and transcendence (and, as a consequence, time). But perhaps we could no longer even speak of immanence and transcendence then? Perhaps these terms should be left to metaphysics? Perhaps we should, quite simply, speak of a human encounter in temporal difference? An encounter marked by the incessant return of revolutionary time?

## Mimesis, Imitation, and Strategic Displacement

How, we must ask ourselves at this juncture, can such encounters be achieved? How can we create (at least) two worlds? Within our current culture of sameness—our culture of the one—is it possible to somehow arrest the movement of repetition so as to break out of its regular patterns, its reproduction of the same? Do we, in other words, have the means to transcend the current paradigm, to establish a culture of difference?

These questions will be addressed in more concrete terms later in this book, but let me already take a brief look at the strategy that Irigaray proposes as she herself begins the work of constructing a world of (at least) two. As David Wood has noted in *The Deconstruction of Time*, any philosopher who wants to seriously challenge previous paradigms and who envisions a new beginning of sorts—a radical renewal of our most basic assumptions—needs a proper method to do so.[39] From Descartes to Kant, from Hegel to Derrida, attempts to change the premises of philosophy and our very outlook on the world have depended on a renewal of the way in which we go about doing philosophy. As is well known to readers of Irigaray, she suggests (in her early work) that we displace and alter the culture hitherto known to us through *mimesis*. But what does this mean, and why would a mimetic strategy help us achieve change?

I want to suggest in what follows that the method of mimesis in Irigaray's work functions as an antidote to a culture of sameness. I will argue that it does so precisely by introducing a different model of time into the very practice of philosophy. I hope to have shown already that the questions of sexuate difference and time go hand in hand in Irigaray's work. I will now attempt to show that this is so not only as far as the content of her thought is concerned, but that the formal-methodological aspects of her work similarly depend on what I have called revolutionary time. If Descartes tried to establish a new beginning (and a stable foundation) for philosophy by erasing all that had been known to him thus far, Irigaray instead wants to renew and question some of the paradigmatic tropes of philosophy (the very notion of stable foundations being one of them) by mimetically revisiting (and thus revising) the Western philosophical tradition. Rather than erasing the past, she thus returns to it and repeats it, but in doing so she brings to the surface its own blind spots, and is therefore able to achieve a thoroughgoing displacement and renewal of the Western philosophical canon. Remember what we have said already: returning ultimately amounts to reclaiming. But let me, again, retrace my steps, in order to more carefully elucidate the function of mimesis in her work.

We have seen that Irigaray characterizes our current culture as one that mimetically repeats or imitates the same at the expense of difference and the other (man reproduces himself through, precisely, an eternal mime). But as we shall see, she simultaneously *prescribes* mimesis as an antidote to this dead repetition, if by mimesis we understand a kind of laughter or ironic displacement, an attempt to repeat the known to render it unknown, to turn the familiar into wonder, and the past into a future as of yet unknown—if, in other words, we by mimesis understand not repetitive imitation but a revolutionary movement of return and displacement. I want to follow this mimetic movement of return and examine its capacities for renewal and revolution.

If the Greek term *mimesis* most commonly is understood as imitation or representation, it is important to note that already the Greeks acknowledged that mimicry involves a degree of alteration and variation.[40] This is why Plato was so wary of mimesis in his discussion of poetry and art in the *Republic*.[41] As is well known, the Plato of the *Republic* warns us of the deceptive and potentially dangerous nature of artworks, basing his argument on the assumption that they are twice removed from the ideal forms. As imitations or images of the sensible world, they are mere copies of copies—twice removed from reality—and therefore necessarily less true and trustworthy than both the forms and the sensible objects of the world.[42] Aristotle held mimesis in higher esteem and gave it a central position in his own theory of art in his *Poetics*.[43] If Plato (to put it schematically) associated mimesis with epistemological and moral decay, and his student emphasized its ethical potential, both were well aware that mimesis by no means simply reproduced or copied what it was meant to represent, but that the meaning or affect represented necessarily was displaced through the very act of imitation or representation.[44] Even for Plato, it can't be entirely true that art would be a mere copy—this would hardly render it dangerous enough to warrant the expulsion of artists and poets from the just city. Art is illusion in a much deeper sense—it exceeds that which it was meant to depict. This is why theorists of aesthetics in our own age have had to address the question of what might have been lost in art during times of mechanical reproduction.[45]

Using the terminology of machinery that I have already established in my discussion of Irigaray above, we might say that two kinds of mimesis appear in her work. On the one hand, there is mimesis understood as imitative copying of the same—the repetitive noise or smooth silence of the machine, which lacks rhythmic variation and alteration (and, of course, sexuate difference).[46] On the other hand, there is mimesis understood as a poetic style or strategy—one that would enable rather than foreclose alteration and displacement. This latter kind comes closer to what has been said so far about nature than it does to the machine-like aspects of human culture, and it is more similar to revolutionary time than it is to cyclical or linear time—both of which, as we have seen, end up repeating the same. As always with Irigaray, the boundary between nature and culture is ambiguous. Poetic language, art, and the kind of philosophy that challenges the Western tradition through mimetic displacement (her own philosophy; a philosophy of sexuate difference)—are similar to the rhythms of nature insofar as they do not repeat, they do not function according to a logic of the same, but rather set into motion a cyclical movement that stirs this logic, that draws it into a whirlpool where the repetitive pattern of such a logic is disrupted, dispersed, and made visible in the process.

I will have reason to say more about this—the revolutionary aspect of what we might broadly call poetic language—in my discussion of Kristeva in the next chapter. It should then become clearer how it is that poetic language (or mimesis) creates displacement precisely through a "return" to its own material conditions of possibility—the corporeal dimension (what Kristeva calls the semiotic) that was repressed as we entered into the linear paradigm of the symbolic order. This, in short, should provide the conceptual apparatus needed to argue that revolutionary time depends on a return into the past and to the body, a re-membering—the work of memory and anamnesis that we examined in relation to Irigaray's work at the beginning of this chapter. Such a return—understood here in terms of mimesis—always and necessarily involves a displacement of sorts. It is, precisely, a return that provides us with a future in that it avoids repetition of the past to which it returns.

In an interview from 1975—a year after *Speculum* was published—Irigaray proposes that mimesis be used as a strategy to begin to question the systematicity of patriarchal discourse, to destroy its discursive mechanism, to laugh in its face and unearth its tendencies for exclusion and its affinity for repetition: "To play with mimesis is thus, for a woman, to try to recover the place of her exploitation by discourse, without allowing herself to be simply reduced to it . . . so as to make 'visible,' by an effect of playful repetition, what was supposed to remain invisible: the cover-up of a possible operation of the feminine in language."[47] We see here precisely the notion of mimesis as a form of anamnesis: a making visible the invisible that lies at the foundation of all that is visible. Man has rendered himself positive (or visible) by turning woman into a negative (or invisible), and this very operation—one that presents itself not as an operation but as an effect of a natural state of affairs—is what makes discourse operate in the first place. Through mimesis Irigaray seeks to uncover what has been covered over: the exclusion of the feminine from the symbolic order and the fact that this very exclusion is what organizes such an order in the first place.

This feminist strategy of making visible that which has remained invisible—or unspeakable—is echoed in the title of Gwendolyn DuBois Shaw's monograph *Seeing the Unspeakable: The Art of Kara Walker*.[48] Her reading of Kara Walker's seminal piece *The End of Uncle Tom and the Grand Allegorical Tableau of Eva in Heaven* (1995) speaks to several of the issues Irigaray treats in her discussion of mimesis.[49] Walker's haunting, life-size silhouettes all engage the past with dark sarcasm, appropriating racial and sexual stereotypes "in order to make her audience 'see the unspeakable.' "[50] Upon entering the piece, originally installed at the Whitney Biennial and mounted much like a curved cyclorama, the viewer is faced with the uncanny effect of seeing their "own outline being projected onto the gallery wall,"[51] such that the shadows cannot be dismissed as belonging to a distant past. The Antebellum drama unfolding on the curved wall, evoking violent and sexualized vignettes loosely referencing Harriet Beecher Stowe's 1852 sentimental novel *Uncle Tom's Cabin*, casts a long shadow into our present reality, haunting the viewer, like a mirror held up to reflect the underbelly of our own contemporary racist culture, and the fantasies that keep it alive.

In an essay reflecting on Walker's artwork in relation to Kristeva's concept of revolt, Amy Ray Stewart highlights this capacity of Walker's to return to the repressed of our collective-traumatic past to displace that same past, redressing it through a space of witnessing and re-memory, in the present.[52] The incessant return that takes place in Walker's imagery is the return of revolt, a remembering that is also a re-membering in the sense of renewal and rebirth (more about this in the next chapter). Stewart notes that "Walker's visual return to the cultural repressed is . . . achieved through the intimate work of sublimation."[53] Walker's artwork, which she describes as a "trauma aesthetic," in other words "cultivates a revolutionary space of sublimation."[54] In her book *Head Cases: Julia Kristeva on Philosophy and Art in Depressed Times*, Miller compares sublimation with the psychoanalytical process of working through, and describes the latter as "a form of nonidentical repetition, in which a repressed memory, perhaps of a traumatic event, that has been repeating itself through neurotic symptoms is remembered and repeated in a way that is fundamentally modified . . . ideally resulting in a capacity in the analysand to accept certain repressed elements and eventually to be freed from the cause of the debilitating repetition."[55] This, she argues, is why Kristeva "accords literature and other artistic endeavors a potentially liberatory effect."[56] I want to argue that it is this repetition with a modification that is at stake in Irigaray's methodology of mimesis. If sublimation for Kristeva has to do with our capacity to return to the repressed in order to make it present and ultimately transform it, then this very capacity to transform through displacement is what mimesis amounts to for Irigaray.

If the shadows in the Platonic cave (a place to which Irigaray will invite us to descend—more on this in chapter 9) signal illusion, Walker's silhouettes confront us with the darkest of truths in our collective unconscious, and force us to stare American racism in the face. As such, they remind us of something Irigaray too often omits or even denies, namely that the work of critical mimesis also must involve confronting the unbearable whiteness of feminist historiography. If "woman" on Irigaray's account has been rendered a negative mirror image of man—and if the work of mimesis seeks to uncover what has been covered over—the life-size silhouettes in Walker's monumental piece are like photograph negatives, they "express a void: an unknowable black hole, a kind of blank darkness, which is signified by an outer contour line."[57] As Robert Storr puts it in his analysis of Walker's *oeuvre*: "if in the Eurocentric tradition blackness has historically been the shadow that whiteness casts, what is the shadow of blackness? A still darker, more alarming enigma? Unruly negations of negation spiraling into a maelstrom of absolute otherness in which all bearings are lost and from which there is no escape—a black hole at the core of Western culture?"[58]

But Walker, like Irigaray, carefully avoids uncritical repetition of such enigmas. The irony that brings their work together, the playful repetition that allowed Irigaray to laugh patriarchal discourse in the face—what Hélène Cixous famously named "the laugh of the Medusa"[59]—is what gives life and subversive power to the cutouts in Walker's work too: "if you stare long enough and hard enough and deep enough into the abyss, the shadow's shadow cracks a starting smile," Storr notes with reference to her work, and adds that they "smile back at you and know where you are, who you are, and with whom you are sharing the raucous, bitter jokes that are the legacy of American bigotry and immemorial racism."[60] And this smile, this laughter, this ironic appropriation and re-membering of the bodies and voices that have been rendered invisible and silent—dismembered—gleefully echoes the past but is not reducible to the past. As Cixous puts it in her classic text, "in spite of the enormity of the repression that has kept [women] in the 'dark' . . . the future must no longer be determined by the past. I do not deny that the effects of the past are still with us. But I refuse to strengthen them by repeating them, to confer upon them an irremovability the equivalent of destiny, to confuse the biological and the cultural. Anticipation is imperative."[61] Mimesis is the work of return and remembering, but it is also the work of re-membering. It is not merely a symptom or return of the repressed, but the gesture of giving a body back to that which has been repressed, dismembered, rendered negative and invisible. And as such it is also the work of anticipation, subversion, transformation. It is the work of imagining a different future, re-envisioning both past and present, repeating otherwise.

The strategy employed by both Irigaray and Walker is not without risks, of course. We have seen already that it has generated decades of lively feminist debates about Irigaray's alleged essentialism—her mimetic return has been perceived as reinforcing stereotypes and buttressing biologistic views about women and sexual difference. Similarly, Walker's work has been harshly criticized by those who worry that her imagery legitimizes derogatory racial stereotypes, and who see Walker as betraying her race. In 1997, Betye Saar and Howardena Pindell (two established African American artists) objected strongly and publicly to Walker's artwork, expressing concern that it catered "to the bestial fantasies about blacks created by white supremacy and racism."[62] The line between mimesis as repetition and mimesis as displacement is fine, and there is no obvious measure by which the two can be distinguished. The heavy sarcasm—the laughter—of Irigaray and Walker's respective work seems to me crucial as we try to trace that line. If indeed "Walker's initial contribution to cutting-edge art was to turn that sharp edge away from the future and point it toward the past," as Storr has suggested,[63] then such a turn marks what I see as a powerful attempt at wielding a count-er-history—or counter-histories—and it is marked by anticipatory revolt. As the poet Kevin Young puts it, the "exploding pickaninnies, nursing mammies, and amputated Negroes" that inhabit her work are far from passive victims: "the figures on the walls of the galleries have given us back some sense of the revenge of those amputated selves—they have taken up arms, as it were."[64]

This conception of mimesis as a kind of playful—and revolu-tionary—repetition comes close to Butler's notion of performativity.[65]

And when Butler discusses the phenomenon of drag in *Gender Trouble* and elsewhere, she too has had to grapple with why we ought to see drag not as reinforcing and promoting stereotypical views about gender and sexed embodiment, but rather as a critical challenge to those very views. One of the central aspects of Butler's notion of performativity is the claim that it "does not assume that there is an original which such parodic identities imitate. Indeed, the parody is *of* the very notion of an original . . . gender parody reveals that the original identity after which gender fashions itself is an imitation without an origin" (GT 175). She thus posits a challenge to the Platonic notion of mimesis as imitation of an original form. As we will see in chapter 9, this is precisely what Irigaray too attempts to do. There, I will offer a thoroughgoing critique of the metaphysical belief in a single and stable origin by stressing the ontological primacy of both time and difference and by pointing to the plurality of our beginnings (through the claim that any culture that sees the paternal function as its sole origin is bound to repeat itself, while a culture that acknowledges its heterogeneous beginnings is capable of change). Revolutionary time understood as a perpetual return to our own maternal-material conditions of possibility—to the fact that we are all engendered and born—thus offers an alternative to the origin-copy-logic on which our current culture of sameness depends.[66]

First and foremost, Irigaray challenges the traditional trope that woman is a mere "copy" of man, that she is his mirror image, his lesser half. Moreover, she stresses the fact that woman—in that she has two "lips" that continuously touch each other—is inherently manifold in her very own being, and that this internal multiplicity escapes the very logic that posits an (abstract) origin-original at the foundation of any sensible fact: "We live by twos beyond all mirages, images, and mirrors. Between us, one is not the 'real' and the other her imitation; one is not the original and the other her copy," she writes in her lyrical essay "When Our Lips Speak Together."[67] By "being two," woman challenges the very logic of the one (a logic that takes the phallus as its paradigmatic model), and hence the very idea that everything can be reduced to a single and selfsame origin. Mimesis as a movement of return does not hinge on the idea that we return to a stable origin or *archē*. Revolutionary time is not meant to retrieve some essential gender identity or a static notion of sexuate difference. That sexuate difference must be understood as a relation (and a temporal one at that) means precisely that it is marked by variation, and that each manifestation of such a relation is singular and flexible.

Irigaray's own mimetic language seeks to articulate this flexibility. She aims to express the multiplicity that has been regarded as "improper" in our culture: the in-between rather than dual opposites; the ambiguous rather than the clearly defined; fluidity rather than solidity; the morphology of touch rather than the paradigm of sight.[68] She asks: "How can we speak so as to escape from their compartments, their schemas, their distinctions and oppositions: virginal/deflowered, pure/impure, innocent/experienced . . . How can we shake off the chain of these terms, free ourselves from their categories, rid ourselves of their names? Disengage ourselves, *alive*, from their concepts?"[69] She grounds her own unstabilizing philosophy in female morphology and in the fluidity and multiplicity that she associates with the female body: "Between our lips, yours and mine, several voices, several ways of speaking resound endlessly, back and forth. One is never separable from the other. You/I: we are always several at once. . . . One cannot be distinguished from the other; which does not mean that they are indistinct."[70]

If women have been doomed to "fuse" with everything they encounter, or to "imitate whatever comes close" in chameleon fashion, women are also capable of challenging the expectation upon them to imitate, and they can do so, precisely, through deliberate imitation.[71] Insofar as they have remained outside of discourse, or at least at the margins of culture, insofar as they are considered excessive and as "guardians of nature"—bearers of the body that must remain on the outside in order for male discourse to reach its ideal and disembodied form—they have the capacity to alter this very discourse: "if women can play with mimesis, it is because they are capable of bringing new nourishment to its operation," Irigaray asserts.[72] Women provide an opening—they bring corporeal elements into language and bend open a tautological system that has been closed off through the repetition of (male) sameness. Women, in other words, introduce difference, and therefore also time. And *écriture féminine* revolutionizes language through a movement of return—revolutionary time.[73]

In *Revolution in Poetic Language*, Kristeva describes mimesis as "internally dependent on a subject of enunciation who is unlike the transcendental ego in that he does not suppress the semiotic *chora* but instead raises the *chora* to the status of a signifier."[74] To play with mimesis—to create works of art or poetry among other things—amounts to acknowledging the heterogeneity of language: its affective and embodied roots (the semiotic *chōra*) on Kristeva's account; sexuate difference and fluidity on Irigaray's. A disembodied view of language "could only produce . . . a tautological discourse . . . the path thus programmed is circular and merely returns to its thetic point of departure," Kristeva writes (RPL 59).[75] Both Kristeva and Irigaray view mimesis as an escape from a tautological-linear discourse that closes up in a selfsame circle. By introducing heterogeneity through a critical mime they inscribe nonlinear time and alteration into discourse: transformation into the future is achieved through a creative variation and re-membering of the past. But the work of artists such as Kara Walker also forces us to grapple with the fact that both Kristeva and Irigaray have inherited from Beauvoir a blindness to issues of race. Their Eurocentrism contains and reproduces its own blind spots and shadows, ones that we must be careful not to uncritically reproduce. We will have reason to return to Walker in the next chapter, to yet again explore and examine the critical force of her work of mimetic return, and what it might add to our reading of Kristeva and Irigaray on questions of time and difference.

## Conclusion

In this chapter I have examined Irigaray's philosophy of sexuate difference, and tied it to the thematic of time. I have sought to show that revolutionary time is intimately linked to Irigaray's non-hierarchical model of sexuate difference. In her work, Irigaray elaborates a systematic critique of linear-progressive time as that through which male subjectivity becomes construed as disembodied rationality, such that man repeats himself in an eternal mime, foreclosing female subjectivity and future horizons of change. Irigaray's engagement with the question of time thus amounts to attributing subjectivity to woman, freeing her from her captivity in and as a passive-receptive space or object.

I have tried to show that the culture of sexuate difference that she calls for—one that can be grounded neither in linear nor cyclical models of time, but that depends instead on the movement of return and displacement that I develop in this book as a whole—is the condition of possibility for novelty and change; the injection of life and aliveness into human discourse and existence. Put differently, we might say that what is at stake is movement, and the possibility for movement. A culture of sameness is, as I have sought to explain in this chapter, a static one—it reproduces itself in its own frozen image and this indifferent imitation lacks the creative force of mimesis understood as displacement and differentiation. I traced this more subversive form of mimesis—which characterizes Irigaray's own critical methodology—to Walker's artistic practice and the mimetic displacement that takes place there. My engagement with Walker was in part motivated by a desire to draw attention to some of the blind spots that mark both Irigaray's and Kristeva's work, namely the manner in which the ideology of whiteness repeats itself in their respective corpus.

For both Irigaray and Kristeva, the mimetic-displacing movement of revolutionary time is tied to an inscription of material elements in language. Irigaray consistently speaks of the urgency of returning to our material-maternal roots, to the sensible realm (the sound of language through hearing and through the voice, the texture of language through touch and the tactile register); and Kristeva urges us to make visible the affects and drives that make discourse possible while, nevertheless, having been to some extent excluded from it.

In the next chapter, I want to turn to Kristeva in order to substantiate and develop the need to return to the past and to the body in order to instigate renewal and change. By examining her work in this context, I hope to deepen several of the themes examined so far. I will speak again of revolution as I examine the various instances in which she speaks of revolt and the time of revolt. I will trace the movement of return yet again, and tie it not only to mimesis or poetic language, but also to the work of anamnesis in psychoanalysis, and the interrogation inherent in critical reflection and thought. And I will, finally, speak yet again of a self who necessarily is embodied and marked by difference from the start—a heterogeneous self in constant movement, oscillation, and change.

## 3

# Revolutionizing Time

I hope to have made it clear that revolutionary time, as much as it involves a movement of return, does not merely repeat the past but functions instead as the condition of possibility for futurity understood in terms of alteration. So far, I have discussed this primarily in light of sexuate difference and the generative-differentiating powers of nature and of a world inhabited by (at least) two. I will turn now to Kristeva, in order to develop a theory of time more explicitly grounded in a quest for political change.[1]

From her early *Revolution in Poetic Language* to the more recent *The Sense and Non-Sense of Revolt* and *Intimate Revolt* Kristeva's work has been concerned with a revolutionary politics of sorts.[2] Her politics is, however, not in any simple way emancipatory. It seeks to displace established systems of meaning, taking the heterogeneous affective body as its point of departure. It also does not engage directly with the traditional structures of political institutions, but emerges at the crossroads between psychoanalysis and aesthetic expression—a realm that she describes as *intimate*. As Cecilia Sjöholm has noted in a book that seeks to map Kristeva's political thinking through a careful analysis of her early radical work in the *Tel Quel* group and in the wake of 1968 France: "Kristeva's project is unique in that it consists of a systematic displacement of the political from the universal (or public) domain to the singular and intimate spaces of signification."[3]

Kristeva's ethical and political discourse is rooted in a critique of the modern unified and stable subject. She endeavors to articulate a theory of subjectivity and agency grounded in the psychoanalytical view of the subject as inherently divided, unconscious, desirous, and embodied. Throughout her corpus, she highlights the need for revolt and revolution. As Kristeva has pointed out repeatedly, Albert Camus famously formulated the modern version of the *cogito* as follows: "I rebel, therefore we are."[4] She too ties revolt to intersubjectivity and, at the same time, to the life of the mind (recollection, interrogation, and thought) (IR 6). "In forcing me towards the other in me," Sjöholm suggests in her discussion of Kristeva, revolt "will push me towards an alterity that will force me to question, interrogate and think, activities that in themselves must be considered the beginning of all politics" (KP 112). As we will see in what follows, Kristeva indeed turns to critical thinking (understood also as self-reflection) as the locus from which a revolutionary politics of sorts can begin to unfold.

Worrying that the Camusian version of the *cogito* renders the present stable and the future predictable, Kristeva ventures to bring it one step further: Camus's formula, she notes in an interview, is "a placid and definitive 'we are,' as opposed to revolt that's simply taking its course. Rather say: 'I revolt, therefore we are still to come.' If we don't keep this possibility open, the indefiniteness of the revolt May '68 represents, there is nothing left to do but to submit to the all-encompassing power of calculation and management that perpetuates the end of history" (WL 42).[5] An important theme from my reading of Irigaray emerges again, namely the worry that calculation and calculative management will lead to dead ends, to an impasse of the future.[6] Kristeva's notion of revolt is evidently rooted in an aspiration for future possibilities and change, but she consistently emphasizes the undecidability of the future, and stresses that subjectivity is inherently marked by becoming (a subject, precisely, *in process*). Revolt, for her, carries the seed of the unknown; the yet-to-come; the unprecedented (which means that the outcome might be "worse" than where we started, that movement forward not always implies progress, improvement, or amelioration, but rather an open-ended process of becoming—issues to which I will return both in what follows and in the conclusion). But, we must ask, what exactly does Kristeva mean when she speaks of revolt? And what does it have to do with time?

In both *The Sense and Non-Sense of Revolt*, *Intimate Revolt*, and in several of the interviews published in *Revolt, She Said*, Kristeva provides an etymological explanation of the meaning of revolt. She explains that the Latin term *volvere*, which is at its origin, had little to do with politics at the outset. The evolution of the word is marked by a set of terms indicating movement, at first, and then various aspects of space and time. Kristeva brings forth its association with "circular movement and, by extension, temporal return" or just "time" (we recognize, of course, the usage of the term "revolution" to describe the cyclical movement of the celestial bodies—which especially for the Greeks was intimately connected to time), and she goes on to note that it simultaneously carried spatial meanings such as "volume," "mass," and "thickness" (SNS 1–2). The etymology thus interestingly demonstrates that whenever time is conceptualized in terms of cyclicality or revolution (rather than linearity), there is an implicit connection between temporal movement and corporeality or materiality (a connection that I will examine in more detail in the section on the past in this book). Gradually, the term came to signify change and mutation, and eventually, more specifically, political change and revolutions of the state.[7]

Revolt, as Sjöholm has pointed out before me, must thus be understood in temporal terms: revolt represents "return in the sense of repetition, not of the same but in the form of a continuous displacement" (KP 110). Through displacement and alteration, renewal becomes possible. "There is a necessary repetition," Kristeva explains, "but beyond that, I emphasize its potential for making gaps, rupturing, renewing."[8] To tie it back to my discussion of her essay "Women's Time" in the opening chapter, the third generation of feminists would be one capable of revolt, if by revolt we understand a movement of return that, through displacement and alteration, generates renewal while acknowledging the unpredictable status of the future (that we are "still to come").

In her analysis of the concept of revolt, Kristeva aligns herself with Freud, for whom, she claims, "the word 'revolutionary' . . . has nothing to do with moral, much less political, revolt; it simply signifies the possibility that psychoanalysis has to access the archaic, to overturn conscious meaning" (SNS 15).[9] She claims to understand "rebellion as access to the archaic" and, evoking Marcel Proust, calls Freud "a revolutionary in search for lost time" (SNS 16). What, we must ask, is going on here? Why would our accessing the archaic (through psychoanalysis) lead to the overturning of conscious meaning? And why should we view psychoanalysis as a search for lost time?

In many ways, this book as a whole is meant to unpack these remarks. I will devote the section on the past to an extensive discussion of the status of the "archaic" that Kristeva speaks of here—and thematize it in terms of the temporal-material figure that the maternal, on my reading, represents in both her and Irigaray's work. For now, I want to focus on the temporal aspects of the very movement of return, and begin to think about the capacity of such a temporal return (or revolt) to overthrow existing structures and produce new horizons of meaning. I will do so by looking at some aspects of Kristeva's work on psychoanalysis and language, and add my own reflections on memorial art, as I further elaborate the concept of revolutionary time.

## Returning to the Body . . . and the Soul

In my analysis of time and difference in Irigaray, what was at stake was the possibility of recuperating a sexuate culture that would challenge the lifeless repetition of a culture of the same. Kristeva is not as quick to characterize our culture as one of *sameness* (as I have already noted, she puts less emphasis on the question of sexuate difference than Irigaray does), but she nevertheless often suggests that Western culture and thought is *one-sided*, and that it needs an injection of *life* (or what she calls semiotic affect) in order not to stagnate. Because of this one-sidedness, our culture is marked by a repetition of sorts, and this results in the death of culture, or in a culture of death. Just like Irigaray did in her discussion of sexual sameness, Kristeva sees this one-sidedness and the repetition that it leads to as intimately linked to a linear temporal paradigm: our emphasis on linear progress leads to the erasure of life in that it depends on an attempt to overcome the finitude of life (I will discuss this idea in more detail in my discussion of the metaphysics of presence in the next chapter). To "inject life" and "avoid stagnation" does, importantly, not merely amount to assuring survival: modern technology has, after all, turned survival into little more than plugging a collection of organs into a machine. In the name of life, we often come to efface the vitality of life; and through our outright denial of death, we ironically establish a culture of death. How, then, is this one-sidedness articulated in Kristeva, and through what means does she suggest that it be overcome?

In *Revolution in Poetic Language*—her first sustained engagement with the concept of revolt—Kristeva speaks at length of the sacrifice that founds our culture: "Sacrifice sets up the symbol and the symbolic order at the same time, and this 'first' symbol, the victim of a murder, merely represents the structural violence of language's irruption as the murder of soma, the transformation of the body, the captation of drives"

(75). The symbolic order (social norms and laws, symbolic structures, language, culture) is in other words achieved through the sacrifice of preverbal bodily drives, and on Kristeva's account our repression of such heterogeneous drives is precisely what gives rise to a culture of death and repetition. Or, as Butler puts it, "the denial of the body . . . reveals itself as nothing other than the embodiment of denial."[10] Psychoanalysis has taught us that repression and denial generate repetition—the repressed eternally returns. Because the symbolic order, on Kristeva's account, is installed at the expense of a corporeal dimension that remains hidden in the process of symbolization (one that symbolization nevertheless depends on in order to carry meaning) it is prone to repeat itself, to lack vitality, to resist change.

Kristeva's elaboration of the relationship between the semiotic and the symbolic is probably the most famous aspect of her thought. Put as simply as possible, she formulates two modes of production of meaning within the signifying process: the semiotic is the mode through which bodily drives and affect make their way into language; the symbolic expresses an organized system of syntactic signs.[11] While some discourse (scientific, logical, philosophical) is paradigmatically symbolic and other modes of expression (such as body language, poetry, and music) lean more heavily on the semiotic, no meaning can be produced unless both modes are implicated, to a greater or lesser degree.[12]

Language is, in other words, always infused with affect, but much of the language that we use when we analyze or describe the world around us quite successfully hides its own material conditions of possibility. In "Women's Time," Kristeva notes that language follows the logic of linear time (206). As is evident from the passage quoted above, she views language as structurally violent, since it is based on an initial repression ("murder") of the semiotic, of soma, of the body. The very language that posits rigid distinctions between, say, body and mind (the Western philosophical language with which we are all too familiar), functions according to a logic that renders invisible its own somatic conditions. As I have already discussed at length, it is through a repression of the body that linear time has been construed and that transcendence has been elaborated. A critique of such a linear-teleological temporal model depends on a return to the body, and hence also to what Kristeva calls the semiotic dimensions of language and meaning.[13]

In Kristeva's work, poetic language emerges as that which keeps semiotic aspects of signification alive, and she views this as the precondition for the "survival and revolution" of the social order, confronting, "through time, the different 'soma' that are sacrificed for the social group's survival" (RPL 80–81).[14] Poetic language offers an alternative to survival as maintenance: its revolutionary status is achieved precisely through its capacity to inject both life and death into an all-too-repetitive symbolic order. The "revolution" of which Kristeva speaks occurs both *in* poetic language (insofar as the latter is a return to semiotic modes of articulation), and *through* poetic language (insofar as it is the means through which a revolution on the level of society might take place).

Revolt, for Kristeva, is a movement of return that is meant to retrieve the forgotten or lost continent of the body and bodily drives—a dimension that to a large extent has been repressed in our language and culture. More specifically, it is aimed at retrieving the *maternal body*, since it is the mother that, on Kristeva's account, organizes our early heterogeneous affects and drives (I will discuss this at length later). To return to the maternal body amounts to two things: it re-authorizes the past as a dynamic process (contra metaphysical accounts of a long-lost idealized past in the form of a disembodied God or a selfsame idea, or any other notion of a singular *archē* or mystical origin); and it re-inscribes the body and its drives into any account of human beginnings and subject formation. Both, on my view, are necessary for the elaboration of a future not already defined by past and present ideological agendas.

But by urging such a return, don't we risk positing the body as a stable essential ground, much like the mystical origin, or *archē*, of the Western metaphysical tradition? And would this not lead us to repeat a tradition that not only views the body as a locus for repetition and immanence but that subsequently associates women and other minorities with such temporal stasis? Let me repeat that I deliberately have chosen the term "revolutionary time," rather than terms such as "women's time" or "feminine time," precisely in order to signal that this return to the body is necessary not only for women but for all human beings. If the sexual division of temporal labor depended on man's repression of his own embodiment and the subsequent reduction of woman to mere body, my point is that this very division can be disrupted if and only if we all acknowledge our own embodiment and that we are from bodies born. This is why, as we will see in the chapters on the past, a return to the maternal body, for example, in no way is aimed at reducing women to mothers. To the contrary, it is what makes possible women's liberation from the strictures of motherhood. In a culture marked by revolt and return, men could no longer put the burden of their embodiment on women, and white women could, importantly, not put their burden of embodiment on men and women of color. The weight of such repression-oppression is what needs to be lifted for our culture to be alive.

To be sure, this inevitably means that, while we all must return, it does matter who returns, and why. Our positionality within structures of privilege matters, the degree to which we have been made to carry the burden of embodiment (or not) matters. We clearly need ways to distinguish conservative appeals to the past of the colonial-patriarchal tradition from radical appeals to the counter-histories of the oppressed. And as Paulo Freire has noted, "the oppressors, who oppress, exploit, and rape by virtue of their power, cannot find in this power the strength to liberate either the oppressed or themselves. Only power that springs from the weakness of the oppressed will be sufficiently strong to free both."[15] In other words, while we are all tasked with the work of return, those who have been oppressed by our current temporal paradigm (women, people of color, queer folk . . .) hold epistemic privileges that allow them to more readily engage in the movement of return in a manner that avoids reestablishing archaic structures.

When Kristeva aligns herself with the Freudian idea that revolt is the ability to access the archaic so as to overturn conscious meaning, she is thus by no means urging us to return to some original-normative and stable *archē* or ultimate beginning. I take her to say that conscious meaning is meaning that has suppressed its past and present material conditions of possibility and that this, as we saw in the previous discussion of Irigaray, leads it to repeat itself in an eternal mime of the same. Only if we bring back to the surface those unconscious dimensions hitherto repressed (affect, drive, and we should add sexuate difference to the list), can the past become alive (not reduced to an *archē*), the present dynamic (not reduced to selfsame presence), and the future unpredictable (not reduced to a *telos*). Only then, in other words, do we actually speak about time and change.

For both Kristeva and Irigaray, the temporal model that they seek to develop in their respective work—what I have chosen to call revolutionary time—is thus meant to revitalize a culture hitherto marked by disembodiment and repetition, and to do so without positing a false distinction between female immanence and male transcendence. Sjöholm has noted that the temporality of revolt is one "in which the singularity of the corporeal subject finds a proper mode for its transformations."[16]

In Kristeva's own terms, it is meant to establish "a society that is alive and developing, not stagnating. In fact, if such a culture did not exist, life would become a life of death, that is, a life of physical and moral violence, barbarity. This is a matter of the survival of our civilizations and their freest and most enlightening components . . . an experience of revolt may be the only thing that can save us from the automation of humanity that is threatening us" (SNS 7). Revolt, in other words, is meant to restore the vitality and heterogeneity of what we might call a living culture: a culture not reduced to the automatic repetition of dis-embodied speech; a culture that revitalizes the singularity of each human life. As Noëlle McAfee has put it: "Someone who lacks any semiotic energy might as well be, perhaps must already be, dead. . . . The less touch people have with semiotic forces, the less they are able to thrive, change, and live."[17]

Revolt is, in other words, an antidote to automated life (which, importantly, by no means amounts to saying that it is an antidote to death or finitude). Kristeva notes that it indicates "what is most alive and promising about our culture" (IR 5), and that it "might keep our inner lives alive" (SNS 8). She emphasizes that a culture of revolt "is indispensable, both to psychic life, and to the bonds that make society hang together, as long as it remains a live force and resists accommo-dations . . . it assures the possibility of a human group's 'survival' " (WL 38). Rebellion "is a condition necessary for the life of the mind and society."[18] Revolt, in other words, seeks to reinstall a living psychic space—psychic life if you will—and it does so through a movement of return. "Without it, neither the life of the mind nor life in society is possible," Kristeva asserts, and adds: "I mean 'life' here, and not just maintenance, repetition, management" (WL 12). Without the movement of return, life is reduced to mere repetition. Life is without time, outside of time, reduced to a two-dimensional line.

What is Kristeva speaking of here? Why this urgency to install a living psychic space? What would it mean that our society is deprived of psychic life? How is the issue of the psyche related to that of the body? And what does it all have to do with the question of time? In the opening chapter of *The Sense and Non-Sense of Revolt*, Kristeva asserts that revolt is in peril in our postindustrial and postcommunist democracies, because we are submerged "in the culture of entertainment, the culture of performance, the culture of the show" (SNS 6). Ours is a consensus society; a regime of the spectacular; a normalizing order; a world where the human body has been reduced to an assemblage of organs to be sold on the illegal market, and where the mind is anaesthetized by remote-controlled images and antidepressants.

Kristeva diagnosed this society already in *New Maladies of the Soul*, where she tried to tackle the manifold symptoms that such a society has produced and keeps reproducing. The overall contention of that book is the worry that what we call "the soul" is in peril in a society dominated by "psychiatric medicines, aerobics, and media zapping."[19] As is clear from the examples Kristeva offers here and elsewhere, her critique is by and large aimed at contemporary Western cultures. The consumer of the spectacle that such cultures produce and rely on, Kristeva explains, is one "who has run out of imagination."[20] Such a consumer is thus quite literally one who is deprived of futurity, who lacks the capacity to imagine the not-yet and the to-come. Kristeva examines the automated speech of her own depressed patients, the repetitive behavior of obsessional neurotics, and the mute resistance of what she calls phantasmatically inhibited people, as she depicts a modern world inhabited by alienated and lost souls. A society so driven by the idea of progress has instead collapsed into the repetitive mindlessness of what Beauvoir called cyclical time—it is indeed deprived of a future. The deep paradox here is that a culture that is founded on a repression of the body has deteriorated into one that, put simply, lacks soul, and is left with nothing but bodies: bodies to perfect, bodies to satisfy, bodies to be looked at, bodies to please, bodies that labor away in sub-human conditions or that are made into market commodities. "The body," Kristeva contends, "conquers the invisible territory of the soul."[21] As we have seen, the repressed eternally returns, and, as it turns out, it returns with renewed force.

When Kristeva says that we should establish a living psychic space—when she calls for a revival of the human soul—she is thus evidently not referring to the disembodied Cartesian-Christian soul. Her notion of the soul comes closer to that elaborated and celebrated by the ancients: the soul "allows you access to your body and to other people," Kristeva explains.[22] While being an internal space, the soul is a space that, insofar as it is alive, connects us with others and with our living bodies. To have a vital psychic space means to be capable of intersubjective relations, to desire, and to feel affect—all of which we need in order to sustain a living and vibrant culture. As McAfee has noted, there is "a very odd logic in society-as-anesthetic: it fulfills desires while simultaneously stripping the subject's capacity to desire."[23] The mechanical, repetitive speech of the depressed—a speech that perhaps could be compared to the disembodied and sexually neutral "noise" of the machine in Irigaray's essay—is devoid of desire and thus devoid of a link to imagined futures.[24]

It is interesting to note that Kristeva chose as the closing chapter for *New Maladies of the Soul* the essay that I have pointed to as the paradigmatic place to turn to for an analysis of her views on time—namely "Women's Time." It seems as if she wants to say that the ultimate "antidote" to the kind of maladies that she had set out to examine—maladies that follow from a separation between body and soul and the subsequent disappearance of both body and soul—would be the temporal approach that she associates with the third generation of feminists in that text. It should be no less surprising that the opening chapter of her trilogy on the powers and limits of psychoanalysis—a series that she herself describes as an attempt to grapple with human experience and existence in a society where psychic life is under threat—treats the question of time and its relation to subjectivity (SNS 1–19). If psychic life is established through an ongoing return to the soma (understood here as a locus for affect and drive—not as a mere possessor of organs that are convertible into cash), we need a temporal model to organize such continuous return. What I have tried to show is that revolutionary time gives us precisely that. If transcendence and freedom traditionally have been conceptualized as an *escape* from the body, we see that these concepts, on Kristeva's account, instead depend on a *return* to the body (a body that, importantly, possesses a living psychic space). Only as embodied beings do we have time. It is through the body that transcendence—understood here as a horizon of possibility for futurity, not as a flight into a metaphysical and disembodied beyond—is possible.

## Intimate Revolt: The Time of Psychoanalysis

If Kristeva's early work was concerned primarily with the revolutionary potential of poetic language (she started off as a linguist and literary critic), her work since the 1980s gives an equally central revolutionary role to the practice of psychoanalysis. If much philosophy had depended on a dualism between body and soul, "the Freudian notion of the psyche challenges this formerly presumed dualism and . . . several aspects of psychoanalysis cross the boundary between body and soul and explore various elements that transcend this dichotomy."[25] Psychoanalysis, in other words, seeks to overcome the one-sidedness of a progressive-linear culture in that it brings together two seemingly separate realms and actively draws from the realm that has tended to go unnoticed in a culture overdetermined by rational disembodied thought.

Psychoanalysis, for Kristeva, is a practice that "permits a renewal of the whole subject" (SNS 29). On her account, it is a practice based on "the questioning and displacement of the past," and its main task is to open up for a new future: "The future, if it exists, depends on it" (IR 5). Intimate revolt should, in other words, be understood "not in the sense of transgression but to describe the process of the analysand's retrieving his memory and beginning his work of anamnesis with the analyst," hence evoking "the movements of repetition, working-through, working-out internal to the free association in transference," which, in turn, "permits a renewal of the whole subject," and therefore contributes to "the construction of a veritable culture where displacement constitutes its source and essence" (SNS 28–29). Remember the Freudian claim that our access to the archaic would allow us to overturn conscious meaning.

Intimate revolt, for Kristeva, has profound political potential in that it offers us a future, the possibility for transformation. The intimate, in Kristeva's work, becomes the bearer of a lost revolutionary tradition—a tradition that carries a promise for renewal and change. Our return to the archaic is by definition an attempt at liberation. The revolt offered by psychoanalysis makes perpetual rebirth possible, first and foremost through the work of memory. "Freud founded psychoanalysis as an invitation to anamnesis in the goal of a rebirth, that is, a psychical restructuring," Kristeva explains (IR 8).

But what does it mean that psychoanalysis provides rebirth or a second birth? In what sense are we renewed through psychoanalytic treatment? The psychoanalytic cure is clearly limited as a political means to achieve collective change. But it nevertheless illuminates what it might mean to understand time as a perpetual movement of return. The analysand returns to a long-lost past—to the dark continent of their individual prehistory. They do so, however, not in order to retrieve an ideal vanished universe but precisely to work through, to process, and to move on, in the sense of liberating themselves from repetitive patterns of behavior and the neurotic return of the same.[26] The aim, in other words, is to reconstruct and revitalize a past that has been frozen in an idealized or traumatic image. What is at stake is not so much an eternal return *of* the repressed as an ongoing return *to* the repressed. The latter would ideally put an end to the former. We would return not in order to linger in the past or repeat it but to make possible new beginnings and a future different from our past. In Kelly Oliver's terms, revolt is "a return or questioning and displacement of the past, the old law, for the sake of renewal in the future."[27] Kristeva herself describes the psychoanalytic cure as "an infinite quest for rebirths," and labels it a "supreme guarantee for renewal."[28]

We should note, however, that the renewal of the subject offered through psychoanalysis by no means amounts to reinventing oneself in the sense of erasing or forgetting one's past in order to establish an unrecognizable self that is once and for all freed from the traumas and fantasies of the past. First of all, the psychoanalytic cure is (to the dismay of many) a slow process. This is in part why Western linear-progressive culture tends to fault it for not being efficient enough. In a society of antidepressants, we seek fast results and prefer to forget our past in order to secure future achievements and immediate success in the present. With our eyes peeled at short-term solutions, we repress old wounds and rush through the present, with the result that we lose the present altogether (I will discuss this need to "slow down," to experience the present, in its unfolding, in the section on the present). Psychoanalysis—which is a practice that requires that we return, both in time and over time—provides renewal not in the sense that we forget our past but, rather, that we come to terms with our past, that we process it, that we integrate it so as to live with it without compulsively repeating it. Psychoanalysis, in other words, embodies the feminist desire to simultaneously remember and make change, allowing for continuity and rupture both at once.

Some would nevertheless ask if revolt, viewed in this way, really is a phenomenon that allows for change. Doesn't it merely aspire for change while, in fact, typically reestablishing the status quo? Is psychoanalysis ever really about renewal and change, or is it more often a process that seeks to establish the "we are" of the Camusian *cogito* (or the stable meaning produced by an equally stable theoretical framework) rather than the "we are still to come" of Kristeva's vision?[29] And who is the "we" implied here? If we speak of revolt in straightforwardly historical terms, in the context of sociopolitical revolutions and times of turmoil, is the movement of return not also bound to repeat itself, to reproduce the same, to (despite all efforts to do otherwise) resort to violence and reestablish the very power structures that it was seeking to challenge (a normative "we"), thus failing to establish anything truly new? The question of novelty will be the focus of my discussion in the conclusion of this book, but I want to address some of these questions already here, since this will allow me to flesh out in further detail and concreteness what I take Kristeva to mean when she speaks of revolt, and how it, in turn, relates to what I call revolutionary time.

∞

Kristeva acknowledges that, more often than not, revolutionaries protest against power only to subsequently reinstall some version of the very structures they were seeking to confront. This is in part due to the fact that revolutionaries fail to continuously interrogate and question the values that they themselves are attempting to put in place, which is what revolt as return would amount to. These revolts are not pursued according to the logic of return but simply follow the traditional linear-progressive movement of time. Teleology as ideology forecloses renewal and change: "As for the future," Kristeva laments, "ideologies that promise you something are bankrupt . . . the new automated world order doesn't grant the possibility of any other future."[30] Insofar as revolutions follow this linear logic, they are therefore bound to more often than not simply repeat the past:

> Very often political movements have tried to abolish old values in order to replace them with new ones, but without questioning these new ideas. For example, the French Revolution was against the Ancient Regime. As a consequence the Third-Estate ceases to question itself. This is why the bourgeois revolution initially turns the rule over to the guillotine, before turning to moral order. Thus, you can see how the French Revolution becomes a betrayal of the initial movement of revolt. If you take the Russian Revolution, things are even clearer. The Russian Revolution established a totalitarian regime which betrayed the revolt, because the rebellion against the old bourgeois world forgot to question the new values that it put in its place.[31]

Revolt without the return that critical thinking involves paves the way for totalitarianism. In *Intimate Revolt*, Kristeva stresses this danger: "I can never sufficiently emphasize the fact that totalitarianism is the result of a certain fixation of revolt in what is precisely its betrayal, namely, the suspension of retrospective return, which amounts to a suspension of thought" (6). That the French revolutionaries rejected close to everything that had hitherto been in place—in a gesture similar to the Cartesian attempt to "raze everything to the ground"—only led to the all-too-familiar Reign of Terror.[32] The radical attempt to establish an entirely new beginning so common to modern revolutions easily collapses into a violent conservatism of sorts (modernity—*Neuzeit* in German—is defined precisely as a new time or as the time of the new). Certain kinds of worshipping of the future are therefore bound to violently foreclose the future in their very aspiration for and focus on it (think, for example, of futurism). And if Descartes wanted to erase all that was known—in a rhetorical-strategic gesture that prior to anything else abolished the body from the realm of certainty—Kristeva is seeking to recover that very body (one severed from the head in the guillotines too) in an attempt to bring affect back into a political discourse that, in its aspiration for purity, could lead to nothing but lethal cycles of violence.[33]

Thought without soma is dead. And it is bound to repeat exactly that which it aimed at erasing: the repressed eternally returns. While the linear model of time gives priority to the future, it paradoxically yields not novelty but repetition because it is governed by an abstract ideal that delegitimizes present practices and stories past—an ideal, in other words, that denies the heterogeneity of lived embodied experience. The two models described by Beauvoir are, as I stressed already in my reading of Irigaray, more similar than they might have seemed at first glance.

I want to propose that the continuous interrogation that Kristeva calls for (and that is the cornerstone of Freudian psychoanalysis) is integral to the concept of time that I am developing here. I want to again emphasize that such interrogation, importantly, seeks not to erase the past, but rather to reclaim, re-member, and integrate it. As long as we conceptualize the movement of time as a progressive line, we are bound to repeat history, to produce the same stories, and reproduce the same subject positions. Linear time, as we have seen, closes up in a selfsame circle, excludes the possibility of creation and rebirth. It fails to provide the reflective (or self-reflective) moment that the movement of return is meant to establish. It is only if revolt follows the movement of return, and if it is accompanied by incessant interrogation—which in turn is intimately bound, I should add, to encounters with alterity and difference—that it might produce new discourses and new subjectivities. As we have noted already, it matters who returns, how they return, and for what purpose they return. For return to be revolutionary, it cannot simply confirm and reinforce dogma or dominant modes of being. And we should recall, in this context, that we need to grant epistemic privilege to the oppressed, such that revolutionary time avoids buttressing current power dynamics and conserving the status quo. As Freire, again, reminds us: "Who are better prepared than the oppressed to understand the terrible significance of an oppressive society? Who suffer the effects of oppression more than the oppressed? Who can better understand the necessity of liberation?"[34] On his account, revolt is ultimately about the future, and should be hopeful, anticipatory, indeed prophetic. It "affirms women and men as beings who transcend themselves, who move forward and look ahead, for whom immobility represents a fatal threat, for whom looking at the past must only be a means of understanding more clearly what and who they are so that they can more wisely build the future."[35] Put differently, we must return in order to begin anew, and to allow for a future that breaks with past injustices and modes of violence.

In an interview, Kristeva asserts that "it's precisely by putting things into question that 'values' stop being frozen dividends and acquire a sense of mobility, polyvalence, and life" (WL 12).[36] For Freire too it is this "putting things into question" that is at stake in revolutionary movements. He speaks of a "problem-solving education," indeed, as the title of his seminal book suggests, a "pedagogy of the oppressed," as what is needed for change to come. While Sjöholm has argued that revolt, for Kristeva, "implies return and displacement rather than production of something new and unpredictable" (KP 114), and that it "institutes a temporality unconcerned with the 'new,' with progress, or with the creation of new imaginary collectivities" (KP 120),[37] I want to argue that the movement of return, for Kristeva, is indispensable for the possibility of a different future. Sjöholm stresses that "the future of the revolt" must be understood not as a "futural or a projective vision, but the establishment of a displacing return, a permanence of the function of negativity, questioning and interrogating, challenging and reconstructing given presuppositions" (KP 113). I want to emphasize instead that it is precisely this that makes revolt capable of providing us with a future (although, indeed, one that is not frozen in a preconceived vision or form). The very displacing movement of return is, as Sjöholm herself ultimately concludes, what allows for change to occur and for the future to remain open. It is true that Kristeva is not concerned with progress in the sense of a linear progression toward an already defined goal.[38] Such progressive movement would not offer future horizons but would, instead, project itself onto what she has called the "future perfect," or a "paradoxical temporal structure" (WT 202), and would thus become totalitarian and uniform. The future, just as much as the past, must always be accompanied by ongoing interrogation and critical thought, by "permanent revolution," as Kristeva herself puts it (WL 12).[39]

Blind celebration of anything will inevitably lead to the terror of the guillotines or the banality of evil that Arendt famously described in *Eichmann in Jerusalem*.[40] But Kristeva's rejection of ideological-teleological progress cannot be reduced to a refutation of futurity; she simply teaches us that we are better off accepting the unpredictability of the future—since our failure to do so results in the instrumentalization of the present of which I have spoken already—and that futurity and change depend on a movement of incessant interrogative return and displacement, or revolutionary time. Grosz, who has noted that the past "is the condition for infinite futures," also argues that a "project of radical politics, and thus of feminist radical politics, remains how to envisage and engender a future unlike the present, without being able to specify in advance what such a future entails."[41] It is through interrogation and imagination only that we are "reborn," and that new horizons can be produced.

Let me expand on what I said about psychoanalysis earlier in this chapter. To be in analysis is to bring into sight the hidden side of that which is most familiar to us—our selves. By tarrying with this hidden side, by allowing it to become a question (just like Augustine became a question to himself), we may establish a living psychic space and reduce the ballast that hindered renewal in the first place. Growth depends on curiosity; on the willingness to ask uncomfortable questions and to think critically about what may seem obvious; and, perhaps most importantly, to approach these questions without an already established answer or solution in mind. In the most basic terms, this amounts to critical thought, and ultimately also to the decolonization of thought. A culture of revolt requires that we pay close attention to our own situatedness in structures of power—especially those of us who hold privilege within the current structures. We should note, however, that far from all thought that takes place in academia—the factories for critical thought of which I myself am part—achieves this. Academia is of course colonial-patriarchal through-and-through. And we know all too well how often the answer or results weigh heavier than the questions. That philosophy is a love of wisdom, rather than the possession of wisdom, is an ancient insight that many of us seem to have forgotten. Naïveté is no longer a virtue, and the aporetic no longer a position worth aspiring to.

The question that we must ask is if a scientific discourse (psychoanalysis included) that privileges good answers over deep questions is one capable of renewal, or if it is bound to merely repeat the same "wisdoms" over time (we get the answers we were seeking, leaving little or no room for surprises and obstacles along the way, with the result that research—or analysis too heavily burdened with theoretical presuppositions—becomes predictable). Oliver stresses that the capacity that revolt has for renewal depends on its interrogative potential and aporetic stance: "Intimate revolt depends upon this ability to continuously question, which Kristeva calls a rebirth perhaps because it recalls a childlike wonder and ravenous desire to ask questions."[42] Ongoing and childlike questioning provides a model for revolt irreducible to ideological agendas or a teleological belief in linear progress. If a fixed agenda would be achieved once and for all we would, in fact, no longer be unfolding temporally. "I will return at the end of time," Jesus proclaimed, and he meant this quite literally: the arrival of a Messiah as the ultimate solution to all problems puts an end to all time and change.[43]

Kristeva diagnoses our options as follows: "we can either renounce revolt by withdrawing into old values or indeed new ones that do not look back on themselves and do not question themselves or, on the contrary, relentlessly repeat retrospective return so as to lead it to the limits of the representable/thinkable/tenable" (IR 7). She opts for the latter, of course, urging us to nourish a culture of revolt: "Rather than falling asleep in the new normalizing order, let us try to rekindle the flame (easily extinguishable) of the culture of revolt" (SNS 9). The very movement of return, on her account, makes impossible an ultimate or final goal in the sense of fulfillment or completion. No political agenda can be realized and put in place once and for all. Revolt is a "dialectical process" without end, "a state of permanent questioning, of transformation, change, an endless probing of appearances."[44]

## Re-Membering the Past: Memorial Art

The movement of return that characterizes revolt is meant to re-member a past that always risks falling into silence, but aims subsequently to move beyond it. If we forget the past we are bound by repetition, but if we cling to it we repeat it too. As we saw already in the previous chapter, the perhaps most fruitful attempts at this kind of re-membering have occurred within the realm of art and literature. In *Head Cases*, Miller sets out to examine the role that artistic expression and experience play in Kristeva's work in the context of our modern melancholic culture.[45] On the one hand, she focuses on Kristeva's critique of modernity as a culture of the spectacle, one that proliferates images without content and leaves us numb and motionless, zapping away in front of our televisions or getting lost in a two-dimensional landscape of glossy billboards and idealized representations. The "new maladies of the soul" that we discussed earlier in this chapter are symptomatic of this culture where countless and contentless images, as Miller puts it, "make the temporality of everyday existence skip eternally like a needle on a record, repeating without progressing."[46] On the other hand, Miller offers an analysis of how it is that images simultaneously can function as a counter-force to such a culture of the spectacle. Kristeva, she suggests, "accords the artistic image a potentially liberatory effect" in that it can "generate recuperative, if not redemptive, iterations of meaning."[47] The image, to put it in the Arendtian terms used by Miller, provides the condition for the possibility of a "second birth," through its capacity to interrupt, reorganize, and fragment the deceptive claim to seamless unity so characteristic of the culture of the spectacle.[48] As Kristeva herself puts it in a brief prelude to *The Severed Head*: "the only resurrection possible may be . . . representation."[49]

Art, for Kristeva and for Miller, "provides a safe space for reopening the depressed subject or culture up to signification and creation," in that it has the capacity to offer a middle ground of sorts between the complete asymbolia of depression, on the one hand, and the full coherence of the spectacle, on the other.[50] Put differently, we might say that art and aesthetic experiences offer an alternative to the binary extremes of not being able to imagine anything at all (depression), and being so lost in imagination that we are reduced to a state of distraction (the culture of the spectacle). Either no images, or too many images. Both of these extremes ultimately involve repetition, whereas art opens up a different kind of temporality—a temporality of return, revolt, or, as Miller puts it, "the temporality of Proust's madeleine and of Freud's *Nachträglichkeit*."[51]

If art in general allows for temporal return, memorial art, or monuments, do so most deliberately, and often with explicit reference to loss and trauma. Miller devotes a brief section of her book to an analysis of monumental art, and uses language that echoes what we have said so far about the re-membering of return and its potential to instigate renewal and change. How, she asks, "can the loss be witnessed or exposed, rather than repressed, but in such a way that at the same time the healing process and political transformation can begin?"[52] She expresses skepticism of the way Americans relate to and represent their past and present suffering and injustices: "In the United States, the process, when it is undertaken at all, seems to be one of disavowal and repression. Either the phenomenon—we might take slavery as an example—is not memorialized at all, or it is commemorated through a grandiose act of atonement that crudely exalts the victims rather than acknowledging the mistakes behind their victimization."[53] This failure to revisit and re-member the darkest corners of our past in complex terms ultimately binds us to repeat that same past, such that human lives in the present come to not matter, and future opportunities for reconciliation and social change are foreclosed. As Frederick Douglass put it in "What to the Slave Is the Fourth of July?" from 1852: "America is false to the past, false to the present, and solemnly binds herself to be false to the future."[54]

So what might it mean for Americans to revisit their past in such a way that it need not be repeated? How break the seemingly cyclical arch that spans from the slave trade to lynching to Jim Crow to our own present plagued by mass incarceration and senseless police shootings of brown and black folk? Miller expresses astonishment by the fact that "no American artist has proposed—or at least been supported in an effort to construct—a countermonument to . . . the country's shameful past, such as the institution of slavery or the mass killing of American Indians."[55] Since the publication of her book, however, the National Memorial for Peace and Justice has been raised in Montgomery, Alabama, in 2018. It was initiated by the Equal Justice Initiative, a nonprofit organization founded by Bryan Stevenson, and is dedicated to the victims of American white supremacy. As Campbell Robertson wrote in the *New York Times* just days before its inauguration, the monument "demands a reckoning with one of the nation's least recognized atrocities: the lynching of thousands of black people in a decades-long campaign of racist terror."[56]

Inspired by the Holocaust Memorial in Berlin and the Apartheid Museum in Johannesburg, the piece catalogs nearly 4,400 acts of lynching of Black people across the South. Eight hundred steel columns hang from a roof, each carrying the name of an American county where people were lynched, and the names of those being lynched. Robertson notes: "The columns meet you first at eye level, like the headstones that lynching victims were rarely given. But as you walk, the floor steadily descends; by the end, the columns are all dangling above, leaving you in the position of the callous spectators in old photographs of public lynchings."[57] The monument thus invites—indeed forces—the viewers to reflect on the effects of racial oppression and our implication in acts of injustice in our own present, not for a moment allowing for the typical "grandiose act of atonement" Miller spoke of above.

At the same time, it is clear that the creators of the monument don't intend to shame the viewer into a state of paralysis: "I'm not interested in talking about America's history because I want to punish America," Stevenson notes in an interview, "I want to liberate America."[58] Recall Miller's claim that Kristeva "accords the artistic image a potentially liberatory effect" in that it can "generate recuperative, if not redemptive, iterations of meaning."[59] The hope, in other words, is that our re-membering of the past, through an engagement with this kind of piece, might allow us to reckon with our present, such that a different future becomes possible. Works of art such as these allow us to return to a past that all-too-often has been repressed or even denied, but this in turn must be coupled with present acts of resistance.

In a meditation on what he too calls revolutionary time in the context of the Black Lives Matter movement, Nicholas Mirzoeff notes that the cycles do "not complete until wrongs have been righted, which in this case means reparations for the 'social death' of slavery."[60] Mirzoeff quotes David Roediger, who, in thinking about Reconstruction in the United States after the abolition of slavery, in fact defines the time of revolution specifically as "a cyclical time of liberation, of abolition, and of mechanisms of redress."[61] The National Memorial for Peace and Justice does remind us that revolutionary time is not linear, and, as we will see in the next section of this book, that its movement must always start in a present marked by relational and engaged praxis. Each of the columns making up the piece therefore has a duplicate, intended to be distributed to the counties all over the country where the lynchings took place. People in these counties can request them so that they can be raised there—and many have—but they must first show that "they have made efforts locally to address racial and economic injustice."[62] When we said earlier that it matters *who* returns, and *why*, this is ultimately what is at stake. An uncritical return, one not already grounded in a desire and demonstrable effort to change the status quo, will merely serve to preserve past injustices and wrongdoings. It will repeat and induce a state of paralysis—a culture of death—rather than promote a vital culture of revolt and change.

Another example of a monument-like attempt to revisit the darkest corners of American history so as to offer a commentary on our present and, perhaps, crack open a different future, is Kara Walker's piece *A Subtlety*, installed in Brooklyn's legendary Domino Sugar Factory just prior to its demolition in 2014. The piece features a massive and glistering white sugarcoated sphinx-turned-mammy—silently residing over the vast refinery—as well as a procession of boys made from melting dark molasses, all carrying bananas or baskets, limbs slowly dripping onto the floor. Although it was not commissioned as such, this monumental piece is clearly a monument of sorts, re-membering and responding not only to the building and its history, but more broadly to the history of slavery, which is deeply embedded in the sugar trade. In a short video produced for the official website of the installation, Walker speaks of "a slave trade that traded sugar for bodies and bodies for sugar."[63] And the full title of the piece ("A *Subtlety*, or the *Marvelous Sugar Baby*, an Homage to the unpaid and overworked Artisans who have refined our Sweet tastes from the cane fields to the Kitchens of the New World on the Occasion of the demolition of the Domino Sugar Refining Plant") speaks loud and clear to the historical context that forms the backdrop of this monumental installation.[64]

Walker explains that she chose the Sphinx because "it's emblematic of a ruin," and she wanted to "evoke the kind of loss that ruins represent."[65] Like the Egyptian pyramids with which we tend to associate the sphinx, and which are awe-inspiring to the point of making us forget that they were in fact built by slaves, the factory sphinx is all but subtle in her massive appearance, made up of thirty-five tons of sugar, and requiring thirty-two crew members to bring her to life. Walker returned back through thousands of years of sugar-making history as she researched the piece, and a particular part of that very history could be felt in the space that housed the exhibit. By 1870 more than half of the sugar in the United States was refined there, and at the time of the exhibit the walls were still dripping with sweet stuff, the odor of which told a more bittersweet story. Not quite a Proustian madeleine evoking memories of time lost, but viscous molasses forcing upon the viewer the return of the repressed.

Walker's piece is a counter-monument of sorts—refusing to monolith-
ically commemorate events past in such a way that onlookers are allowed
"to move on with their lives while the memorial does the remembering
for them."[66] It is marked by its own disappearance: the melting molasses
of the boys' limbs is deeply uncanny, and the building itself was fully
demolished at the conclusion of the exhibition. As a counter-monument,
it serves to comment on the insidious ways that racism is alive and well
in our present, rather than turning it into an issue of the past. As in
all of Walker's works, including the one we looked at in the previous
chapter, it powerfully appropriates and brings to their extreme racial
stereotypes. Curator Nato Thompson describes the sphinx as "a hybrid
of two distinct racist stereotypes of the black female: She has the head
of a kerchief-wearing black female, referencing the mythic caretaker of
the domestic needs of white families, especially the raising and care of
their children, but her body is a veritable caricature of the overly sexualized black woman, with prominent breasts, enormous buttocks, and
[a] protruding vulva that is quite visible from the back."[67]

As onlookers of this awe-inspiring, sugarcoated sphinx—Walker's
own rendition of ancient pyramids or other such imposing monuments—
we are confronted with our own role in perpetuating the objectifying
and sexualizing gaze that keep such racial stereotypes alive. The piece
further thematizes the way in which our culture of the spectacle plays a
role in perpetuating racist violence, in that Walker invited her audience
to take snapshots of themselves posing in front of the sphinx, and the
photographs—often depicting white men posing in ways that confirm
rather than confront the sexualization of the Black woman embodied by
the sphinx—make up what remains of the piece today, after the factory
has been demolished.

❦

Miller takes a brief look at counter-monuments in her book, including
Jochen Gerz and Esther Shalev-Gerz's Monument Against Fascism, which
was installed in 1986 in Harburg, a suburb of Hamburg. I want to end
my discussion of art in relation to the time of return by taking a closer
look at this as well as another piece by Esther Shalev-Gerz, whose work
I have followed for many years, and with whom I worked on an exhibit
in Stockholm in 2002.[68]

In 1979, the city of Hamburg started a public discussion about raising a monument against fascism. Seven years later, Esther Shalev-Gerz completed the piece together with Jochen Gerz. A column, twelve meters high and one square meter at the base, was erected in a busy square in the city. The surface of the column was covered with a thin layer of lead, and passers-by were invited to sign their names as a gesture and manifestation against fascism. As the surface was covered with signatures, it was gradually lowered into the ground, so as to create space for more inscriptions. In 1993, after seven lowerings, the column vanished completely and only a plaque remained in the ground: "In the long run," it said, "it is only we ourselves who can stand up against injustice."

The column, during the seven years that it was still visible, became a public forum of sorts. In a place where people were literally passersby, anonymous faces, passing each other without further notice or attention, it became a space for reflection and active participation, a space where, if only for a moment, people could stop and see each other, engrave their names, look at the signatures, tributes, insults or graffiti of others, make a standpoint, leave traces behind. And during the years when the column was visible the political situation in Germany changed—the fall of the Berlin wall, the reunification, the resurgence of neo-Nazis—leaving the column as a kind of memento of contemporary Germany. Social change and experiences were cemented into the ground and into the memory of the citizens of Hamburg. The traces on the column were like rings of a tree; evidence of time passed, perforated in lead and in the collective memory of the participants.

Similar to the melting molasses and the imminent destruction of the space that housed Walker's *A Subtlety*, the very idea of this monument is its own nonexistence, its disappearance as object. Yet this invisible monument is by no means one of absence. Commenting on the piece, Jacques Rancière writes that it "signifies that the memory of the horror, and the resolve to keep it from returning, only have their monument in the wills of those who exist in the here and now . . . The monument is buried by those who take upon themselves the task that it symbolizes."[69] We are reminded that history cannot be reduced to a series of past events. It comes to life in the present and through present acts, and these acts are the condition of possibility for a future different from the past it was meant to commemorate. A monument against fascism could just as well have delved into the horrors of the past—presenting forever inscribed names of victims or freezing past events in an archival image as if fascism was a problem of the past. But this monument seeks instead to underline that past instances of fascism are a concern for us mostly insofar as we risk repeating them anew, in our present. The column could be seen as reflecting its own location and becoming, one could say, a "portrait" of Hamburg between 1986 and 1993. Moreover, it questions the very notion of memory that monuments traditionally are constructed to evoke. Or, as formulated by the artist herself: "we simultaneously evoked the past and the present, installing 'forgetting' in a place meant for 'remembering' and thus establishing, in the memory of each participant, through the act of public participation, a fleeting, subjected and fragmented memory."[70]

In the spring of 2005, the sixtieth anniversary of the liberation of Auschwitz was commemorated with an exhibit at the City Hall of Paris. Shalev-Gerz was invited to interview sixty survivors, asking them about their life before the war, the arrest and deportation, their time in the camp, and their present life. These "last testimonies" were pre-sented on sixty individual screens, unedited, the shortest two hours and the longest nine hours in length. Headphones on, seated at four long wave-shaped tables running through the room, each visitor could hear the stories at their own pace, leaving room for reflection. This kind of unmediated narration is the only way, according to Arendt, in which we can even try to understand the tragedy of the Holocaust. Kristeva writes that it is "through the narrative itself, and not through some particular understanding, analysis or rationalization of that narrative, that Arendt believes we will be able to contemplate the horror of the Holocaust."[71]

At the end of the exhibit room three big screens were showing an edited version of the testimonies, where all the talking had been left out, leaving just the moments of silence, the in-betweens, the instants of reflection dividing words and sentences. A raised eyebrow, tearing eyes, lifted shoulders, smiles. The moments of remembrance, condensed and repeated through the silence between words that disappear in writ-ten testimonies, add to the testimony a human dimension—a semiotic, embodied layer; or the silence or pause of breath that Irigaray so often urges us to revisit. By presenting these ruptured testimonies—the very ruptures that turn the testimony into something more than an image of a frozen past; that give it an affective dimension; and that therefore in turn disrupt a blind repetition of the past—the artist brings our attention to the very moment when the past is brought into the present. Frozen, yet dynamic time. Rifts in the repetitive movement of cyclical time and in the incessant projection forward of linear time. Rifts produced by a return to the quietude of a body and a semiotic register that say more than a thousand words.

## Conclusion

If the sexual division of temporal labor depended on man's repression of his own embodiment and the subsequent reduction of woman to mere body, this very division can be disrupted if and only if we are willing to acknowledge our shared embodiment and that we are from bodies born. This chapter, therefore, examined the very movement of return that constitutes revolutionary time, and the way in which it is a movement of return to a corporeal register. I focused on Kristeva's concept of *revolt*—which appears throughout her corpus—to reflect on the specific ways in which revolutionary time is a time of return, and how this movement of return allows for differentiation and alteration rather than a repetition of the past. I emphasized the role of psychoanalysis, language, and art in this context, elaborating on the ways in which these practices are loci in our culture where revolutionary time comes to life in concrete ways. For Kristeva, as we have seen, what is at stake is ultimately not just to revive corporeal dimensions of human life, but also to revitalize psychic life in the face of the automated nature of the Western modern lifestyle. In this chapter I explored the capacity of revolutionary time to disrupt these dimensions of modern life, as well as the political discourse that accompanies them.

Both Kristeva and Irigaray view linear time as grounded in an initial repression or amnesia, which results in an eternal return of the same. The traditional linear metaphysical paradigm hinges upon two core ideas: that there is a single origin (*archē*) and a single goal or end (*telos*). In the three chapters included in the present section, I have begun to sketch a model of time irreducible to these two poles or ends. Revolutionary time allows us to revisit the past in order to make possible a different future, but neither the past nor the future can be reduced to a single origin or a given end. My task in the chapters that follow will be to provide a more detailed account of revolutionary time, and I will do so by examining the three modes of time that we have known hitherto, but that will come to carry different meanings when time is viewed as a movement of return rather than as linear motion from the past into the future. These three modes are present, past, and future, and they will be examined in this order.

As should hopefully be clear from my introductory remarks, and from the kinds of examples that I have provided in the present chapter, a return to these three modes of time from the perspective of revolutionary time carries profound ethical and political weight. From a feminist point of view, I am trying to disrupt the sexual division of temporal labor that has granted man a subject position and reduced women to bodies outside of time; and bring the body back into our discourse about time, subjectivity, and human experience. In critical dialogue with Kristeva and Irigaray, I have also suggested the need to think beyond the categories of "man" and "woman" that pervade their work, both to include non-binary sexuate identities, and to draw critical attention to the intersection between sexual difference and other forms of difference, such as colonial and racial difference. From a broader political point of view, I aim at establishing a model of time that will allow for change, and that will provide us with a working model for engaging with the past and history in ways that allow us to integrate the past without repeating it in the present. This, I argue, is the condition of possibility for imagining a different future.

PART III

# THE PRESENT

Fundamentally, to begin the practice of love we must slow down and be still enough to bear witness in the present moment.

—bell hooks

The point of departure must always be with men and women in the "here and now," which constitutes the situation within which they are submerged, from which they emerge, and in which they intervene. Only by starting from this situation—which determines their perception of it—can they begin to move. To do this authentically they must perceive their state not as fated and unalterable, but merely as limiting—and therefore challenging.

—Paulo Freire

# 4

# The Problem of the Present

As I begin to trace the movement of time sketched in the previous section as revolutionary time, I will take the present as my point of departure. In the spirit of Freire's words in the epigraph to this section, it seems to me appropriate to begin in the here and now of our present. Given what I have said so far, it would indeed seem contentious to begin with the past only to progress forward via the present to the future. This would reinforce the linear model of time I am seeking to reject. Instead, I want to begin in the present, pursue a movement of return into the past, and finally (and only very briefly) examine the effects of such a return for our thinking about the future.

There are additional reasons to begin in the present. As I hope to have convinced the reader through my discussion in the opening chapters of this book, the sexual division of temporal labor that has marked so much of our human history—the culturally assumed separation between cyclical and linear time—empties the various temporal modalities of the vitality that they would need to remain dynamic, flexible, and unpredictable. I have argued that the past has been either idealized or repressed; that the future has been made to fit into visions and projects always already defined in advance; and that the present, to use the imagery provided by Kristeva, no longer is inhabited by living and loving subjects but rather by mass consumers numbed by antidepressants and cable TV. As we seek to reauthorize the past in order to make possible a different future, it is crucial to note that such a task must be pursued in the singular. The point is, precisely, to resist the temptation to posit an ultimate and universal origin or *archē* to which we all ought to return. Such a universalizing move would only repeat the traditional gesture of metaphysics. This is why Freire insists that "the point of departure must always be with men and women in the 'here and now' "[1]—not with humans in general (although we should certainly include those who identify neither as women nor men). What is at stake is the continuous movement of return that each singular person would pursue—a task that could never be finalized and completed once and for all, and one that necessarily must start in the present.[2] This is what the injection of aliveness that both Kristeva and Irigaray call for amounts to, and it depends on continuous interrogation and evaluation, through present acts (praxis).

By beginning in the present we might avoid universalizing abstractions in that the analysis takes as its point of departure the singularity of each lived present. As Irigaray articulates it in *Sharing the World*: "The world that we can share is always and still to be elaborated by us and between us starting from the perception and affirmation of what and who we are as humans *here and now*."[3] Just as Shalev-Gerz's monument against fascism had to be buried by those who took the task that it symbolized upon themselves, the world can only appear between those who inhabit it, here and now. As Freire notes in a passage proceeding the one quoted in the epigraph: "since people do not exist apart from the world, apart from reality, the movement must begin with the human-world relationship."[4] This is why I believe that we must begin in the present as we try to envision a temporal model that we—women and men and those identifying with neither of those terms—might be able to share.

It seems that the present is the tense that naturally would remain most vital, even when the past and future tenses have been frozen or rendered immobile by an all-too-rigid linear model of time. Precisely because of its fleeting character, however, the present is in fact the temporal tense that has suffered the hardest blows within a tradition that seeks to capture the movement of time in a rigorously straight line. While standing at the heart of our traditional notion of time, presence has simultaneously been thought of as that which escapes the movement of time: the everlasting eternal mode that metaphysical transcendence seeks to achieve in its overcoming of time and temporal change. In what follows, I will explore the specific ways in which the present has been rendered immobile, and begin to articulate how we might bring life back to the present.

To begin, I will offer an engagement with Derrida (and, by extension, Heidegger), in order to formulate the stakes involved in "the problem of the present." Drawing from Derrida—one of the most famous critics of the metaphysics of presence—I argue that unchanging presence not only is impossible but also undesirable, since it posits a fundamental threat to the very concept of life. By turning to Irigaray, however, I argue that the metaphysics of presence more appropriately should be described as a metaphysics of *absence*, since it in fact deals not with the ever-fleeting present ("here and now") but rather with an always-already final and defined past ("there, then, and beyond"). If Derrida (and Heidegger) sought to develop an account of time that circumvents presence altogether, Irigaray's critique of the metaphysics of presence (and the logic of identity that it implies) takes as its point of departure a commitment to "saving" presence from its metaphysical baggage. Her work, as I see it, seeks to articulate a logic of difference grounded in presence, but this is a notion of presence that, importantly, differs from that which has been privileged within the metaphysical tradition, precisely because of its inseparability from difference and differentiation—its being a living rather than static present.

Derrida, as so many before him (Heidegger included), thematizes time and finitude first and foremost in terms of mortality and death. I want to problematize the view that finitude primarily or solely would be a question of death, by adding to the discussion of finitude questions of natality and birth. The human condition of birth has commonly been ignored in accounts of time and finitude, and I argue that this one-sided focus on death and negativity feeds into the very logic that the critics of metaphysics are trying to reject.[5] I contend that the forgetting of birth leads us to cover over a fact that Irigaray and Kristeva (and many feminist thinkers with them) see as their task to uncover; namely that finite and embodied life necessarily is engendered and sexed. I will begin to articulate the philosophical and political implications of this argument here, and return to it with more precision and concretion in the chapters on motherhood in the next section of this book.

While Derrida and Irigaray respond somewhat differently to the tradition that they criticize, it is nevertheless important to note that they share a commitment to the idea that time is a necessary condition for existence. Irigaray's attempt to recuperate presence is, importantly, not an attempt to overcome temporality or finitude. On the contrary, her project seeks to establish the irreducible status of both time and difference. Derridean deconstruction could be described as "a revision of the logic of identity" that so forcefully has marked the history of Western thought, and this revision is essentially achieved through a thoroughgoing analysis of existence as being necessarily temporal.[6] Metaphysical presence must thus be understood as intimately linked to a notion of identity or sameness—and with the decolonial critique of presence in mind we might add that it is tied to the zero line of Greenwich time (European time) as well as the zero point of epistemology (European "reason").[7] Given what I have said so far about Irigaray's project, it should be clear by now that her emphasis on difference, on the one hand, and her critique of a certain linear-teleological conception of time, on the other, must be understood as two sides of the same thought. As I will try to show, any serious critique of the metaphysics of presence must therefore simultaneously be a critique of the logic of identity or sameness.

## Metaphysical Presence

In his essay "Différance," Derrida suggests that "the privilege granted to the present . . . is the ether of metaphysics."[8] And in "*Ousia* and *Grammē*," he expresses this same idea, noting that "the entire history of philosophy" has "been authorized by the 'extraordinary right' of the present" and that, "from Parmenides to Husserl, the privilege of the present has never been put into question."[9] Everything is thought in terms of presence, even non-presence or absence: "The past and the future are always determined as past presents or future presents," Derrida notes (OG 34). Heidegger, too, highlights the central role of presence in the metaphysical tradition, emphasizing that the Greek term *ousia* means both being and being-present, and that the two meanings have been conflated, in an unacknowledged way.[10] Being, Derrida explains, is "already determined as being-present," yet this determination remains un-thematized within the Western philosophical tradition (OG 47).

The question of time has thus always been inscribed into the question of Being, yet Being has also precisely been understood as that which is exempt from time. We know, from Hegel, that time "is the being which, in that it *is*, is *not*, and in that it *is not*, *is*."[11] The temporal present can, in fact, never be captured or maintained. Its very nature is to pass away, to be negated in the same moment as it comes into being. Within the framework of time, the present is that which never itself *is* as present—this is the riddle that has fascinated and troubled all those who have taken upon themselves the task of understanding the nature of time. It drove Aristotle to wonder if there really is such a thing as time: "Some of it is past and no longer exists, and the rest is future and does not yet exist; and time . . . is entirely made up of the no-longer and not-yet; and how can we conceive of that which is composed of non-existents sharing in existence in any way?"[12] Augustine puts the problem similarly: If "the present is time only by reason of the fact that it moves on to become the past, how can we say that even the present *is*, when the reason why it *is* is that it is *not to be*? In other words, we cannot rightly say that time *is*, except by reason of its impending state of *not being*."[13] Temporal presence is, from the outset of all philosophical thinking about time, defined in terms of absence, and the task of ontology, we might say, has been to "save" presence from this condition of always already becoming absent or past. Being, to put it simply, has been conceptualized as exempt from and immune to time: if the sensible realm is subject to change, the intelligible is posited as residing beyond such instability.[14]

Derrida identifies this division between temporal change and non-temporal presence as organizing Western philosophy from Aristotle to Hegel (OG 44). As Martin Hägglund puts it, we have come to subsume "time under a nontemporal presence in order to secure the philosophical logic of identity."[15] Selfsame Being (identity as presence in itself) can only be thought and grasped if exempt from the succession of time.[16] Since time never truly *is*, Being must be posited as somehow other than time, or immune to time. Augustine, for example, makes a distinction between "eternity which is forever still" and "the ebb and flow of things in past and future time."[17] In an attempt to explain the everlasting perfection of an unchanging divinity, he posits eternity as that in which "nothing moves into the past," where "all is present," once and for all.[18] The metaphysical tradition crucially hinges on this distinction between the static presence of Being (level of ontology and conceptuality) and the temporal character of becoming (level of the ontic, sensible, or empirical).[19]

It is precisely this distinction that Derrida refuses: a deconstructive logic must assume the irreducibility of time. He posits *différance* as that which never *is* and never can *be*. *Différance*, he asserts, cannot be thought "on the basis of the present, or of the presence of the present," but must rather be articulated in terms of a "past that has never been present" (Df 21). It not only escapes presence and essence as such but, more importantly for Derrida, it "threatens the authority . . . of the presence of the thing itself in its essence" (Df 25–26). It is thus one of many

Derridean terms designated to undo classical ontology: he asserts that the "determination of Being as presence or as beingness . . . is interrogated by the thought of *différance*" (Df 21). Put differently: *différance* undermines the very possibility of a selfsame identical present, since it inscribes a trace that eludes "that which might maintain it in presence" (OG 65).[20]

Through a careful reading of a footnote from Heidegger's *Being and Time*, Derrida scrutinizes and ultimately rejects the idea that a critique of classical ontology first and foremost would depend on the replacement of the "vulgar concept of time" (our everyday understanding of time as succession) with some other (presumably more authentic) concept of time, or rather temporality (such a replacement would be the task of Heidegger's own fundamental ontology, contra classical ontological accounts).[21] Derrida concludes that "an *other* concept of time cannot be opposed to [the vulgar concept], since time in general belongs to metaphysical conceptuality. In attempting to produce this *other* concept, one rapidly would come to see that it is constructed out of other metaphysical or ontotheological predicates" (OG 63).[22] While we must grant that Heidegger manages to avoid the problematic distinction between eternity and temporality, he nevertheless posits a fundamental opposition between primordial (ecstatic) temporality and derivative (vulgar, common) time. And while we thus no longer are said to "fall" from non-time to time, "the passage from one temporality to another" is nevertheless determined as a "fall" of sorts (OG 63). Derrida argues that Heidegger, who had set out to take apart the metaphysical oppositional structure, in fact ends up with a new "fundamental axis: that which separates the authentic from the inauthentic and, in the very last analysis, primordial from fallen temporality," and hence that he is guilty of the most "'essential' operation of metaphysics" (OG 63). Heidegger, to put this differently, sets up yet another dichotomous-hierarchical distinction of the kind that organizes the very tradition he had set out to disrupt.

Derrida, instead, wants to grant ontological status to our everyday understanding of time as succession. As I have noted, time has traditionally been subsumed and rendered immobile under the rule and self-determination of presence. But as Derrida points out, time plays the double role of "belonging as much to the de-limitation of metaphysics as the thought of the present, as to the simple overturning of metaphysics" (OG 62). Since Aristotle, time has, in other words, been both submitted to and subtracted from the privilege of the present. It has both settled and unsettled the domination of presence. It is both at the heart of and that which escapes and undermines a tradition concerned with presence. It is exactly this "play of submission and subtraction" that unfolds through the question of time that, according to Derrida, "must be thought as a *formal rule* for anyone wishing to *read* the texts of the history of metaphysics" (OG 62). Herein would lie the key to deconstruction—that reading of metaphysical texts that Derrida devoted his own philosophical career to pursuing.[23]

## Metaphysical Absence

Irigaray, in turn, describes the philosophical desire for presence as a "dream of man's, deferred to an immemorable past or future," while she herself argues that "nothing remains the same, not even in death" (FAMH 157–58).[24] Like Derrida, she denies the possibility of a selfsame present beyond the unfolding of time: "That there would be—in an age-old past or an unforeseeable future, in a time before or after time—a sameness eternally able to make itself present," is a false fantasy that has haunted man for ages (FAMH 158). But Irigaray first and foremost aims at showing that the metaphysical tradition, in fact, never really speaks of presence at all. She does not only express a worry that the present has been understood in non-temporal terms, as selfsame Being or eternity (which is in large part Derrida's concern), but she also brings our attention to the fact that such a reduction has robbed us of presence altogether. If temporal presence is that which never truly *is*, and if the non-temporal model of everlastingness has been articulated in terms of presence, such everlastingness is, in fact, nothing other than *absence*.

The metaphysical notion of presence can, in other words, not have been modeled on presence at all, but looks instead like an imitation of the past. Within a linear model of time, the past is that which can be grasped, known, and contemplated upon.[25] Perfect ideas and self-sufficient gods can really only be thought of in terms of a completed past (or perhaps also as an idealized future horizon already inscribed in a teleological economy). I want to stress that the view of the past as completed or self-identical hinges upon a *linear* model of time. If we—like Kant or Hegel for example—see history as teleological and universal (Kant calls the necessary progress toward maximal freedom the *ruse of Nature*, while Hegel speaks of the *cunning of Reason*), then the past can indeed be completed. Benjamin has argued that such a view of the past and of history depends, precisely, on the idea that we could stand outside of history, like a God or a divine creature, who somehow escapes the movement of time (it depends, in other words, on access to a position of selfsame presence). As David Couzens Hoy has pointed out in his lucid reading of Benjamin's "Theses on the Philosophy of History": "Universal history is written from outside or at the end of history. But we are always only ever *in* history, and its end is always in a future—one that will never come."[26] According to Couzens Hoy, Benjamin maintains that history has no *telos*, and he illustrates his point by pointing out that the angel in Paul Klee's painting *Angelus Novus* is facing backward. It should be noted, however, that while the angel is facing toward the past (and this allows him to see that history is full of victims and barbarism rather than universal progress), he nevertheless is moving forward. Benjamin, in other words, also views history as linear.

Wood, too, has pointed out that the privilege of presence depends on a linear notion of history as progress: "History is the unbroken transmission and development of meaning. Contingency, plurality, death, breaks, circles, regressions are all to be appropriated within a wider continuity. Progress, truth, wisdom, freedom, and so forth are all names for what history is or can be made to generate."[27] We might say that the metaphysics of presence is an ideology of sorts—just like I described linear time as an ideology in the previous chapters of this book. They are, again, flip sides of the same coin. As we will see in my section on the past—and as should be clear already from what I have said so far—the return to the past that characterizes revolutionary time as I perceive it allows us, precisely, to undermine any notion of linear movement forward, as well as any notion of the past as completed. What I hope to show in what follows is that it allows us to think—and live—presence in non-ideological terms.

It is not a coincidence that the metaphysics of presence tends to be framed by the belief in an absolute origin (*archē*) and an ultimate end or goal (*telos*). As Wood notes: "Origin and end are equally examples of this value of presence."[28] The "presence" of the Western tradition is in fact crafted on these two extremes—an absolute and stable past or an ultimate and predictable future—never on the undecidable and fleeting "present" of time. God, in Irigaray's own words, is that figure who is "everywhere present and never there" (BEW 13). Absolute presence is nothing but absolute absence. And while the metaphysical thinkers themselves would hardly acknowledge this, it is exactly about the absent that they have been speaking all along.

This can be illustrated by the figure of the feminine, insofar as it has been articulated in terms of lack. For woman, absence is "the condition for entry into presence"—like time, she only "is" insofar as she "is not" (FAMH 52). And the same can be said about other minorities too. Racial and ethnic multiplicity is routinely reduced to the "*non*-white" or "*non*-Western"—that which *lacks* reason or resources or rights. Queer desire is framed as a "phase" that will *pass*, or as a *dead end*. And people with disabilities are indexed as *lacking* the proper capacities for mobility, thought, self-sufficiency, and so on. The fully present ultimately takes the shape of a productive-reproductive white able-bodied man, autonomous and upright, sovereign and strangely disembodied.[29]

I want to suggest that the dichotomy between presence and absence stands at the heart of a logic incapable of thinking difference (sexual, racial/colonial, and other forms of difference) beyond hierarchical dichotomies. The possibility of thinking difference otherwise (and in the context of sexual difference specifically, the possibility of thinking *sexuate* difference) depends on our thinking time as that which would help us overcome the rigid opposition between presence and absence. This, in my mind, is why we need a feminist critique of the metaphysics of presence, but one that not merely rejects or negates presence but that rather elaborates presence differently, as always already shot through with absence (and absence, similarly, as shot through with presence). As we saw in chapter 2, Irigaray responds to sexism not by erasing sexual difference (in the name of equality articulated in terms of neutrality), but by arguing that it has been erased all along, and that we therefore need to rethink it, in terms of sexuate difference (a non-oppositional relation between the sexes; a relation that does not reduce woman to lack or absence or other to same). Similarly, she endeavors to criticize the metaphysical tradition of presence not by escaping presence altogether, but by establishing that said tradition never has been able to think presence other than as absence, and that a proper critique of such tradition therefore depends on our rethinking the relation between presence and absence in non-oppositional terms.

When, in her later work, Irigaray takes on the challenge to write her own philosophy—to construct an ontology of two rather than merely deconstructing a metaphysics of the same—she therefore does so not by denying or rejecting presence, but by returning to and reclaiming the present in terms that resonate with what I have called revolutionary time. We might say that she seeks to provide an account of presence injected with aliveness (which, among other things, is to say that she elaborates the question of presence by turning to the body and to human relations). No doubt, Irigaray shares Derrida's worries about the metaphysics of presence. But instead of solely focusing on the domination and privileging of this present, she thus conversely points to the manner in which the metaphysical tradition in a certain sense also has covered over the present, leaving us with an illusion of presence which in reality is nothing but a rigid and dead (*rigor mortis*) version of the past. This is, of course, in part due to the fact that the present really only comes into being by becoming past. But the point, for Irigaray, is to try to think—and live—the "becoming past" (and the "coming-into-being") of the present instead of the "being" of presence, since such "being" in fact always already would be a "having become past." Eternity, for Irigaray, would be an everlasting past, a frozen or idealized timeless horizon of the "there" and the "beyond."

The answer to the problem of the present is, in other words, not to reject presence altogether, but rather to reclaim it in different terms, to offer a different explanation of what it means for something or someone to "be present." We must not throw the baby out with the bathwater: the "bad" presence of the metaphysical tradition can only be criticized and undermined insofar as we offer an alternative account of presence— one that stands not in opposition to time but rather at the very heart of the incessant unfolding of time (this would, again, be similar to her treatment of sexual/sexuate difference). The point is not to reduce time to (non-temporal) presence or eternity, but rather to sustain all three dimensions of time—present, past, and future—in their interdependence and internal oscillation.

This is, precisely, the work that revolutionary time is meant to achieve. To reduce time to the two dimensions of past and future would, in my mind (and this seems to be implied by Irigaray), be to reduce time yet again to a two-dimensional line, and we would thus repeat the traditional metaphysical move, one that can harbor oppositions only according to an either-or-logic of rigid dualisms.[30] The point, instead, is to think time beyond the dichotomies of presence and absence.[31] Presence understood in this way might allow us to think the undecidability of the in-between (a crucial category for Irigaray). If the Western philosophical tradition has separated everlasting presence from time, and if the latter has been conceived as a line leading from the past into the future, it seems that the task would be not only to bring presence back from an eternal beyond, but also to reinscribe the present into the very structure of time, without giving it the priority and the rigid form that it has been given hitherto.

Both Derrida and Irigaray stress the role of finitude in their respective critiques of a tradition that privileges presence, but they do so rather differently. In what follows, I will say something about why finitude not only is *impossible* but also *undesirable* to overcome, and then articulate a critique of the idea that finitude exclusively is a matter of mortality and death, arguing, instead, that one must think finitude on the basis of both birth and death.

## To Be Finite Is to Have Been Born

While the dream of everlasting presence is grounded in the desire to overcome our finitude (be it the philosophical search for eternal ideas or the religious hope for resurrection), I want to argue, instead, that it inevitably results in a thoroughgoing destruction of vitality and aliveness. In an attempt to escape the inherent vulnerability of mortal life we in fact lose life and the temporality of life. The perpetual presence that man is striving for can really only be understood in terms of death, violence, or the annihilation of life. Commenting on the work of Jean-Jacques Rousseau, Derrida claims that "pure presence itself, if such a thing were possible, would be only another name for death."[32] In *Radical Atheism: Derrida and the Time of Life*, Hägglund has pursued this idea as it runs through the work of Derrida, pointing not only to the impossibility of eternal presence but, more radically still, to the *undesirability* thereof:

> What traditionally has been figured as the most desirable—the absolute being of God or the immortality of the soul—is here figured as the most undesirable: as the pure indifference of death that would annihilate the impure difference of life. . . . If there can be nothing without the spacing of time, then all metaphysical ideas of something that would eliminate the spacing of time are ideas of something that would extinguish everything.[33]

The notion of absolute life, celebrated and longed for by metaphysicians of the past two millennia or more, is in a certain sense inseparable from death. Or, as Adriana Cavarero puts it, "only a perspective that is obsessively focused on death can in fact read existence in terms of totality."[34]

To be fully present is to not be at all. Absolute *presence*, as we have just seen, amounts to nothing but absolute *absence*. The finitude of human life is exactly what makes life vital. To live is to be vulnerable and finite, *to be temporally determined*. The most dangerous threat to life is thus not death per se, but rather immortality or positive infinity. As Butler points out: "Ironically, to rule out death for life is the death of life."[35] Or, as Jacques-Yves Cousteau puts it in his book on aquatic life: "Immortality cannot survive," since death is fundamental to evolution, and evolution is fundamental to survival and life.[36] If finitude traditionally has been seen as a "negative limitation that prevents us from having access to the fullness of being," the deconstructive insight is that finitude, on the contrary, "is an unconditional condition that makes the fullness of being unthinkable as such."[37] It is the horizon upon which life and survival are possible. We might recall the idea expressed by Freire in the epigraph to this section, namely that movement is only possible if we start in the here and now, insofar as the latter ("here and now") are understood not as *limiting* conditions, but precisely as *challenging* conditions (our irreducible situatedness) that make movement possible in the first place.

The fullness of being, on this account, is not just impossible to cognize, but it is unthinkable and even undesirable, since it in fact amounts to death (insofar as the condition for life is finitude): "Mortality is thus not a lack of being that it is desirable to overcome," Hägglund explains. "Rather, mortality is the possibility for both the desirable *and* the undesirable, since it opens the chance of life and the threat of death in the same stroke."[38] In *Specters of Marx*, Derrida gives this formula a rather dramatic edge: "absolute life, fully present life, the one that does not know death," is, he asserts, nothing but "absolute evil."[39]

Aesthetic and literary examples of this double-edged aspect of life are abundant. Think, for example, of Aylmer in Nathaniel Hawthorne's short story "The Birthmark," who cannot but feel "shocked" by the little hand-shaped birthmark that brings imperfection to the face of his otherwise perfect wife.[40] An alchemist and scientist by profession, Aylmer endeavors to remove the crimson hand that so stains her cheek, by treating it with a refined dose of the elixir vitae that he has invented for this purpose.[41] If only "the birthmark of mortality" could be removed, he reasons, Georgiana would be immaculate and "fit for heaven without tasting death."[42] But as Georgiana herself notes early on in the novella:

"the stain goes as deep as life itself."[43] There is no life without mortality, and perfection is but another word for death. Once mortality is removed, we reach not immortality but immediate death. This is illustrated by the transformation Georgiana goes through once the elixir goes into full effect and the birthmark disappears: "The fatal hand had grappled with the mystery of life, and was the bond by which an angelic spirit kept itself in union with a mortal frame. As the last crimson tint of the birthmark—that sole token of human imperfection—faded from her cheek, the parting breath of the now perfect woman passed into the atmosphere, and her soul, lingering a moment near her husband, took its heavenward flight."[44] Because of his longing for selfsame presence, Aylmer has to face the absence of that which he most loves. Presence, again, reverts into absence. More than being a moral tale, the story tells us something about the irreducibly temporal character of life. It is said of Aylmer that "he failed to look beyond the shadowy scope of time, and, living once for all in eternity, to find the perfect future in the present."[45] In search for presence beyond the here and now, we lose precisely the presence of the here and now. And while the latter kind of presence might seem imperfect, it is the only kind compatible with life and living beings.

∽

While critics of the metaphysical tradition (Heidegger, Derrida, and others) have focused on death as the necessary horizon for temporal life, Irigaray importantly adds that it is not only in our attempts to eliminate *death* that we undermine the movement of life, but that life and aliveness also depend on the fact of *birth*. Our denial thereof is the flipside of the same coin: temporal life not only passes away or ceases to be but also perpetually comes into being. That time passes means that temporal life is marked, time and again, not only by an *end*, but also by *beginnings* (note the plural—what is at stake here is not an ultimate or stable *archē*). Life is indeed *finite*, but as such it is not only *mortal* but also *engendered*.[46] The limits of life are death *and* birth.[47] Both these limits must be understood not as negative limits or limitations but as the condition of possibility for life itself—the *challenge* that makes movement possible (that Freire spoke of in the epigraph). Both birth and death are the horizons upon which the very unfolding of life depends. To be mortal is to be alive as someone who has been born, and to be born is to be alive as someone who will die. Or, as Irigaray herself puts it in *To Be Born*, "Once we are born, we will always remember, even if we are not aware of it, that to live entails the risk of death."[48]

Irigaray consistently brings our attention to the fact that birth has been forgotten and covered over in our culture (I will discuss this at length in part 4 of this book), and ties this emphasis on death to a kind of forgetfulness of life. As we saw in my discussion of revolutionary time in the opening chapters, this repression of life is also a repression of the material conditions of possibility for life—that is, the body, or more precisely, the sexed body. On Irigaray's account, this emphasis on death (and our subsequent attempts to overcome it) is exactly what paves the way for metaphysical presence.[49] She describes man as "preoccupied with death and not with life. Uprooted from his own birth, from his growth, into a world of projections, a world of dreams" (FAMH 122). In critical engagement with Arthur Schopenhauer, she notes that "without death there would hardly have been any philosophizing" (BEW 23), adding (somewhat dramatically) that in Western philosophy "the thought of the world as a living world no longer exists" (BEW 45). What she means by this is, I think, that philosophy and philosophical discourse has been so concerned with the *end* of life—or with that which resides *beyond* life—that it has come to repress our (maternal-material) beginnings (beginnings that, on Irigaray's account, are neither static nor possible to define once and for all—precisely because they remain temporal and, as we shall see, plural).

The result of this, as I have argued from the outset of this book, is a loss of time, or of living/dynamic time. We are left with a purely ideal notion of time—a notion tied exclusively to death and hence to the "de-materialization" of life (if birth is what *gives* us a body, death—in most traditions—is seen precisely as a *liberation* from the body).[50] Time is thus reduced to repetition. Irigaray describes the human as being "cut off from the origin of the evolution of its becoming," and therefore "paralyzed in its development."[51] She prescribes "a constant return" and a "continual movement of backwards and forwards" between the beginning and the end."[52] Without such movement—a movement of return—she worries that we would fail to accomplish our own becoming, "and this quest, which is based on a natural dynamism, risks becoming a going around in circles—a sort of eternal return of the same—in which energy exhausts itself, and which ends in a nothing (of) being."[53] The eclipse of birth results in a loss of life, of becoming, and of time itself. In the metaphysics of presence, the effort to "overcome" time/mortality relies upon our having already overcome (as in made invisible) our being born—the fact of birth.

In her introduction to *The Way of Love*, Irigaray notes that "the wisdom of which these technicians of the logos are enamoured is sometimes a *knowing how to die*, but seldom the *apprenticeship to a knowing how to live*."[54] Now, we might of course add that our knowing how to live necessarily must involve a knowing how to die. And while Irigaray clearly would agree, she is nevertheless eager to emphasize that the intimate tie between life and death also depends on the fact of birth, and that insofar as the latter is disavowed to such a degree that it never quite enters into the discourse of finitude, life becomes reduced to the absolute death of selfsame eternal being. Rachel Jones puts this aptly in her important reading of Irigaray's critical engagement with Plato: "instead of recognizing our beginnings in birth, the philosopher longs for a re-birth of the soul that depends on the death of the body."[55] Knowing how to *live* would thus be equivalent to knowing how to *return*. The man of philosophical discourse—one who inhabits linear time—is dead, "always already and nevermore, from forgetting his own birth" (FAMH 101). That he is "dead" is just another way of saying that his life is a repetition of sorts (recall the repetitive procedure of the machine discussed in chapter 2—a machine incapable of renewal due to its denial of sexuate difference).

Both Derrida and Irigaray are thus trying to respond to and undermine the morbidity of selfsame presence (their insight that our striving for pure life and peace would amount to nothing but a putting in place death and violence—that time would be reduced to repetition, and presence to absence). But whereas Derrida does so by framing finitude as a question of death and negativity, Irigaray seems to say that such a move in part is bound to repeat the one-sidedness of the very metaphysical tradition that he had set out to obliterate. It is only if we understand temporal life as incessantly passing away *and* coming into being—thus only if we acknowledge not only *death* but also *birth* as part of the structure of life—that we can achieve a culture of life and change.[56] Or, as Grosz has put it, time "*makes* as much as it *unmakes* or *decays*."[57] Time, we might say, is not only a negative and destructive force, but also one capable of creation. And to be finite is to have been born.

This may seem like a minor difference between our two thinkers, but it in fact marks a crucial distance between them—one that goes

back to what I said about Irigaray taking as her point of departure life
and living beings (embodied and marked by sexuate difference), while
Derrida first and foremost develops a formal deconstructive logic. To forget
birth is, among other things, to forget the role of women in our culture.
Where Derrida speaks of the *trace* or of *différance*, Irigaray speaks instead
of *woman* or the *feminine*. Woman is indeed the invisible ground from
which life evolves, but insofar as woman is forgotten and silenced, life
is reduced to timeless repetition, and presence loses its living character.
Woman "remains the nocturnal ground and lethal slumber on which
bases [man] erects himself, remains a transparency imperceptible in the
entry into presence. . . . The tie that bound him, as engendered, to this
maternal her [*c'elle maternelle*] breaks. Being can exist as one, can close
itself up in a circle," Irigaray notes (FAMH 97, 99). "Being" is achieved
at the cost of the time of life and of the living. And at the expense of
woman, who gives life.[58]

To reconsider space and time, Irigaray argues, is a work of anamnesis,
a making-visible the forgotten ground from which we all emerge: the
maternal body or the invisible air, which we all breathe and need in order
to exist: "Time thus amounts to remembering the forgetting—that nothing
ever occurs in the same place, that in each instant man changes his air,
that he disappears-reappears all the time, that his becoming obliterates,
and, moreover, corrupts, the air where he takes place, the air thanks to
which he entered into presence" (FAMH 163). We see here how time
and space are intertwined; that a tradition that tries to eliminate space
and materiality also is bound to reduce time to presence, which in turn
amounts to eliminating or immobilizing time altogether.

Irigaray's many attempts to return to our forgotten beginnings—manifest for example in her emphasis on the maternal body—could of course
be understood as a rather traditional metaphysical move toward an absolute
origin or *archē*. The radicality of her trajectory toward our beginnings,
however, lies in her emphasis on their (at least) *dual* nature—therefore
the plural. If the metaphysical tradition has appointed God the Father
or the idea of the Good as an absolute and ever-present origin, Irigaray
consistently underlines the plurality and temporality of beginnings. The
ontological status of both time and difference in her thought distances
her from a metaphysical tradition that privileges *archē* and presence.

I take Irigaray to argue that the *oneness* of Being is as undesirable
as the *presence* of Being. She notes that "a society in neutral mode loses
sight of the line separating life from death. Although life, obviously, is

always sexed, death on the contrary no longer makes this distinction."[59] We can, moreover, arguably die alone, while birth is constitutively and doubly marked by difference: we cannot be born alone, a (m)other is always present.[60] Or, as Irigaray puts it in her meditation on the human condition of being born: "Coming into the world initially means coming from an other."[61] Any logic that sets up a single and original *archē* (God the Father, the idea of the Good) above and beyond the particulars that it is said to produce, is bound to reduce life to mere repetition or to the pure indifference of death. Irigaray notes that "Being's self-identity is suspended beyond space and time," because we have "forgotten that everything always and all the time becomes other" (FAMH 163). To live is to breathe, to change, to alter, to become. To be—understood as being ever-present—is to forget, and to die (FAMH 164).

To attribute to finitude both the condition of death and that of birth helps us, in my mind, to more rigorously think finitude not as a negative limitation of life but rather as a condition for life (what Freire called a "challenge"). Derrida ties the possibility of life to its inherent impossibility (an aporetic figure that makes possible, among other things, the end of possibility). We must by no means reject or deny the negativity inscribed in the movement of time and life—it is indeed irreducible—but it seems to me crucial to think it together with and alongside a generative, creative discourse grounded in the categories of birth and natality. Positing death alone as the unconditional condition does not, moreover, allow us to rigorously criticize the logic of identity and sameness. Two identical copies will still thrust themselves toward their death (think only of cloned beings who are produced in sameness—and thus not quite engendered—but that nevertheless inevitably will die).[62] Birth requires difference.[63] Our birth is thus never a solitary or individual experience. As Lisa Guenther puts it, "the lapse of time between myself and my birth disrupts in advance the possibility of a completely masterful, unified subject," and "birth is passively given to me in a way I do not initially choose or control."[64]

By adding birth (or the having-been-engendered-by-someone) to the structure of finite life, we inscribe difference at the very core of the unfolding of life. And this in turn challenges the linear model of time and the metaphysical notion of presence that accompanies it: "Should Being divide in two, what happens to presence? If this obscure key that opens man's world is broken into at least two parts, what then becomes of man's time, of man in his space-time," Irigaray asks (FAMH 123).[65]

These questions point to the intimate relation between time and differ-ence. And they introduce a thought that runs through all of Irigaray's work: In a world of at least two there can be no selfsame presence. The idealization of selfsame presence is embedded in our current culture of sameness. The cultivation of sexuate difference would prepare ground for presence understood otherwise.

~~~~

In *Being and Time*, Heidegger famously develops his notion of primordial or ecstatic temporality, and describes it as arriving at us from the future. Our task, according to Heidegger, is to affirm our finitude "in an authentic anticipation of death," which is to say that our being is a being-towards-death and that this should be acknowledged.[66] This emphasis on finitude understood in terms of death is inherited both by followers and critics of Heidegger. When Irigaray and others emphasize the role of birth or the category of natality, they by no means sacrifice the future for a simple retrieval into the past. It is true, of course, that my birth is a past event while my death lies in the future, but it is equally true that my death marks an end to my future while my birth (and my continual re-births, to use Arendtian language) constitute the horizon of possibility for a future (or rather, for *futures*) in the first place.

The fact of birth—and our acknowledgment thereof—is intimately tied to future horizons while at the same time serving as a reminder that we are rooted in and indebted to history, the past, and our maternal-ma-terial conditions. It bears witness to the fact that nobody is "thrown" into the world out of nowhere, but that somebody *put* us into the world, that the world was *handed down* to us (this is why Heidegger must begin his account of historicity with a reference to birth). Moreover—and of this Heidegger does not speak—our access to the world is embodied and sexed in nature. The emphasis on birth does, finally, not imply the assumption that I will live forever (it does not assume an "inauthentic" relationship toward my death and finitude, to use Heideggerian language). It is true that it establishes a relationship to the future that exceeds the measure of my own finitude (insofar as it carries a promise for possible future generations), but it importantly does not do so through a denial of my own death or through some attempt at positing my own being above and beyond finitude. It is *as someone born*—not as an all-know-ing sovereignty—that I become aware of my connectedness with (and indebtedness to) past and future generations, and thus precisely with the vulnerability and finitude of my own life and of life in general.

If thinkers of time and temporality have tended to disregard questions of material conditions and history (the argument, again, is easily reduced to a formal or logical analysis), the strength of Irigaray's thinking is that she provides an argument about the irreducibly temporal character of life while, simultaneously, consistently grounding it in a material account of embodied and sexed life, and a historical account of the sexual division of temporal labor. In fact, as this book is meant to show, both Irigaray and Kristeva offer a theory of embodiment through a discussion of temporality grounded in the category of birth, and they are both careful to tie their discussion of time to an analysis of material conditions and power relations. This is why I argue, throughout this book, that an understanding of their respective analysis of time is indispensable for an understanding of their feminist politics of difference and change.[67]

## Conclusion

It is well known that Heidegger, in his formulation of ecstatic time, privileges the future, while Derrida characterizes *différance* as a past that has never been present. Both, in their own way, deliberately try to articulate the movement of time in ways that avoid presence. Their critique of the metaphysical tradition amounts to showing that it has relied on presence both for thinking time (time, on this account, would be seen as a succession of discrete now-points) and for thinking the outside of time (the everlasting presence of immutable Being). Insofar as they view existence as constitutively temporal, they therefore take as their task to think time (or temporality) as irreducible to presence.

I have argued that Heidegger, Derrida, and Irigaray all view time as an irreducible and necessary condition for life. They do so, however, in different ways. Derrida's critique of Heidegger was that he had posited a hierarchical relationship between phenomenological temporality (ecstatic time) and ordinary time (clock time), and in so doing he had allegedly ended up reproducing one of the central aspects of the very tradition that he was taking to task. Following Irigaray, I added that the sexual neutrality of Dasein leads Heidegger to remain within the logic of identity, and that this, in the final analysis, prevents him from thinking time beyond traditional metaphysics. Derrida introduces *différance* as a self-effacing trace that posits a challenge to any notion of selfsame presence. His work allowed us to see why positive infinity not only is impossible but also undesirable, and gave us a good ground for thinking the irreducibly temporal structure of existence. What distinguishes his work from that of Irigaray is, first and foremost, his formal approach to the problem (while she approaches it instead from the standpoint of lived sexed experience and embodiment), and the fact that he, like Heidegger, puts exclusive emphasis on death and mortality (while Irigaray wants to inscribe the fact of birth and natality into her analysis of time and finitude).

In his critique of the metaphysics of presence, Derrida ultimately sought to reject the present—and the possibility of presence—altogether. By turning to Irigaray, however, I have suggested in this chapter that the metaphysics of presence more appropriately should be described as a metaphysics of *absence*, since it in fact deals not with the ever-fleeting present ("here" and "now") but rather with an always-already final and defined past ("there," "then," and "beyond"). I argued that this dichotomy between presence and absence stands at the heart of a logic incapable of thinking sexual as well as racial/colonial and other forms of difference beyond hierarchical dichotomies—a logic that, precisely, reduces woman and other marginalized subjects to lack or absence. A proper critique of such tradition therefore depends on our rethinking difference in non-oppositional terms, which is arguably the central task of Irigaray's own thinking.

Such a task, I have argued, depends on a reconfiguration of finite life as framed not only in terms of death and mortality, as Heidegger and Derrida would have it, but also in terms of birth and natality, such that life—and the living present—can be conceived as always already fluid and heterogeneous. The human condition of birth has commonly been ignored in accounts of time and finitude, and I have argued that this one-sided focus on death and negativity feeds into the very logic that the critics of metaphysics have been trying to reject. I contended that the forgetting of birth leads us to cover over a fact that both Irigaray and Kristeva see as their task to uncover; namely that finite and embodied life necessarily is engendered and sexed.

But is there, we must ask, really a way of thinking or approaching the present not in terms of absence or the past, but as it unfolds "here and now" (which, as I hope to have made clear in this chapter, would not be the same as grasping or holding onto the present, in the sense of freezing the movement of time)? Would Irigaray's attempts to "reclaim" the present lead her to repeat the very tropes of the tradition against which she turns, or is she able to distance herself from the metaphysical tradition of presence? If Derrida wondered whether or not we could think time outside of a metaphysical framework, we must ask ourselves whether presence—perhaps the most central of all metaphysical concepts—can be thought in non-metaphysical terms. With these questions in mind, we must now look more carefully at the specificity of Irigaray's critique of the metaphysics of presence, and elucidate the notion of presence that she offers as an alternative that not only exceeds but also challenges the set of assumptions that I have described in these opening reflections on the present.

## 5

# Temporalizing the Present

One of the deep challenges in our Western capitalist culture is our ability—or rather inability—to *be in the present*. We are slaves of our calendars; experience most precious moments through the lens of a camera (so that they are eternally inscribed memories before they are even cognized); we plan out the future in perfect detail; obsess about what we could have done differently; prepare our funerals and decide who will inherit our possessions when we die; try to anticipate and control any given situation; complain that things used to be better in a long-lost idealized past; document the growth of our children without really experiencing it in proximity, as it unfolds. In our attempts to render things ever-present, we lose the present. The fact of the matter is thus that we live mostly in the past or in the future—rarely in the "here and now" of the present. And, as we saw in the opening chapter of this book, our "living" in the past or in the future amounts to freezing these temporal dimensions in an idealized or ideological frozen image, which means that they in fact are not "lived" at all, but rather projected.[1]

For Irigaray, as should be clear by now, we must differentiate between the everlasting presence of a metaphysics of presence on the one hand (one that, in fact, has nothing to do with presence but rather with the past and with absence—it is exactly never here and now but always there, then, or beyond), and the fleeting presence of temporal life on the other hand (one that, according to the very nature of time, is bound to be ever-changing, always-disappearing, self-effacing). If the former is understood in terms of eternity and selfsameness, the latter unfolds within a life both engendered and finite, a life marked by alterity

135

and alteration. Put differently, if the former depends on the dichotomy between linear and cyclical time, the latter might materialize within the framework of revolutionary time. And if there is anything about time that the metaphysical tradition has tried to reject, it is exactly this present, insofar as it is understood as that which continuously comes into being and passes away, and hence never can be sustained over time, in a lasting way. The challenge, it seems, is not exactly to seize the day, but rather to let the day pass, to experience it in its passing. And, in a sense, to slow down, to be mindful of the movement of time, to be, as we say, "in touch" with life in its unfolding. How, then, might we begin to reclaim the present in such temporal terms? How might we begin to tease out the possibility of being in the present not in terms of Being, but instead in terms of (mindful and attentive) becoming?

In what follows, I will offer three examples of how Irigaray attempts to bring our attention back to the present: first through her (daily) practice of yoga, then through her (also daily) practice of writing poetry, and finally through her reflections on love and intersubjective relations. While I hope to unearth some of the most powerful aspects of the living present that inhabit Irigaray's thought, it will also become evident what a difficult task it is to think presence beyond metaphysics, and to speak of the movement of time without arresting it in a frozen image of the now. Perhaps this is because we are still confined within a linear model of time—a model that conditions the very language with which we speak. Perhaps there are no already established practices that fully escape the linear model of time that has been the paradigm for so long. Following Irigaray, I will nevertheless make an attempt to identify such practices—if for no other reason than to reveal some of the challenges that such a revolutionary project is bound to encounter.

## Breathing Life into Presence:
## The Praxis of Yoga and Pranayama

In *Between East and West*, Irigaray expresses a thought that should be familiar by now: Western metaphysics, she writes, corresponds to "an ill-considered sacrifice of the body and of the universe to a coded and codeable knowledge outside a *present* act, to a truth that is valid in all times and all places" (34). Universalized abstraction depends on an escape from the body and from singular experience in the present. As the title of her book suggests, she turns to Eastern cultures and traditions—and more specifically to the practice of yoga in such traditions—in search for an alternative to this Western sacrifice of the body and of present acts.

Before we examine Irigaray's attempt in this context to revitalize presence through the practice of breath in yoga, it should be noted that this text has been subjected to criticism from interlocutors who read it as homogenizing and idealizing "Eastern" cultures in a way that ultimately serves to "other" those cultures and reduce them to one and the same, in a manner that ends up reproducing—although in the context of cultural and racial difference rather than that of sexual difference—the very logic that Irigaray has devoted her career to critiquing. Her overly simplistic and generalizing characterization of "Eastern culture" is arguably Orientalizing and runs the risk of reducing the irreducibly different to a logic of sameness.[2] While I am interested in examining her discussion of yoga here, I want to flag this problematic orientation of her work, and reject in the strongest terms her homogenizing tendencies in this context.[3]

Through the practice of yoga, Irigaray begins to explore what it would mean to be, or rather to become, *in the present*. This occurs most importantly through the active practice of breathing (*pranayama*)—a practice that brings attention to that which defines temporal life: breathing begins when we are born and ends with our death—"living is equivalent to breathing" (BEW 74); "to breathe also means to be" (FAMH 62)—yet most Western traditions fail to acknowledge the importance of air and breath.[4] If God was "everywhere present but never there" (BEW 13), air, precisely because it is always there, "allows itself to be forgotten" (FAMH 8). That the fire of the Platonic cave would not burn without air symptomatically tends to go unmentioned. And in her most extended engagement with Heidegger, with the telling title *The Forgetting of Air in Martin Heidegger*, Irigaray argues that air, in his work, "remains the unthought resource of Being" (FAMH 14). Through the practice of yoga we become aware of the rhythmic movement of our own breath and of life as such. *Pranayama* puts us in touch with the time of life and of the living.

Irigaray explains that the practice of yoga aims, "among other things or principally, at realizing the immortality or the eternity of the self and the world here and now" (BEW 37). The practice of renunciation, sought out by Hindus and Buddhists across the world, "does not signify—sacrificing oneself for a hypothetical immortality or eternity but bringing them about here and now" (BEW 35). What we do when we elongate our breath in yoga is that we strive to "prolong" life (in the sense of slowing down, being in touch), without trying to attain immortality or a life beyond life. To bring about eternity "here and now" would mean exactly to affirm the infinity of finitude, while the sacrifice of "oneself for a hypothetical immortality or eternity" would mean nothing other than sacrificing mortal life to attain eternity, which—as we have seen—amounts to death. The point would thus not be to put a halt to breath (this would, literally, entail death) but rather to extend each inhale and exhale and to cultivate breath in an effort to "extend" finite life in the moment.

But in Hindu texts such as the Vedas, the Upanishads, or the Bhagavad Gita we learn the obvious, namely that Eastern traditions, no less than Western ones, strive for immortal life and timeless being. Is the difference between the two traditions then simply that immortality or eternity is sought "here and now" in the yogic tradition, while Western metaphysics hopes to achieve it in a transcendent beyond? And would this difference really make a difference? Are these yogic traditions not in fact repeating the fundamental trope of a Western metaphysical tradition that attempts to escape time and finitude, resorting to the ever-present presence of Being?

What makes the difference, according to Irigaray, is that Eastern traditions (and more specifically the Hindu yogic tradition that Irigaray focuses on in her work) rather than escaping the time of life and of the living, strive toward a cultivation of human time and life "in harmony with that of the universe" (BEW 37). The yogis may practice renunciation, but they do not, according to Irigaray, separate themselves from "the economy of the living universe, notably the vegetal" (BEW 35). As Sara Beardsworth puts it in an essay that puts into conversation yogic and psychoanalytic theory and practice, yoga is about "the cultivation of nature through nature's growth."[5] The Western dualism between nature and culture, or body and soul, finds no counterpart in Eastern traditions, according to Irigaray. Speaking of Buddha, she points out that he "tries to become pure subject but on a model forgotten by us: pure subject means here breathing in tune with the breathing of the entire living universe" (BEW 36).

That individual consciousness rises to universal consciousness carries a different meaning for the yogi than for the Western metaphysician. Universality does not imply the neutral knowledge of an ever-present God, nor a single truth valid at all times and everywhere, but rather the living character of our shared universe, a communion of sorts, between a variety of beings sharing breath. The term *yoga* means "to yoke" or "to bind together," and in Irigaray's work the yogic tradition comes to represent the possibility exactly of tying together the sensible/corporeal with the transcendental/divine/spiritual. The notion of a "sensible transcendental" is important in her own work at large, and represents exactly the possibility of thinking the two together, contra a metaphysical tradition that has separated them along a mind-body dualism.[6] That my model of revolutionary time depends on bridging such a gap we have already seen. Yoga would be a practice that could undo the strict dichotomy between cyclical and linear time. Through the cycles of breath we would achieve growth and renewal, a rebirth of sorts.

Yoga is, as we have seen, not an attempt to retain the breath or live without breathing. It aims at elongating the breath, but also at harmonizing my breath with that of my fellow yogis, and to, in turn, harmonize it with that of the trees, the earth, even the cosmos. As Beardsworth notes, it "can contribute to the construction of singularity and community."[7] Yoga is the cultivation of both vital and spiritual breath, the union of body and soul, the channeling of the cyclical rhythmic movement of the living world—a world in which we, as humans, are included.[8] This all means that breath can be a political practice of sorts, if indeed it brings together communities of breathers who are otherwise different. Elisha Foust, for example, examines "the political potential of Luce Irigaray's theory of the breath" by turning to the example of Christian and Muslim women "who turn their silent individual breath into a public, physical female presence so as to bring peace to war-torn Liberia."[9] In her analysis of the film *Pray the Devil Back to Hell,* which chronicles interfaith peace efforts on the part of women who have lived through the horrors of war, she draws from Irigaray's "The Way of Breath" (from *Between East and West*) precisely to show that breath has connecting powers, ones that can provoke real social change.

We might add that yoga and breathing exercises have been used in a variety of places where a bodily practice for healing bodies torn apart by conflict and war is acutely needed. I am thinking, for example, of Project Air, a Rwandan initiative that offers yoga classes to HIV-positive survivors of the systematic rapes that took place in the 1994 genocide.[10] Another example is Urban Yogis, a New York City-based program that brings ashtanga yoga to urban communities seeking to heal from the traumas of gun violence and other forms of inflicted injury. As Beth

S. Catlett and Mary Bunn—who have firsthand experience with both of these initiatives—have noted, yoga (especially as it is practiced in Western yoga studios) is a praxis riddled with first-world privilege, yet it has a tremendous capacity for connecting communities and making healing from traumatic experiences possible.[11] We might add, of course, that not only yoga but breath as such is a practice marked by privilege. Think only of all the people who do not have access to clean air. Or of Eric Garner's repeated "I can't breathe"—under the chokehold of a police officer for whom Black life did not matter, and in a world where Black folks are suffocating due to the lack of the vital air many of us take for granted.

In her discussion of yoga and yogic breath (*pranayama*), Irigaray emphasizes the centrality of daily practice rather than withdrawn contemplation: "the present, temporality, the relation between the instant and immortality or eternity is constituted by *acts*, and not only by words, logical and grammatical conventions, already coded meaning, a prioris, etc. These acts . . . are not simply repetitive . . . they vary . . . from one day to another, because the present time changes from one day to the next" (BEW 32–33). Because acts cannot be universalized—because they are necessarily singular and temporal—they produce variation rather than a repetition of the same. Beardsworth describes yoga as a tradition where "theory and practice are not separated," noting that this means that the practice is "not merely instantiating or implementing the theory but also constituting and altering it," and that this in turn means that it is "never rigid or fully stabilized."[12] We see here yet another example of the need to start through praxis in the present, in "experiential modalities"[13] rather than theoretical reflection far removed from our lived and living present.

And yet, while I myself have experienced the transformative power of such everyday practice, I must admit that this example leaves some questions to be answered. The practice of yoga does not seem to satisfactorily address, much less resolve, the temporal-philosophical problems with which we are faced here. While it is clear that these Eastern traditions in many ways challenge the Western eclipse of nature and the time of life and growth; while their emphasis on daily acts and the rhythm of breath injects movement and vitality into a present that the Western philosophical tradition may have perverted into an always already defined (*dé-finir*) finished past; and while they pay more careful attention to the connection of body and soul rather than the hierarchy between them; they are nonetheless founded upon the desire to experience *Moksha* (in

Hinduism) or *Nirvana* (in Buddhism)—the *liberation* from *samsara*, or the cycles of death and rebirth, of temporal life.

Are we then bound to ultimately fall back on a metaphysical structure that privileges timeless Being; one that strives toward immortality or eternity; one that ultimately aims at suspending the present to an everlasting and non-changing presence? Is any attempt to think through the question of time bound to return to the domination of this everlasting present?

## (Re)presenting Becoming:
## Poetry as a Practice of Presencing

I want to look briefly at another example of Irigaray's attempt to "reclaim" the present in temporal terms. It is well known that her work is marked by a thoroughgoing critique of language, as exemplified in the quote above, where she urged us to revitalize a present "constituted by *acts*, and not only by words, logical and grammatical conventions, already coded meaning" (BEW 32). In her analysis of language, Irigaray often turns to the verb (and, as an extension, the verbal) as the part of speech that allows us to express the flux of time.

In an essay on the verb from her early linguistic work, *To Speak Is Never Neutral*, she differentiates three types of verbs, exemplified by the infinitives *to live*, *to absorb*, and *to give*. It is the first one that interests me here, since I think that Irigaray's discussion of the verb *to live* sheds interesting light on what I want to call a *living present*—a temporal present that might evade the metaphysical logic with which we are grappling here.[14] If Derrida arrives at life (and death) through a *formal* critique of the Western metaphysical tradition, Irigaray importantly takes as her point of departure *lived* (and sexed) experience in order to arrive at a logical argument about time and difference. Perhaps this is one of the most profound differences between Irigaray and the deconstructive tradition: her feminist thought *begins* where other thinkers might *arrive*—in an account precisely of life and beings whose lives are marked by sexuate and temporal difference.[15]

Examining the verb "to live," Irigaray notes that it "implies an animate subject, not necessarily a person, who would undergo the activity more than carry it out," thus suggesting that living is passive and intransitive: it is a condition that we experience and which we can assume,

but with respect to which we cannot quite be seen as agents; and no
object (direct or indirect) is involved when we undergo the "activity" of
life.[16] Because no object is involved here, the activity of *living*, Irigaray
suggests, is in some sense incompatible with a traditional temporal scan.
Let me quote her at length here, in a passage that ends by echoing the
Aristotelian edict that to *be*, for a living being, is to *live*:

> *To live* implies a constant actuality that cannot be assimi-
> lated to a present whose existence is thinkable only through
> the separation from a past or a future. The action is always
> in the process of happening; the condition is always in the
> process of coming about. Neither is ever repetitive or able to
> be anticipated, because neither is ever complete. *To absorb*
> and *to give*, as infinitives, do express incompleteness, but they
> are not incompatible with a temporal scan related to the
> object. It is the presence of the object that means an action
> can be considered complete, and therefore repeatable, and
> predictable. . . . The possibility of the existence of a present,
> past or future character of an action is posited only on that
> condition. What appears to be the impossibility of rupture or
> of reiteration in the pure dynamic of *to live* comes from the
> absence of the object. . . . One could sum up by saying that
> *to live* is comparable to *to be*, whereas *to absorb* and *to give*
> belong to the domain *to have*.[17]

For living beings, the three modes of time are necessarily co-implicated,
and cannot be fully distinguished from one another. Our present is folded
into past and future horizons. And, as we shall see later in this chapter,
this is why any relation between *two subjects* (note the distinction from
a relation between a subject and an object) depends on a model of time
where the continuity between its three modes *remains uninterrupted*.
This does, of course, sound similar both to Bergsonian duration and to
Heideggerian ecstatic temporality, but as we will see in what follows,
there are some central differences between Irigaray's model of time and
that of the classic phenomenologists.

Life must, according to Irigaray, be understood as an ongoing
and always incomplete unfolding of present acts. The present, here, is
importantly *not* reducible to a repeatable past or a predictable future.

It is understood first and foremost as an incompleteness that can never be completed. If *différance*, for Derrida, was a past that had never been present, the living present, for Irigaray, is incompletable, unrepeatable, and unpredictable. Such a present can by no means be equated with the everlasting presence of the metaphysical tradition (it is not a present that will never become past), nor with some discrete "now" in a series of separate now-points. The infinity of this present must be understood not as the positive infinity of eternity but rather as the negative infinity of time. We might say that life is *infinitely finite*. Irigaray opens her essay by tying verbs to the enunciation, while she argues that substantives dominate the utterance, and she goes on to describe enunciations as "always infinite, unfinished."[18] I take it that infinity, here, cannot be meant to signal immobile perfection. It is, rather, a term that implies the incessant movement of time, the unfinishability or the infinitely undecidable structure of temporal unfolding.

Irigaray's critique of (Western) languages (she in fact looks mostly at the Latin languages) is that they are structured according to a linear-tele- ological logic (remember that Kristeva made a similar remark in "Wom- en's Time"). She has argued that our usage of words tends to annihilate difference and that it fails to capture becoming insofar as it "hardens up and closes off," thus exhausting our capacity to create anything new.[19] She often describes language as "tautological," as a "monologue" that "closes up in a circle," as speaking "with itself alone," as being, therefore, "always already in the past" (WOL 32). Language, like time, is confined by (repetitive) circularity or (teleological) linearity—each of which on my reading is the flip side of the same logic. A language that speaks oneness (the speaking subject in our culture is, on Irigaray's account, a male subject, while woman is reduced to the object of speech[20]), and that seeks to establish presence over and above temporal change (our desire to speak an everlasting "objective" truth), is part of a tradition that, as we have seen, reduces presence to absence, to a finalized and already-said (and therefore in some sense already-dead) past.[21]

Such a language repeats itself indefinitely, it is one in which "'brothers' reply to each other in one same tone," and that encoun- ters "no contradiction coming from a female other whose voice would be different" (FAMH 140). I do not intend to offer a fully developed account of the significance and implications of Irigaray's critique of (patriarchal) language here. Others have already taken on such a task and dealt with it compellingly. I would merely like to stress and discuss the fact that Irigaray turns to language not only as the (negative) source of a logic of sameness and presence, but also (insofar as we develop a language different from the one that has dominated Western discourse) as a potential (positive) locus for the establishment of a living present understood temporally. If language as we know it is objectifying and "dead," the language that she calls for is dynamic, vibrant, and alive.

Irigaray has noted that the substantive has a tendency to immobilize time; that time becomes "imprisoned with the thing that the substantive designated in a supposedly immortal or eternal denomination" (WOL 62). The verb, as opposed to the noun, is that of which the tense can be modulated, that which articulates becoming without reducing it to proper names and definitions, to static being, as we have just seen. But in our culture, Irigaray argues, the verb "disappears, fades away, is forgotten in the substantive. Speaking then loses a large part of its creative function in the present" (WOL 39). Speaking aims at *naming*, at providing *definitions*, at giving things reality through *concepts*. We recognize this worry from my discussion of Kristeva in chapter 3 of this book: if language becomes too symbolic, if it subdues semiotic rhythms and movement to the point of erasure, it becomes paralyzing.

Verbs, in Irigaray's view, have the capacity to express transformation, temporal change and becoming, without violent appropriation. But the "verbal" has been diminished in our culture: we are a mono-logical society that celebrates proper names over and above the open and undecidable character of verbs and dialogical discourse. When philosophical language, for example, gets expressed predominantly in the form of written treatises, it loses its corporeal dimensions (voice, tonality, emphasis, and so forth), as well as its immediate encounter with the other (the dialogue form).[22] According to Irigaray, we have diminished our chances to truly encounter the other through language: discourse as we know it *speaks* sameness (it is, according to Irigaray, predominantly masculine in character), and *bespeaks* the other (I speak "of" you when naming you), while failing to speak *with* them. It reduces the other to a graspable and analyzable object or thing, placed outside the movement of time and beyond the unfolding of a reciprocal relation. I will return at length to the question of time and presence as they unfold within the *relation*. But let me first briefly examine Irigaray's own writing—more specifically her poetic writing—in light of the problem of (temporal) presence.

∞

We have seen how Irigaray turns to yoga as a meditative practice based on "present acts" and the flow of breath. For twenty years or so, she has been practicing yoga on a daily basis. Similarly, Irigaray has written one poem every day for more than two decades. These daily testimonies, some of which were published in both English and French in 2004 under the title *Everyday prayers / Prières quotidiennes*, establish for her yet another praxis that attempts to enter into the presence of the here and now without reducing it to a frozen image of the there and beyond of a finalized past or an idealized future. In the preface to her collection of poems, she notes that they "celebrate life" and that her poetic writing "seeks to preserve and promote a *phuein*, a becoming, which does not divide itself from nature," thus recalling what she saw as the capacity in yoga to cultivate the presence of breath as a becoming with and alongside nature, as opposed to a separation from and appropriation or domination of it.[23] She wants to establish a language that remains "faithful" to the continuous movement of nature: "To speak about nature," she writes, "it would be better to avoid metaphors and allegories which assimilate it to our world," and she stresses the importance of not separating "form from matter."[24] Irigaray celebrates poetic language as a "less rigid and less definitive" form of expression than scientific or philosophical discourse, and points out that the poem, instead of "immobilising anything . . . tries to return each living being to its becoming, with a respect for its blossoming."[25]

In the context of her own poetry she introduces what she calls a "living substantive" as the part of speech that best captures the temporal movement of nature. Echoing Heidegger, she notes that "the clouds will cloud, the wind will wind, the summer will summer," and so on.[26] If common discourse "generally entrusts the permanent to the substantive and the transitory to the verb," she here suggests that, in her poetry, "discourse unfolds in another way," since a "living substantive, and not a fixed concept . . . preserves the duality of the subjects, the temporality of subjects. A substantive can also take the place of the presence of the other, him or her, if it avoids imprisoning in a definitive dwelling."[27] Substantives are thus not necessarily imprisoning or appropriating on her account. The "living substantive," just like breath in yoga, is meant to allow the speaking (and listening?) subject to harmonize with the rhythms and movements of nature rather than freezing or fixing them in a final form.

We should note, however, that while these "living substantives" may not be violently appropriating, they nevertheless assume a certain "appropriateness" about the very movement they are meant to describe.

That the clouds will cloud—here as well as in Heidegger—signals that there is a particular activity that clouds are expected to "achieve," and that the term "clouding" would be able to appropriately capture this movement, as if the movement itself was reducible to a representation. Irigaray asserts that

> . . . *physis* has a "proper" *arché*, a proper space-time of unfolding, and that to submit it [*elle*] to man's *architechné*, his language, amounts to bowing its destiny to an inappropriate form of unfolding, to suspending this destiny within a factitious blossoming, and to leave *physis* out, a remainder still. A resource that resists technocratic power and that can only unfold according to its proper motion. When man returns to draw on it, he exhausts it as factitiously as he makes it blossom artificially. He cuts off both himself and it from its reserve store, tearing it away from the motion of unfolding that follows its *arché*. (FAMH 88)

I think she is right to mourn the loss of the rhythmic movement of nature due to the technocratic language of our logocentric culture and, to be sure, much could be done to establish a more profound and balanced relationship between human activities and our natural surroundings. But I find it problematic that she ascribes a proper *archē* to nature, as if it could be defined once and for all (the point, as I see it, would be precisely to reject the fantasy of such *archē* and propriety).

As far as language is concerned, it seems to me that it is bound to in some sense arrest the movements of nature (to reduce it, precisely, to the discourse of the proper), and that this is true at least to some extent of poetic language too. While the latter might be more directly "in touch with" or "in tune with" or able to "voice" the oscillating rhythms of nature and materiality—the "music" that unfolds in poetic language and of which I will speak at length as I turn to Kristeva's discussion of the semiotic *chōra* in chapter 8 of this book—it nevertheless seems to me that the very function of language (be it poetic, technocratic, philosophic, or everyday language) is to in some sense "grasp" that which it is meant to describe and thus "arrest" its gestation or movement. Language objectifies. And insofar as it seeks to represent, it makes present that which is ever-changing in nature. Irigaray's gesturing toward the need to develop a nonappropriating (and nonlinear) language is both powerful and important. But her own tendency to slip into a discourse of "the proper" or "the appropriate" shows us how difficult such a shift indeed would be.

What we have seen in my earlier discussion of Kristeva, however, is that poetic language—in virtue of its openness toward the semiotic—carries the potential to "revolutionize" more rigidly assertive discourse, and the culture that such language reflects. This is, of course, not a thought invented by Kristeva or Irigaray. Poetry has always been the "other" of philosophy, a discourse that carries revolutionary and subversive potential. This is precisely the reason why Plato wanted to ban it from the just city. What is unique about Irigaray's turn to poetry is, in my mind, her thoroughgoing attempts to bring poetry *into* philosophy (rather than it being an *external challenge* to philosophy). From her dissertation to her most recent books, her philosophical discourse is profoundly poetic—which may well be why so many find her difficult to read (and why her work has been described as non-rigorous by some). Think only of the long poetic prologue of *To Be Two*, the lyrical and dialogical discourse of *Marine Lover*, or the morphologically infused writing of her essay "When Our Lips Speak Together." These texts—and so much else in her corpus—defy our common distinctions between theoretical and fictional genres, and they are performative examples of the "sensible transcendental" of which she herself speaks. In these texts, form is indeed inseparable from content. They not only speak *of* the sensual, the fluid, the in-between. They *speak* these themes and terms; they force the reader to experience and to touch them, and to be touched by them. As such they have the potential to offer us a different kind of presence; a presence constantly on the move, in flux, alive and breathing, unfolding through our encounter with those texts.

I will turn now to Irigaray's discussion of intersubjectivity and relationality in order to conceptualize presence more explicitly on the basis of difference and differentiation. This will allow me to subsequently articulate the ethical stakes of my discussion of time and presence, as I tie the question of temporality to that of otherness, or alterity.

## Time for Love: Presence as Co-presence

As we have seen, Irigaray is more than anything worried that a culture based on one subjectivity alone—the male culture of sameness in which we find ourselves on her account—is bound to repeat itself indefinitely. What we should be able to add, at this point, is that this movement of repetition is intimately bound to the privileging of selfsame presence: "Entry into presence already constitutes the appearing of a repetition," Irigaray explains (FAMH 135). Time and difference, as I have argued, must be thought together: only then can presence be thought as a living mode of time, as a process of becoming. The problem with the Parmenidean paradigm is not only that Being would be *static*, but also that it is *one*. Irigaray's ontology of becoming radicalizes the Heraclitean emphasis on flux. It is an ontology of becoming that simultaneously is an ontology of difference. Without alterity, there can be no alteration or change. And without the flux of time, conversely, otherness is annihilated. This insight is probably one of the most unique aspects of her work—and one of the main reasons why it is such a fruitful place to turn as we attempt to think presence in a way that would challenge the traditional metaphysical account.

The deconstruction of the metaphysics of presence is, in other words, necessarily also a deconstruction of the logic of identity and sameness.[28] As we have already seen, Irigaray's critique of metaphysical presence cannot be distinguished from her critique of a culture that can think sexual difference only within a logical framework of identity (a culture, in other words, that reduces woman to the other of man, and, we might add, despite the fact that Irigaray herself never does so, that fails to think sexuate identity beyond the dualistic model of woman and man). Irigaray's great insight is that non-temporal presence and sexual sameness are flip sides of the same metaphysical coin: the copula "is constructed by man as *one* path, *one* project, and *one* conveying that unites him with himself as selfsame, in his world, with no alliance or exchange between two that are different" (FAMH 125). In a culture of sameness, anything different from male subjectivity is viewed as lack or absence: "the feminine finds itself defined as lack, deficiency, or as imitation and negative image of the subject."[29] Difference, as we have seen, becomes reduced to an oppositional logic of presence and absence, and woman is bound to be associated with the latter; a deficient male, castrated and lacking, robbed of the possibility of cultivating her own subjectivity and desire (she is, again, only present *as absent*).[30]

Man, on the other hand, comes to view himself in terms of presence, fully "equipped" and self-sufficient, a being whose self-conscious mind gives him access to the ever-present beyond of a vertical transcendence understood as eternal divinity or ideal forms—a consciousness exempt from the movement of time; a synthesizing transcendental ego or unity of apperception who experiences time from a position outside of or beyond time (read: outside of or beyond the body—the latter being left for woman to uphold).[31] We live under the illusion of a disembodied and universal cogito; a masculine subject, disguised as a neuter, upon which subjectivity is crafted, and which consequently defines woman as negation and lack. Such a notion of subjectivity or consciousness escapes time and erases (sexuate) difference since it inscribes all relations into a logic of identity and sameness (it is, precisely, a *unified* subject).

What I have argued already must now be fleshed out more concretely and explicitly. There is an immediate relation between our desire to think presence as static and everlasting (the non-temporal presence of classical ontology) and the patriarchal desire to grant (temporal) subjectivity to man alone in a move that reduces woman to a (spatial-embodied) object marked by lack. Classical ontology, in other words, depends on the sexual division of temporal labor of which I have spoken at length. Selfsame presence can only be thought if contrasted with a symmetrically opposed absence. In our culture, as I have already noted, woman carries this burden of absence (as do other marginalized subjects). The disembodied (male) subject depends on an embodied (female) object to uphold its unity. This logic would be interrupted if we were to posit (at least) *two* subjectivities, irreducibly different yet equally "present" insofar as both would be granted subject positions. Neither sex, in other words, could be burdened with the embodiment of the other, and neither could be reduced to a negative mirror image of the other—which is to say that we would need to challenge the disembodied ideality that the linear model of time and the subsequent notion of selfsame presence depend on.

The "presence" of such subjects could, moreover, no longer be thought as fullness, wholeness, or selfsame everlasting infinity or plenitude, since the (at least) twofold nature of existence necessarily undercuts the infinite nature of existence (sameness and selfsame presence are, again, flipsides of the same coin).[32] Any idea of alterity is bound to abolish selfsame presence. And any idea of selfsame presence is bound to abolish alterity. This follows from the fact that selfsame presence (or positive infinity) posits a totality. Absolute presence and irreducible difference are mutually exclusive. Difference, in fact, necessarily implies finitude (and vice versa, since to be finite is to have been born and thus engendered). Finitude implies alterity and differentiation. If the classical metaphysical account places oneness or sameness on the ontological level (Being is, importantly, one and selfsame) while difference and plurality are seen as ontic contingencies, Irigaray's account thus amounts to saying that we are two on the level of ontology (whether we acknowledge this or not) but one on the ontic level (insofar as our culture has reduced the horizon of two to a logic of presence and absence, making room for one subjectivity—male in essence—alone). An ontology of non-temporal sameness breeds a culture available to one subject alone.

Irigaray often speaks of "an ontology founded on 'being two'" (BEW 101), and of the irreducible and ontological status of sexuate difference.[33] If Western metaphysics has repressed *time* in an attempt to solidify presence and rid itself of mortality and change (Being is understood as exempt from time and change—this was what Heidegger took issue with in his 1927 magnum opus) it has, in the same stroke, forgotten the irreducible status of *difference*, granting privilege instead to self-contained wholeness and oneness (Being is, similarly, understood as one). My claim is, in essence, that to acknowledge the irreducible status of time and difference alike amounts to overthrowing the core assumptions of this entire tradition. It is not exactly clear if we would still be speaking of "ontology" when doing so, since Being per definition would have to be understood in terms of becoming, and since alterity and alteration would stand at the very foundation (or rather non-foundation) of all that is (or rather becomes). Irigaray's insistence on our forgetfulness of (sexuate) difference goes hand in hand with her claim that the time of life has been lost. Time and difference are, again, irreducible and inseparable.

It is only because Irigaray inscribes difference on the level of ontology that she would be able, if at all, to posit presence in temporal and "living" terms.[34] An understanding of Irigaray's emphasis on the present as a temporalized, living present thus depends on some further insight into her claims about difference, or more specifically, sexuate difference. In order to create a living present, we must, as we have already seen, make possible a relation *between two*, a horizontal relation of proximity that has little in common with "intersubjectivity" as it has been conceived within the tradition that Irigaray turns against (a tradition that, on her account, never actually has made room for *two subjects* and that thus really only has been able to articulate subject-object-relations). I have already begun the work of unpacking what a world of (at least) two might look like. At this point, I want to substantiate my deconstruction of immanence and transcendence from chapter 2 in this book, and express in more detail what a relationship between two might amount to. Let me therefore turn to Irigaray's later work on love and relationality in order to examine yet another way of exploring presence in terms of becoming or, to be more exact, in terms of *co-presence*.

∞

In *The Way of Love*, Irigaray suggests that "another relation to space and to time becomes necessary" if we want to establish subjectivity in terms of intersubjectivity, if we want to be two in the proper sense of the term, and approach the other without appropriating him or her (81). How can I say *I love you* without reducing you to an object? How might I express my love to you while respecting your difference from me—the fact that you will always remain unknown to me? How to love you without defining you, without trying to make you *mine*? These are questions that echo through books like *I Love To You*, *The Way of Love*, *To Be Two*, and *Sharing the World*. Irigaray notes that "making you my property, my possession, my *mine* does not accomplish the alliance between us. This act sacrifices one subjectivity to another."[35] The result of the positing of a selfsame copula is a world where the subject can exist only in relation to an object—be it an object of love—and this in turn reduces love (and human interaction more generally) to a possessive relation. You who are mine. You whom I can know and name, whose alterity I can annihilate. What is at stake is the possibility of *two* subjectivities, and more importantly, for Irigaray, the possibility of *sexed* subjectivities.

In what might be broadly construed as her ethical work, Irigaray emphasizes the need to return to a horizon of *two*, and she often does so through the example of love. At stake is the possibility of a non-appropriating relationship between two subjects irreducible to one another. A crucial implication of her emphasis on the two is that the relation between them, insofar as it no longer follows a subject-object-logic, necessarily also refuses a self-other-logic. While the relation is described in terms of *asymmetry* (sexuate difference is, importantly, never reducible to mere complementarity), it nevertheless has little in common with the Levinasian notion of absolute alterity. Irigaray does not posit a *self* vis-à-vis an *Other*, but is careful to point out that both subjects within the relation are "other" to one another (this is precisely the difference between sexual difference as we have known it hitherto, and the sexuate difference that Irigaray urges us to cultivate).[36] In Irigaray's view, relationality has hitherto been articulated in terms of and from the point of view of a (male) selfsame *subject* of presence, who stands in relation to a (female) *object* defined in terms of lack and absence. Our task, according to Irigaray, is to think relationality beyond such dichotomies, and this would depend on a cultivation of sexuate difference.

The relationship between two (irreducibly different) subjects is characterized by a time of life and therefore has the potential to undermine static presence and appropriation or ownership, since "a subject, still living, is *ungraspable* and, moreover, *changes all the time*" (WOL 84, emphasis mine). Living subjects, as opposed to static objects, can never be defined once and for all: "A living being," Irigaray notes in *Sharing the World*, "is irreducible to a thing. It cannot exist once and for all, neither in itself nor toward the other or the world."[37] In her earlier *To Speak Is Never Neutral*, she expresses a similar thought: "Living beings, insofar as they are alive, are a becoming."[38] If there is an "ought" at all in Irigaray's ethics of sexual difference, it would be something like "you ought not to appropriate the other, you ought to let them be in their irreducible becoming as other." This might sound much like the Kantian dictum to not treat others as means to an end, but it essentially amounts to saying that the other ought to be treated as a temporal subject, and that their time is irreducible to mine. If time depends on perpetual return, and if we each return to our own beginnings and material conditions, then the unfolding that constitutes each life cannot be reduced to the unfolding of another. Our becoming is, and must remain, singular.

In *The Way of Love*, Irigaray writes that without "a cultivation of life, no encounter or dialogue is possible between living beings" (165). Such a dialogue (inasmuch as it is, in fact, a dialogue, and not a monologue formulated by a "subject" addressing an "object") is understood as necessarily unfolding in the present (not the everlasting presence of a metaphysics of presence but, rather, an ever-changing temporal present—a living present). If the encounter does not take place in dialogue, there is, according to Irigaray, "no question of becoming nearer . . . proximity is . . . defined through an object and not by a movement of approximation between subjects. And *this object is already in the past, not in the present or in the future*" (WOL 26, emphasis mine). Again, we see that the (static) object is defined not in terms of presence but rather as an absence of sorts, as a being always already in the past, elsewhere.

Love, in Irigaray's view, "always requires staying in connection both with becoming and the present" (WOL 17). Further, she notes that "difference remains the *condition of presence* and the *source of becoming*" (WOL 171), and that man "comes to presence through his capacity for entering into a relation" (WOL 85). Our culture of sameness has hitherto prevented us from "being with the other in the present" (WOL 48), which is to say in openness and reciprocity (neither fusion nor symmetry). The opening of a culture of difference and becoming will thus allow us to enter into "a being-with different from a complicity and a sharing in an already constituted same" (WOL 48). A "being-with" marked by difference is a "being-here" in the sense that the relation remains open (not already established in the past, nor already projected into the future). We are reminded of hooks's words that served as an epigraph to this section: "Fundamentally, to begin the practice of love we must slow down and be still enough to bear witness in the present moment."[39] Love requires time, a sharing of time, and our being present to attend to the singularity of the other of the relation. hooks's words appear in a discussion of Buddhism and her own spiritual practice of love, and it is colored throughout by temporal language. But while love for hooks is a practice of bearing witness to presence, this has nothing to do with everlastingness or stasis. Rather, love on her account is a transformative practice, an experience of rebirth and renewal—it is a matter of shattering habits and the status quo, so as to give room for change, revolutionary change. And such change, through the practice of love, does not live in a time to come, but begins in the present moment, and with our acceptance that "the present moment is the appropriate time."[40]

We have already seen that (temporal) presence (posited here as distinct from the everlasting present of the one and the same) necessarily is incomplete and in constant transformation. We might now add that such presence must be understood in terms of *co-presence*: its incompleteness is in part due to its being *shared*. Being is always *being-with*, or even *becoming-with*, which in turn means that presence is marked not only by the differentiation of temporal flux, but also by difference or alterity. We are thus able to further substantiate what I have said already, namely that time and transcendence depend on plurality and intersubjectivity. Without an other, there is no time. It is only with an other that we are able to transcend (the other, in other words, is not a *threat* to but rather a *condition* for my transcendence). Time and difference—alteration and alterity—are co-implicated and co-dependent. This has profound ethical implications. Only a subject aware of their own becoming can approach the other reciprocally, by acknowledging their own incompleteness (the fact that we are not whole, not fully present, and not fully transparent). If we forget or repress this incompleteness—by positing a selfsame autonomous transcendental subject—time freezes, on Irigaray's account, and becomes a time of death, or of the past, rather than a time of the present and the living (hooks uses similar language, and ultimately describes this state as a state of fear and paralysis—our incapacity to love and be loved). The relation as such is thus annihilated; reduced to the (violent) appropriation of an object by a subject.

Here, we can articulate the "time of life" as reciprocal oscillation between *living* and *loving* subjects. As we have seen, this would depend on an entirely new elaboration of the categories of space and time: "To go toward one another requires the elaboration of other space-times than those in which we, Westerners, are accustomed to living," Irigaray proclaims (WOL 19). We need a new model of time—what I have called revolutionary time—to establish intersubjectivity in reciprocal terms. And this, Irigaray tells us, would allow us the "possibility of *arriving in the present, of being in the present, of being capable of co-presence*" (WOL 48, emphasis mine).

How, then, can we approach the other *as other*? How can we love in a way that respects and cultivates difference? Irigaray, who describes love as the "safeguard of life and time,"[41] shifts the focus of the problem and, again, articulates it in terms of time: "All too often," she writes, "sacramental or juridical commitment and the obligation to reproduce have compensated for this problem: how construct a temporality between us? How to unite two temporalities, two subjects, in a lasting way?"[42] She suggests that time is that which unfolds *between* us. Time sustains a spacing between two subjects, simultaneously holding them together and keeping them apart. Each subject, to remain a subject without being reduced to (or reducing the other to) an object, must respect this temporal spacing that opens up as an abyss between subjects irreducible to one another ("you are a mystery to me"), at the same time as it unites the two and holds them together ("I love you, who are a mystery to me").

If we close off the gap that time opens between us, we will have reduced the two separate worlds that Irigaray sought to establish, and we will come to inhabit a world of sameness, a world devoid of both time and love. We see, again, that the metaphysics of presence is intimately intertwined with a (patriarchal) culture and world of sameness. Such a world would be precisely what metaphysicians of presence had always been seeking (one marked by wholeness and eternity) and it is, on Irigaray's account, in a certain sense the world in which we presently live (one marked by the timeless repetition of the same). What is lost in such a world is time and difference. And presence understood not as the absence of time but as the living encounter between two living and loving subjects irreducibly kept apart—and put in touch—by the incessant oscillation of the temporal abyss that opens up between them. Time, in other words, is the condition of possibility for an encounter to take place, to take place in the present. And without such encounter, conversely, there is no time, no living time, no co-presence or becoming-with.

In *I Love To You*, Irigaray brings our attention to the temporal movement of love. In saying "I love you," I make a claim that reduces my lover to an object of possession. "I love *to* you" is a gesture rather than an act of ownership and appropriation. It is a constant asymptotic "towards" that respects the irreducible temporal space between two separate beings. The title of another of her books, *The Way of Love*, can be understood in similar terms. Love is a path, but it does not lead to an already defined end. It is the path between you and me, always there between us, assuring our connectedness, but also the separation between two subjects that can never become one, nor same (nor once and for all present).

Closeness and intimacy, on this temporal-differential account, do not result in the collapse of one subject into the other (love, in other words, does not result in, or even aim at, fusion). If love sometimes has been understood as an attempt to *overcome* difference, Irigaray instead turns to love as a place where difference has a chance at survival: it emerges exactly out of the insight that the other is and will remain fundamentally foreign to me.[43] Recall the Aristophanic myth from Plato's *Symposium*, where the lover longs for fusion with his or her second half, and where the very object of love is understood as a previously lost part of the self. Desire, on this account, is conceived of as a striving for originary (but lost) wholeness or oneness.[44] Stanley Rosen, however, reminds us that selfsame oneness—just like presence—not only is impossible but also undesirable, insofar as it undermines the very possibility for life: if "Eros were to succeed in making one from two, he would not heal human nature, but destroy it."[45] Time and difference are irreducible. It is not a coincidence that the "fulfillment" of love so often coincides with death. Romeo and Juliet or Tristan and Isolde: their complete(d) unity (love understood as "becoming one") is perhaps possible in and as death alone.

Temporal distance is thus the prerequisite both for life and for there to be any relations at all. But Irigaray's critique of metaphysical presence, and the selfsameness that follows from it, is, as we have seen, grounded not in a rejection of presence altogether but rather in a revival of presence understood in temporal and relational terms. At stake in our relation to the other is exactly the possibility of entering into presence—or co-presence—with them.

## Conclusion

In this chapter I have sought to broach the problem of the present in terms that move us away from metaphysical presence, focusing instead on present acts, on a praxis of presencing, and on breathing life into the present as it unfolds in the here and now of our lived experience. I have examined Irigaray's commitment to "saving" presence from its metaphysical baggage. To this end, I have explored three of Irigaray's own attempts to engage in the praxis of presencing, namely yogic breath, poetic writing, and loving relations.

First, I explored *pranayama*, or yogic breath, as a daily practice that situates presence firmly in the body—contra a metaphysical tradition that not only has separated body and mind, but that consistently has articulated presence as a disembodied beyond or transcendent that escapes the fluctuations of embodied change. In search for a living present, Irigaray thus turned to these yogic traditions and their breathing practices, insisting on presence as embodied, riven by the oscillation of inhalation and exhalation, and marked by an attunement to our social and cosmic surroundings—other breathing beings.

Second, I examined Irigaray's critique of phallogocentric language as one that is prone to freeze life and becoming into a stilted objectivizing form—the substantive—at the expense of verbal registers of language that are better disposed to giving voice to the ever-changing flux of life. Again, in her search for the living present, Irigaray thus sought to develop a language of the verbal (of movement and transformation) through her own daily practice of poetic writing, and the subsequent elaboration of a language that can speak women without reducing them to objects of knowledge. What was at stake in this chapter was precisely to think a living present always already exceeding the presence-absence dichotomy that we saw in the previous chapter as organizing the very conception of metaphysical presence (and the inevitably sexuate nature of that dichotomy).

Third, therefore, I elaborated a model of presence as co-presence, through an engagement with Irigaray's later ethical writings on love and intersubjective relations, as well as, briefly, hooks's discussion of love as an attention to presence. Here we saw again the necessary link between time and difference—alteration and alterity—and were able to see more concretely this link as it appears in the loving relation between two who are irreducibly different.

I will end this section on the present by turning, in the next chapter, more explicitly to a discussion of the ethical and political stakes of rethinking presence in relational terms. First, I want to raise some issues that I see with Irigaray's account of co-presence. Then I will offer a close reading of Kristeva's ethical project, which she develops on the basis of a psychoanalytic account of subjectivity rooted in the unconscious. Finally, I will turn to Kristeva's analysis of Freud's conception of the unconscious as being timeless. This will allow me to return to the issue of revolutionary time, and to reflect upon the nature of presence within the model of time that I have developed so far.

# 6

# An Ethics of Temporal Difference

Irigaray's critique of positive infinity and the logic of identity is, as we have seen, grounded not in a *rejection* of the present but rather in a *return to* presence understood in temporal and intersubjective terms. This view, I have argued, brings about four aspects of her understanding of time that distinguish her account from previous ones: (1) the metaphysics of presence should more appropriately be described as a metaphysics of absence—it has in fact robbed us of the experience of presence altogether; (2) finitude must be understood not just as a question of death and mortality but also as conditioned by birth and natality; (3) non-metaphysical presence must be grounded in a living and ever-changing here and now marked by praxis or what I have called presencing; and (4) presence must be understood as co-presence, which is to say that it appears only between two subjects that are different.

It seems, in other words, like we have found a way in which to think presence otherwise, and as a challenge to the metaphysical tradition of selfsame everlasting presence, in the interrelation and encounter between two subjects-in-difference. One problem, however, remains to be addressed: while Irigaray stresses that each subject, as a living subject, is ungraspable and ever-changing, she nevertheless (especially in her later work) speaks of difference in terms of "what is proper to each one" and "appropriate to oneself," and she propagates a "faithfulness to what is proper to one."[1] The encounter with the other, for Irigaray, is described as a departure *and a return*. The encounter between two always culminates in a return to oneself in her work, and the ethical status of this encounter depends on my capacity to encounter the other without prohibiting *them* from the subsequent return to *their* self and *their* world. This is what it would mean for me not to appropriate the other, but let them be *as other*. But what, we must ask, is the status of this "self" to which we are called to return? The present chapter seeks to bring the question of presence into relation with questions of subjectivity and intersubjectivity. If revolutionary time is a return not only to the past but also to the self (understood as embodied, finite, born, and riven by the movement of time), and if the self is always already partaking in a relation—indeed constituted through that relation—then we need a more robust account than we have offered so far both of subjectivity (selfhood) and intersubjectivity (relationality).

## On the Propriety of Self and Other

Irigaray, as we have just seen, stresses the need to attend, in our loving encounters, to "what is proper to each one" and "appropriate to oneself." The ethico-political stakes of positing a "proper self" are clear: Irigaray wants to defend the integrity of each subject so as to avoid the kind of appropriation and violation that hitherto has marked human relations. To be faithful to one's integrity, to one's "proper self," is to resist the masculinist logic of appropriation, and to protect oneself from all kinds of violence (from subtle acts of discrimination to physical abuse). But the language of the "proper" simultaneously signals a kind of sovereignty or autonomy that runs counter to the temporal account I have just developed. It signals a view of the self as unitary, a self that coincides with itself, in selfsameness.

We see here, in my mind, a version of the essentialism of which Irigaray so often has been accused. It is not so much a *sexual essentialism* that prescribes characteristics to each gender as it is a kind of *singular essentialism* that falls short of fully accounting for the consequences of the irreducibly temporal status of human existence. If Irigaray more than most stresses the irreducibility between the sexes, she fails—at least in her account of love—to address the irreducibility of self to self. The relentless and restless division of time in fact undermines the possibility of the proper or a unity of the self. This is true for me just as much as it is true for the other (I am, importantly, an other too). Time not only divides me from or creates an abyss between me and the other—it incessantly divides me from myself, as I come into being and pass away.

A critique of the transcendental ego forces us to rethink the self as constitutively divided, never proper or sovereign or autonomous. Each and every time that we "return" to ourselves, we are bound to find a different self than the one we departed from—not merely because the encounter with the other has changed us (which is of course also true), but more fundamentally because the incessant movement of time has done so too. Of course there is a certain measure of continuity—we still do and should continue to speak of a "self" insofar as some things remain the same (or at least similar) over time; without this sense of continuity we would feel shattered. But this continuity is nevertheless marked by change and continuous variation (as I noted in the introduction, time is that which provides continuity and discontinuity both at once).

Irigaray is right to emphasize the impossibility of defining, knowing, or owning the other. But she does not, in my mind, sufficiently stress the fact that the irreducibility of the other—the fact that we can never fully know them—is an ontological rather than an epistemological problem.[2] Because the other is temporal, they are bound to constantly change. Similarly, we must add, I too am bound to change because of my temporal existence. In her later works, Irigaray does not sufficiently acknowledge that I, as an other, and as a temporal being, always already am and continue to be other and unknown to myself. If the other is a mystery to me, I too am a mystery to myself. The Augustinian "I have become a question/problem to myself"[3] can only properly be understood in light of the Socratic injunction to "know thyself," inasmuch as what Socrates means by this is that we must "know" that we cannot know at all.[4] The "self," just like the "other," remains (and must remain) a riddle and a question, an ongoing aporia, and this is one of the conditions of human existence, insofar as we are finite (and, we might add with Irigaray, insofar as we are sexuate). It follows necessarily from our understanding of the subject as temporally constituted, which makes impossible the return to a "proper" self as well as the respect for the "integrity" of the other. The self can never be "proper" because it continuously becomes "other," insofar as time divides it from within. And the other cannot be "properly" respected in their "integrity," because they, too, constantly alter and change.[5]

Of course, a more generous reading of Irigaray might see her language of propriety as a reference to our capacity to remain faithful to our very potential for becoming. The return to the "proper" self would, on such a reading, amount precisely to embracing our becoming (or our becoming-with). Such a reading is consistent with her attention, in her earlier work, to the abyss that time and difference opens up not only *between* subjects, but also *within* each individual subject, precisely insofar as we are sexed. I am specifically thinking of her morphological account of women as always already at least two (more than, or not, one), split through the multiplicity of their genitals (the labia and folds, as well as erogenous zones), as described in her essay "When Our Lips Speak Together," published in *This Sex Which Is Not One* (the title of which illustrates what I am trying to get at here). While this essay in particular has been criticized for what might be read as a kind of biological essentialism (because of her emphasis on genitalia, and her insistence on the specificity of *female* genitalia), it seems to me a rather fecund place to turn for thinking propriety in less unified terms, and for broaching questions about the fragmentation of the self.

Does the speech of those lips offer a challenge to the "language always already in the past" so much criticized by Irigaray (WOL 48)? Is it here that we might search for presence beyond metaphysics? In the breath of those other lips that mark the beginnings of becoming, by breathing life into beings? Irigaray characterizes woman as that being who is never one or selfsame, who is "indefinitely other in herself," who "always remains several . . . because the other is already within her": "within herself, she is already two—but not divisible into one(s)—that caress each other."[6] Elsewhere, she notes that the patriarchal tradition has defined woman as "restless" and "unstable," and remarks that "it is quite rigorously true that she is never exactly the same," since woman, more so than man, is affected by and changes with the cycles of time and of nature.[7] In a different formulation, she states that the "becoming of women is never over and done with, it is always in gestation."[8] These are moments in her work that signal a very serious challenge to any and all accounts of unified selfhood, and that do so in ways that yet again tie an intimate knot between time and sexual difference.

Let me turn now to Kristeva's work, in order to deepen and pursue the ethical concerns developed here. If Irigaray is willing to recognize the internal division of women that marks them as always already irreducible to the one and the same, Kristeva will give universal status to this very quality of the subject (regardless of its gender), and insist on the ethical implications of such division from within. Her psychoanalytic insights about our constitutive internal strangeness will help me shed light on above questions, and should allow me to develop what I call an ethics of temporal difference. Kristeva's theory of subjectivity—which is one deeply rooted in psychoanalytic theory—carefully accounts for the irreducibly temporal structure of the human self and her others.

## Becoming Two: Encountering the Stranger Within

Like Irigaray, Kristeva has written a great deal about intersubjective relations, and she often elaborates the question of time in intersubjective terms. Time and again, she examines the dynamics of love, most prominently of course in her book *Tales of Love*, but also elsewhere. She too views love as the affirmation of irreducible difference, not as fusion or merging. And this difference between loving subjects is, throughout her work, articulated in temporal terms. In the epigraph of her book *Time and Sense*, for example, she quotes a passage from Proust's *The Captive*: "Love is space and time made perceptible to the heart."[9] When we love we become aware of the time and space (the distance) that unfolds between us; that we are separate and finite even in the most intimate moments of proximity.

In *Tales of Love*, Kristeva offers an interpretation of Aristophanes's tragicomic myth from Plato's *Symposium*, in which love/desire is described as resulting from the splitting apart of an earlier version of the human that was round, whole, and made up of two rolled into one (men consisted of two males, women of two females, and androgynes of a male and a female). As a consequence of their hubris, Zeus split them apart, and since then humans have wandered the earth in a constant search for their second half, longing to be whole again.[10] In her reading of this passage, Kristeva suggests that the original whole being is incapable of love. He "admires himself in another androgyne and sees only himself, rounded, faultless, *otherless*," she writes.[11] Kristeva not only points to the absence of an *other* in this original schema (i.e., its narcissistic structure); she also notes that the androgyne is *"outside of time"* or *"timeless."*[12] The androgynes in the Platonic myth are content and free from the "curse" of desire, but this very freedom is, in Kristeva's view, nothing but another curse, since it places them outside of time. There is nothing to move them. They are trapped in the dead time of sameness.[13]

If the Aristophanic story was narrated at a banquet of love, Kristeva speaks elsewhere of the "banquet of hospitality" of which all foreigners or immigrants dream, a banquet of "guests who soothe and forget their differences," one where we are all alike and equal. But she stresses, again, that such a banquet would be "outside of time" (SO 11). As we have seen, without difference there is no time; without time, there is no difference. And life, as we know, depends on both in order to unfold.

I will focus here on the book by Kristeva that most explicitly tackles questions of otherness and ethics/politics, namely *Strangers to Ourselves*. Here, Kristeva traces the concept of foreignness from ancient Greek tragedy and the Bible, via Medieval and Renaissance literature, to Enlightenment philosophy and twentieth-century thought. By recognizing the foreigner within ourselves, Kristeva suggests, "we are spared detesting him in himself" (SO 1). And our confrontation with the foreigner is equally a confrontation with our own unconscious—"that 'improper' facet of our impossible 'own and proper'" (SO 191). It is only in relation to the other that we can come to know ourselves in our fundamental strangeness. What is at stake here is something other than simply "acceptance of" or "respect for" those different from us. "Living with the other, with the foreigner," Kristeva writes, "confronts us with the possibility or not of *being an other*" (SO 13). It forces us to imagine and confront our very own strangeness. And by ascribing foreignness to each and every one of us, Kristeva hopes that we may get rid of the category of foreignness as such: "The foreigner is within me, hence we are all foreigners. If I am a foreigner, there are no foreigners," she asserts in what has become a paradigmatic and much discussed passage (SO 192).[14] Kristeva aims at a notion of foreignness that cuts across all national, cultural, religious, or other boundaries. We are all foreign, all different, hence not foreign at all.

In what follows, I want to examine Kristeva's analysis of foreignness in this context, so as to broach, yet again, the question of time and temporal change. While this text most obviously is an attempt to pursue the ethical implications of a theory of subjectivity grounded in the psychoanalytic notion of the unconscious, I want to draw attention to an implicit theme that follows from such a view of subjectivity and intersubjective relations. Kristeva's characterization of the human subject as inherently divided by unconscious drives is, on my reading, grounded in an account of the human being as *sexuate* and *temporal*. As we shall see, her analysis of the unconscious as that which splits us from within is pervaded with temporal language throughout. And this temporal language is explicitly linked to questions of birth and sexual difference, and to what I have called revolutionary time.

Just like Irigaray, Kristeva urges us to "not seek to solidify" the other; to not "turn the otherness of the foreigner into a thing"; not give it "a permanent structure"; but to sketch, instead, "its perpetual motion" (SO 3). But if both thinkers stress the irreducible strangeness of each and every other—and if both do so by highlighting the perpetual motion and change that others undergo (that they are temporal, and hence, as we have seen, impossible to define)—Kristeva carefully ascribes this strangeness (again understood in terms of temporality) to the self as well: "Strangely, the foreigner lives within us: he is the hidden face of our identity, the space that wrecks our abode, the *time* in which understanding and affinity founder" (SO 1, emphasis mine). Differences *between us* and the difference that resides *within each of us* are both tied to the incessant movement of time. Time creates a distance between us and within us. If transcendence for Irigaray occurred between two sexually differentiated subjects (the sexually other being opaque and unmasterable on her account), Kristeva speaks instead of "an alterity immanent to the human being."[15] By this she means that the *self* is opaque and unmasterable. When she speaks of "strangeness" and "foreignness," she has the transcendental opacity of the self in mind. And this transcendental opacity, I argue, is a constitutive feature of our self-relation *and* our relation to others.

If modern ethics typically is seen as concerning the relation of self to other, Kristeva retrieves an ancient notion of ethics that takes as its point of departure the relation of self to self, or the imperative of self-knowledge as the ethical task *par excellence* (let us remember, however, that the Socratic injunction is that we must "know" that we cannot achieve complete knowledge: since transparency is not attainable, ethical life is bound by an aporetic structure). Ethical discourse in ancient Greece was pervaded with an emphasis on the human being as constitutively divided (there was not yet even a notion of subjectivity proper, or of the unified sovereign self that we moderns take for granted), and ethical life amounted as much to establishing harmony and balance between the various aspects of the soul as it was concerned with establishing such balance or equality between the individuals of any given community.[16] The view that the human being is heterogeneous—that we are desirous, spirited and rational at once—stands at the foundation of Greek ethical thought, and Plato famously argued that the heterogeneity of the human self parallels that of the human community (hence the correspondence between city and soul, or *polis* and *psuche*).[17]

Kristeva implicitly draws from this tradition as she elaborates her own ethics, which takes as its point of departure the psychoanalytic view of the human subject as constitutively divided. Just like the ancients, she sees it as an ethical task to strike a balance between the different parts of the psyche, without therefore attempting to *unify* them altogether and once and for all (this would, indeed, be an impossible undertaking).[18] The ethical task par excellence would, in other words, be to recognize and come to terms with our internal strangeness (I will return to the question of what it would mean to "come to terms with it" in what follows). Only then would we be able to approach the other differently: "Henceforth, we know that we are foreigners to ourselves, and it is with the help of that sole support that we can attempt to live with others," Kristeva explains (SO 170).[19]

I take "to live with others" here to quite literally mean being *alive* with others and affirming their *aliveness* in return. The living presence that I have articulated in terms of co-presence ("being-with") appears in Kristeva's thought as a kind of co-presence between me and the other and, simultaneously, with the "other" that resides within me, inasmuch as I am constantly divided by time ("becoming-with"). If we view the movement of return that this book is meant to elucidate in terms of revolutionary time as a psychoanalytic process of anamnesis (returning to the archaic—to the body and to unconscious drives—but also to oneself), this return to the self is for Kristeva thoroughly marked by instability and provisionality: "The individual, in this return to him or herself, experiences division, conflict, pleasure and jouissance in this fragmentation," she states in an interview.[20] The return to the self must, as we have seen, be marked by perpetual interrogation and revolt: it can never be a serene homecoming to a stable and harmonic dwelling. And it is, precisely, a return to heterogeneity; to a sexed and finite body; to a corporeal field of both pleasure and pain.

Kristeva consistently challenges the transcendental subject and its alleged unity. Her subject in process/on trial (*sujet en procès*) is marked by heterogeneity and cannot attain full sovereignty or autonomy. The psychoanalytical notion of unconscious drives and internal strangeness/dividedness is, for her, the *sine qua non* for any theory of subjectivity.[21] To say that we are unconscious amounts, among other things, to saying that we are embodied beings; beings inhabited by affects and drives. But this, in turn, amounts to saying that we are mortal beings, temporal beings,

beings divided by incessant temporalization. The unconscious subject is, in Kristeva's own words, "desiring, desirable, mortal, and death-bearing" (SO 182). "What," she asks, "if there was no other Authority than to recognize the mortality at work in the speaking subject?"[22] The focus, here and elsewhere, is thus placed on those aspects of human life that are a consequence of our temporal existence (we have seen that only temporal beings desire and are desired, and only temporal beings are finite or death-bearing).

Our own "foreignness," on Kristeva's account, is "that 'improper' facet of our own impossible 'own and proper'" that splits us or divides us into heterogeneous beings (SO 191). The "proper" has been rendered "improper" by the unconscious. That which is most familiar to us (our self) is bound to also be unfamiliar, even unknown. This is the very logic of Freud's discussion of the uncanny—a discussion to which Kristeva returns repeatedly and which she treats at length in the closing chapter of *Strangers to Ourselves*. In his essay "The Uncanny," Freud describes the uncanny (*unheimlich*) as "that class of the frightening which leads back to what is known of old and long familiar."[23] Through a reading of E. T. A. Hoffmann's short story "The Sand-Man," Freud suggests that our encounter with the uncanny through literary texts or other aesthetic expressions can bring back to memory the phase of our individual development that corresponds to a certain "animistic stage in primitive men," and that "residues of animistic mental activity within us" therefore are brought into consciousness: the uncanny is "something repressed which *recurs* . . . the prefix '*un*' ['un-'] is the token of repression."[24] We experience uncanniness when we *return* to a repressed memory, or when repressed memories *return to us* by way of association later on in life.[25]

The two examples that both Freud and Kristeva give of the uncanny is our confrontation with death ("our unconscious refuses the fatality of death" [SO 185]), and the female sex ("the entrance to the former *Heim* [home] of all human beings . . . the place where each one of us lived once upon a time in the beginning" [SO 185]).[26] Uncanny strangeness is thus accomplished when "*death* and the *feminine*, the end and the beginning . . . break through" (SO 185)—an equation that should be familiar by now. Birth, death, and sex are all key aspects of finite and desirous life: life engendered; life sexed; life marked by the incessant movement of time. And these are categories that we all experience, that we all share, insofar as we are living beings. They are the strangeness that we all carry within; the temporal structure that divides each of us yet brings us together as "equals." We are all "same" in that we are all born, finite, and sexed.

Kristeva ends *Strangers to Ourselves* by speaking of "a weakness whose other name is our radical strangeness" (SO 195). This "weakness"—I take it to quite simply be a synonym for the incompleteness that marks human life (that we are finite and sexed)—is a boundary or limit which, rather than being defined in negative terms, must be seen as a horizon of future possibilities: the limit that makes life, and life with others, possible. We hear echoes again from Freire's claim that the present situation is limiting in the sense of challenging—that which makes movement possible. And this in turn comes close to how Irigaray often describes sexuate difference—a horizon or limit that serves as an opening, and that which makes our relation with the irreducibly other possible. Erotic and death-bearing at once—the root of desire and of life itself—our internal strangeness is our sexed embodiment and the unfolding of time that we all experience: a universally shared condition that nevertheless makes us irreducibly singular and different.[27]

The universality of our foreignness is what compels Kristeva to perceive it as a powerful ground for ethics: "After Stoic cosmopolitanism, after religious universalist integration, Freud brings us the courage to call ourselves disintegrated in order not to integrate foreigners and even less so to hunt them down, but rather to welcome them to that uncanny strangeness, which is as much theirs as it is ours," Kristeva proclaims (SO 191–92).[28] She suggests that the ethics of psychoanalysis—what I propose to call an ethics of temporal difference—implies a politics, a new kind of cosmopolitanism that cuts across governments, economies, and markets.[29] "On the basis of an erotic, death-bearing unconscious, the uncanny strangeness . . . sets the difference within us in its most bewildering shape and presents it as the ultimate condition of our being *with* others," she notes (SO 192). The task, as we have seen, is to be with others without appropriating them.[30] And this being-with—which, if it is to be reciprocal, must be a becoming-with—is not only conditioned by our internal strangeness but depends on our acknowledgment thereof. To "come to terms" with our internal strangeness therefore amounts to actively returning to that place—or that time—which is both familiar and foreign to us.

We might, in other words, say that the cosmopolitanism elaborated by Kristeva in this text and elsewhere—a cosmopolitanism of the uncanny and of internal strangeness—is very similar to what I described as a culture of revolt in the previous section of this book. The ethical relation is one that begins with a movement of return: a return to that most hidden side of our abode with which we are at once at home and on completely foreign ground. This means that presence understood as co-presence always already involves a movement of return. Not a return to a stable and selfsame (fully present) "proper self," but a return precisely to the improper that is our most proper, in the sense of our most own: unconscious drives and the intimate intertwining of soma and psyche. Ethical life depends on a return to the finite and sexed body that is our common yet irreducibly singular ground, the unstable ground that makes us all strange and opaque. Revolutionary time, again, is not a return to the same, but a passage through an always unmasterable past that opens us up to heterogeneity and the possibility for transformation and renewal in the present.

It seems important to note, however, that I take issue with Kristeva's claim that the universality of our shared foreignness cancels out foreignness altogether, since I worry that it moves way too fast past what we might call the unequal distribution of foreignness, or what Butler has referred to as the unequal distribution of precarity.[31] Kristeva risks to disregard the tangible (and often painful) experience of exclusion that "others" (in the sense of oppressed or silenced others) in our society, after all, share. As Sara Ahmed strives to show in her essay "The Skin of the Community: Affect and Boundary Formation," which is an explicit engagement with Kristeva's work on these issues, "the deconstruction of the host/stranger opposition requires not that we distribute strangeness to everyone (we are all strangers with an equal duty to recognize others as strangers), but that we recognize how strangeness is already *unevenly distributed*."[32] Or, as she puts it in the conclusion of her essay: "A politics of opening up the community cannot be achieved simply by saying 'we are all strangers,' or by the good will of the national subject. We must acknowledge how others have already been recognized as *stranger than other others*,[33] as border objects that have been incorporated and then expelled from the ideal of the community."[34]

Put simply, Kristeva addresses one side of the problem—our unwillingness to realize, affirm, and recognize our own strangeness and temporal rivenness—but she fails to properly bring attention to the consequences of the structural and hierarchical divisions that are the hallmark of the neoliberal-colonial-patriarchal world in which we live. Is it really the case that the otherness of those outside of us would evaporate if only we could recognize our own internal strangeness? And can we ultimately think our own internal strangeness outside or independently of those power structures that have constructed and defined otherness based on discrimination and oppression? More specifically, what would it mean to insist on our "shared" foreignness without a robust analysis of the role that race (and racism) plays in this context? These are questions that deserve critical attention, and I hope to address them more directly in a separate project.

## (Un)timely Revolutions:
## The Timelessness of the Unconscious

What I have suggested so far is that a theory of subjectivity grounded in the psychoanalytical notion of the unconscious implies an understanding of the human subject as necessarily divided by time. But how, we must ask, does this align with Freud's famous claim that the unconscious is *timeless* in nature? If time traditionally has been viewed as located precisely in consciousness, how are we to think time once we have established that the subject is *unconscious* and ever only present as *being-with-others* (or even *becoming-with-others*)? Kristeva raises this very concern in *Intimate Revolt*: "If we emancipate ourselves from the 'symptom of "being conscious,"' what about time? . . . What do we do with time, by definition conscious, if we postulate an unconscious psyche" (27, 33)?[35] These questions bring her straight to what she calls the Freudian "scandal" of the timeless (*Zeitlos*). In what follows, I want to look closer at this notion in Freud, and at Kristeva's analysis of it, in order to elucidate the relation between the unconscious, revolutionary time, and what I have called the living present. This should help me to further deepen my claim that a theory of subjectivity grounded in the unconscious paves the way for an alternative elaboration of presence and even of time as such.

Kristeva notes that the early Freud keeps with the classic philosophical thesis that time is a given of consciousness, but that, starting with *The Interpretation of Dreams* (1900), "the unconscious as well as the id" begin to "enjoy a temporality called *Zeitlos* (timeless)" (IR 30). Freud himself says notoriously little of this concept. It is introduced in passing in his essay "The Unconscious" from 1915. Here, Freud attempts to establish the special properties of the unconscious, and he states that one such property is that the processes in the unconscious system "are *timeless*, i.e., are not chronologically ordered, are not altered by the passage of time, indeed bear no relation to time whatsoever."[36] He acknowledges that his description of the unconscious might come across as both "obscure" and "confused,"[37] yet when he revisits the notion of timelessness five years later in *Beyond the Pleasure Principle*, he does not provide much more clarity:

> As a result of certain psycho-analytic discoveries, we are to-day in a position to embark on a discussion of the Kantian theorem that time and space are "necessary forms of thought." We have learnt that unconscious mental processes are in themselves "timeless." This means in the first place that they are not ordered temporally, that time does not change them in any way and that the idea of time cannot be applied to them.[38]

What we are to make of these allusive remarks remains contested. Freud himself simply reiterates that his own understanding is limited: "I know that these remarks must sound very obscure, but I must limit myself to these hints."[39]

Both references to the timelessness of the unconscious appear in what is usually described as Freud's metapsychological work.[40] Freud himself saw metapsychology within the field of psychoanalysis as analogous with metaphysics in the field of philosophy. As Adrian Johnston puts it, "the metapsychological domain contains the aggregate of a priori principles that must be in place at the outset for the initiation of analytic interpretation as such."[41] Does this imply that the timelessness of the unconscious would be Freud's version of metaphysical presence? Or, given the reference to Kant above, does the characterization of the unconscious as timeless establish a parallel between the Freudian unconscious subject and Kant's transcendental unity of apperception? Does the timelessness of the unconscious imply precisely a subject somehow *exempt* from the movement of time: a subject that would *constitute* but not be wholly *constituted* by time and temporal movement? As should probably be clear from what I have said so far about the psychoanalytical theory of subjectivity, my unequivocal answer to these questions is *no*. Let me develop this in further detail.

There should be no doubt that Freud's statement about the timelessness of the unconscious offers a challenge to any traditional account of time. If Freud's theory of the unconscious was a "Copernican revolution" of sorts (SO 169), this revolution is, according to Kristeva, nothing other than "a revolution of the conception of time" (IR 28).[42] She ascribes "an incomparable originality" to "the Freudian *Zeitlos*" (IR 30–31). It is, in her view, different from all previous attempts to conceptualize time, from Aristotle and Augustine to Kant, Hegel, Nietzsche, Bergson, and Heidegger.[43] The unconscious, Kristeva explains, has "its own time" (IR 31). We saw already in chapter 3 that Kristeva turns to Freud as a "revolutionary of lost time," and that the psychoanalytic notion of revolt as return colors her own work throughout. In his book *Time Driven: Metapsychology and the Splitting of the Drive*, Johnston similarly characterizes Freud's "dethroning of the self-transparent, rational subject" as such a "radical rupture in the history of ideas" that it is worthy of the epithet *revolutionary*.[44] But he raises the same set of concerns that I raised in my discussion of revolution in the opening chapters of this book: "All revolutions naturally appear novel when contrasted with the status quo against which they react. However, at the same time, all revolutions also contain the seeds of their own destruction. If successful in overthrowing the previous theoretical regime, a revolutionary theory immediately runs the risk of becoming as complacent as its predecessor. Although this observation is itself practically a truism, the revolutionaries frequently become the new tyrants."[45]

How can psychoanalysis avoid stagnation and complacency? How can it avoid cementing the ideas that it invented precisely in order to bring life to the sedimented? How are we to assure that the Freudian theory of the unconscious—one that allegedly was formulated as a *critical response* to the metaphysical tradition of presence that I have described above—does not posit yet another version of metaphysical presence, articulated precisely in terms of a "timelessness" embedded at the core of the human psyche? Does the Freudian revolution amount to nothing more than a removal of eternity from the "there" and "beyond," by placing it instead at the heart of the "here" and "now" of finite life?

In order to address these questions, I will have to do some of the clarifying work that Freud himself avoided. What, we must ask, does it mean that the unconscious is "timeless"? Is this timelessness similar to or different from the selfsame everlasting presence that I have described here as a core feature of the metaphysical tradition? According to Freud himself, as we have seen, unconscious processes are timeless because they "are not chronologically ordered, are not altered by the passage of time, indeed bear no relation to time whatsoever."⁴⁶ Or, in the later formulation also quoted above, their timelessness is explained by the fact that "they are not ordered temporally, that time does not change them in any way and that the idea of time cannot be applied to them."⁴⁷ Unconscious processes defy causality and chronology. Most of us have experienced some version of this when we dream: dreams rarely follow the linear narrative logic of real-life, real-time events. But is this really to say that the unconscious processes are eternally stable and ever-present, or does it rather mean that they do not fit neatly into the notion of time with which we are familiar? Does the unconscious truly lie *outside* of time, or is it rather structured by a *different temporal order* than the one we tend to take for granted?

Kristeva describes its timelessness as a "time outside time," which implies not a *non-time* but, precisely, a *time* outside of time, a time different from the time we know, a time, perhaps, that challenges our common notion of time. Following Freud, she stresses that the timeless breaks the *linearity* of time: it is "a rift" in "the linear time of consciousness" (IR 25, 30). And indeed, she notes, the timeless "has nothing to do with the belief in a life beyond, a time beyond, an eternity beyond" (IR 31). In the essay "New Forms of Revolt," she underlines this distinction: time-lessness, she argues, "does not characterize the mystical *nunc stans*"—a term philosophers often use to refer to the "eternal now" at the heart of the metaphysics of presence—but rather, as she puts it, "the *temporality* of the unconscious."⁴⁸

With Kristeva's remarks in mind, I want to suggest that the term "timelessness" is somewhat misleading, since it implies an *exemption* from any form of temporal movement. What Freud is trying to do, it seems to me, is to articulate a notion of time that has little in common with our current view of time: a temporal model that, precisely, would be impossible to label "temporal" from within our current temporal paradigm. The Freudian revolution, as we saw in chapter 3 of this book, "has nothing else to seek or find but lost time" (IR 42). In her analysis of the timeless in *Intimate Revolt*, Kristeva suggests that we translate the term *Zeitlos* to, exactly, "lost time" (IR 42). Is Freud trying to retrieve a lost notion of time? A time different from the one that has come to dominate Western philosophical discourse? Derrida defends this view: "The timelessness of the unconscious is no doubt determined only in opposition to a common concept of time, a traditional concept, the metaphysical concept: the time of mechanics or the time of consciousness. We ought perhaps to read Freud the way Heidegger reads Kant: like the *cogito*, the unconscious is no doubt timeless only from the standpoint of a certain vulgar concept of time."[49]

But if the timeless in fact *is* temporal, albeit of a different temporal order than conscious time, then what kind of time is it, and how might it be related to revolutionary time? To explore the relationship between the timelessness of the unconscious and revolutionary time helps us better understand why Kristeva would tie the Freudian *Zeitlos* to her own analysis of revolt understood as a movement of perpetual return. With this in mind, we must look at the context in which Freud's discussion of the timeless occurs. His remarks on the *Zeitlos* in *Beyond the Pleasure Principle* immediately follow his discussion of our tendency to compulsively repeat repressed memories of infantile sexual life.[50] If we do not *remember*, we *repeat*. When we remember, we experience our memories precisely as belonging in the past (they thus have a place in linear time), but if the memory is repressed, we experience it time and again (we repeat it), and each time it is experienced as unfolding in the here and now of the present: the repressed memory affects our present life and is experienced *as present* rather than as the past event or wish that it in fact represents.[51] Freud makes it very clear that this not only is a neurotic pattern; it is in fact common in most people, and we see examples of it in children's play, or in our tendency to experience the same obstacles in one relationship after another.[52]

It is his observation of this *compulsion to repeat* that leads Freud to suggest that there exists a death drive "beyond" the pleasure principle already established in his earlier writings,[53] and it is this death drive that Freud as well as Kristeva associate with timelessness. As Kristeva puts it: "While human existence is intrinsically linked to time, the analytical experience reconciles us with this timelessness, which is that of the drive, and more particularly, of the death drive."[54] This death drive paves the way for and is governed by a discontinuous temporality, a time incompatible with linear progress, a time of repetition or, as Freud himself puts it in implicit reference to Nietzsche, a "perpetual recurrence of the same thing."[55] That the unconscious is timeless is really only another way of saying that because some memories are repressed (because they are unconscious), the relationship between past and present is of an oscillating, nonlinear kind. This in turn means not only that our past shapes our present, but also that the opposite is true; that our past is continuously shaped by the present through which it can be accessed and retrieved. Or, as Johnston puts it: "the repressed past resurfaces in the manifest text of consciously accessible material—that is, the past shapes the present. But, simultaneously, the contextual parameters of the subject's present retroactively alter the very past which supposedly influences this same present."[56] While repressed memories are not yet conscious, they need a catalyst in the present to appear even in their repressed form: "fresh mnemic traces behave like a Trojan horse for repressed childhood desires . . . the past overdetermines the present only insofar as the present inadvertently provides the past with certain opportune openings, namely, materials possessing associational connections to repressed contents," Johnston explains.[57]

The term that Freud uses to describe this retroactive process is *Nachträglichkeit*, or deferred action.[58] Jean Laplanche and Jean-Bertrand Pontalis explain that the notion of *Nachträglichkeit*—rarely used explicitly by Freud, but developed at length by Jacques Lacan—was meant to convey "that the subject revises past events at a later date and that it is this revision which invests them with significance."[59] Alison Stone offers a lucid explanation: "When I remember (reproduce) long-dormant elements from my personal past, I bring them into the present and thus place them into a new set of connections—new causal connections and new connections of emotional significance. This changes the significance of these elements for me; and this, by a ripple effect, changes the whole web of significance that connects and constitutes the elements in my personal past."[60] The past attains meaning retroactively, as we return to it, through a recollective practice that changes the very past to which we return.

While Freud viewed *Nachträglichkeit* as a mark primarily of neurotic temporality, Lacan maintains that it in fact is an integral aspect of the very process of psychoanalytic interpretation.[61] What the analyst does is to retroactively reconstruct and reinterpret past events in order to integrate them in the present. Irigaray retrieves this notion of *Nachträglichkeit*, viewing it precisely as a critical tool through which Freud can be read against himself, and more specifically as a leverage point that would help us formulate a critique of the metaphysics of presence. In the opening essay of *Speculum of the Other Woman*, she notes that Freud "destroys a certain conception of the present, or of presence, when he stresses secondary revision [*l'après-coup*, or *Nachträglichkeit*], over-determination, repetition compulsion, the death drive, etc."[62] What Irigaray seems to suggest is that the repetition that stands at the heart of both neurotic symptoms and the analytic cure as such represents an alternative temporal model, one that would challenge the privileging of presence and that would instigate a retrospective return to the past so as to make possible a different future.

We should begin to see a structure similar to that which I have articulated throughout this book: The timelessness of the unconscious brings about a perpetual movement of retrospective return. Just like (female) cyclicality traditionally has been seen as the non-time that (male) linearity needs in order to appear as time (in the sense of progress), the timelessness of the unconscious could easily be regarded as the silent yet determining ground that makes conscious time possible but that in itself is viewed as, precisely, non-time. If we, instead, recognize that the *Zeitlos* is atemporal *only if viewed from the standpoint of conscious-linear time*, we should be able to characterize the repetition and retrospective return that governs the unconscious not as a dead repetition of the same but rather as the condition of possibility for renewal and change.

Kristeva frames her discussion of the timeless by highlighting two features unique for the very psychoanalytic theory that had discovered it: on the one hand, the *heterogeneity* between drive and meaning (or between energetic and hermeneutic); and on the other, the inseparability in analysis between theory and practice, the fact that analysis always already is a *technique*, a *praxis* (and that it therefore takes place *in the present*). The task of analysis cannot simply be to make conscious what was unconscious and thus subsume the timeless under the rule of linear time. What is at stake, instead, is *integration*. The work of anamnesis—the praxis that psychoanalysis is and that is a work of perpetual return—amounts to linking the timeless of the unconscious (repetition, drive) with conscious time (linear progress, meaning). The result? Revolutionary time. A time of ongoing return that nevertheless always involves rebirth, renewal, and the indeterminacy that analysis in a certain sense always amounts to. As Kristeva notes: "without this unfathomable temporality and the psychical modulation that it implies, there is no reason—thus no possibility—to carry out the upheaval of the intimate that is re-volt in the sense of continual rebirth or interrogation" (IR 42).

In order to describe the timelessness of the unconscious in terms of revolutionary time, we have to further explain why it is that the movement of return would involve renewal rather than monotonous and changeless repetition. We have seen that such renewal would depend on sexual difference. But is such difference present here? In an essay titled

"Time and the Witch: Femininity, Metapsychology and the Temporality of the Unconscious," Alan Bass pursues a reading of the Freudian timeless, taking as a clue Freud's own labeling of metapsychology as a *witch*—a female irrational figure who might provide some clarity to the otherwise murky realm of the instincts. Following Derrida, Bass views the *Zeitlos* not as non-time but as a time that appears to be atemporal only from the standpoint of linear-progressive (i.e., conscious) time. He ventures to explicitly tie this "other" time to primary processes and drives, to primary narcissism and auto-eroticism, to the early relationship with the mother: in short, to what he calls a pre-Oedipal "feminine" phase. Metapsychology, he claims, is a feminine figure (a witch), deployed to map out the repressed of our culture: its feminine beginnings, the repetition-differentiation that stands at its very foundation but that nevertheless remains invisible to the point of erasure. If Freud himself had compared metapsychology to metaphysics (and if his references in the metapsychological papers often are precisely philosophical), Bass brings attention to the fundamentally *non-philosophical* nature of metapsychology, and argues that the metapsychological concept of time offers a challenge to those models developed in the (male) philosophical tradition. He attributes this subversive difference to its feminine character:

> Metapsychology must be feminine, must be a witch, in order not to be philosophy, i.e. in order to penetrate to the almost primary "feminine" phases of which we first see evidence in the unsuccessful repressions and regressions of philosophy. . . . And this too, is why Freud must repeatedly say that the unconscious is atemporal, and yet make so many hints about the temporality of the unconscious, for if temporality is the temporality of consciousness, of philosophy, it can be related to an unconscious temporality only as a repression of it. We now have some evidence that this might be so, because all of Freud's references to the temporal factor that "may turn out to be of great importance" occur as unexpected consequences of the investigations of the primary instinctual phases and of the femininity, which even when "secondary" (feminine masochism, secondary narcissism) regresses so close to the primary phase that these primary phases are always discovered by investigating the feminine phases.[63]

What Freud does, in other words, is to specifically define "the relationship of philosophy to psychoanalysis in terms of the repression of a certain view of time," and this repressed notion of time—the timeless—is, Bass argues, intimately linked to femininity.[64] So much so, he claims, that only a female figure, a non-philosophical one at that (the "witch" of metapsychology), could provide some clarity regarding the status of such temporality. We saw this already in my discussion of the uncanny: *death* and the *feminine* are those aspects that are most hidden yet most familiar to us—those that give rise to recurrence and repetition and a time different from linear time.

The *Zeitlos*, in other words, is governed by death and femininity. In the extreme, Kristeva explains, it is "the time of death" (IR 31). But she is careful to point out that such a "time of death" by no means is the equivalent of "a dead time, or a time of nothing, or a time for nothing" (IR 31). It is, importantly, not dead repetition, nor is it self-same eternity. The timeless, Kristeva concludes, "has nothing to do with the belief in a life beyond, a time beyond, an eternity beyond" (IR 31). This time of death, which is not dead time, inscribes death into the very movement of life: "biology itself is accompanied by a thanatology," Kristeva writes (IR 32). Remember that the timeless was discussed in the context of the death drive already in Freud. Kristeva regrets that "a linear and basically paradisiacal conception of life in our religious and scientific tradition makes us habitually subtract this thanatology from the logic of the living" (IR 32). We might add that such linear paradigm also has subtracted the feminine (and birth) from this same logic. That the timeless defies linear progression amounts to saying that its negativity—the thanatology that is its driving force—must not be reduced to or confused with (Hegelian) negativity ("if you take this term to mean the dialectic triad that presides over working out and sublimation" [IR 32]): the *Zeitlos* is "inscribed against any teleology," Kristeva explains (IR 33). The "timeless" is thus not "non-time" in the sense of eternity, but an "unbound" time that, while connected to the archaic in the sense of an early "feminine" phase, nevertheless does lack a *telos* or a specific aim. The "timeless biothanatology" disrupts the teleological movement of linear time. It cannot be reduced to a single end. And in this sense it remains open to the unpredictability of the future. As such, it inscribes unpredictability at the heart of analysis—and this is precisely why analysis as revolt avoids the complacent tyranny that Johnston was worried about in his discussion of psychoanalysis as revolution.

# Conclusion

Already in the previous chapter, I argued that a dynamic notion of presence depends on our attending to lived practices, the most promising of which was rooted in loving relations. I suggested, with Irigaray, that we must think presence in terms of what I called "co-presence," and being in terms of "becoming-with." But to fully understand the nature of such intersubjective relations—and to tease out the ethical stakes in insisting on both time and difference as necessary for thinking intersubjectivity in non-appropriating terms—we needed a more robust understanding of the self in its relation to others. In the present chapter I have thus examined the question of subjectivity in both Irigaray and Kristeva, stressing the need for a model of subjectivity that takes seriously the fact that the human subject lacks unity: that we are heterogeneous and temporally riven, constitutively strange and estranged.

If Irigaray's insistence that we return to the proper self raised some concerns regarding our capacity to render radically temporal both the subject and intersubjective relations, I turned to Kristeva, whose insistence on the divided nature of the self and the work of the negative that it entails allowed us to yet again examine the possibility of thinking presence (and co-presence) in non-metaphysical terms. I examined—through a temporal vocabulary—her claim that we are strangers to ourselves, through a reading of Freud's work on the uncanny. I traced in her discussion of our internal strangeness the potential for an ethics of temporal difference. But I also raised some concerns regarding the political implications of her argument, and the lack of a robust intervention into dynamics of power, which leads her to ignore the crucial fact that some strangers are, as it were, stranger than others.

I then scrutinized her commitment to the Freudian idea of the timelessness of the unconscious. While it looks suspiciously metaphysical, I ultimately argued that it posits a challenge to the metaphysics of presence by, again, elaborating a notion of presence fundamentally different from that espoused in the Western canon. It is thus my contention that the "timelessness" of the unconscious has a lot in common with revolutionary time, and that it inscribes into the movement of time a form of presence that, because it is shot through with both libidinal impulses and the negativity of the death drive, remains dynamic rather than static. In this sense, it brings into the very structure of revolutionary time the "living present" discussed in the previous chapter.

Through a perpetual movement of return (a movement that, importantly, begins in the present), analysis is meant to provide us with a dynamic present not stilted by repressed memories and compulsive repetition. As Stone puts it in her discussion of the "organic unity" of time that comes to the fore in the psychoanalytic practice: "the past organizes each individual's openness to the future, but the future as it unfolds reciprocally shapes and re-shapes each individual's past. The present acquires a living, vivid character as past and future intersect."[65]

Kristeva urges us to familiarize ourselves with the timelessness that resides within us, to encounter the negative as it unfolds within us: "Perhaps in the end it is a question of our own capacity, as analysts and analysands, to be personally sensitive to the various configurations of the Zeitlos and let it be known how much our identity—conscious, unconscious, biological—is a function of the timeless, this major modality of the unconscious," she notes (IR 42). The point of analysis as intimate revolt would, in other words, not simply be to establish linear time over and above the timeless. To bring consciousness to our past amounts not merely to separating it out as belonging, precisely, in the past. It must simultaneously be a matter of bringing awareness to the role that the present plays in our accessing and interpreting the past. As Freud himself noted in "Remembering, Repeating and Working-Through," the task of the analyst is to study "whatever is *present* for the time being on the surface of the patient's mind," and to employ "the art of interpretation mainly for the purposes of recognizing the resistances which appear there, and making them conscious to the patient."[66]

The task is, of course, also to recognize that the past to a certain extent remains (and must remain) lost, hidden, uncanny. As Stone puts it, "there is always more in the past than can be made present," and the past "retains an excess over the present."[67] Kristeva ends her analysis of the Zeitlos by suggesting that the timeless would allow us to reconcile "with the experience of our own loss" (IR 42). What has been lost is that early "feminine" phase vis-à-vis which the Oedipal structure is already secondary. The Zeitlos is in other words intimately linked to the first relation of all, the prototype for relationality as such, and for love as I have analyzed it in this chapter: "we may read the time*less*ness of the unconscious as the inevitable repression of this deferral which we first saw as the 'femininity' which is very close to those primary phases on which all sexual life is built," Bass notes.[68] It is to this fundamental loss that we must now (re)turn, as we revisit the place of birth ("the entrance to the former *Heim* of all human beings . . . the place where each one of us lived once upon a time in the beginning"), in order to make possible rebirth and new beginnings. The time has come to revisit the very locus of the uncanny and of our own internal strangeness: the maternal body that is so familiar and yet so foreign to each and every one of us.

# PART IV
# THE PAST

How can a man be born when he is old?
Can he enter a second time into
his mother's womb, and be born?

—John 3:4


I enter it as a woman who, born between her mother's legs, has time after time and in different ways tried to return to her mother, to repossess her and be repossessed by her, to find the mutual confirmation from and with another woman that daughters and mothers alike hunger for, pull away from, make possible or impossible for each other.

—Adrienne Rich

# 7

# Returning to the Maternal Body

I have argued so far that revolutionary time is a movement of perpetual return into the past that, because it is marked by alteration and differentiation, remains open toward the future. In the previous section, I examined the present from which this movement of return begins, and I articulated such a present mode of time as distinct from metaphysical presence in that it is a present always already marked by temporalization and difference: a living present. I have stressed, moreover, that the movement of return is a return not only to the past but also to the body—the very body that was repressed in the construction of a linear temporal paradigm. In what follows, I want to examine this body in further detail, in order to develop a thought that has already been introduced at several occasions: the body to which we return is itself inherently temporal. To return to the material conditions of our existence amounts, in part, to recognizing that materiality, rather than being some static and stable ground (an all too common feminist worry), in fact is constitutively temporal and prone to change.

I will develop this thought through a discussion of a particular body with a particular cultural and philosophical baggage, namely the *maternal* body. This is, I argue, an especially fruitful place to turn, and this is so for several reasons: (1) the maternal body has, perhaps more than any other particular body, been covered over (or, in a different register, idealized) in our culture, and this very repression is, we might say, what organizes and perpetuates a more general repression of our embodied condition (we saw this in my discussion of the category of birth in chapter 4); (2) by bringing attention to the mother and to her active role in procreation-creation we are able to articulate a critique of the idea that origins are one and selfsame (the metaphysical idea of a stable foundation or *archē*); (3) it is through their association with maternity and procreation that women, as we saw in my reading of Beauvoir, have been made to carry the burden of embodiment, and it is as mothers that women have been seen as doomed by repetition: it is, therefore, to the mother that we must turn in order to provide an account that does not perpetuate this reduction, and that liberates women from such associations; (4) the maternal body, on my reading, illustrates powerfully our capacity for renewal, which makes it a fertile place to turn for a discussion of time and change; (5) maternity is a topic often discussed by Kristeva and Irigaray, and I want to show that their emphasis on the maternal is tied to their concern with questions of time; and (6) the maternal body has been a locus for dispute within feminist philosophical discourse, so to discuss the question of motherhood will help me situate Kristeva and Irigaray's work—and my discussion of time—within the larger field of feminist thought.

## Feminism and Motherhood

Since Beauvoir's early analysis and critique of patriarchy as a system that, among other things, reduces women to mothers and confines them to the realm of reproduction, in *The Second Sex*, feminists have been wrestling with the question of whether birth and motherhood pose a threat to or promote women's liberation. In an early assessment of this tension in feminist thought, Mary O'Brien suggests that feminist theory as such in fact starts "within the process of human reproduction."[1] Almost three decades later, Imogen Tyler notes that birth "remains a pressing political question for feminism."[2] To be sure, many of the topics so pertinent to feminist philosophy—from emancipatory issues such as reproductive rights, the right to work and equal pay, and women's health, to more conceptual concerns such as the ones treated in this book—force us to return to questions of birth, reproduction, and motherhood.

Beauvoir's analysis of women's lived experience, which is clearly guided by an awareness that women have played and continue to play an all-too-important role in reproduction and child-rearing, has been formative, especially for early feminist debates about birth and motherhood.[3] For Beauvoir, one of the foremost reasons for the oppression and othering of women is their role in procreation, which has locked them in a state of immanence, and prevented them from embracing their human capacity for transcendence and freedom. She "cautions women against assuming the role of mother and getting caught in the trap of reproducing the species at the expense of other projects."[4] Her own commitment to a feminist-existential emancipatory project that seeks to liberate women from such a state of facticity is thus tied to a critique of the institution of motherhood as we know it. It is telling that her chapter on motherhood opens with a twelve-page discussion of abortion, and offers only two pages on the experience of giving birth (SS 524–35 and 547–49).[5] While Beauvoir's rejection of motherhood has been overstated, and interesting analysis has emerged that paints more complex and ambivalent a picture of her views on motherhood,[6] it is clear that for Beauvoir reproductive labor as we know it represents an obstacle on the path toward women's liberation.

To be sure, the social expectation that women become mothers is far-reaching and powerful. As Christine Battersby puts it, "whether or not a woman is lesbian, infertile, post-menopausal or childless, in modern western cultures she will be assigned a subject-position linked to a body that has perceived potentialities for birth."[7] And such compulsory obligation is, of course, intimately tied to social and economic inequalities between women and men, such that women's liberation ultimately rests on their capacity to reproduce without being swallowed up by the demands of maternal labor; their right to embody motherhood in ways that challenge traditional norms and expectations; or their ability to reject motherhood altogether. Women's "troubling talent for making other bodies"[8] continues to haunt those who are now or are about to become mothers, those who choose not to be mothers, those who struggle to become mothers, or those who have given birth but don't identify as mothers.[9]

Both Kristeva and Irigaray have been under fire for their emphasis on motherhood, particularly with regard to their alleged equation of maternity with femininity.[10] Critics have suggested that such equation risks to reduce women to the biological function of motherhood. Butler, to give an example to which I will return at length, speaks of a "compulsory obligation on women's bodies to reproduce" (GT 115). Kristeva herself has noted that "it seems . . . difficult to speak today of maternity without being accused of normativism, read: of regression."[11] Our ambivalence vis-à-vis the status of the mother is manifested in the attempts, on the one hand, to articulate female subjectivity independently and outside of motherhood and, on the other hand and at the same time, the widespread feminist call for female genealogies.[12] Such ambivalence would be the consequence of a patriarchal society that simultaneously has reduced women to mothers and robbed them of mothers, assuring that women remain domesticated and, if challenging this role, that they do so under the impression that they are the first of their kind. Women, within such a patriarchal framework, are reduced to mothers but lack mothers of their own.[13] And the reduction of women to motherhood is far from straightforward. Nancy Tuana has convincingly argued that women, paradoxically, have been simultaneously reduced to the role of mothers and robbed of their role in procreation. From ancient Babylonian and Greek creation myths, via the biblical Genesis to modern science, the female power to give birth has been both over-emphasized (as a way of establishing women's inferiority to men) and under-emphasized (as a way of denying such female power and appropriating it onto an all-powerful masculine divinity or medical-scientific establishment).[14]

How, then, can one reclaim and revive female genealogy without ascribing motherhood as the one and only mode of subjectivity available for women? How return to the mother without reducing women to the function of motherhood? Throughout this book, I have argued that such a return would be necessary for the establishment of a temporal model that rather than seeking to *overcome* its material conditions of possibility instead remains in constant and vibrant *interrogation* with and *return* to such beginnings. But how, again, can we return to this maternal dimension without imprisoning women there once and for all? How return without getting stuck in the past, or without repeating the metaphysical mistake of seeking to establish a stable origin or originator?

In the chapters in this section I will argue that these are questions that both Kristeva and Irigaray try to tackle in their writing. Our task, in the words of Irigaray, is to "not again . . . kill the mother who was immolated at the birth of our culture" but, instead, "to give life back to that mother, to the mother who lives within us and among us" (BAB 18). Or, as she puts it in her poetic-autobiographical meditation on her relationship to her own mother: "what I wanted from you, Mother, was this: that in giving me life, you still remain alive."[15] The language of aliveness should be familiar by now, but let me nevertheless remind us that what this means, for Irigaray as well as for Kristeva, is our avoiding being reduced to an idealized image or a teleological function, such that we can embody, instead, heterogeneous becoming. In that same autobiographical account, Irigaray stresses that women, especially in relation to men, far too often have been trapped "in a single function—mothering,"[16] and elsewhere she emphasizes that "women must construct an objective identity model enabling them to situate themselves as women and not merely as mothers," criticizing the "still common practice of reducing the woman to motherhood."[17] Kristeva, similarly, asserts that what we need "in the West today is a reevaluation of the 'maternal function,' seeing it not as explosive and repressed but as a source of practices considered to be marginal (such as 'aesthetic' practices) and a source of innovation"—which, I take it, is another way of saying that the mother must remain alive, in a state of becoming and openness, but also that motherhood entails much more than reproduction and care.[18]

In what follows, I argue that neither Kristeva nor Irigaray reduce woman to the function of motherhood but that, instead, they return to the maternal partially to free women from this very reduction. By bringing the mother out of the shadows, they provide women with a past (a genealogy of their own, a community of women, a history hitherto repressed) and, simultaneously, with a future (in the sense of liberating them from pre-defined roles and positions—from Motherhood, or a certain definition of motherhood, as the only form of subjectivity available to them). They seek to offer an account of motherhood "beyond all the masks," beyond the "mirror reflection"—letting the frozen image of the Mother "thaw" and "melt" into a heterogeneous-temporal and singular lived experience of motherhood and motherhoods-to-come.[19] In the chapters in part 4, I will trace the place to which revolutionary time returns. And yet, as should become clear in the course of what follows, the place to which we are called to return is not really a "place" at all. This "lost foundation" is, in fact, no foundation.[20] It is, as I will argue, *itself* an expression of revolutionary time.

It is, in my mind, the *future* that is at stake when Kristeva and Irigaray speak of the maternal, and it is more specifically the possibility of *temporal change* that depends on a return to it. The maternal principle to which they urge us to return must be understood not as a stable ground but as a locus for renewal. This return is thus importantly not aimed at preserving some essential notion of motherhood: it is one that makes possible new beginnings, allowing for a future pregnant with change and transformation.

In the closing chapter of *Gender Trouble*, Butler offers a critical reading of Kristeva, where she specifically attacks her view on the maternal and the semiotic *chōra*. Butler ends her critique with the following remark, one that is meant to describe what would happen if we *stopped* focusing on the mother the way Kristeva does: "The culturally constructed body will then be liberated, neither to its 'natural' past, nor to its original pleasures, but to an open future of cultural possibilities" (GT 119). I will attempt to show that these words, contrary to what Butler intended, are an accurate description of what would happen if we *did* return to the maternal the way Kristeva and Irigaray attempt to do; that such an "open future" in fact is precisely what they are aiming for through their repeated return to the maternal in our culture.[21]

The implication of their retrieval of the maternal is twofold: First, it situates Kristeva and Irigaray within a materialist tradition and allows them to articulate and inscribe a morphological-phenomenological legacy of embodiment contra merely constructionist or discursive accounts. Second, it gives them ground to re-articulate time as inseparable from space and thus to challenge and overcome the deep-rooted tradition that divides time and space alongside a mind-body dualism. If, as I will argue here, the maternal body to which they return is described not only as *corporeal* but also as a *temporal* principle, then we are forced to think through the intimate relation between temporality and materiality in ways that will come to transform the very materialist tradition that they themselves often are understood to represent.[22]

Both Kristeva and Irigaray speak of matricide. But their own attempt to trace a maternal genealogy—the movement of return this book seeks to trace—bears witness to a loss that (if appropriately mourned) perhaps could be overcome. Through the act of recovery the maternal takes on new meanings, thus becoming incompatible with traditional views on motherhood—views that have served to define and erase the mother in one and the same act. Moreover (and this is perhaps the most crucial point for my purposes here), the very retracing of the lost mother is, simultaneously, a retracing of time lost—a time that has been covered over by the linear construction of time that has come to dominate and structure our culture.

Multiple questions will surface during this journey: What constitutes the "maternal" that both Kristeva and Irigaray so often refer to? To what (if we can still speak of "whatness" here) is it that we must return, and how has it initially been covered over and forgotten? Is this return a temporal one? Does it necessarily consist of retreating into the past? Or does this return offer a revolutionary politics of the kind we discussed in the opening chapters? While Stone describes maternal time as "distinctly past-centered" in that the experience of motherhood, on her account, brings us back to our own archaic beginnings and the repressed bond to our own mother,[23] Lisa Baraitser, in *Maternal Encounters*, postulates a radical priority of the future—as well as the tropes of interruption and disruption—in her discussion of maternal time.[24] My own analysis in what follows ultimately privileges neither the past nor the future, but is precisely an attempt to think them together, in terms of revolutionary time.

I will begin by briefly and schematically looking at the disappearance, repression, loss, or murder of the mother, and the mourning (or is it melancholia?) that this loss has provoked. In the next two chapters, I will then turn to Kristeva and Irigaray, respectively, examining the role of the maternal in their work, and fleshing out its relationship to space and time. I will ultimately argue that the maternal must be understood first and foremost as a principle of temporalization. My reading of both Kristeva and Irigaray will unfold through a close engagement with Plato. I have several reasons for engaging with Plato here. The most obvious is perhaps the fact that both Kristeva and Irigaray, when they first introduce the mother as a figure in their own thought, do so with reference to Plato (Kristeva by appropriating his term *chōra*, as described in the *Timaeus*, and placing it at the center of her thought on the semiotic; and Irigaray by a journey into the Platonic cave of the *Republic*, which on her reading becomes strongly associated with the maternal womb, the *hystera*).[25] Plato is, moreover, an interesting figure to turn to since, for many feminists, his thought is seen as marking the beginning of the metaphysical tradition that was examined in the chapters on presence, and it would consequently be in his dialogues that we should trace the inauguration not only of the privilege granted to the present but also the paternal-teleological-linear thinking that revolutionary time is meant to challenge and undermine. But as should become evident in what follows, Plato plays a much more complicated role in this temporal drama than we might think, and we will have much to gain from returning to his discourse and retrieving the forgotten maternal from within it. I want to show that some aspects of the Platonic corpus are much more in line with Kristeva and Irigaray's projects than they themselves have acknowledged. I therefore also turn to the moments in which our two thinkers criticize Plato in order to suggest that it in fact is here, in the Platonic dialogues, that the time of return was articulated in the first place. But before spelling this out in more detail, let me begin by examining the claim that the maternal has been lost, or covered over, in our culture.

## Mothers Lost: Matricide

Kristeva has been accused of what may seem like two contradictory flaws by feminist theorists. On the one hand, she is said to put too much emphasis on the maternal body, leaving little or no space for women to develop subjectivities other than that of motherhood. On the other hand, she is accused of having knowingly sacrificed the maternal by emphasizing the necessity of separation from the mother (in her psychoanalytic-developmental account) and by allegedly idealizing the imaginary father. In both cases, she appears to be a representative of a phallocratic symbolic order that reduces women to mothers only to then exclude them from the realm of symbolization altogether.[26]

There is no doubt that Kristeva, faithful as she is to the Freudian model of individuation, inscribes what we might call *matricide* as a necessary condition for subject formation. The little child must separate from the mother in order to gain access to discourse, and this separation is (fantasmatically of course) experienced as murder. Kristeva describes matricide as "our vital necessity, the sine-qua-non condition of our individuation," and notes that "the loss of the mother is a biological and psychic necessity, the first step on the way to becoming autonomous."[27] The mother is, however, not entirely "left behind" or excluded from the socio-symbolic pact. Kristeva never fully separates the maternal-semiotic from the paternal-symbolic. The interdependence between the two is one of the underpinning structures of her thought (one often missed, and one to which I will return at length). The semiotic and the maternal traces in language emerge, time and again, in poetic language and other creative discourses. While healthy separation from the mother is necessary, Kristeva thus insists on the importance of remembering and integrating our relationship to her, even as we distinguish ourselves as individuals:

> I would say that we must not repress this archaic relationship
> to the mother, this phase (or mode of symbolization) that I
> have termed the "semiotic." Instead, we must endow it with
> its own expression and articulation while not holding it back
> from the sort of "symbolic" and more intellectual manifestation

that can bring it into our awareness. In fact, all *creative* activity . . . presupposes the *immanence* of libido and the symbolic process along with their dialectalization and harmonization, if you will. Innovation is never the repetition of the paternal discourse or a regression to an archaic mother.[28]

The maternal, for Kristeva, is thus intimately bound not only to the creation of a child, but to creative activity in general. In both instances (procreation and artistic creation) she emphasizes the necessity of a *dual* foundation—both maternal and paternal—and notes that the two continuously coexist.[29] If matricide is necessary for subject formation, it is nevertheless always in some sense partial, and a continual *return* to the mother is in fact equally necessary for creation and the possibility of novelty and change.

Kristeva is, importantly, speaking of matricide in more ways than one. I would like, here, to focus less on the matricide of individuation and shed light instead on a thought that runs through Kristeva's entire corpus, and that is even more prevalent in the thought of Irigaray. Both speak of a (patriarchal) culture guilty of "killing" the mother, of turning the womb into a tomb where our maternal origins can be put away and forgotten, eternally eclipsed by the sole male creator, originator of (the) all. While the process of individuation depends on a separation from the mother (based on the fantasy of a matricide nevertheless never fully realized or final), our cultural repression of the maternal is far more problematic, and politically charged. In *In the Beginning She Was*, Irigaray expresses concern that women have been robbed of their generative powers, and that this in turn has been covered over and forgotten in our masculine culture: Why, she asks, "has [man] likened the woman's part in generation to a simple nourishing environment, keeping for himself providing for the germ of individuation? And how does it happen that this error has remained ignored for so long?"[30]

As I suggested at the outset of this chapter, I will argue that both Kristeva and Irigaray view this loss of the maternal as a loss of the kind of temporality that I have developed in this book.[31] The repression of the maternal on a cultural level (and the subsequent understanding of origins as being solely paternal in nature) coincides, in my view, with that same culture's instituting of time understood as a line. Our returning to and uncovering of the maternal hence plays a dual role: in the first place it allows us to rediscover and give life back to a figure whose presence in our culture would undermine the very notion of linear time, and second, it is integral to that movement of time understood not as line but as, precisely, repeated return, and must thus be sustained ongoingly to keep the movement of return going.

Kristeva notes that "phallic idealization is built upon the pedestal of a putting-to-death of the feminine body,"[32] and Irigaray claims that "our society and our culture operate on the basis of an original matricide" (BAB 11). Both revisit the primitive myth in Freud's *Totem and Taboo*, revealing "the evacuation of the maternal" since, as Kristeva claims is clear from the subtext of the Freudian myth, "one has to get rid of the domestic, corporeal, maternal container . . . in order to establish the symbolic pact" (SNS 21). Irigaray makes a similar observation: "When Freud, notably in *Totem and Taboo*, describes and theorizes about the murder of the father as the founding act for the primal horde, he is forgetting an even more ancient murder, that of the woman-mother, which was necessary to the foundation of a specific order in the city" (BAB 11).[33]

Irigaray speaks of a male "monopoly on family benefits," and explains: "The mother (is the) becoming of (re)production which is progressively 'sublated,' raised, refined. She is idealized, but only by being reversed" (PH 315). She notes, further, that "women are, today, orphaned, without she-gods, goddesses."[34] In the preface to *Key Writings* she asserts that "the pre-Socratic masters began to construct Western logic starting from the oblivion of her—woman, nature, Goddess," and she expresses that her own "criticism of Western culture above all concerns the forgetting of her."[35] In her more recent *In the Beginning She Was*, she explores this theme even more systematically than she has in previous works, describing the mother as having receded "into darkness," and stressing the importance of retrieving-remembering the forgotten maternal: "it is necessary, for us, to cross back over a culture constructed from the necessities of the unique—one, identical, same, equal, etc.—masculine subject and find again the one who was in the beginning: the mother."[36] One could, of course, give a variety of examples of this collective repression. The ancients established the long-lasting view that woman is a mere passive receiver while man is the agent in procreation. Aeschylus, for example, articulates the following: "The woman you call the mother of your child is not the parent, just a nurse to the seed, the new-sown seed that grows and swells inside her. The *man* is the source of life—the one who mounts."[37]

There is a vast literature on the loss of the mother in our culture. Beauvoir has given a detailed account of how the role of women in procreation has been reduced to passive receptivity, from Aristotle to Hippocrates to modern science (SS 21–48).[38] It was only in 1883 that the details of the union between sperm and egg (and thus the understanding that they play an equally active role in fertilization) were worked out by the Belgian zoologist Edouard van Beneden (SS 25), but the association of woman with passivity by no means disappeared just because science changed, and it remains strongly imbedded in our culture to this day.[39] Many accounts point to an interesting yet perplexing fact, namely that woman is *robbed* of her active role in procreation (she is allotted a docile role as a mere receiver and nurse) while, at the same time (as a consequence?) being *reduced* to the function of motherhood and the natural realm. Both aspects are based on a double repression of sorts: the forgetting of woman as mother and, at the same time, the forgetting of woman as irreducible to the function of motherhood. We have seen this in my discussion of Kristeva and Irigaray already at the beginning of this chapter, and we see it developed and examined at length by thinkers such as Cavarero, Tuana, and Sherry B. Ortner, to mention but a few.[40]

Cultural and individual amnesia surrounding the maternal is a core issue for both Kristeva and Irigaray. Miglena Nikolchina has suggested that Kristeva's work be seen as "a theoretic rehabilitation of the maternal figure."[41] Kristeva herself first and foremost addresses our forgetfulness by showing how the work of anamnesis can occur through the practice of psychoanalysis and art or poetic language. The latter, she asserts, "maintains and transgresses thetic unicity by making it undergo a kind of anamnesis, by introducing into the thetic position the stream of semiotic drives and making it signify" (RPL 60).[42] She goes on to state that symbolic language "constitutes itself at the cost of repressing instinctual drive and continuous relation to the mother," while, on the contrary, "the unsettled and questionable subject of poetic language (for whom the word is never quite uniquely sign) maintains itself at the cost of reactivating this repressed instinctual maternal element."[43] The focus, here, is on the way in which *language* is paternal in nature, and the fact that the symbolic order constitutes itself by repressing the pre-linguistic dyadic relationship between mother and child.[44] Insofar as both Kristeva and Irigaray trace a matricide of sorts in language, we might say that culture as a whole (understood as a set of discursive practices) depends on it. If "culture" traditionally has been situated in contrast to and even in opposition with "nature" (keeping in mind of course that this very distinction is a cultural one), and if the latter most commonly has been associated with the maternal ("mother earth," "mother nature"), the sacrificial logic becomes evident.

Both Kristeva and Irigaray's work could thus be described as obituaries of sorts. Irigaray mourns a maternal space that has been perverted, "turned inside out, or truncated" to fulfill an old (masculine) dream of symmetry/sameness (PH 248). In search for universals, for the purity of eternal truths and idea(l)s, we have turned our back on the materiality from which we all emerge—the maternal womb, mother earth, embodiment, sexual difference. Time and again, Irigaray revisits the maternal body, suggesting, as we have already seen, that this "exile" in which we live our calculated and calculating lives is "a universe of death"[45] that forgets the fertile soil from which difference arises: "The spirit, in its perfection, does not thrust its roots deeper into the earth. It destroys its first roots. Its soil has become culture, history, which successfully forget that anything that conceives has its origins in the flesh" (FG 109). Or, as she puts it in critical dialogue with Aristotle, "mother-matter affords man the means to realize his form."[46] What then, she asks, "is to be made of matter?" (PH 345). We will, she insists, need to return to it one day. "But by what path?" (PH 344). How overcome this forgetfulness?

Irigaray understands castration anxiety in light of the already-cut-off-umbilical-cord: a wound, she laments, never spoken of, since "the scar of the navel is forgotten," since there is no memory of this original loss (BAB 16).[47] The morning of our culture can thus not be properly mourned: "In more ways than one, it is really a question . . . of a 'loss' that radically escapes any representation. Whence the impossibility of 'mourning' it," she writes in *Speculum*.[48] The lost object is inscribed as negation or lack, silent yet threatening. "Threatening because it is silent, perhaps?" (BAB 16). Strictly speaking, our culture is thus incapable of mourning. It is a melancholic one. A strange obituary indeed . . .[49]

## Other Mothers: A Colonial Maternal Continent

Before I turn to a more careful and systematic reading of the return to the mother as it unfolds in Kristeva and Irigaray's work, it seems essential to take note of the fact that feminist discussions of motherhood—including those that we find in these two thinkers—have perpetuated normative assumptions about mothers as Western, female, straight, white, middle-class, and able-bodied. As Kaila Adia Story has noted, "the dominant portrayal of what is, and what it means to be a 'mother' . . . remains locked within a reductive and imaginary prism of white supremacy, heteronormativity, and sexism."[50]

To be sure, we must challenge the all-too common assumption that motherhood is altogether "natural," and that nature somehow privileges some birthing bodies over others in hierarchical fashion. It is, I think, no coincidence that TERF feminists such as Janice Raymond combined deeply held transphobic views with intense suspicion of assisted reproductive technologies—both couched in the name of "real" and "natural" women, allegedly under attack by medically created "artificial" women. As Sophie Lewis has pointed out in an important article mapping the shared roots of transphobia and feminist critiques of surrogacy, for scholars like Raymond, "transition surgeries and contract pregnancies were two facets of a seemingly omnipotent 'male' war on or invasion of the 'female.'"[51] With a growing body of work in trans-studies, and with increased visibility of queer, non-binary, and trans bodies, the age-long association of women with gestation and birth, and the concomitant assumption that all birth parents are mothers, is coming to an end. Critical work on motherhood will inevitably have to pay more attention to experiences that trouble and disrupt such associations, descriptively and normatively.[52]

Kristeva and Irigaray both lag behind in this regard, as the accounts they offer by and large take as their point of departure normative motherhood. With this in mind, it seems important to say a few words about those "other mothers" that have suffered from even more acute forms of erasure than the ones Kristeva and Irigaray seek to render visible in their respective bodies of work. And while my reading of Kristeva and Irigaray will focus primarily on what they *do* say about motherhood rather than what has been omitted, I want to nevertheless name that such erasures take place in their own discussions of motherhood, and that these erasures add yet another complex dimension to the issue of what it would mean to "return" to the maternal body. What maternal body are we speaking of here? What maternal experiences do they appeal to as they urge us to return? And how might the erasures that mark their own work come to shape the very movement of return, and the futurity that it allows for? I am gesturing toward these questions here so as to allow for them to reverberate in the chapters that follow.

In light of this, let me note, in this context, that there is an overwhelming tendency in feminist work on motherhood—including, again, Kristeva and Irigaray's work—to discuss maternal experience as if it was racially neutral, which is to say that it has mostly been treated from an implicitly white standpoint. As Dorothy Roberts points out in her seminal *Killing the Black Body*: "The feminist focus on gender and identification of male domination as the source of reproductive repression often overlooks the importance of racism in shaping our understanding of reproductive liberty and the degree of 'choice' that women really have."[53]

Since Roberts set out to correct this imbalance, and to account for the manifold ways in which Black women's reproductive lives have been subjected to insidious forms of white supremacist violence and injustice—ranging from the ideology of Mammy and white slave-owners' widespread use of rape for the purpose of impregnating Black women, to forced sterilization and scientific experiments devoted to proving the biological inferiority of Black folk, to the contemporary stereotyping of Black mothers as immoral, neglectful and domineering welfare queens, media stories about hopelessly defective crack babies, and massive racial discrepancies in maternal health care and infertility treatment—a body of work has emerged that speaks specifically to racial dimensions of reproduction, and racist tendencies in the literature on motherhood.

Echoing Kristeva's call for complex and ambivalent accounts of motherhood that refuse both the idealized image of the Virgin Mother and the degrading image of mothers as passive vessels (I will say more about this in the next chapter), Patricia Hill Collins, for example, calls for accounts of Black motherhood that reject the "mother glorification" that she attributes to "Black men who routinely praise Black mothers, especially their own," as well as the social stigma of the "bad" Black mother, such that Black motherhood can be described in more complex and multifaceted terms, as the "fundamentally contradictory institution" it in fact is.[54] We need, in other words, to make more widely available and visible counter-narratives that depict the lived experience of Black motherhood in all of its richness and uniqueness, not just in terms of inequity and oppression.

For Collins, as much as motherhood for many Black women comes at the expense of their own freedom, she is careful to point out that for many, it remains "a symbol of hope" and an "empowering experience," and it can "foster a creativity, a mothering of the mind and soul, for all involved."[55] Again, we see that this appeal and return to motherhood is far from stilting or oriented toward preservation or nostalgia about our past. Rather, what is at stake is the future—our capacity for change and the power of creativity. But let us be reminded that such change must not come about through the othering of some mothers so as to make possible the liberation of those mothers who more easily fit normative ideas and ideals about motherhood.

## Conclusion

Having already argued that the movement of return involved in revolutionary time is a return not only to the past but also to the body—the very body that was repressed in the construction of a linear temporal paradigm—in this section on the past I examine this corporeal register in further detail. To return to the material conditions of our existence amounts, in part, to recognizing that materiality, rather than being some static and stable ground, in fact is constituted by temporal processes and change. In the present chapter, I have begun to develop this thought through a discussion of a particular body with a particular cultural and philosophical baggage, namely the maternal body.

I have thus briefly outlined what I see as the issues at stake in returning to a lost maternal continent. First, I examined some of the difficulties involved in broaching issues of motherhood as a feminist, given the paradoxical ways in which women have been both *reduced* to mothers and *robbed* of their capacity to mother, which means that the recuperation of motherhood is a precarious and risky task from a feminist point of view, one that both Kristeva and Irigaray nevertheless take on. Second, I surveyed the role of *matricide* in the work of these two thinkers, and began to sketch the gestures of erasure, amnesia, and even violence that the mother has been subjected to in Western-patriarchal thought. Finally, I also flagged some of the erasures that take place within Kristeva and Irigaray's own thinking about motherhood and maternal experience. Paradigmatically, these erasures serve to posit motherhood as implicitly straight, cis-gendered, and white, thus disregarding the diverse experiences of motherhood that arise from the margins, and the need to return to and recuperate *that* lost continent—the other mother—which remains largely invisible in their work.

Ultimately, I have suggested that Kristeva and Irigaray's respective return to motherhood in no way is motivated by a conservative-nostalgic-foundational agenda, but rather represents an attempt to free women from a very specific set of idea(l)s regarding motherhood, and that this attempt is marked by a desire to open up future horizons for embodying motherhood otherwise. I have yet to support these claims at length, and this will be the task at hand in the next two chapters. The question that we must ask has been eloquently articulated by Nikolchina: "If the phallus has taken, theoretically, the place of the logos, whatever could be the reality that this shift inverts?"[56] What is it that has been covered over and forgotten? If we don't even know what it is that has been lost, retrieving it will be a hard task indeed. We must, therefore, turn to the accounts given by Kristeva and Irigaray, respectively, in order to define more concretely the nature of this loss, and our chances to breathe life into the lost mother once again.

# 8

# Motherhood According to Kristeva

Kristeva's earliest thematization of the maternal appears in her doctoral dissertation, *Revolution in Poetic Language*, which appeared in French in 1974.[1] It is here that she first articulates her influential, and also criticized, notion of the *semiotic chōra*, associating it with the maternal body and early heterogeneous drives.[2] Drawing from, while at the same time modifying, established psychoanalytical views on childhood development, she articulates her own account of subject formation and language acquisition. Her most important departure from Freud and Lacan is her thoroughgoing emphasis on the early relationship between mother and child, a relationship that she often describes as symbiotic, although as we shall see it is marked by alterity from the outset. In her 1980 text *Powers of Horror*, she deepens the thoughts articulated in the dissertation, bringing further attention to a mother-child relation that, as she puts it, is marked by *abjection* (the distinction between subject and object has not yet been developed, and Kristeva articulates this ambiguity in terms of an "abject"). As far as the question of the maternal is concerned, these texts first and foremost examine what we might call maternal residual traces in language. Poetic language in particular is described as being shot through with semiotic elements, and therefore as exhibiting maternal elements (more or less repressed memories from our early relation with the mother) that would be more thoroughly concealed in non-poetic language. As I argued in chapter 3, this capacity on the part of poetic language to retrieve and express semiotic drives and affect is what makes it *revolutionary*: it enables a transformation and vitalization of language and the symbolic order.

Kristeva picks up the Greek term *chōra* from Plato's *Timaeus*; a dialogue that more than anything deals with the very question of beginnings, as it narrates the story of how the cosmos and its living creatures were created.[3] In what follows, I will turn both to the Platonic text, and to Kristeva's engagement with it, in order to trace the meaning and significance of *chōra*, and to point to some difficulties and issues surrounding it.[4] I want to examine Kristeva's account and description of the semiotic *chōra* in order to clarify what I think she means by the maternal, and to tie it to the question of temporality in ways that I believe undermine the charges of essentialism raised against her on this point.[5] If *chōra* most commonly has been understood as a "receptacle" or "container" (and both Plato and Kristeva do use these terms),[6] what I will show in what follows is that *chōra*, and the maternal body that both Plato and Kristeva associate with it, is far from a receiver passively awaiting penetration or fulfillment. I will, instead, emphasize the *temporal* characteristics that both thinkers ascribe to it, and this will, in turn, allow me to elaborate a more nuanced account of the relationship between materiality and temporality than the one we get from a paradigm that opposes cyclical and linear time.

## Plato's *Chōra* Revisited: Receptacle or Revolutionary?

Put most simply, *chōra*, for Kristeva, is the articulation of primary processes and drives.[7] We may say that it is the material from which language emerges, and yet, as I hope to show, to characterize it merely as "material" is both problematic and inaccurate, on Kristeva's as well as on Plato's account. Kristeva explains that all discourse "moves with and against the *chora* in the sense that it simultaneously depends upon and refuses it" (RPL 26). It is a "preverbal functional state that governs the connections between the body (in the process of constituting itself as a body proper), objects, and the protagonists of family structure" (RPL 27). As such, it represents an "instability of the symbolic function in its most significant aspect—the prohibition placed on the maternal body (as a defense against autoeroticism and incest taboo). Here, drives hold sway and constitute a strange space that I shall name, after Plato . . . *chora*, a receptacle."[8] Kristeva underlines the role played here by pre-symbolic drives, and she emphasizes the fact that such drives are experienced by a not-yet-subject connected to and oriented toward the mother (not yet differentiated from her). Both Kristeva and Plato characterize *chōra* in maternal terms: Timaeus, in Plato's dialogue, famously likens it with a "mother" [*meter*] and a "wet-nurse," drawing on female connotations distinct from the paternal demiurge and creator present from the outset of his story.[9] For Kristeva, the maternal body is "the ordering principle of the semiotic *chora*" (RPL 27). Had the mother not been there to harbor and organize the wealth of affects and drives of the early psychic space, the experience might have been so overwhelmingly disorienting that we would have all been doomed to psychosis. The mother, in other words, provides the first space in which semiotic meaning can be produced.

One could object that such an account problematically seems to divide a pre-symbolic, drive-ridden, natural, passive, maternal mold or receptacle from a symbolic-logic, cultural, active, paternal force of creation, with the consequence that we, again, essentialize such categories along gendered lines. Many feminists have indeed responded in such a way.[10] Such concerns, however, I see as stemming from a misconstrual of what Kristeva means when she speaks of *chōra*, and moreover a misunderstanding of the meaning and function of this ambiguous concept as it appears already in Plato. I want to return, therefore, to both Kristeva and Plato, in order to show that *chōra* is neither passive nor essential (if by essential we mean static), and that to the extent that it is "natural" the latter must not be understood as in any way *opposed* to "cultural," but rather as always already *integral* to and in *mutual dependence* with culture and symbolization. Moreover, I will show that *chōra* is not merely spatial, but also—and more importantly for my purposes here—temporal. It is through my emphasis on the temporal aspects of the maternal *chōra* that my reading is distinct from most previous readings.

Let us recall the function of *chōra* in the Platonic dialogue: Timaeus has recounted the creation of cosmos (the all), as it was brought about by the good god (the demiurge, the father) in his own (perfect) image. Already at the outset, we encounter a creation rather different from that of the Judeo-Christian tradition. The demiurge does not create the world *ex nihilo*—his act is rather one of bringing order to that which lacks order: "the god thus took over all that was visible, and, since it did not keep its peace but moved unmusically [out of tune] and without order, he brought it into order from disorder, since he regarded the former to be in all ways better than the latter" (Tm 30A). We learn two things already at this early point of the dialogue: First, that matter existed *before* the creation we are about to witness, and second, that this matter *moved*, albeit in a disorderly manner. If matter moved and was subject to change before the demiurge began his work, then matter was temporal before the "creation" of time. The world is not exactly created then, but rather ordered, organized. And similarly, time is not exactly created, but rather given a shape that can be counted or measured. Put differently, creation is understood *qua* ordering, and has little in common with the Judeo-Christian notion of genesis *ex nihilo*. The act of creation is a matter of calculation and ordering, of mixing things together according to certain proportions, and of separating things out according to mathematical formulas. As is implied by the very opening words of the dialogue; what ultimately counts is the act of, precisely, counting: "One, two three . . ." (Tm 17A).

Later on in the dialogue, when Timaeus has given a detailed account of the different steps of this calculative ordering, and consequently the coming-into-being of the universe as we know it, and the "creation" of time and the heaven, he stops, as it were, and recalls that the cosmos came about not only in virtue of the activity of the divine intellect, but rather through its mixing with *necessity*, or what he here calls "the wandering cause" (Tm 48A), and later will name *chōra* (Tm 52A).[11] Let me quote Plato at length at this important juncture, a passage which John Sallis has brought our attention to as one of several new beginnings in this dialogue about beginnings, and one that marks the beginning of the chorology—the discourse on *chōra*.

> So if anyone is to declare how the all was in this way genuinely born, he must also mix in the form of the wandering cause—how it is its nature to sweep things around. In this way, then, *we must retreat*, and, by taking in turn another, new beginning, suited to these very matters, just as in what was before us earlier, so too in what is before us now, *we must begin again from the beginning*. We must get a view of the nature itself of fire and water, and air and earth, *before the birth of heaven*, and of their affections before this. For at present *none has yet revealed their birth*; but on the contrary, we speak to people as if they knew fire, whatever it is, and each of the others; and *we set them down as principles*—as elements or "letters" of the all—whereas it would not be at all suitable for them to be likened with any degree of likelihood even to the forms of "syllable," at least not by a man who was even the slightest bit prudent. (Tm 48A–C, emphasis mine)

First of all, this passage exemplifies the movement of return that I have outlined throughout this book. The term "retreat," the translator points out, is a form of the Greek term *anachorein*, "which literally means to go back to one's space or *chora*."[12] New beginnings depend on a movement of return. Derrida writes that "the discourse on the *khōra* . . . is inaugurated by a new return [*retour*] to the origin: a new raising of the stakes in the analytic regression. Backward steps [*retours en arrière*] give to the whole of the *Timaeus* its rhythm. Its proper time is articulated by movements which resume from even farther back the things already dealt with farther back."[13] Such a return thus demands that we push beyond what we previously thought of as the beginning.[14] Timaeus, who has given an extended account of the nature of the four elements and their relation to one another, here acknowledges that, in fact, "none has yet revealed their birth," but that we rather speak of them as if we knew, without actually knowing. The question, then, remains as to what they were and how they were interrelated before the birth of heaven, i.e., before paternal-divine interference, and before the beginning of time in its measured sense.

It is important to note that the issue at hand is the extent to which we *speak* about things as if we knew their beginning, and that we do so by setting them down as *principles*. Timaeus speaks of letters and syllables—the very building blocks of language. We liken the natural elements with linguistic elements, as if they were a social construct like language. And yet, Timaeus tells us that such likening is inappropriate, that there is something about the natural elements that escapes and precedes language. And, as we know from so many interlocutors of this dialogue, the deep problem concerning *chōra* is exactly the extent to which it cannot be spoken of, the extent to which language fails when we attempt to bespeak it.

This, of course, is exactly what is at stake in Kristeva's work. In a footnote, she raises the question of whether the receptacle in fact is "a 'thing' or a mode of language" (RPL 239n12). The "revolution" that she ascribes to poetic language is really quite literally a revolution (as I explored the term through the language of "return" in the opening chapters of this book). She seeks out and underlines early (preverbal) traces as they emerge in avant-garde modern literature—the ways in which poetic language allows us (in fact forces us) to return to the pre-linguistic space-time that the maternal element (*chōra*) in her work represents—one that transcends and threatens language and yet is internal to and necessary for it to emerge and transform. By contrast, she explains how linguists and philosophers, in approaching language and subjectivity, tend to repress and deny these very maternal-material (and, as we shall see, temporal) beginnings through a kind of repression or a calculation forgetful of the heterogeneous character of the drives and primary processes, and their role in subject- and language-formation.[15] It is at this juncture, for Kristeva, that *chōra* is introduced as that time-space which contains the repressed semiotic elements, eternally returning in dreams and artistic discourse. Poetic language "reminds us of its eternal function: to introduce through the symbolic that which works on, moves through, and threatens it," and in so doing, it becomes "the ultimate means" for the "transformation or subversion" of the symbolic, "the precondition for its survival and revolution" (RPL 81).[16]

But is *chōra*, for Plato as well as for Kristeva, not just a silent ground then? The condition and soil, the receptacle (or, as in Kalkavage's translation, "molding-stuff") that passively awaits and makes itself available for a paternal demiurge or speaking subject who occupies it in order to impose its own law and name on it? And if this is so, is it not then deeply problematic that both Plato and Kristeva associate such a ground with the feminine, with the maternal body, with women? This, again, is the standard critique. But we must look more closely at what *chōra* actually means for the two before we can assume the validity of such charges.

What, for example, does it mean for *chōra* to be a receptacle? Could this be understood in non-passive terms, as different from mere receiving? In Plato, the term *chōra* (translated as Space) is intimately related to (if not the same as) *ananke* (necessity, second cause, material elements). It signifies both materiality and spatiality. It is important to note, here, that for the Greeks, Space (capitalized here as in the dialogue to mark the distinction from what we tend to understand by that term) had little in common with the Cartesian homogenous or geometrically neutral space that we tend to associate it with today. Matter and space, in the Greek context, cannot be thought separately. Space cannot be emptied of matter—we are not dealing with pure conceptual form. *Chōra*, therefore, cannot be thought of as an abstraction. It is irreducible to intelligible categories—this is exactly why it is so difficult to bespeak. What is at stake is the possibility of thinking expansion in non-mathematical terms, outside of the Cartesian model so familiar to us.[17] Such a space is only "neutral" insofar as it stands *between* (or beyond) the intelligible and the sensible—it itself belongs to neither of these realms, but rather constitutes a third kind. Its neutrality must thus not be understood as pure availability or receptivity, but rather as that which refuses (and therefore challenges and even undermines) dichotomization.[18] The creator depends fully on the second cause. He pleads for its collaboration, convincing it (or her) to be his ally (Tm 48A). I take it that we are called to understand *chōra* as that which (actively) imposes itself as a limit vis-à-vis the intellect (or, on Kristeva's account, language).[19] It is not as if *he* (the demiurge) imposes his laws on *her* (*chōra*). She dictates her own laws.

Moreover, and this is crucial for my reading (and, as I see it, for Kristeva too), by virtue of being "materialized" or even "embodied," this kind of Space is *alive*, it *moves*, it is *animated* (in contrast to Cartesian space which, qua abstract, is lifeless and immobile). Timaeus himself is very careful to underline this point. While *chōra* is introduced first and foremost as necessity, it (or she) is by no means stable or solid. She introduces movement (sweeping and rhythmic in nature) and difference (the causes are, importantly, two). And since *chōra* is there from the very beginning (or prior to all beginnings), movement and difference are given ontological status in Plato's text. There was never a selfsame universe on this account. The cosmos is marked by movement, alteration, and alterity from a beginning that precedes all beginnings.

*Chōra* names the expanse, the opening implied in the act of creation or generation, of beings coming into being. In the thrust of origination, the origin is no longer self-contained: it overflows beyond itself. The very possibility of fecundity relies on the availability of an opening. A self-contained entity cannot, per definition, be an origin (a point the consequences of which I will return to as I look at the work of Irigaray).[20] By introducing *chōra*, Timaeus reminds us that if the paternal demiurge would be the sole creator, living beings would be mere copies of selfsame Ideas, or *eidos*. The demiurge alone could create nothing but copies. Thanks to *chōra*, reproduction becomes *creative* rather than *repetitive*, and we see that it is the maternal, not the paternal function that introduces variation and temporal flux. Let me repeat that for an origin to originate it must differentiate itself from itself. An origin is abundance with regard to itself—it is that which cannot contain itself. This comes close to what Socrates associated with aliveness at the beginning of the dialogue—when he urged his interlocutors to give life to the city of speech (Tm 19B–C). Socrates, however, described the movement and expansion of the city in terms of struggle, contention, and war. Timaeus, at this point, offers an alternative account of movement and expansion—one grounded in generation and birth. Both accounts, importantly, tie movement and expansion to time and temporal matters such as birth and death.[21]

Contrary to what has often been assumed, and to what Timaeus himself claims, *chōra* is, in my view, therefore a *morphous* and *morphizing* Space. It orders the elements through a kind of rhythmic and sweeping movement. And as this movement is being described we begin to take note of the complex chronology with which creation is taking place. We learn that the creative ordering of the demiurge not simply emerges out of chaos, but that the pulsating movement of *chōra* already has ordered the elements in a certain manner "even before the all was arrayed and came to be out of them" (Tm 53A).[22] The chorology offers an elaboration of movement understood in primary terms. Movement is not secondary to stillness or selfsame perfection. *Chōra* is likened to an "instrument that produces shaking"—an image that brings to mind a musical instrument, one producing rhythms and harmonies, what Kristeva calls "semiotic rhythm" and what she believes "gives 'music' to literature" (RPL 29, 63). While Timaeus, at an earlier point, specifically stated that the matter present prior to the work of the demiurge "moved unmusically and without order" (Tm 30A), this new beginning and the introduction of *chōra* sheds new light on and qualifies his previous remarks.

In her insightful reading of the *Timaeus*, Louise Burchill traces the appropriation and usage of *chōra* in French philosophy from Derrida to Jean-François Lyotard. Let me quote her at length here, in a passage that I think reveals the essence of my argument at this juncture, and that will allow me to subsequently turn back to Kristeva. Responding to the way in which French theorists have come to characterize and criticize the Platonic *chōra* for being an amorphous and non-differentiated "originary spatiality," Burchill urges us to pay closer attention to the Platonic text:

> After all, the archaic spatial matrix that Plato describes in the *Timaeus* as a moving "irrational" configuration, without "measure or order," refractory to the dominion of the transcendental forms and ever-rebel to an imposition of geometric objectivity, is surely somewhat difficult to identify with the "homogeneous space" of metaphysical "pure presence"—or, for that matter, with an inert, passive support docilely awaiting the impression of virile forms. Even the specific attribution

of "amorphousness" that Plato uses to underline the formal indetermination of a "space" ever eluding a stable nomination while simultaneously displaying a constant motility and imbalance of "forces," clearly cannot be equated with the homogeneity, isotropy, or "passivity" proper to a space *partes extra partes*, but would seem, quite to the contrary, to open up a conception of "space" resolutely "marked" by an ontological undecidability.[23]

Burchill continues to argue that the ultimate aim of these French theorists (Kristeva included) is to secure "their own understanding of the 'site in which differentiation in general is produced' in terms . . . not of an 'originary space' but of an 'originary time' (on condition that the term 'originary' here be distinguished from any and all notions of a punctiform pure origin)," and that such "originary time" has been thought through in terms of "the feminine."[24] Rather than replacing "originary space" with "originary time," I would argue that what is at stake, already in Plato, and subsequently in Kristeva, is an attempt to think space and time together; that the proto-temporalization, as Burchill herself will come to suggest, "may be understood to carry, in a certain manner, space within itself—much as rhythm can be defined as the articulation of space and time."[25]

We have already seen that *chōra* is likened with an instrument that produces shaking. Rhythm and vibration, we must add, cannot be thought without or beyond materiality and embodiment. Already in the Pythagorean tradition, rhythmic pulsation was viewed as formative of matter. Vibration is that which *informs* creation. Music, we know from Plato's *Republic*, is formative (of both body and soul) in the same sense as gymnastics is.[26] Insofar as *chōra* introduces rhythmicity, Plato seems to suggest that existence is irreducibly spatial and temporal; that temporality and materiality must be thought together. As we will see, this is precisely what the maternal on my reading is meant to articulate. I will return in more detail to how rhythm carries spatio-temporal articulation in Kristeva. But let me already now begin to tease out the ways in which this structures her own reading of the *Timaeus*.

When first introducing *chōra* as a concept in her own work, Kristeva describes it as "a *motility* that is *as full of movement as it is regulated*," and further specifies that it is "an *essentially mobile* and extremely provisional articulation constituted by *movements* and their ephemeral stases" (RPL

25, emphasis mine). In *Powers of Horror*, she again emphasizes the mobile aspects of *chōra*, as she characterizes it as " 'primal' pulsation."[27] For her, as for Timaeus, the *moving* character of *chōra* is crucial. What are the implications of this emphasis on movement—present both in Kristeva and Plato? Kristeva explains:

> We must restore this motility's gestural and vocal play (to mention only the aspect relevant to language) on the level of the socialized body in order to remove motility from ontology and amorphousness where Plato confines it in an apparent attempt to conceal it from Democritean rhythm. The theory of the subject proposed by the theory of the unconscious will allow us to read in this rhythmic space, which has no thesis and no position, the process by which significance is constituted. Plato himself leads us to such a process when he calls this receptacle or *chora* nourishing and maternal, not yet unified in an ordered whole because deity is absent from it. (RPL 26)

While Kristeva worries that Plato is ontologizing motility, I would argue that this is exactly what takes place in her own work too. But Plato is not, as Kristeva suggests, *undermining* motility by *imposing* ontology upon it (the latter understood statically, as everlasting Being). As I have tried to show, he is, instead—and this they have in common—granting onto-logical status to motility, which is to say that Being always already moves, that Being is temporal, that Being, put simply, is becoming or flux. Such a reading of course challenges the entire characterization of Plato as a dualist who believes in essential forms, and this is exactly what Timaeus's discourse on *chōra* does: it shakes "Platonism" from within its own logic (if by "Platonism" we mean a tradition that assumes a singular cause or origin, selfsame, atemporal, and one). As Kristeva notes (and as is true for her own work too), the chorology shakes such a "Platonism" precisely by vehemently insisting on the interdependence between maternal and paternal function: The demiurge is characterized as a generative principle that overflows beyond itself, that remains open, and that cannot be fixed as an utmost or ultimate beginning without beginnings of its own. The movement *from* the paternal creator takes place *in* the maternal *chōra*. And while the latter traditionally has been withheld in passive silence, both Plato and Kristeva highlight the fact that the "from" and the "in" are one, that they always must be thought together, that they are both vocal and active, endowed with creative powers.

Kristeva also reveals a Platonic acknowledgment and retrieval of a certain rhythmic motility in language (and in culture at large), which in turn challenges the alleged stability and unity of language and the paternal law. Such a retrieval, however, does not aim at introducing brute chaos or disorder, but rather a rhythm that continuously structures and orders language through repetition, "starting over, again and again" (RPL 26), the movement of return that allows us to sustain the tension inherent in language, the fact that it is semiotic *and* symbolic, maternal *and* paternal. Two causes, standing together, co-dependent, never mutually exclusive. And yet, the difficulty of thinking and articulating such a dual cause is manifest in the very discourse of Timaeus, who must begin anew, again and again, never quite able to capture the event of creation other than in a language "difficult and obscure" (Tm 49A), a "strange [*a-topos*] and unusual narration" indeed (Tm 48D), a speech without a proper place, a proper voice, a discourse never quite finished, lacking closure, aporetic in nature, a "bastard reasoning . . . hardly to be trusted" (Tm 52B). Timaeus is always grappling for yet another beginning, retrieving further back into the unknown and unspoken. In a beautiful passage, he attempts to capture *chōra*, and ends up likening it with "the very thing we look to when we dream" (Tm 52B), thus recalling the intimate link between the semiotic *chōra* and the unconscious, emphasized by Kristeva throughout her work.[28]

In a footnote, Kristeva further articulates the importance of motility in this context, and raises a set of concerns regarding the tendency that she again sees in Plato to reduce and ontologize it, since he brings the pre-symbolic "back into a symbolic position," with the consequence that "rhythmicity will in a certain sense be erased" (RPL 239–40n13). As I see it, however, rhythm is never erased in the chorology. As I have tried to show, Timaeus's discourse is a logos in crisis. It is fragmented, self-obliterating, and self-annihilating. And yet, it is as if Timaeus tried to bring our attention to the fact that it is precisely when faced with this lack of clarity that we find the highest manifestation of human logos. Something unique about our discourse is expressed and disclosed here, namely its constant attempts to trace and expose its own limits by moving beyond them. The limits cannot be known a priori, they are exposed exactly by being transgressed time and again. Timaeus's discourse is one that oscillates around its own limits—hence its rhythmic character and its similarity with the temporality of return (it moves to the outside—to a beginning before all beginnings—only to then bounce back to the inside in search for new beginnings). While Kant subsequently has warned us of this uniquely human desire to understand or articulate that which lies beyond the limits of our reason, Timaeus seems to embrace such a tragic desire. What nevertheless makes him different from the philosophers criticized by Kant is his thorough and explicit awareness of his own shortcomings, his acknowledgment of the inherently excessive and unspeakable character of that which he nevertheless attempts to bespeak.

Rather than suggesting that this marks his discourse as poetic—understood in opposition to philosophical discourse—I want to suggest that here, as is common in Plato, we see an example of philosophy akin to poetry (which is ironic, of course, given Plato's own critical views on poetry). That discourse which is able to sustain perplexity is, according to Timaeus himself, musical, or in tune (Tm 55C). The irregular movement of *chōra* is musical. This is why, despite his many shortcomings, Timaeus manages to do exactly what Socrates had demanded at the beginning of the dialogue: to describe the city (even the cosmos) in its *aliveness*, as that which *moves*, as he undertakes to disclose the very structures of life and of the living, through a discourse in tune with the rhythmicity and heterogeneity of life itself. It is no coincidence that the chorology is followed by a long phenomenological account of the entire field of becoming—embodiment, desires, pleasures, pains, diseases, decay, death—of singular bodies, as they come into being and pass away. While Grosz, like most interlocutors, has characterized *chōra* as an intermediary "whose function is to explain the passage from the perfect to the imperfect, from the Form to the reality,"[29] I want to suggest, instead, that this third kind importantly points to the *continuity* between the two—the fact that life is form *and* matter, symbolic *and* semiotic. Just as Kristeva has stressed the necessity of bringing to light semiotic aspects of language—this would be the revolution that poetic language might bring about—Plato too seems to argue that this rhythmicity in language is what gives it life and aliveness.

This brings us to a full articulation of why the rhythmic aspects of the semiotic must be understood in terms of temporality. Maria Margaroni has noted that the usage of the term *chōra* "enables Kristeva to conceptualize" the intersection of corporeal, linguistic, and social forces "both spatially (as the 'in-between' produced by the ambiguous relatedness of two always already socialized bodies: that is, the body of the not-yet-subject and that of its [m]other); and temporally (as the beginning before 'the Beginning,' the mobile origin 'before' the imposition of 'the Word')."[30] What I want to emphasize here is not so much the fact that *chōra* chronologically precedes "the Beginning" (the latter understood as the imposition of the paternal law), but rather the motility and temporality of *chōra* as such. Kristeva explains that "the semiotic *chora* is no more than the place where the subject is both generated and negated" (RPL 28), echoing Timaeus, who had suggested that *chōra* is "that *in which* these things individually show themselves as always coming into being and again *from which* they perish" (Tm 49E–50A). What could such a "thing" or "place" be other than time, or *chrōnos*: that which comes into being and passes away; that through which life is both generated and negated as we are born and die?

My argument is that *chōra*—in confronting us with a kind of time before time; time perceived as not-yet-measurable or countable—introduces to us time understood not in terms of measured regularity and calculated progress but rather as rhythmic oscillation, alteration, and displacement (a time of return). Rather than being non-ontological, then, we might say that *chōra* gives us an ontological foundation that is a non-foundation—it suggests the irreducibility of time and motility. Or, as Margaroni puts it, "the beginning itself is reinscribed *as* a process."[31] Language replaces the time of *chōra* with linear time: "The sign," Kristeva announces, "represses the *chora* and its eternal return."[32]

Through Timaeus's introduction of the second cause, we are made aware that the complexities of human life cannot be reduced to the movements of the celestial bodies alone. If our concerns lie solely with the head—spherical like the planets and the stars—we would be content with the preliminary account of time as measurement, as counting. But insofar as we care about human life in its fullness and complexity (which includes, for instance, embodiment and sexual difference, not just the head or the intellect alone), then we must turn to the irregular motion of *chōra*, to its eternal return, to revolutionary time.[33] Kristeva does associate *chōra* with the maternal body, but this does not, in my view, mean that she characterizes it as that which simply eternally escapes discourse, or that she essentializes the maternal in terms of a silent yet constitutive ground upon which the symbolic order is to be raised. I want to argue, instead, that she turns to *chōra* because of the way in which Plato describes it as corporeal and temporal both at once. The maternal body to which Kristeva urges us to return must be understood exactly

as a principle manifesting the inseparability of time and space—a point
that I will develop in what follows.

The specificity of Kristeva's work does not, in my mind, simply
amount to her emphasis on the material aspects of the origins of language and the subject, but rather the way in which she refuses to let
time and matter part ways, the way in which, for her, such a materialist
foundation always already is a temporal-material foundation.[34] Margaroni
describes *chōra* as "a materialist economy of the Beginning that permits
Kristeva to displace all transcendental forms of origin (the Word, the
divine *nous*, subjective will), at the same time, forcing us to rethink our
assumptions concerning the passivity and chaotic nature of matter."[35]
The maternal—for Plato and Kristeva alike—is thus no brute matter
waiting to be penetrated and impregnated. It is the locus of birth and
new beginnings. Marked by motility, ever-changing in nature, she is
time and generates temporal beings. A living rhythm to which we must
return if we want to nourish a culture of life and change rather than
one always already marked by repetition and death.


## Flesh Flash: On Time and Motherhood

Allow me, more specifically, to turn to Kristeva's characterization of
the maternal, in order to deepen my claim that it is a site that must
be understood in temporal terms, and to respond to some of the most
central feminist claims raised against her. As Butler has pointed out,
the "classical association of femininity with materiality can be traced
to a set of etymologies which link matter with *mater* and *matrix* (or the
womb) and, hence, with a problematic of reproduction."[36] She continues
to explain that matter either explicitly has been associated with reproduction, "as a site of *generation* and *origination*," or implicitly "generalized
as a principle of origination and causality": "In both the Latin and the
Greek," she concludes, "matter (*materia* and *hyle*) is neither a simple,
brute positivity or referent nor a blank surface or slate awaiting an external signification, but is always in some sense temporalized."[37] We know
this from the *Timaeus*, where we noted that the temporal movement of
*chōra* in some sense undermined its alleged status as a merely passive or
amorphous receiver. But what I want to show in what follows is that the
temporalization of matter must be understood not merely as generation
or origination—as the metaphysical tradition described by Butler would

have it—but that there are uniquely temporal aspects of materiality, ones that cannot be reduced simply to a logic of reproduction, and that in fact challenge causality as we tend to understand it. And yet, I want to do so precisely by returning to the mother.

In "Stabat Mater"—arguably her most important essay on maternity—Kristeva addresses the feminist view that she has reduced woman to the function of motherhood while simultaneously excluding the mother from the symbolic pact altogether.[38] She also clarifies what her own attempt to revisit the maternal amounts to:

> We are caught in a paradox. First, we live in a civilization where the *consecrated* (religious or secular) representation of femininity is absorbed by motherhood. If, however, one looks at it more closely, this motherhood is the *fantasy* that is nurtured by the adult, man or woman, of a lost territory, what is more, it involves less an idealized archaic mother than the idealization of the *relationship* that binds us to her, one that cannot be localized—an idealization of primary narcissism. Now, when feminism demands a new representation of femininity, it seems to identify motherhood with that idealized misconception and, because it rejects the image and its misuse, feminism circumvents the real experience that fantasy overshadows. The result?—a negation or rejection of motherhood by some avant-garde feminist groups. Or else an acceptance—conscious or not—of its traditional representations by the great mass of people, women and men.[39]

This passage, placed at the very beginning of her essay, needs some careful unpacking. I will do so by way of following the trajectory of the essay as a whole, one that in its very structure incorporates the two polar aspects of motherhood in our society: on the one hand the most idealized and phantasmatic of them all—the figure of the Virgin Mary—and on the other hand what Kristeva herself refers to as "the real experience that fantasy overshadows"—a poetic account of pregnancy and birth-giving grounded in her own personal (and hence singular) experience thereof. Kristeva, who neither wants to reject motherhood altogether (like the avant-garde feminists), nor accept its traditional representation (like the great mass of people), addresses the problematic reduction of femininity to what she calls *maternality*, and suggests that it represents a "masculine appropriation of the Maternal" integral to "masculine sublimation" (SM 236). The male subject would, as it were, try to tame maternal power through an act of appropriation—one maybe most clearly exemplified by a Socratic philosophy of midwifery.[40] "Phallic power," Kristeva writes elsewhere in *Tales of Love*, "would in short begin with an appropriation of archaic maternal power."[41]

But what about the actual mother? Is she ever real? And is there a way of approaching and articulating that reality? Kristeva asks if there is "something in that [phantasmatic] Maternal notion that ignores what a woman might say or want," and suggests that if there is, it should come as no surprise that "when women speak out today it is in matters of conception and motherhood that their annoyance is basically centered" (SM 236). While most of Kristeva's own thought on motherhood is situated within essays dealing with male authors and artists such as Marcel Proust, Louis-Férdinand Céline, Stéphane Mallarmé, Comte de Lautréamont, Giotto, or Giovanni Bellini, and the way in which sublimated forms of the maternal spring up in their respective work, "Stabat Mater" is her most explicit attempt to delve beyond the phantasmatic idealization of primary narcissism and instead articulate—from a woman's point of view—the very real experience of motherhood (to the extent that it can be experienced and articulated in a "real" way within our socio-symbolic context).

What, we must ask, is motherhood for Kristeva? How is this dark continent experienced and articulated? She opens the poetic-experiential part of her essay with one capitalized word—FLASH—followed by a qualification: "instant of time or of dream without time" (SM 234). From the very outset of her essay, the experience of motherhood is articulated, first and foremost, in temporal terms. And two notions of temporality surface: the instant (a rupture, we might say, in the seamless flow of linear time), and the timeless (which, as we saw in my discussion of the Freudian *Zeitlos* in chapter 6, is equivalent to revolutionary time rather than being a term for selfsame perfected eternity). In *This Incredible Need to Believe*, Kristeva calls "the maternal experience of temporality . . . a *duration with new beginnings*"—a characterization that sounds much like the "living present" that I have elaborated in this book.[42] And in the opening chapter of *Powers of Horror* she, again, uses the image of the flash: "forgotten time crops up suddenly and condenses into a flash of lightning an operation that, if it were thought out, would involve bringing together the two opposite terms but, on account of that flash, is discharged like thunder. The time of abjection is double: a time of oblivion and thunder, of veiled infinity and the moment when revelation bursts forth."[43]

The two types of time thus recur, both illustrated by the flash. On my reading, this flash is yet another instance of what I have called revolutionary time: the "instant" and the "timeless" amount to a movement of return marked by renewal and regeneration. This passage, moreover, brings forth another important aspect of maternal temporality, one that also should remind us of what has been said so far: it avoids the teleological movement of (Hegelian) synthesis ("bringing together the two opposite terms") and, instead, sustains difference and heterogeneity within the double time of abjection. Returning to "Stabat Mater," we find the articulation of this thought in the only other capitalized passage, this time consisting of two nouns—WORD FLESH—kept together or separate by no other term, no middle third that would allow them to merge. WORD FLESH: the paradigmatic opposites of a (patriarchal) cultural domain where, in Irigaray's words, paternal language can be instituted if and only if the "fertility of the earth is sacrificed" (BAB 16). Maternal time—integral to the very experience of motherhood—is one that respects and sustains difference and heterogeneity, challenging the linearity of (Hegelian) synthesis.[44] In addition, it challenges and bridges the gap between word and flesh (linear and cyclical time?), introducing instead the perpetual movement of return that denies neither of these aspects and that, for this very reason, can bring about renewal and change.

Kristeva describes the maternal as an "ambivalent principle" (SM 234–35) or a "see-saw" (SM 258), and notes that Christianity—"the most refined symbolic construct in which femininity . . . is focused on *Maternality*"—has attempted "to freeze that see-saw," to "stop it, tear women away from its rhythm, settle them permanently in the spirit" (SM 234, 259). She sees the very figure of Mary as an example of how motherhood has been cemented in a frozen image—pure (untouched) and infinite (immortal)—completely lacking both corporeal desire and the oscillating rhythms of maternal temporality. The consequence of such idealization is addressed by Irigaray: "The problem is that when the father refuses to allow the mother her power of giving birth and seeks to be the sole creator, then according to our culture he superimposes upon our ancient world of flesh and blood a universe of language and symbols that has no roots in the flesh and drills a hole through the female womb and through the place of female identity" (BAB 16). Patrilinearity is installed through a word detached from flesh (with word God created the world in the Hebrew Genesis), and woman is left with no other identities accessible to her than Maternity in its idealized form.[45]

As Kristeva has noted elsewhere, woman as mother is either *absent* or *idealized*: she is either depicted as a *hole* (the meaning of the Hebrew word for woman, *nekeva*) or as a divine or royal *whole* (in the form of the Virgin Mother).[46] The maternal to which we are called to return can be neither of these figures. As Kristeva sets out to search for the "lost time" of motherhood,[47] she seeks to articulate the reality of motherhood—or rather (and crucially) *a* reality of motherhood, namely her own—without thereby turning the mother into an essentialized or solidified figure. As we saw in my discussion of presence in part 3, revolutionary time avoids both absolute presence (idealization) and absolute absence (repression). It is conceived, precisely, as a temporal model that undermines these two extremes, and that refuses to reduce women—and mothers—to one or the other. Neither idealized nor forgotten, the mother, on Kristeva's account, is at once temporal and refuses the separation of word and flesh. Kristeva thus brings attention to the fact that we should view time not as an *escape* from the body (as in our linear paradigm), but as *dependent* on embodiment. Let me develop this thought as I respond to some criticisms raised by Butler in the final chapter of *Gender Trouble* (101–19).

## Temporalizing Mat(t)er:
## On the Interdependence Between Semiotic and Symbolic

In her reading of Kristeva, Butler raises what I see as two major concerns: first, she is skeptical of the subversive potential and emancipatory status of the semiotic as articulated by Kristeva; and second, she worries that Kristeva's alleged attempts to delimit "maternity as an essentially precultural reality," as she puts it, will lead to a reification of motherhood that precludes "an analysis of its cultural construction and variability" (GT 103). Butler worries that we would fail to see that this "outside" very well may be the effect or product of the very law or order from which it is said to be excluded. Put differently, "repression may be understood to produce the object that it comes to deny" (GT 119).

While I think Butler's worries are important—she in fact articulates some central and difficult challenges for feminist thought today, many of which have yet to be resolved—she misses the target due to some fundamental misconceptions of Kristeva's thought that run through her argument. The most important one, I think, is the characterization of Kristeva as someone who speaks of an unspeakable outside that is *prior to* and *opposed to* culture and the symbolic order. Kristeva's whole project, in my mind, is exactly a sustained attempt to *avoid* such oppositional and exclusive structures, which is why she consistently describes the semiotic and the symbolic as *co-dependent, co-existing, intertwined* (which is to say that they are irreducible to linear time). To further deepen this point, let me quote Beardsworth, who illustrates it by way of comparing Kristeva with Kant:

> Not only are intuitions without concepts blind—in Kristeva, semiotic content without symbolic form is mute, invisible, and deprived of a history. But concepts without intuitions are empty—in Kristeva, a linguistic, symbolic universe deprived of connections with the infrasymbolic representations of exposure to otherness, separateness, loss, and death, is one without meaning or values.[48]

Kristeva herself explains that the alleged exclusivity between the two realms is "relative, precisely because of the necessary dialectic between the two modalities of the signifying process, which is constitutive of the subject. Because the subject is always *both* semiotic *and* symbolic, no signifying system he produces can be either 'exclusively' semiotic or 'exclusively' symbolic, and is instead necessarily marked by an indebtedness to both" (RPL 24). When Butler speaks of the semiotic as "distinct from," or "in opposition to" the symbolic—descriptions that will come to inform the central claims of her own argument—she thus misconstrues a central aspect of Kristeva's work (GT 104, 114). To repeat what I have said already: for Kristeva, no meaning can be produced unless *both* modes are implicated, to a larger or lesser degree.[49]

Butler is by no means alone in characterizing Kristeva's work in this way. While Jacqueline Rose, to mention another example, begins by acknowledging that there is "no strict demarcation" between semiotic and symbolic, and that "the semiotic has to work through the very order of language it defies," she nevertheless goes on to claim that Kristeva's emphasis on the relation between mother and child "immediately produces a split between the order of the mother and of the father, giving to the first the privilege of the semiotic and separating it out from the culture in which it is inscribed," and then criticizes her for placing "the realm of the senses . . . outside of all history and form."[50] She worries that Kristeva assigns to the semiotic "the status of origin," and that she places it "beyond language,"[51] despite the fact that Kristeva has made it clear that "the position which takes the semiotic as heterogeneous does not arise from a concern to integrate some alleged concreteness, brute corporeality, or energy-in-itself into a language suspected of being too abstract. . . . *This semiotic is without primacy and has no place as origin.*"[52]

The semiotic, Kristeva insists, is a condition for *and* a product of the symbolic. The two are thus simultaneous and co-dependent:

> Although originally a precondition of the symbolic, the semiotic functions within signifying practices as the result of a transgression of the symbolic. Therefore the semiotic that "precedes" symbolization is only a *theoretical supposition* justified by the need for description. It exists in practice only within the symbolic and requires the symbolic break to obtain the complex articulation we associate with it in musical and poetic practices. (RPL 68)

She goes on to say that the semiotic "is always already social and therefore historical" (RPL 68), and that the semiotic *chōra* "is always already inevitably and inseparably symbolic" (RPL 96). There is thus nothing biologically "pure" about it, as Butler and others suggest, and the very question of (temporal) primacy is complicated by the manner in which Kristeva articulates the relationship between semiotic and symbolic.

We are, in other words, faced with a complicated chronology here, perhaps somewhat similar to the one we encountered in Plato's *Timaeus*, where time turned out to exist before it had been properly created. Kristeva goes from stating, early in *Revolution in Poetic Language*, that she wants to "keep the term *semiotic* to designate the operation that *logically and chronologically precedes* the establishment of the symbolic and its subject" (RPL 41, second emphasis mine). And yet, later on she will claim that while the "semiotic functioning is discernible *before* the mirror stage, *before* the first suggestion of the thetic," as signifying practice it nevertheless "always comes to us *after* the symbolic thesis, *after* the symbolic break" (RPL 68, emphasis mine). The interdependence between the semiotic and the symbolic thus complicates the question of causality. It is, as we see here, not at all clear that the semiotic precedes the symbolic, nor however the other way around, exactly because one cannot exist without the other.[53]

This thought might be explained by the very temporality of return: to "return" to the maternal or the semiotic does not simply mean to travel "backwards" in time, as this would assume a linear understanding of time as progress. The kind of oscillating movement at stake here cannot be thought of or articulated in simple causal terms. And this is why the semiotic lacks primacy, why it has "no place as origin." If we take seriously the interdependence between semiotic and symbolic, and if we think both in temporal terms, no such thing as a stable or singular origin can exist. We have seen already that the retroactive logic expressed here (articulated in my discussion of *Nachträglichkeit* in chapter 6) challenges and undermines both metaphysical presence and linear time, installing, instead, revolutionary time as that which propels us to seek a future through a perpetual return to our past, where our return to the past is always already shaped by our present.

It is interesting to note that Chanter, who takes very seriously the interdependence between the two realms and the implications thereof, does so with a reference to Kristeva's understanding of time: "The way in which Kristeva thematizes the problem of time suggests the need not only to continually rethink and revise feminist strategies, but also to reconceptualize the idea of history to which we unthinkingly appeal when we dub a certain thinker ahistorical."[54] Sjöholm, who also pays attention to the question of time in Kristeva's work, repeatedly emphasizes the interdependence between the two realms in her book *Kristeva and the Political.*[55] The judgment of Kristeva as an essentialist thinker may well be the result of a failure to see the role that time plays in her thought.

Kristeva herself concludes that we have to "represent the semiotic . . . as a '*second*' *return* of instinctual functioning within the symbolic, as a negativity introduced into the symbolic order, and as the transgression of that order" (RPL 69, emphasis mine). Such a return and negation, she explains, should not be confused with a Hegelian dialectic: "This explosion of the semiotic in the symbolic is far from a negation of negation, an *Aufhebung* that would suppress the contradiction generated by the thetic and establish in its place an ideal positivity, the restorer of pre-symbolic immediacy. It is, instead, a *transgression* of position, a reversed reactivation of the contradiction that instituted this very position" (RPL 69). The tension is kept in place, as is the difference that it generates. And the two positions are never mutually exclusive, never "pure."[56]

From the outset of her critical response to Kristeva, Butler brings our attention to what she sees as a subversive failure in her work: "By relegating the source of subversion to a site outside of culture itself, Kristeva appears to foreclose the possibility of subversion as an effective or realizable cultural practice" (GT 112). She complains that Kristeva reinforces the hegemony of the paternal law, and suggests that, following Kristeva, "a full-scale refusal of the Symbolic" would be impossible, and that "a discourse of 'emancipation'" would be "out of the question" (GT 109). First of all, I am not sure what a "full-scale refusal of the Symbolic" would mean, whether it is possible on Butler's own account, and whether it is even desirable.[57] For Kristeva, as we have seen, poetic language is "the ultimate means of its [the symbolic order's] *transformation* and *subversion*, the precondition for its *survival* and *revolution*" (RPL 81, emphasis mine). Subversion, on her account, means *transformation*, not complete breakdown or erasure. The latter is both impossible and undesirable. And the aim of poetic language, as I read her, is therefore not to *destroy* the symbolic order, but rather to allow it to *survive*—a term which I suggest that we must understand quite literally as the sustainability and injection of *life* and *aliveness* into discourse, as opposed to a kind of mechanical and dead discourse that would reproduce itself eternally and exclude alterity and alteration altogether.[58] In fact, Kristeva warns us of the potential danger inherent in the transgressive element of artistic creation, and calls for a "structurally necessary protection, one that serves to check negativity, confine it within the stases, and prevent it from sweeping away the symbolic position" (RPL 69–70). We recognize the sweeping movement ascribed to *chōra* in the *Timaeus*, one that simultaneously shakes beings into their appropriate place and sweeps them into the "prodigious river" of sensible life (Tm 43A). The point, it seems to me, is to give room for the roaring current that keeps us alive and sensible, but to avoid drowning in that river or entering the land of schizophrenia.[59]

I take it, moreover, that Kristeva's acknowledgment of the impossibility of a "full-scale refusal of the Symbolic" has to do exactly with the fact that the semiotic, for her, lies precisely *not* outside or beyond the symbolic in the sense Butler wants us to think. It is exactly because it is always already *part of* the symbolic order (formed and deformed by it) that the semiotic is bound in some sense to fail; that it cannot fully undermine it (although we should note, again, that such "failure" is no real failure, since complete demolition of the symbolic in any event would not be desirable). Similarly, it is because of this interdependence that the symbolic, in turn, can never fully rid itself of the semiotic; why semiotic drives and rhythms are bound to resurface and reemerge in language no matter how much we try to repress and silence them.

If we take seriously Kristeva's attempt to think the semiotic and symbolic as standing together—just like the two causes were standing together in the *Timaeus*—we will begin to see not only the emancipatory potential of her work, but also how it cannot be said to assume a self-identical or essential "outside" that governs yet somehow escapes language. Kristeva does not, as Butler suggests, call for a fully finalized "liberation . . . from the shackles of paternal law"—such a liberation would, as Butler herself has carefully pointed out, be the equivalent of psychosis for Kristeva (GT 119). There is no "negating or denying the symbolic" for Kristeva, since without it the speaking subject "would be incapable of doing anything" (RPL 63). This by no means implies that the symbolic order is static or unchangeable. The presence of semiotic drives forces signification to renew itself, and the more we allow ourselves to return to and carve out a space for semiotic drives, the more we will be able, not to destroy, but to alter and transgress the Law—this is why poetic language carries political and revolutionary weight.[60] And this, of course, is completely in line with Butler's own Foucauldian analysis of the power of discourse. As she herself states in the opening pages of *Gender Trouble*: "Obviously the political task is not to refuse representational politics—as if we could. The juridical structures of language and politics constitute the contemporary field of power; hence, there is no position outside this field, but only a critical genealogy of its own legitimating practices" (GT 8).

What Kristeva calls for is a more integrated and balanced relationship between the two modalities of language: semiotic *and* symbolic. The interdependence between the two is, for her, a fact. The question remains whether we are willing to acknowledge and embrace this interdependence and give voice to both aspects. The narrative we saw unfold in Plato's *Timaeus* does, in fact, account for and even celebrate this duality. Most philosophy after Plato does not—which is probably why the passage on *chōra* stands out as such a strange and foreign passage as far as philosophical discourse is concerned. It literally gives voice to that which henceforth will lack a place within philosophy proper, having been relegated into poetic language alone (perhaps the fulfillment of Plato's own alleged desire to exile poetry from the city ruled by philosophers).

A helpful way of problematizing the relationship between semiotic and symbolic, and one that I think clarifies my critique of Butler, appears in Chanter's essay "Kristeva's Politics of Change." Chanter interestingly suggests that the two realms can be compared to the distinction between sex and gender, a division that has been scrutinized and questioned by Butler herself in books such as *Bodies That Matter*. If traditionally sex has been viewed as static and "natural" while gender has been understood as "cultural" and subject to change, Butler was among the first to question this distinction, pointing instead to the fact that sex, too, is constructed and, therefore, subject to change. Chanter asserts that "it is no longer so clear where sex stops and culture starts, since our very definition of sex is always already bound up in cultural assumptions—just as semiotic expression is always already bound up with the symbolic order."[61] Chanter is thus suggesting that "Kristeva's semiotic/symbolic distinction acknowledges the need not only to unsettle the sex/gender distinction"—which would be perfectly in line with Butler's own project—"but also to bring into question received ideas about the difference between nature and culture that often underlie mistaken notions about the ease with which gender can be siphoned off from sex."[62]

Chanter herself, however, only goes so far as to admit that the "truths" of science (and thus of the nature of "sex") must be constantly adjusted in light of new discoveries (the way we conceptualize reproduction, for example, inevitably changes with the rapid development of reproductive technologies, and so motherhood too is bound to change). I would push the logic one step further, and turn her epistemological argument into an ontological one. What is at stake, in my view, is the very definition of nature as something static, something that repeats sameness (a notion that would remain intact even if our *knowledge* of some particular aspects of nature—such as the status of reproduction—changes), while culture is viewed as subject to change and variation (it is not only our *knowledge* of culture, but culture *itself*, that is understood as ever-changing). As we saw already in the opening of this book, and as I will emphasize again when I turn to Irigaray in the next chapter, the very distinction between static nature and a culture of change is undermined and perverted by the temporal logic that is unleashed as we return to the maternal body.

∽

Let me pause here to note some consequences of this for the very status of embodiment and corporeality as they have been treated both by
the metaphysical tradition and by Butler in her critique of Kristeva. As
we compare the metaphysical tradition with a feminist anti-essentialist
account à la Butler we are, in my mind, faced with something like a
paradox with regard to the question of the body. Schematically speaking,
we might say that the traditional mind-body dualistic account treats
the body with suspicion exactly because it changes, because it is finite,
because it is temporal. If the body is associated with the sensible and with
phenomena, the mind, by contrast, is aligned with the intelligible, which,
in turn, is perceived as eternally perfected, as immutable and exempt
from the movement of time and from decay. If the body is "natural,"
then we might say that it is nature, on this account, that changes, while
the human mind (or the soul) remains intact. The latter, as we know, is
given priority and comes to represent the truth. The body, consequently,
is viewed as a "problem" to be solved: Cartesian skepticism originates in
the untrustworthy status of bodily sensibility.

If the metaphysical tradition grants privilege to selfsame Being,
contemporary feminist critics are prone instead to esteem becoming, since
they view in it the potential for change and liberation. When Beauvoir
introduced the category of gender by stating that we are not born but
rather *become* women, she did so not only as an attempt to show how
patriarchy has "created" women, but also as a gesture toward the possibility for change: if we have *become women* we can *become otherwise*; no
essential circumstances define us as such (to use Butlerian language we
might say that if gender is *done* it can just as well be *undone*[63]). For *this*
tradition, paradoxically, the body (sex) becomes a problem too: Butler's
critique of Kristeva—and many subsequent feminist critiques of Irigaray—is exactly that their respective philosophies allegedly posit the body
as a pre-cultural essence that imprisons us. On this account, the body
("sex") comes to represent static essence while the mind ("gender") is
seen as a cultural category capable of transcendence and transformation.
Nature is thus viewed as static while culture is subject to change. It is,
arguably, this very view that *Bodies That Matter* (and Butler's work as a
whole) sets out to complicate.

If the metaphysical tradition grants privilege to non-temporal Being
while its feminist critics prefer temporal becoming, both end up mar-
ginalizing the body (the former sees in the body a locus for undesirable

change, while the latter regards it as problematically static). A feminist theory striving to reevaluate and recover the body without ascribing to human subjects essential sexed characteristics would, in my mind, have to draw the best from both traditions: the metaphysical insight that bodies change, and the feminist insight that change can be liberating. It should be clear how viewing matters in this way has practical implications for example thinking trans embodiment without appealing to dualist and essentializing conceptions of sexuate identity and embodiment. The lived reality of trans folk puts pressure on feminist theory to think embodiment in constitutively temporal terms, and to render flexible and open to transformation not only conceptions about "culture" and "gender," but equally so "nature" and "sex."

I want to again emphasize that nothing is immutable and eternal. Both nature and culture are finite and in a process of becoming. To "become woman" (using again the famous expression from Beauvoir) does not mean that we are just socially constructed and lack material bodies. It means that our bodies are in constant becoming *and* that culture imposes normalizing modes of becoming upon us.[64] And this, in turn, means that we are free but by no means sovereign or autonomous. We are, literally, subjects-in-process, and as such we are both *submitted to* and *capable of* change. The body, as I have already suggested, is a limit but not a negative one. It is a limit understood as a horizon of possibilities: insofar as we are sexed (to have a body is to be sexed), we are able to become and to flourish. Without sexual difference, we would merely repeat ourselves infinitely, and would thus be more dead than alive.[65]

If critics of Irigaray have worried that her emphasis on sexuate difference imprisons us in a dualist framework that fails to account for the manifold genders and sexualities that are a lived reality, we might read Irigaray as emphasizing sexuate difference exactly because a world of two would make possible multiplicity, whereas the paradigm of the same (which we have hitherto been confined to) forecloses multiplicity altogether in that it can produce nothing but an identical mime or copy. Thinkers who seek to embrace plurality and multiplicity are, in her mind, bound to fall short of this ambition, since they remain within the logic of the same: it is only if they *first* acknowledge the duality of sexuate difference that they might proceed to theorize or live multiplicity in the true sense of the term, beyond the binary. That bodies are temporal and sexed is, again, not a negative limitation but a horizon of possibilities: "The duality of the sexes allows modifications, transmutation, transpositions, so that a relationship can happen," Irigaray suggests in one of her early essays.[66]

What I have tried to show is that Kristeva, contrary to what Butler suggests, views the materiality of the body and of language as a dynamic process, one marked by rhythm and oscillation. Insofar as the body is alive it is no stable entity or essence. We might thus say that bodies, on Kristeva's account, *materialize* (a notion articulated by Butler in *Bodies That Matter*). But if Butler understands materialization first and foremost in terms of social construction, the focus for Kristeva, as I have tried to show, is the temporality of matter itself: that bodies change and that change is embodied. And that any account that separates "culture" from "nature" by positing one as stable and the other as being in constant flux is unable to properly think the complex relationship between two realms that are both subject to infinite temporalization.

∽

Before turning to Irigaray in more detail, we must however address two important questions raised by Butler in her critique of Kristeva: why choose the figure of motherhood to speak of repressed aspects of discourse; and is it the case that this maternal can be assumed to be "repressed"—or is it not rather a "compulsory cultural construction," one that assumes "the female body *as* a maternal body," as Butler has suggested (GT 115)? At this point I want to turn again to "Stabat Mater," and the way in which I proposed that we read this essay as an account of maternity expressed in terms of temporality.

Butler asks: "What grounds, then, does Kristeva have for imputing a maternal teleology to the female body prior to its emergence into culture" (GT 115)? As we have seen, the term "prior" would need some elaboration and qualification here. As I have argued, there is no simple relationship between "before" and "after" or "inside" and "outside" for Kristeva.[67] That said, however, Kristeva herself does make what looks like a distinction between the archaic mother of the semiotic *chōra*, on the one hand, and the idealized and fantasmatic mother that emerges out of the symbolic order as mere symbol, image, or icon, on the other. While both depend on the symbolic order, it does seem like the former is somehow more "authentic" or "originary" than the latter.[68] As we have seen, Kristeva did not want to reject motherhood altogether (like avant-garde feminists), but she also did not want to accept its traditional representation (like the great mass of people). It seems as if she wants to say that the maternal body is *both repressed and compulsory*, depending on what we mean when we speak of it.

Let me begin by addressing the latter of these two: The "traditional representation" of motherhood—I think Kristeva would argue in agreement with Butler—is compulsory in ways that delimit women and ascribe to them a predefined set of expectations upon which their subjectivity depends. This narrow (yet universalized) notion of maternity is thus something that Kristeva is as critical of as Butler. As I see it, it is not the case, as Butler suggests, that Kristeva assumes "a true body beyond the law" (GT 119). In fact Kristeva, in line with Butler, describes embodiment as a process of signification. The human body, she asserts, cannot "function biologically and physiologically, unless it is included within a practice that encompasses the signifying process. Without such a practice, the body in process/on trial is disarticulated; its drives tear it up into stymied, motionless sectors and it constitutes a weighty mass. Outside the process, its only identity is inorganic, paralyzed, dead" (RPL 101). The alleged "true body beyond the law" would be nothing but a piece of dead meat. Matter, to use a Butlerian expression, in this case would not matter.[69]

But at the same time it should be clear by now that the maternal body (understood otherwise) in fact *is* repressed, and that Kristeva finds this repression or loss problematic. Insofar as we speak of maternity as a certain kind of corporeal-temporal experience—manifested in the rhythms and oscillations that emerge through the semiotic modality of language—it is, on Kristeva's account, to a large extent made invisible to the point of erasure (matricide) in our culture. It is when speaking of this kind of maternity—the repressed version—that we must ask why we should keep using the image of the mother, instead of just speaking of a different kind of language or temporal experience, if that is what ultimately is at stake.

The point, as I see it, is not that all women are or should be mothers, but rather that all human beings, at least as of yet, are of mothers born. Our refusal to acknowledge our dual origins is exactly what installs the patrilineal conception of time that has come to dominate Western discourse. At stake, then (as we have seen already in my discussion of Irigaray), is our own acknowledgment of being born, of having been generated, of springing forth from a dual origin. Through the figure of the mother, we are able to rethink the relationship between temporality and corporeality—not, as one might think, through a reductive equation of the maternal with corporeality and the paternal with time—but exactly thanks to the way in which the maternal body brings our attention to the *continuity* between time and matter. That time is embodied and that bodies are temporal.

This, on my reading, was what Timaeus was trying to express as he introduced *chōra*, which is why he inevitably resorted to maternal images when doing so. And this, in my view, is what Kristeva is seeking to express in her work, which is why she returns to the notion of *chōra* and then further elaborates her concerns with language, embodiment, and time, using the maternal body as her point of departure. As she herself suggests in one of her early essays: "Rhythm, a sequence of linked instants, is immanent to the *chora* prior to any signified spaciousness: henceforth, *chora* and rhythm, space and time, coexist."[70] The introduction of *chōra* thus allows Kristeva (and—perhaps more surprisingly—Plato) to challenge any traditional notion of *archē* as stable and selfsame and, more importantly, as being inherently paternal. By including the maternal function in our account of our beginnings we assure that beginnings be seen both as mobile and plural (more about this in the next chapter).

We can also say, following Burchill, that "it is precisely to the extent that the 'images' conveyed by the tradition show a singular association of women [and even more so, mothers] with space (or, conversely, of space with a 'feminine principle') that these images constitute such a propitious source for the philosophers seeking to formulate another 'articulation' of what is named 'time.' "[71] On this account, the very attempt to re-articulate spatiotemporality in ways that challenge the millennia-long tradition of separating time and space (associating the former with the self-conscious mind, while ascribing embodiment to the latter), inevitably forces us to return to the very place where this division has been inscribed and assumed; to, as it were, reclaim that place in corporeal-temporal terms. Burchill continues:

> It would then be the fact that "women" have traditionally been linked to space—i.e. to an order "outside of time" and, hence, "outside of the sign"—that explains why "the feminine" [or maternal], as a conceptual persona translating this socio-historical link into a thought-event, is able to schematize a "process" that seeks to circumvent the categories of metaphysical discourse establishing presence as the value determining the complicity of time and the sign.[72]

Kristeva herself, as we have seen, ascribes what she calls "*rhythmic agency*" to the maternal, and puts it in contrast with "time as evolutive *duration*," explicitly characterizing the former as "metered time, spatialized, volume rather than line."[73] What we get, by turning to the maternal body, is what we might call a three-dimensional account of time not simply reduced to a uni-directional line. The two parallel columns of "Stabat Mater"—one depicting the lived and embodied (three-dimensional) experience of motherhood, the other unraveling and deconstructing an idealized (two-dimensional) image of Maternity—could be seen as representing these two versions of time: the rhythmic volume and the evolutive line. The former, Kristeva explains, is bound to crop up "to remind one of what is at work beneath repression: the cost at which repression (duration—or history, to put it briefly) achieves its goal as the fulfillment of a sociocultural contract."[74]

Such eruption, while incapable of destroying the social contract altogether and once and for all in a Butlerian manner (not that I take Butler to strive for this—far from it—but it seems as if it is what she demands of Kristeva), in my mind has significant emancipatory and transformational potential. Put differently, it is *revolutionary*. It moreover challenges and reformulates what we thought of as maternal in the first place—allowing us to rethink not only our relationship to our mothers, but also to time and space as intrinsically inseparable. What comes to bind *word* and *flesh*—just as *chōra* in the *Timaeus* allowed for a passage between concepts and living bodies—is the *flash* that is time and space at once: revolutionary time. Three capitalized terms structuring Kristeva's own experience of motherhood: WORD. FLESH. FLASH.

## Conclusion

In this chapter, I have sought to provide as detailed as possible an account of what Kristeva means when she speaks of motherhood, and tie it to the theme of temporalization that runs through this book. I started with a paradox, namely that the maternal is both idealized and repressed in our culture, and traced Kristeva's attempt to offer a three-dimensional middle ground—one where the singularity of an embodied maternal experience can be expressed, temporally.

Kristeva's attempt at returning to the maternal body famously takes as its point of departure a concept from the Platonic corpus, namely *chōra*. This concept first appears in Plato's *Timaeus*, and is put to use by Kristeva in *Revolution in Poetic Language*, where it is explicitly associated with the maternal body. While it may seem strange that Plato serves as an interlocutor for Kristeva's discussion of motherhood, in this chapter I have offered a careful analysis of why and how she returns to his work in her own search for the lost mother in our culture. I have examined Kristeva's account of *chōra* in order to clarify what I think she means by the maternal, and to tie it to questions of time and temporalization in ways that I believe undermine the charges of essentialism raised against her on this point. If *chōra* most commonly has been understood as a "receptacle" or "container," through my somewhat idiosyncratic reading of Plato I have shown that *chōra*, and the maternal body that both Plato and Kristeva associate it with, is far from a receiver passively awaiting penetration or fulfillment. Instead, I emphasized the temporal characteristics that both thinkers ascribe to it, and this, in turn, allowed me to elaborate what I believe is a more nuanced account of the relationship between materiality and temporality than the one we get from within the linear-cyclical paradigm.

Subsequently I offered a novel interpretation of Kristeva's account of motherhood in her essay "Stabat Mater"—one that ultimately shows that, here too, a reading of Kristeva that emphasizes her attention to time and temporal matters allows us to revise our understanding of her work and to cast new light on her famous elaboration of the lived experience of motherhood. Refusing the dichotomy between an idealized version of motherhood (embodied in the Virgin Mother) and the rejection of motherhood (the feminist notion that liberation depends on a refusal of it), Kristeva sets out to articulate a conception of motherhood that straddles such dichotomies, liminally, by way of radically temporalizing the very experience of motherhood rather than (again) reducing mothers to passive-spatial receptacles. My argument here thus mirrors my claim in the section on the present that women have been reduced to either presence or absence, and that such reduction is the result of our current temporal regimes and paradigms. This has, inevitably, tainted our understanding of motherhood too (in patriarchal and feminist accounts alike), and I read Kristeva as attempting to offer a more three-dimensional account of motherhood, irreducible to such false dichotomies.

Finally, I moved on to offer a critical reading of Butler's analysis of Kristeva on the topic of motherhood, as it appears in the final chapter of *Gender Trouble*. At stake here was, again, to read Kristeva as refusing dichotomies and dualisms—including that between symbolic and semiotic—and to show that her insistence on the simultaneity and co-dependence of these two registers is tied to her insistence on the time of motherhood as being neither linear-progressive nor cyclical-repetitive, but rather revolutionary. My analysis here served to clarify how and why our return to the maternal body in temporal terms allows us to articulate a more complex account of embodiment in general as always already marked by becoming and change. As such, my analysis of motherhood in this chapter can hopefully be helpful for thinking embodiment beyond maternal embodiment, such as when we grapple with trans embodiment and issues having to do with the relationship between sex and gender more broadly construed. While Kristeva's explicit analysis has limitations in this regard—as we saw already in the previous chapter—her work nevertheless offers important resources, especially if we take seriously the temporal language embedded in her analysis of motherhood.

Let me turn now to Irigaray's return to the mother, which, like Kristeva's, will unfold through a reading of Plato. Irigaray too returns to the *Timaeus* in her search for mothers lost, but more importantly and explicitly she invites us to descend into the mythical cave from Plato's *Republic*. Our journey, however, will not end there. The time has come to embark on a rather labyrinthic expedition, as we unravel, again, the nature of the return that revolutionary time entails.

# 9

# Motherhood According to Irigaray

If Kristeva organized her search for mother (and time) lost around the early semiotic-symbiotic relationship between mother and child (a relationship that we have articulated first and foremost in terms of its residual traces in language and symbolization), Irigaray, in her search for the buried mother, moves beyond that early founding of the socio-symbolic order in search for our most archaic beginnings. When speaking of the maternal, she does so, on the one hand, by envisioning a pre-patriarchal kind of terrain, one not yet severed by a masculine logos; and on the other hand through examples of pregnant embodiment, as opposed to the early relationship between mother and (already born) child. She revisits the womb ("the primal place in which we become body" and "that first nurse") and the placenta ("that first home" and "primary safety zone"), as she elaborates what she has famously coined the placental economy (BAB 15–16).[1]

Readings of Irigaray and Kristeva tend to differentiate the two by claiming that the latter accepts the traditional psychoanalytic view of primary fusion between mother and child, followed by a separation made possible by the paternal law, while the former more rigorously emphasizes originary difference and thus the fact that separation need not take place. It is true that Irigaray often explicitly emphasizes the heterogeneous relationship between mother and child already *in utero*. This is the most important implication of the placental economy, here articulated by Hélène Rouch in an interview conducted by Irigaray:

First of all, I'll digress to look at psychoanalysis, which justifies
the imaginary fusion between a child and its mother by the
undeveloped state of the child at birth and by its absolute need
of the other, its mother. It's this fusion, implicitly presented as
an extension of the organic fusion during pregnancy, which,
it would seem, simply has to be broken in order for the child
to be constituted as subject. The rupture of this fusion by a
third term—whether it's called the father, law, Name of the
Father, or something else—should facilitate entry into the
symbolic and access to language. This third term supposedly
avoids the fusion that would lead into the chaos of psychosis,
and is said to guarantee order. But surely all that's needed is
to reiterate and mark, on another level, *a differentiation that
already exists during pregnancy thanks to the placenta*, and at the
moment of birth, as a result of the exit from the uterine cavity?
It seems to me that *the differentiation between the mother's self
and the other of the child, and vice versa, is in place well before
it's given meaning in and by language*, and the forms it takes
don't necessarily accord with those our cultural imaginary
relays: loss of paradise, traumatizing expulsion or exclusion,
etc. I'm not accusing these forms of the imaginary of being
wrong, but of being the only ways of theorizing what exists
before language. It makes one wonder about this remarkable
blindness to the process of pregnancy, and especially to the
particular role of the placenta, even though nowadays they're
quite familiar.[2]

Rouch's comments here serve as a starting point for Irigaray's own
relational ontology of difference. The point is that the placenta offers
an *organized economy*, and as such it inscribes otherness from the very
beginning (Irigaray even speaks of an *ethical* relation on the level of the
fetus).[3] While the commonly held view is that the placenta is half-ma-
ternal and half-fetal, it is in fact a tissue independent of both mother
and child, one that plays a mediating role between the two. Irigaray
thus challenges the traditional view that subject-formation takes place
through the entry into language (and that all is chaos and fusion prior
to that point), and develops instead a theory of subjectivity—and intersubjectivity—independent from the thetic break so central for Kristeva.

As I hope to have shown in my discussion of Kristeva, however, she also acknowledges the originary status of heterogeneity insofar as she ascribes temporal-differentiating character to the earliest relationship between mother and child. While it is true that she speaks of matricide as a vital necessity, and while she puts more emphasis on the entry into the symbolic order than Irigaray does, her thinking can nevertheless not be reduced to a traditional psychoanalytic account about primary fusion or wholeness.[4] As Kristeva herself has noted: *"there is an other* right from the beginning."[5] And the many instances in which she ascribes rhythmicity, heterogeneity, sweeping movement, and temporal change to our pre-oedipal relations attests to the fact that she, like Irigaray, challenges any notion of originary wholeness or oneness.[6] *Chōra*, as we have seen, is for Kristeva an ordering principle, just like the placenta is for Irigaray.[7]

Irigaray, too, turns to Plato to bespeak the matricide that founds our culture. It is on this aspect of her work that I will focus primarily in what follows, and more specifically on the theme already examined in the previous chapter, namely the temporal aspects of the maternal, and the fact that these elements specifically have been lost and must be retrieved if we are to establish a vital culture of change and renewal. While I point to several similarities between Kristeva and Irigaray in this context, it should be clear that their respective return to Plato is distinctive, and that their motivations for turning to the Platonic corpus are quite different. Kristeva finds a concept (or rather a non-concept, since *chōra* is explicitly described as such) in Plato's work that she appropriates or assimilates into her own for reasons already stated in the previous chapter. In the process she raises several critical concerns, but her engagement with Plato is not first and foremost critical in nature—she uses his work rather as a springboard to develop her own theory of poetic revolution and subject formation. Irigaray's work can also be described as appropriative—she uses the cave allegory in Plato's *Republic* in order to articulate some core aspects of her own philosophical program—but her act of appropriation is in part meant to say something very critical of, precisely, the way in which Plato (among the other male canonical figures with whom she engages) has founded his own thought on an act of appropriation (in this context an appropriation of motherhood specifically).

If Kristeva finds the remedy for our archaic loss in Plato's corpus (*chōra* is exactly that to which we must return in order to give life back to the mother), Irigaray instead ascribes to his philosophy (and in this context the famous cave allegory from the *Republic*) the poison that killed the mother in the first place. Or, as Jones puts it, the myth of the cave "is archetypal insofar as it inscribes forgetting of the maternal, and consequently of sexual difference, into the foundational structures of western metaphysics."[8] While Irigaray's reading, moreover, focuses on a very specific passage from the Platonic corpus, we might say that what is at stake for her is to expose the predicaments of the entire philosophical tradition that has followed (her critique, we might say, is aimed more at "Platonism" than at Plato himself). Despite their different motivations and strategies, however, I find it fruitful to juxtapose their respective engagement with Plato in order to draw out some central similarities in what they have to say about the maternal, our return to it, and the temporal dimension associated with it.

In my reading of Irigaray, I will primarily focus on her essay "Plato's *Hystera*," which appeared in *Speculum of the Other Woman*, published the same year as Kristeva's *Revolution in Poetic Language*.[9] Both books, as I see it, contain the seeds for the central arguments elaborated by these two thinkers in their work to follow, and so I find it fruitful to return to these works in an attempt to understand their projects at large. So, let us again return to the beginning, as we search for our (maternal) beginnings.

## Plato's Cave Revisited: An Impossible Metaphor

In "Plato's *Hystera*," Irigaray offers a rather unconventional reading of the famous myth of the cave from book 7 of Plato's *Republic*.[10] It seems worth noting that *Speculum of the Other Woman* is a book the very structure of which follows a movement of return, as Irigaray begins with a reading of Freud and ends with a critique of Plato. In-between these two long chapters are several shorter ones that treat some of the most canonical of Western philosophical texts.[11] And yet, she opens the final essay by suggesting that the myth of the cave—the famous passage from Plato's *Republic* that she is about to deconstruct—"is a good place to start" (PH 243). A starting point it is, yet one that will reveal itself to be no beginning at all. From the outset, Irigaray urges us to be cautious as we enter the mythical cave: "Read it this time as a metaphor of the inner space, of the den, the womb or *hystera*, sometimes of the earth—though we shall see that the text inscribes the metaphor as, strictly speaking, impossible" (PH 243). Wherein lies the impossibility of the metaphor? Why is this beginning no beginning at all? And what might it nevertheless teach us about our lost maternal beginnings?

The passage is widely familiar: Socrates envisions "an image of our nature in its education and want of education," and goes on to depict humans as prisoners "in an underground cave-like dwelling with its entrance, a long one, open to the light."[12] Tied since childhood by their legs and necks, the prisoners, who are "like us,"[13] are released by the philosopher and dragged into the light of the world outside, where they come to realize that what they had taken to be real and true was nothing but shadows projected on the back wall of the cave. What they have known hitherto, as Irigaray puts it, has been nothing but "phantoms, fakes or, at best, images" (PH 300), while the world outside houses the forms or ideas (*eidos*) of things as they truly are. The journey out of the cave is a journey away from our perceptions of an ever-changing temporal-material realm of becoming to true knowledge about the everlasting eternal-abstract realm of Being.

Clearly, Plato's text does bring images of childbirth to mind. Delivered by the philosopher-midwife, the prisoners are released into the world of ideas, leaving the dark realm of shadows behind. While Plato himself uses the word *antron* (cave) rather than *hystera* (womb) to name the underground dwelling, he was clearly not unaware of the similarities between the journey he describes and the event of childbirth. His description of the strenuous and disorienting passage into the world above is remarkably similar to the laborious journey of the infant out of the womb and birth canal.[14] It is worth noting, however, that while birth is naturally a *descent*—the force of gravity delivers us toward the earth—the journey here is depicted as an *ascent* toward the world above. On Irigaray's reading, the prisoners of the cave defy gravity as they ascend into the realm of ideas. They are all able to pass through the little dividing wall within the cave, which, according to Irigaray, "can be passed only by sublimation" (PH 283), and so the world becomes "peopled by ghosts" (PH 282), by people whose bodies have been sublated into "air, smoke, vapor" (PH 283)—pure spirit?[15]

Something has been reversed—and indeed we see this very reversal reflected in current mainstream birthing practices where birth rarely is allowed to follow the course of gravity (as was the common practice when midwives were still in charge and birthing stools were used), but has been placed in the hands of obstetricians who, precisely, place laboring women in a passive horizontal position such that they can deliver the newborn "against" gravity, with the help of epidurals, forceps, and other man-made tools. As Adrienne Rich has pointed out, these changes are the result of a move away from a female culture of midwifery to a male culture of medical obstetrics.[16] We might say that Plato's work offers a philosophical precursor to such shifts in birthing practices. Recall how Socrates describes his philosophical vocation in the *Theaetetus*: "My art of midwifery is in general like theirs [real midwives]; the only difference is that my patients are men, not women, and my concern is not with the body but with the soul that is in travail of birth."[17] The birth witnessed here is not a birth of the body, and it is articulated precisely as a voyage *away* from the material realm.

For Irigaray, such an ascent is a form of death rather than an event of birth. In an attempt to escape the finitude of the body in search for eternal truth, the philosopher instead escapes life, since finitude is a condition for life. And as a consequence, the mother becomes reduced to a container for fake offspring: "Engendering the real is the father's task, engendering the fictive is the task of the mother—that 'receptacle' for turning out more or less good copies of reality" (PH 300).[18] The womb left behind—and the mother thus forgotten—becomes a tomb in which Plato, on Irigaray's reading, buries the "fake offspring" reflected on the back wall of the cave (PH 255). Meanwhile, the world above is a world of selfsame ideas that crucially have *not* been engendered at all: "*The offspring of Truth become bastards*," Irigaray notes. "No one knows what origin, what originating being to attribute them to. Orphans of a simple, pure—and Ideal—origin" (PH 293). Irigaray associates this disembodied ideal with a paternal figure who, she claims, "will hold the monopoly on procreation" (PH 274), as he "copulates himself indefinitely without any alteration" (PH 347). Copulation in sameness leads to the pure copula of Being, which bans alteration, difference, and change. As the machine in Irigaray's essay "The Female Gender," it "never creates or engenders life" (107). What we have before us is the kind of technological mimesis that repeats sameness, rather than the subversive or revolutionary mimesis of which we spoke in chapter 2 (in relation to the artwork of Kara Walker) as a creative repetition of difference, a process of displacement, playfulness, and alteration.

As we have seen, in "The Female Gender," Irigaray points to the fact that nature, because it "always has a sex," is generative and ever-changing, while the machine, which "has no sex," is bound to eternally repeat itself (FG 107). She thus challenges the stereotypical conception of nature as static or essential, vis-à-vis a dynamic culture of change. We may say, as we turn to Plato again, that the sensible is the realm of becoming and change while the intelligible is that static realm safe-guarded against the instability of temporal becoming.[19] And yet, such a parallel immediately falls back into the age-long equation of culture and change, since, while the sensible at first glance may be thought of as "natural," it in fact cannot be understood in such terms on Plato's account at all. As we have seen, the sensible realm is rather described in terms of artifact and performance—a man-made artificial world that points to culture more than anything. Nature, Irigaray asserts, will henceforth be relegated to the world above, and "will be solved in this way. By means of comparisons, analogies, metaphors which claim to make her present, to represent her, with a 'bonus' of truth if you like, but you could equally say with a 'bonus' of fantasy. By eclipsing her" (PH 277).

If the cave represents the maternal womb, and the journey toward the truth necessarily involves our turning away from the cave and the mother-matter that it represents, then clearly the founding moment of philosophy involves a denial of the mother's engendering powers. How, Irigaray asks, "can one return into the cave, the den, the earth? Rediscover the darkness of all that has been left behind? Remember the forgotten mother?" (PH 345). But given Socrates's own emphasis on the need to *return* to the cave, it is not at all clear how the journey constitutes *matricide*, or how it would lead us to *forget* our maternal origins. The task of the philosopher is, after all, to make the laborious journey *back* into the cave, time and again. How are we to make sense of this important fact? How does Irigaray account for the movement of return that is so crucially inscribed in the Platonic myth?

We must recall that something is upside-down in this story. If we simply equate the cave with the maternal ("womb"), we forget that "the figure given to the father's potency might have been *inverted by being inscribed*" (PH 301), and that the "place the man had once inhabited must be mimicked by turning it inside out and back to front and by gradually raising it up" (PH 284). The cave-like dwelling, with its back wall down below and its path leading upward, toward the opening that lies above, is indeed a complete reversal—a mirror image—of a womb, whose back wall lies *above* the opening which in turn is placed *downward*.

The cave, Irigaray insists, "is a mere reversal, a project of figuration" (PH 249). This inversion, however, has been carefully covered over: "It must, absolutely must, not be known how much the procreation of the 'son,' of the logos, by the father, owes to inversion. Nor that the mother is the place where that inversion occurs" (PH 310). Irigaray insists that we pay close attention to "the 'like' and 'as if' that have always already been at the bottom of such scenography" (PH 279). We must, in other words, be aware that the story narrated here about the importance of leaving images behind in order to access reality, as a story also *is* an image, an allegory, a metaphor. Now, we have already seen Irigaray suggest that such a metaphor is "impossible." We should be better equipped, at this point, to explore its alleged impossibility in further detail.

As she returns to the cave-womb of Plato's allegory, Irigaray shows the complexity with which the perversion of the womb has taken place.[20] Her essay does not simply characterize the cave as a (natural) womb to which we must return in order to reclaim a female or corporeal legacy denied through the philosophical journey out of the cave (a legacy that, as it were, would have been left behind inside the cave). Through a series of disorienting and perplexing reversals, Irigaray instead shows her reader that the cave, far from being an "original womb," in itself already is a mirror image, or a copy: "In cave or 'world' all is but the image of an image. For this cave is always already an attempt to re-present another cave, the *hystera*, the mold which silently dictates all replicas, all possible forms" for "*this cave is already, and ipso facto, a speculum*" (PH 246, 255).

Understood in this way, the cave is merely a stage set up in order to conceal the place of actual engendering.[21] The womb is indeed a tomb—not only because it produces "fake offspring" but also because it quite literally is a site of repression set in place to eclipse our maternal beginnings. The maternal has thus been reduced to a projection screen, a mute surface upon which images and stories can be projected only to subsequently be dismissed as imaginary or false. It is this very mechanism that Irigaray seeks to uncover and challenge. She articulates the stakes of this challenge particularly clearly in the interview "The Power of Discourse and the Subordination of the Feminine," where she speaks of

> . . . the necessity of "reopening" the figures of philosophical discourse—idea, substance, subject, transcendental subjectivity, absolute knowledge—in order to pry out of them what they have borrowed that is feminine, from the feminine, to

make them "render up" and give back what they owe the feminine. This may be done in various ways, along various "paths." . . . One way is to interrogate *the conditions under which systematicity itself is possible*: what the coherence of the discursive utterance conceals of the conditions under which it is produced, whatever it may say about these conditions in discourse. For example the "matter" from which the speaking subject draws nourishment in order to produce itself, to reproduce itself; the *scenography* that makes representation feasible, representation as defined in philosophy, that is, the architectonics of its theatre, its framing in space-time, its geometric organization, its props, its actors, their respective positions, their dialogues, indeed their tragic relations, without overlooking the *mirror*, most often hidden, that allows the logos, the subject, to reduplicate itself, to reflect itself by itself. All these are interventions on the scene; they ensure its coherence so long as they remain uninterpreted. Thus they have to be reenacted, in each figure of discourse, in order to shake discourse away from its mooring in the value of "presence." For each philosopher, beginning with those whose names define some age in the history of philosophy, we have to point out how the break with the material contiguity is made, how the system is put together, how the specular economy works.[22]

The "value of 'presence'"—the temporal paradigm that dominates our discourse—depends on a repression of our maternal roots. This repression takes place through a sophisticated series of reversals and mirrorings, and woman has functioned as the "scene" on which such reversals have been staged. Whitford notes that, what "has been abstracted from the scene of the cavern is the cavern as screen."[23] And yet, despite this important insight, she goes on to equate the cave with the mother and the ideal world above with the father. Instead, I want to argue that the entire structure that opposes (phantasmatic) cave with (ideal) world is in fact itself a fantasy that covers over that which would lie beyond such dichotomies. As Whitford herself has noted, "the male function takes over and incorporates all the female function, leaving women outside the scene, but supporting it, a condition of representation. The picture of the cavern *represents*, while concealing, the process."[24]

On my reading, we must take seriously the idea that the cave *is representation*, and ask about what it is that it conceals, so as to not reproduce the very structure Irigaray attempts to undermine—namely the division between sensible and intelligible and the equation of the former with maternal materiality and the latter with paternal ideality. The task, as I see it, is not so much to "reconnect" these two spheres (which is what Whitford suggests we should do), but rather to move beyond them to enter an altogether different logic, one in which "maternal" and "paternal" indeed must be thought *together* and *in relation*, but where each of them simultaneously must be thought *otherwise than* and *different from* the spheres and concepts with which they have been associated hitherto (sensible and intelligible, matter and form, passive and active, etc.). I agree, here, with Butler, who has suggested that there would always exist, for Irigaray, "a matter that exceeds matter, where the latter is disavowed for the autogenetic form/matter coupling to thrive."[25] Matter, Butler maintains, "occurs in two modalities: first, as a metaphysical concept that serves phallogocentrism; second, as an ungrounded figure, worrisomely speculative and catachrestic, that marks for [Irigaray] the possible linguistic site of a critical mime."[26]

We must in my view be careful not to look for this "ungrounded figure" inside the cave. The cave is, after all, by no means *outside* the scene, but rather *integral* to it, albeit as that which must be rejected as imaginary or false within the logic of the allegory. We might say that it is the very soil from which the form/matter dualism emerges, and woman, or the maternal, is nowhere to be found on this scene. As Butler suggests, "Irigaray wants to argue that in fact the feminine is precisely what is excluded in and by such binary opposition. In this sense, when and where women are represented within this economy is precisely the site of their erasure."[27] Woman is like a Derridean trace—the *différance* underlying all difference. So, while Whitford explains that the "Platonic myth stages a primal scene in which Plato gradually manages to turn his back, like the pupil/prisoner, on the role of the Mother altogether,"[28] I instead want to argue that the mother has been left behind long before the myth of the cave even begins. Socrates's account is conditioned by a previous repression or exclusion. We know, of course, that the descent taking place here by no means is the first in this dialogue. It all begins with the descent of Socrates and Glaucon entering the port of Athens the previous day.[29] As in the *Timaeus*, beginnings are many, and this makes it difficult to locate the exact moment of repression or locus of displacement.

Insofar as there is an alternative to this logic, it can thus *not* be found within the cave, nor in the outside realm. This, of course, would be to simply stay within the metaphoricity put in place by Socrates, when he suggests that the prisoners of the cave are "like us,"[30] and that the cave is an (inferior) image of the true world above. But what then, we must ask, would be the "outside" made invisible by the performance witnessed? *Of what is the cave a (distorted) mirror image?* The womb, it seems, is eternally elsewhere: nowhere to be found?

The difficulty of locating such alternative points to the impossibility of the metaphor, since it entails that we have no point of reference to turn to, as we unpack the image. To say that someone is "big as a bear" would make little or no sense if we don't have some idea of the size and shape of bears. Similarly, to state that the cave is "like a womb" is an empty statement if we have no insight into the nature of wombs. What we might end up doing, if confronted with such a lack of origin or reference, is to begin with the image we are given—the cave—and conclude that wombs must be much like such caves. Or, as Jones puts it: "If the cave is *like* a womb, the womb by implication is like a cave," and the maternal generative powers have thus been "captured in the deadening image of a frozen rock."[31] A reversed logic that comes to reduce the womb, or the maternal, exactly to the image we are presented with.[32] And this seems to be exactly what has occurred here: *"The fact that semblance has passed into the definition of the proper will have gone unnoticed,"* Irigaray exclaims (PH 297).

When, for the first time in the essay, Irigaray explicitly mentions women, the feminine, and the maternal (all three suddenly appear in the same paragraph), she speaks (critically) of the "ideal of truth" that "in fact is necessary to under-lie and legitimize the metaphors, the figures used to represent the role of women, without voice, without presence" (PH 265). It is this very logic that sets up a structure of oppositional difference and dichotomization, with a notion of "origin" that always already is and will be superior to the "copy" it is said to reproduce:

> The feminine, the maternal are instantly *frozen* by the "like,"
> the "as if" of that masculine representation dominated by truth,
> light, resemblance, identity. By some dream of symmetry that

itself is never ever unveiled. The maternal, the feminine serve (only) to keep up the reproduction-production of doubles, copies, fakes, while any hint of their material elements, of the womb, is turned into scenery to make the show more realistic. (PH 265)

I agree with Butler that Irigaray's mimetic method "has the effect of repeating the origin only to displace that origin *as* an origin," and that, "insofar as the Platonic account of the origin is itself a *displacement* of a maternal origin [his privileging of the world of forms over the cave-womb], Irigaray merely mimes that very act of displacement, displacing the displacement, showing that origin to be an 'effect' of a certain ruse of phallogocentric power."[33] I do not, however, agree that such a reading of Irigaray allows us to assume that "the feminine as maternal does not offer itself as an alternative origin."[34] The challenge, as I see it, is indeed to displace the already displaced Platonic "origin," but this in part would be done so that we could articulate maternity differently than within the already established logic. Irigaray therefore insists that we must replace the universal-paternal origin of Plato's myth (and of Western philosophy more generally) with *irreducibly dual* origins. "Maternal" would have to be something other than "cave-like" (read "inversion" or "lack" or "passive receptacle"). She would have to be thought no longer as "other to same," but as "other to other," and as a subject in her own name and right (as we saw in the discussion of female subjectivity more generally earlier in this book). We would, moreover, have to show that such maternal origins in no way are universal or essential. To simply replace the paternal-patriarchal origin with a female version would hardly change or challenge the logic, and such a displacement would merely lead to yet another metaphysical-foundational account of the kind Irigaray explicitly has endeavored to undermine.

At this juncture, it will be helpful to establish some conceptual distinctions. During a conversation that I had with Irigaray in a seminar at Liverpool Hope University, she distinguished *origin* [*origine*] from *beginning* [*commencement*], explaining that the former is always already cultural, situated and established within the symbolic order, while the latter belongs to the real, escaping discourse altogether.[35] Our culture, she explained, conceals female beginnings and thus prevents women from entering into the cultural sphere on their own terms. Within patriarchal culture, therefore, women lack origins of their own, since origins are always already on the level of logos. Through logos, man substitutes his origins for beginnings. This distinction between origins and beginnings is in fact present already in *Speculum*. There, Irigaray emphasized the "erasure of the beginning [*commencement*]" (PH 312 [390]), and criticized a logic that requires that man too "turns his back on any beginning [*commencement*] that is still empirical, still too material and metrical, and that he receive being only from the one who wills himself as origin [*origine*] without beginning [*commencement*]" (PH 295 [368]).[36] Our beginning, she has noted elsewhere, "is not in language. Which will be interpreted as: it is not. Thus closing up the circle of oblivion" (FAMH 88). And it is precisely through this loss of beginnings that our culture has become marked by repetition and sameness:

> Western man has constructed his subjectivity against his natural origin. He did not work out his maternal beginning but put it into the unthought background of his story and history. To escape a *return* to such a substratum, he has elaborated a culture of men and between men, a culture of the same as he is: father, brother and son, who share the same necessities, the same values, the same world. Wanting to become as man, woman fulfills the secular male dream of concealing sexuate difference. She asks for entrance into a history which has expelled her, instead of *turning back* to the start of our culture, to the moment—for example, to the time of the pre-Socratics—when the process of her exclusion still clearly appears, trying to *start again* with another logic, to enter into history as woman without agreeing to securing anew only its background.[37]

In this passage from *Key Writings*, Irigaray explicitly urges us to pursue a movement of return, a return to our (maternal) beginnings. This, she claims, is necessary if we want a new beginning, a future different from the patriarchal present that we know.

Irigaray's more recent *In the Beginning, She Was* is an even more systematic attempt to account for such beginnings. There, she links beginnings with *engendering* and origins with *creation*, and associates the former with women and goddesses and the latter with men and gods: "In the one," she notes, "she—and She—is at the beginning; in the other, he—and especially He—is at the origin of a world created outside of a

natural engendering, a world in which creatures are organized in a hierarchical manner in relation to an absolute model."[38] If Plato's cave is an
early prototype for the latter, in terms of the logic by which the world
of appearances is seen as an (inferior) copy of selfsame ideas, certainly
this logic culminates with the biblical genesis, where an all-powerful
paternal deity "creates" (rather than "engenders") man in his image—and,
we might add, where woman (at least according to one version of the
text) is created as an (inferior) image of man, made from his ribs. It is
thus precisely through this substitution of origins for beginnings that our
culture has become marked by a repetition of the same in its selfsame
image, and where the relation between the sexes is one of hierarchical
dualism rather than irreducible difference.

Woman, according to Irigaray, is more faithful to her beginnings,
but she lacks a cultural representation thereof, and is thus cut off from
her roots, eternally doomed to homelessness.[39] As I see it, *Speculum* is an
account not only of how this homelessness has come to be the destiny
of women in our culture, but also how it is indistinguishable from a kind
of *timelessness*. What we have lost is not merely a dwelling place, but
the very temporal structure of such a place, which has been erased in
order to give way to a linear time eternally pointing back to one sole
origin. The loss of (maternal) beginnings brings about a loss of time. It
will be my task then, in what follows, to take a closer look at this "loss
of time" as it is articulated by Irigaray in her essay.

## The Substitution of Origins for Beginnings

Let me begin by turning to the title of Irigaray's book: *Speculum of the
Other Woman*, or *Speculum de l'autre femme*. A speculum is the medical
tool inserted into the vagina during gynecological examinations. But it
is also, importantly for my reading here, a metal (a hard white alloy of
copper and tin) used for mirrors, most typically for the mirrors of tele-
scopes and early octants. The speculum is thus used both for examining
the female genitalia, and for observing and measuring the heavenly bodies
in their movement. From a Platonic point of view, we see here a double
reference to time: the unruly rhythmic time of the maternal *chōra*, and
measured time perceived as an image of the sky and the heavenly bodies.

In an interview, Irigaray herself comments on the meaning of
the term speculum in light of the early modern idea of a "speculum

mundi" or "mirror of the world": "It's not simply a question of a mirror in which one sees oneself, but of the way in which it's possible to give an account of the world within a discourse: a mirror of the world."[40] The speculum is that through which we come to understand the world. It is that through which our culture is reflected. It provides meaning, patterns, a discursive lens. But it is not only the Platonic reference that brings us to the question of time. The very source Irigaray provides in the interview—the "speculum mundi"—has temporal connotations. In her comments, Irigaray states that she cannot recall the specific "European works" in which this concept emerges. The most famous example, however, is probably the English doctor and clergyman John Swan's text *Speculum Mundi*, first published by Cambridge University in 1635. The full title is suggestive of the problems addressed therein: *Speculum Mundi: or, A Glasse representing the Face of the World; Shewing both that it did begin, and must also end: The manner How, and time When, being largely examined. Whereunto is joyned an Hexameron, or a ferious discourse of the clauses, continuance, and qualities of things in Nature; occasioned as matter pertinent to the work done in the six dayes of the World's creation.*[41] The "speculum mundi" not only reflects the world, nor the universe at large and the heavenly bodies. It gives us a discourse about our *beginnings*, it combines natural history with theology, and it focuses on the manner and time in which the world was *created*. It is thus not merely that through which we come to understand and make sense of the world. It is also that which gives us access to and understanding of our beginnings, and this is crucial for my own reading of Irigaray's seminal text here.

The second half of the title is clearly a wink to Beauvoir, whose characterization of woman as "the second sex" was well established in France at the time of publication of *Speculum*.[42] But insofar as the other woman of the title also is secondary—a second sex—we must recall yet another Greek connection, one that leads us all the way to the womb-like cave of Plato's allegory: in addition to the feminine noun *hystera* (with a stress on the second syllable) meaning womb, and the neuter noun *hysteron* (same stress) meaning afterbirth, the adjective (with a stress on the first syllable) *hysteros* ($-\bar{e}$, -on) means latter, later, behind, younger, and next. This term clearly has a claim on both temporal as well as causal relations. *Hystera*, most commonly translated as womb, and the etymological root of (female) hysteria, means exactly "second woman," temporally the woman that comes after, or later. The *hystera* of the essay therefore appears already in the book's title, and we are urged to think the (chronological) relation between the speculum-mirror and that which is reflected in the mirror as we read the essay.[43]

The title thus brings our attention not only to the way in which woman has been rendered an image, a flat surface detached from the world of flesh—perhaps an image somehow distorted or perverted, one that fails to reflect a female subject whose body has always already been penetrated and examined, specularized as it were—but also to the ways in which such a reflection, inevitably, is a distortion of time or chronology. In a variety of ways, Irigaray points to the philosophical "desire to reduce the (mother) earth to a flat surface that can be measured by solar projections" (PH 290), recalling the two-dimensional imaginary Mother that we encountered in Kristeva's "Stabat Mater." In Kristeva's essay, we were given an account of motherhood as experienced "beyond" the flat surface to which it traditionally has been exiled, and we found that this account described motherhood in terms of time and rhythm. I want to show, now, that something similar occurs in Irigaray. That the mother, again, is articulated in temporal terms, and that mother lost thus equals time lost—a glossing over of a time different from the traditional patrilinear notion of time. The "beyond" of the logic of the cave would thus be articulated temporally, and just as in Proust's epos our arrival at such a repressed time occurs through retrospective encounter with the mother.

In critical dialogue with Freud, in the opening essay of her book, Irigaray notes that "woman's symbolization of her beginning [commencement], of the specificity of her relationship to the origin [l'origine], has always already been erased, or is it repressed? by the economy that man seeks to put in place in order to resolve the problem of his primary cause [son principe]."[44] Earlier in the same essay, she states that "woman's only relation to origin [l'origine] is one dictated by man's. . . . This is shown, specifically, in the way she is forced to renounce the marks of her ancestry and inscribe herself on man's pedigree [la lignée de l'homme]. She leaves her family, her 'house,' her name—though admittedly it too is only a patronymic—her family tree, in favor of her husband's."[45] Irigaray's return to the maternal is thus twofold. We must return to what seems like a beginning, only to discover that this is a representation covering over our more archaic beginnings (this would be the function of the cave on the present reading, and it is similar to Timaeus's journey). The representation of the womb glosses over our beginnings, which escape representation. In the process, what we gain is an origin, in the cultural sense of the term.[46]

This should remind us of my previous discussion of the phantasmatic aspects of maternity. Just as Kristeva made it clear that the "lost territory" to which we wish to return is but a fantasy—produced by a society that needs this image in order to cover over the reality of singular female experiences of maternity, Irigaray revisits Plato's cave only to uncover the phantasmatic image that founds Western culture and thought. In conversation, she has suggested that "woman has been reduced to the function of mother in order to provide man with an origin."[47] Woman *is* an origin, but *has* none. For Irigaray, as for Kristeva, the maternal function must in other words be understood in a dual sense. On the one hand, as that which has been forgotten and repressed, that to which we must return. This maternal—the singular experience that escapes representation—is *equivalent* to beginnings. On the other hand, as a male reduction of female subjectivity where woman becomes but a function in order to provide man with an origin. This maternal—arguably a male construction that serves to oppress women—*covers over* our more archaic beginnings.

It is with the maternal as with nature for Irigaray: we must return to it but not reduce ourselves to it (as has been the destiny of women within patriarchal culture). We must return to it *on our own terms*. We are back where my discussion of the past started—at the complicated task of providing women with a genealogy of their own without reducing them to the function of motherhood, as this function is understood within our culture. This would, importantly, not amount to equating female subjectivity with motherhood. To the contrary, Irigaray is careful to point out that women simultaneously must "construct an objective identity model enabling them to situate themselves as women and not merely as mothers," so as not to fall prey again to the "still common practice of reducing the woman to motherhood."[48] Just like Kristeva did in the opening paragraph of "Stabat Mater," Irigaray suggests that the options for women in our culture have been either to be *reduced* to mothers or to *repress* the specificity of their sexed identity altogether. The task, as she notes in the final essay of *Je, Tu, Nous*, is to become "women without an *exclusive* subjection to motherhood and without, for all that, being reduced to male identity."[49] Woman, as we have seen, paradoxically becomes *reduced* to an origin at the same time as she is *robbed* not only of her beginnings but also of her own originating capacities. She is reduced to a mother only to subsequently be written out of the story altogether, as God the Father enters the scene as the sole originator. When man "turns his back towards her," Irigaray writes, "he has made a source for himself. He has appropriated, and attributed to himself, the source" (FAMH 63). And this, in her mind, is a crime: "a reduction of the other [and, we might add, of the mother] to nothingness" (FAMH 98).

The task would thus be to try to return to our beginnings. The problem, however, is that philosophy lacks a discourse to articulate such beginnings—they are, as Irigaray puts it in the opening essay of *Speculum*, a "blind spot" for philosophical discourse, and this is especially so for girls and women:

> No return to, toward, inside the place of origin [*le lieu originel*] is possible unless you have a penis. The girl will herself be the place where origin [*l'origine*] is repeated, re-produced and reproduced, though this does not mean that she thereby repeats "her" original topos, "her" origin [*origine*]. On the contrary, she must break any contact with it, or with her, and, making one last turn, by a kind of vault—up one *more* branch of the family tree—she must get to the place where origin [*l'origine*] can be repeated *by being counted*.[50]

Strangely, the translator has omitted one sentence in this passage, which follows after the first sentence quoted here: "C'est bien autrement que la fille, la femme, trouvera une économie du désir (d')origine."[51] Woman's desire for origin, and her original desire, will be found elsewhere, otherwise, beyond the phallic logic. And it is this "elsewhere" or "otherwise" that we are exploring here.

To enter into the symbolic order as a "castrated" being, the girl must thus repress her own beginnings and will, instead, be reduced to an origin/originator for those not castrated. And in so doing, she is forced to participate in a linearity that points back to a singular origin, and she must enter measured time, countable time. As in the *Timaeus*, what is implied here is the necessity of returning to a time *prior* to the measurability of time, a time *preceding* the act of counting. Only then might we find our beginnings. For Irigaray, *repetition of sameness* and the possibility to *count* is what founds the logic of sameness and linear time, and it simultaneously robs us of our beginnings. The (natural) beginnings covered over by a (cultural) origin are, in fact, always already two, irreducibly so (not one plus one), since we all originate from two: maternal *and* paternal function.[52] This, as we have seen, is a central theme of her entire work. Creating *two* worlds, irreducible to one another, would, for Irigaray, be the only possibility to recuperate our beginnings, and with them the maternal body that has been buried in order to establish *an origin*, in the singular (most prominently, of course, through the instituting of *one* solitary God, origin of all, world and humans).[53]

While beginnings might occasionally erupt into symbolic discourse, as we have seen, through for example poetic language, they thus remain largely concealed or repressed. This difficulty of bespeaking our beginnings, understood as irreducibly two, is raised by Derrida in his reading of the *Timaeus*: "Philosophy cannot speak philosophically of that which looks like its 'mother,' its 'nurse,' its 'receptacle,' or its 'imprint-bearer.' As such, it speaks only of the father and the son, as if the father engendered it all on his own."[54] His challenge to philosophy "can be translated thus: let us go back behind and below the assured discourse of philosophy, which proceeds by oppositions of principle and counts on the origin as on a *normal couple*. We must go back toward a preorigin which deprives us of this assurance and requires at the same time an impure philosophical discourse, threatened, bastard, hybrid."[55]

Irigaray, if anyone, has taken on this challenge in profound ways. It is in search for this "preorigin," in her attempt to "go beneath the origin," that she brings our attention to and challenges the invisible-repetitive machinery of the cave.[56] Because just as those prisoners failed to notice the puppeteers hiding behind the wall (and, importantly, they were never made aware of their role in the drama, not even after they themselves had been released from the cave: who are they? who put them there? why?), we too have failed to see the staging and disguise with which this underground stage has become equated with material becoming. In a sense, Irigaray wants to take Plato quite seriously regarding the phantasmatic nature and the spectacle of the cave. And this is exactly why a mere "return" to the cave by no means would provide a solution to the absence of maternal beginnings in our culture.

On this reading, Irigaray thus wants to get us out of the cave just as much as Plato did. The difference between Plato and Irigaray, of course, lies in their respective understanding of the "beyond" of this structure. While it is the world outside, the realm of ideas, that represents truth for Plato, Irigaray takes this world to be part of the same phantasmatic logic—in fact it is the very motor behind it. There are thus two ways out of the cave: the path chosen by Plato, which in fact does not lead "out" as much as just "up" (we are still trapped within the logic of sameness and repetition); or a different path, one that would lead us "through the looking-glass," "out the rabbit hole," to a world where difference no longer is oppositional or complementary, but irreducible, and where change, as a consequence, becomes possible.

Irigaray's text, therefore, functions on two levels.[57] Consider, for example, the following passage:

> . . . it [the journey out of the cave] marks a break with the preceding economy, which must be abandoned as childishness, dreams, insanity. One must turn (around) toward something else, cut short the childish beliefs and language, make a clean break between fantasies and reality. In some way it is necessary *to forget in order to remember what is truer.*
>
> But this transition implies a jump. A fault, a split, which cannot be crossed without risk. One may lose one's sight, one's memory, one's speech that way. And one's balance. (PH 273)

This passage can of course be read as a description of the events as narrated by Plato. And insofar as we understand it as such, we know that Irigaray is deeply critical of it. The forgetting involved in sacrificing a material world for one of pure forms marks the very foundation of matricide on her account. If, Irigaray claims, man seeks to repress his beginnings, "those recollections of the mother and the womb," then "having been foolish (*aphron*), he risks becoming demented (*paranous*)" (PH 278). Contrary to the Platonic idea that knowledge amounts to recollection, Irigaray is thus suggesting that the Platonic search for truth would be premised on an act of forgetting. Anamnesis would, in other words, be a form of amnesia.

But if, instead, we read this passage as a description of what I have called a journey "through the looking-glass" or "out the rabbit hole" (and not as the Platonic ascent into a philosopher's haven of forms), its meaning shifts, and takes on a prescriptive character, one capturing the challenges Irigaray herself has been faced with as she has tried to introduce a logic of difference to a world that is all-too habituated by sameness. To take her political-philosophical program seriously, we would indeed have to "break" with the old economy, perhaps "forget" the language with which we have hitherto communicated, in order to create a new language, a new economy, a new world, a world of two. We may, for a while, lose our sight and balance. We may feel speechless, at a loss for words. To be sure, we would have to give up our "origin" (insofar as it is assumed to be exclusively paternal in nature). But only if we take that risk, only if we are willing to lose ground for some time (by turning, turning around, returning perhaps?), might we break free from the logic of sameness that has kept us hostage for far too long already. And only then, Irigaray seems to suggest, would we be able to again remember our beginnings—always irreducibly plural.

Irigaray is, in other words, addressing the difficulty we are bound to encounter in the transition from seeing women only as "shadows" or "lacks" to affording them their own subjectivity. At present, we have no words to speak about woman—she is a dark continent, a riddle, an enigma, and a stranger—and the event of speaking woman or recognizing her specificity is bound to lead to some confusion and a sense of being at a loss for words.[58] As Irigaray will go on to say about the process (again, seemingly speaking of the Platonic ascent out of the cave, but perhaps also speaking of her own endeavor): "And that cannot be brought about simply by adding a few apt terms, but demands a transformation of the process of discourse" (PH 273). Such a discursive transformation is exactly what Irigaray's own work attempts to realize. And this entails shifting from a speculum that reflects woman as *secondary* (male subject, female object) to one that reflects her as radically *other* (two irreducibly different subjects). The "speculum mundi" of Irigaray's work is one that reflects not one but two worlds. And it is one that depicts not the divine-paternal creation *ex nihilo* but rather elaborates a genesis that depends on plural beginnings.

Irigaray, if anyone, has experienced what the philosopher of the allegory experienced as he returned into the cave in order to enlighten the prisoners who remained down there. Just as he, on Plato's account, was ignored, then laughed at, and ultimately would have been killed (and we recognize, of course, the fate of Socrates here), Irigaray, as a consequence of the very book in which her essay appears, was excluded from her academic institution and, although by no means killed, certainly to some extent silenced and ridiculed (she has since then been largely excluded from French mainstream academia, and her later works are not even published in French).[59] The similarities between our two narrators—Socrates and Irigaray—become evident. But while the former (on Irigaray's account at least) attempted to convince an ignorant world that maturity and wisdom would be achieved through a turn toward the eternal realm of selfsame ideas, Irigaray's task has instead been to free us from this imaginary sameness, insisting that difference—and with difference alteration, change, revolution, unpredictability—is the horizon to which we must (re)turn, if we want to "remain alive and regenerate ourselves as living beings" (FG 107).[60]

## Mother Lost, Time Lost

This finally brings us back to the question of homelessness, and the way in which it relates to timelessness, or a loss of time. Grosz, among others, has claimed that the denial of our debt to the maternal has deprived us of a home: "Men have conceived of themselves as self-made, and in disavowing this maternal debt, have left themselves, and women, in dereliction, homelessness."[61] Of course it is easy to associate the mother with "home"—both in the sense that her body provides a first home for the growing fetus and in terms of the age-long association of women (and especially mothers) with the private sphere. But if we want to challenge such associations of women with space and home—and the very idea that women are mere passive "receptacles" in the realm of procreation—it seems to me important to shift the focus a bit and reflect on how it is that the loss of maternal beginnings not only causes a homelessness of sorts, but also a *timelessness*. In what follows, I want to fully develop the argument that the loss of maternal beginnings brings about a loss of time. What kind of home, and what kind of time, has been lost? And what does it have to do with maternity?

We know, already, that the journey out of the cave, for Plato, amounts to a rejection of temporal existence. As Whitford has noted: "In Plato, the reason for the obliteration is clear: he wishes to obliterate becoming. For Plato, the highest truth—Being, the Good, the Idea—is that which has never been born . . . never been mortal, never been subjected to the vagaries of time and change, never been incarnate, never been *indebted* to an act of intercourse . . . or to a period of dependence on the maternal body."[62] Irigaray herself notes that the paternal figure, representative here of the logic that posits form over matter, the atemporal over the temporal, "is eternal, because he has always refused to be born. His being, as a result, continues throughout time identical to himself. . . . Immutable, unchangeable" (PH 319). And more recently she reminds us again that the erasure of the mother amounts to our entry into the realm of timelessness: "This presence of her . . . is erased . . . by passing to the timeless and insensible level of the idea."[63]

And yet, on Irigaray's reading, it is not as if time or becoming could be found, instead, inside the cave. As we have seen, the cave is but a distorting surface for reflections. Its alleged flux has been revealed as the work of magicians, a perversion of sorts. Just as the maternal, on my reading, must have been repressed prior to our very first descent into the cave—and must be looked for far beyond both cave and ideal world—the disappearance of time (or the reduction of time to a line) coincides with the very logic set in place as we sketch a division between cave and world, sensible and intelligible. We must, again, admit and recognize that our search for a livable time and place cannot be conducted in the darkness of the cave (nor, of course, in the realm of ideas), but rather elsewhere (indeed "elsewhen"), through the looking glass, out the rabbit hole. It may at first appear that the cave—being as it is a representation of the mother-womb—would correspond to cyclical time or even revolutionary time. But given what I have said so far (given, precisely, that the cave is a *representation*) time here has already been sublated to a line, and thus to non-time.

As Irigaray begins, making the myth of the cave her "point of departure" (PH 243), where men have lived "since time began" (PH 244), she underscores the linear nature of the scene: "One is able to only look ahead and forward. Chains, lines, perspectives oriented straight ahead—all maintain the illusion of constant motion in one direction. Forward. The cave cannot be explored in the round, walked around, measured in the round" (PH 244–45). Causal movement forward. Origins (or origin, in the singular) behind. Despite the fact that time in Plato's work—and for the ancients more generally—is typically defined in cyclical terms, the cave dwellers are, she seems to suggest, prisoners of a linear logic: "A phallic direction, a phallic line, a phallic time, backs turned on origin" (PH 245). Since the beginning of time (time as we know it—perhaps this marks rather the end of time; that moment when time becomes reduced to a line?) we are bound to move along a line that points either forward or back, undermining all other directions and preventing us thus from interaction with those next to or around us (making intersubjectivity impossible).

The cave and the world outside (understood, here, as two aspects of the same logic) can indeed be thought of as a line—in fact we know that the very myth narrated by Socrates follows immediately after his account of the divided line[64]—and Irigaray here evokes the ways in which such spatial limitations also reflect a certain temporal paradigm. All this, she signals, is a (male) construct. And while we (and as long as we) perceive of ourselves as moving forward, in fact we all revolve in a circle bound to repeat itself, a self-enclosed movement which, in fact, is no movement at all.[65]

Before we examine Irigaray's argument at this juncture further, let me emphasize that the reading presented here is one quite clearly aimed at the effect the allegory has had on the tradition we call "Platonism," rather than necessarily being an accurate and precise reading of Plato. We must recall that time, for Plato and his contemporaries, by no means is linear. I will not be able to go into the details of ancient views on time here, but it is a commonly held view—and we find many examples of it in the Platonic corpus (perhaps most importantly exactly in the *Timaeus*), that the ancients modeled their understanding of time on the cyclical movement of the heavenly bodies.[66] Linear time as we know it (a time of no return where, for example, we no longer believe in reincarnation) is born with Christianity.

Irigaray describes the cave as "the representation of something always already there, of the original matrix/womb which these men cannot represent since they are held down by chains that prevent them from turning their heads or their genitals towards the daylight" (PH 244). Now, "daylight" can of course be understood, here, from within the structure of the myth proper, as the ideal and ever-present world into which these prisoners eventually are to be released.[67] But if we choose, instead, to think of it as that place, or time, to which an alternative path leads—a place-time that indeed would be the "original" womb (without therefore being an Idea or form, and without being a stable or singular metaphysical origin)—we can make more sense of what follows: "They cannot turn toward what is more primary, toward the *proteron* which is in fact the *hystera*. Chains restrain them from turning toward the origin but/and they are prisoners in the space-time of the pro-ject of its representation" (PH 244). The Greek term *proteron* means before, primary, temporally that which comes first. *Hystera*, as we have seen, not only means womb, not even only second woman (as in the title of the book), but more generally it implies secondariness, posteriority, that which comes after.[68]

If the womb traditionally has been thought of in secondary terms— woman as derivative of man, a kind of secondary and lesser incarnation of him—Irigaray here brings our attention to the fact that the *hystera*, in fact, is primary.[69] It is when this pre-temporal beginning becomes projected or pro-jected (represented in the shape of a cave), that we become prisoners of a linear logic: "A phallic direction, a phallic line, a phallic time, backs turned on origin" (PH 245). And in this process by which the *hystera* is "displaced" or "metaphorized," the actual womb becomes "faceless, unseen, will never be [and can never be] presented, represented as such" (PH 245). And thus we remain prisoners of linear time, or of the timeless: "Unable to turn, turn around, or return . . . with no possible recourse to a first time" (PH 245–46).

In the cave, time is but repetition and offspring are but copies. In the world above, another prison awaits us: "O! *Impoverished present, copula in effigy only, statement in a state of rigor mortis*," Irigaray exclaims (PH 252). In the Platonic universe, we are either "wasting our time" (PH 253) or killing time, and we are putting a "ban on pulsations, rhythmic intervals that are unlike" (PH 252). And "the fiction of the being-present masks the ancestry of its reproduction-production" (PH 256). The emphasis, for Irigaray, is of course the loss of difference, how we are trapped in a logic of sameness. But again and again, this loss is articulated through the lens of time, since difference is differing ("Birth pushed further and further back into an infinity where all differences, and differings, fuse in a blind contemplation" [PH 275]) and deferring ("Difference and deferral are gradually banished in this way" [PH 289]). On such an account, "time, space-time are side-tracked" (PH 256), and "fetishes and ghosts will thus argue over dead time" (PH 252). As we have seen, the loss of sexuate difference is a loss of time. And as the "fiction of the present" is being installed, not only "the time/tense of (re)production of the past" will be forgotten, "but also the future perfect tense, the preterit" (PH 287). "Time is cut up, over and over again, and lost in all kinds of caesuras and scansions" (PH 290). Representation is "*tearing time apart*" (PH 353). The rhythms of nature are covered over and we become cursed with an everlasting day: "The mid-night of the mother would be covered indefinitely by the mid-day of the Father" (PH 349), and life "is thus frozen, for all eternity" (PH 351). But, Irigaray asks, "on what space-time is this sovereign self-appropriation," this "production (of self) without matter, or mother" raised (PH 351)? The aim of the entire machinery set in place, she concludes, "is to tear away the mother's, the earth's function as space-time of (re)production," to push the mother into an "eternal elsewhere" (PH 356). We might add, into an eternal "elsewhen."

Let me pause here for a moment to make clear what is at stake in all this for me. As I have tried to show, Irigaray's mimetic reading of Plato's cave allegory proposes a logic altogether different from that which distinguishes sensible cave from intelligible world. Within the Platonic logic (as depicted by Irigaray), two options are available as far as the question of time is concerned: on the one hand the linear logic of the cave, which is said to represent becoming but which in fact revolves in a selfsame and self-enclosed teleological circle; on the other hand the timelessness of eternal forms in the world above. Following the thrust of my argument at large, the two options are really just two dimensions of the same logic—a logic in which the problem of time and finitude (the fact of birth and mortality) is "solved" by the positing of an ever-present elsewhere (true forms, eternal divinity, selfsame presence). These two poles—which traditionally have been understood as time and eternity—thus turn out to be flip sides of the same coin: on the one hand a *time of death* (a linear time forgetful of its maternal-material dimensions and the horizon of birth) and on the other hand the *death of time* (selfsame eternal presence). This logic as a whole is what produces "fake offspring," since it fails to acknowledge our maternal beginnings, attributing creative-reproductive powers to the father alone.

Some might argue that the true power of Plato's schema lies in the fact that the ideas are not *a-temporal* but, instead, *all-temporal*. Rather than coming into being and passing out of being, they are the persistence of that being, the constancy, which, from the perspective of the cave, may appear to have no time but must in fact be of all time. The truth of time, according to this reading of Plato, is not the *lack* of time but the *full presence of all time*. I do, however, again want to emphasize what I insisted on already in my discussion of metaphysical presence earlier in this book: to posit the full presence of all time amounts to destroying time altogether. Anything "all-temporal" would be exactly "a-temporal." The full presence of anything amounts, as we have seen, to full absence. And the "timelessness" with which we are faced here has little in common with the "timelessness" of the Freudian unconscious.

Instead of merely criticizing the timelessness of the world above, however, Irigaray—in line with what I have argued so far—turns against the logic as a whole, positing the possibility of an altogether different approach to temporal existence. The maternal time to which she (as Kristeva) urges us to return, is one that follows the movement of return, displacement, and alteration as described in this book as revolutionary time. Such time—where each return is singular and different from its predecessor or from that which follows—remains faithful to life and to our heterogeneous beginnings, and it need not posit everlasting non-material presence in a transcendent beyond, since maternal regeneration as such offers an alternative model of immortality grounded in the flesh. Plato himself in fact acknowledged the possibility of a different kind of relationship between time and eternity in a dialogue where Socrates deliberately notes his indebtedness to a woman, namely Diotima: "Pregnancy and procreation instill immortality in a living, mortal being" Diotima tells her young student Socrates in the *Symposium.*[70] Maternal regeneration creates continual new births and new beginnings and allows us to transcend our own limited existence not by calling for an eternal elsewhere in some everlasting beyond, but instead by acknowledging the lived "eternity" of human corporeal regeneration.

Contra Irigaray, however, I want to suggest that our pre-temporal beginnings—that time-place "beyond the mirror" where "pulsations, rhythmic intervals that are unlike" have not yet been banned and done away with, and where movement cannot be reduced to a selfsame circle or a phallic line but is, rather, irregular, non-determined, differing—can be found *within* Plato's own corpus. I have, in fact, already discussed this dimension at length: *chōra* is her name, if at all she can be named, that third kind that undermines the very division between sensible and intelligible, and that cannot be reduced to one or the other. Indeterminate in nature, differing and deferring, she is the very temporalization and sweeping along of Being and beings.

If the maternal—as on Timaeus's own account—in some sense embodies this very indeterminacy, it is no coincidence that both Kristeva and Irigaray call us to return to this figure. If thought of exactly as an active voiced subject, but one who remains open and receptive, susceptive to change and variation, not self-contained and self-enclosed and once and for all frozen in the same rigid shape, the maternal seems to offer what they are both looking for—namely a temporal principle that is not captive and does not hold us captive to the linear time of teleology or in the *rigor mortis* of everlasting presence. What the maternal moreover provides—recalling the placental economy with which I opened my discussion of Irigaray here—is an understanding of time as always already *relational.* The "womb" of which Irigaray speaks in her discussion of Plato is not, *and cannot be,* a singular and selfsame origin. The very notion of motherhood implies a relation. In fact, it implies and assumes more than one relation: that between the mother and her other (the paternal function, broadly speaking, regardless of its sex); and that between the mother and her child(ren).

Butler, as we have seen, has described the "feminine" in Irigaray as a constitutive excessive outside, and the conclusion that Butler draws from this position is that the "feminine," on Irigaray's account, "cannot be said to *be* anything, to participate in ontology at all," since it is "set under erasure as the impossible necessity that enables any ontology."[71] I would like to argue that the "being" of the "maternal"—a term I have chosen to use here instead of the "feminine," precisely because of its inherently relational status—in fact *does* exist, but only insofar as we perceive of it as *irreducibly temporal and temporalizing.* This being is thus never selfsame, never quite in a state of *being*, but rather always in *becoming*, always in change. Indeed, such ontology offers no stable ground. But it does, instead, offer infinite horizons of becoming and differentiation. The task then, would not be to free *chōra* from ontology, but to perceive of ontology as carrying her name. A name which, as we know, continues to change and vary—one that cannot be inscribed once and for all in the presence of a selfsame and everlasting present.

## Conclusion

Irigaray, like Kristeva, turns to Plato to bespeak the matricide that founds our culture. This is most evident in her famous reading of Plato's allegory of the cave, which appears in *Speculum of the Other Woman*, wherein she reads the cave as an inversed and distorted image of the *hystera*, or womb, such that both cave and world outside (as narrated by Plato) come to represent the erasure of our maternal-embodied roots. In this chapter, I have offered a close reading of this essay, focusing on a theme already examined in the previous chapter, namely the temporal aspects of the maternal and the fact that these elements specifically have been lost and must be retrieved if we are to establish a more vital culture.

I have offered an analysis of the philosophical issue of origins (*archē*), suggesting that the metaphysical tendency to stress the singularity and stability of origins leads to a repression of our material-maternal *beginnings*—one that needs to be corrected if we want to maintain a dynamic relation to our individual as well as collective past. The metaphysical obsession with selfsame and atemporal origins has generated the mimetic production of the same so criticized by Irigaray. Man reproduces himself in his own selfsame image and upholds his status as one in this way. And woman subsequently becomes reduced to an enigmatic and lacking other.

To break this logic—to disrupt this mimetic process of repetition and put in its place a process of true engendering that generates singularity and difference—we would, on Irigaray's account, have to challenge traditional philosophical-theological accounts of origins, and their appeal to abstraction, by bringing attention to and complicating our relation to our maternal beginnings, and to our being of mothers born. This entails refuting the logic of Platonic metaphoricity altogether, and it requires that we move beyond both cave and world outside, down the rabbit hole, through the looking-glass, in search for maternal beginnings that are irreducibly plural and temporal, again emphasizing the intimate relationship between difference and differentiation, alterity and alteration. Only then does change become possible. Having thus returned, on a labyrinthic path, to our maternal beginnings, we are now ready to turn to the future. But, as we will see, our turn toward the future will be all but conclusive, even though it is placed in a conclusion of sorts. The end, as we will see, is nothing but a new beginning.

PART V

# THE FUTURE

This is what time *is* if it is anything at all: not simply mechanical repetition, the causal ripple of objects on others, but the indeterminate, the unfolding, and the continual eruption of the new.

—Elizabeth Grosz

When does one decide to stop looking to the past and instead conceive of a new order? When is it time to dream of another country or to embrace other strangers as allies or to make an opening, an overture, where there is none? When is it clear that the old life is over, a new one has begun, and there is no looking back?

—Saidiya Hartman

# A Non-Conclusive Conclusion

## New Beginnings

The central argument of this book has been that the two models of time hitherto available to us—cyclical and linear time—are incapable of producing change and thus unable to actually give us a future. The Enlightenment ideal of progress, based as it is on a temporal paradigm that gives priority to the future (a linear paradigm that functions through a repression of the body and the past, or of cyclical time, and that hence depends on what I have called a sexual division of temporal labor), has yielded not *novelty* but *repetition*. In an effort to shape the future we end up repeating the same. My own model of *revolutionary time*—a perpetual movement of return into the past and to the body—is meant to disrupt the repetitive character of these previous models, and consequently to open the future.

If the future is an "ocean of uncertainty" as Arendt has put it (HC 237), then how can we say anything about it at all? My point, in what follows, is that we cannot, and this is why this conclusion is both brief and tentative. Perhaps it is misleading, then, to treat the question of futurity in the conclusion, since this might signal an aspiration to achieve closure. Let me therefore note again that my remarks in what follows are all but conclusive. Indeed, the end is nothing but yet another beginning. If Irigaray concluded *Speculum* with a beginning that turned out to be no beginning at all (as we saw in the previous chapter), and if she opened that same book by describing the female predicament as that of being destined by an end inscribed already from the beginning (woman would have to "achieve" femininity in line with the path ascribed to her by Freudian psychosexual theory), I see this end of my own journey as an open-ended beginning.[1]

265

I mean this in two ways: First, I see this book as a prolegomena for future research. The temporal model that I have developed here is a starting point indeed. My ambition has been to provide the conceptual tools needed for engaging in further debates about questions of subjectivity and embodiment, the relation between sex and gender, and the status of nature in our culture—all of which are issues not fully or exhaustively addressed in the pages that precede this conclusion. My own analysis is largely limited to time and difference as these are taken up by Kristeva and Irigaray respectively, which is to say that the focus is Eurocentric, not intersectional enough, and that far more attention could be given to issues of class, sexuality, and race—categories that remain marginal in the work of these two thinkers. These are shortcomings of which I am aware, and I can only hope that my discussion may instigate further reflections on these topics in years to come. Second, the temporal model that I have elaborated is one that emphasizes *beginnings* (note the plural), and that precludes any and all attempts to define the future in advance (such attempts, it should be clear, amount to a foreclosure of futurity). It is this aspect that led me to name the temporal model developed here *revolutionary time*. I hope to further elucidate this in what follows.

## Suspended Time, Foreclosed Futures

The question of the future is central for most philosophical thinking about time. If Heidegger defined the human being, or Dasein, as that being whose own being is in question, we might add (with an eye to Heidegger's own privileging of the future) that the human being, perhaps more than anything, is future-oriented. As humans, we try to predict the future (i.e., predictive sciences, forecasting, and prophetic eschatology); we hope to survive in the future (Arendt describes the public world as one created by human hands in order to assure a form of immortality: buildings, monuments, works of art, and stories will all outlast us and make our fleeting finite actions tangible and memorable); and we see the future as a guarantor of our freedom and our capacity to transcend (recall Beauvoir's characterization of woman's emancipation as an act of claiming access to futurity).

The problem with this view of the human as *futural* is that it not only often fails to acknowledge that some humans are denied access to futurity, but it also defines futurity as such in ways that make it bound to perpetually exclude some subjects from gaining access to it unless they sacrifice their specificity and particularity. I have, moreover, argued that our current notion of futurity—a notion by and large dependent on linear time and the transcendence of the body—ultimately serves to repeat the past, which is to say that all humans (even those who see themselves as futural) in fact have lost the future, and with it the very capacity for change.

While Beauvoir was right to claim that women should be granted a place in a time that transcends the present ("let a future be open to her, and she will no longer be obliged to settle in the present"), I have argued, in this book, that she articulated transcendence in a way that made liberation possible only if women became "like men." Indeed, we might add here, only if they became like white, middle class, straight men. As hooks puts it, if feminism is simply construed as "a movement that aims to make women the social equals of men," then this "raises problematic questions" in a world plagued by white supremacy, capitalism, and homophobia: "which men," we would have to ask, "do women want to be equal to?"[2] Liberal-existential feminist projects inevitably run the risk of perpetuating a model of time that reproduces, into the future, already established norms and identities that are premised upon the inherent value of progress, and that evacuate bodily registers of experience from their discourse about time.

If the "present always serves to build the future," as Fanon has suggested,[3] we are reminded yet again that certain folks—not only women but also Black folk, queer and trans folk, poor folk—have been reduced to immanence and presence in the service of building the future of those (white, cis-straight, able-bodied) men who have laid exclusive claim to freedom and transcendence. To become the equals of these men, such marginalized folks have been made to put on a mask (a white mask, a cis-straight mask, a male mask), so as to become "like them." The options are either, at worst, to remain in immanence or, at best, to achieve a transcendence already defined by the white man. But I have argued that neither of these options really gives us time (nor futurity), since they both reproduce and repeat the same in its own selfsame image.[4] A future based on such exclusion is, in other words, no real future at all, precisely because it is "built"—with the master's tools, we might add, echoing the work of Audre Lorde—which is to say that it has lost its potential for unpredictability and open-ended possibilities, its capacity "to bring about genuine change."[5]

In terms of lived reality, what this all amounts to is that some lives are marked by a temporal suspension of sorts. Denise Ferreira da Silva opens her important study *Toward a Global Idea of Race* with a temporal reflection that might serve to illustrate this claim: "That moment . . . between the release of the trigger and the fall of another black body, of another brown body, and another . . . haunts this book."[6] Couple this account of temporal suspension with the response Claudia Rankine received when asking a friend what it is like being the mother of a Black son: " 'The condition of black life is one of mourning,' she said bluntly. For her, mourning lived in real time inside her and her son's reality: At any moment she might lose her reason for living."[7] These reflections bear witness to a bleak temporal reality in which one's relation to past, present, and future is marked by an acute awareness of imminent death and loss. It has been my contention in this book that we urgently need an elaboration of time that permits us to reclaim futurity, and that allows those who have hitherto been excluded from the future to enter into it on their own terms. This is another way of saying that their lives would come to matter, and this would entail that their deaths would matter too, such that they could be properly grieved and commemorated. As Mirzoeff has noted, "when black life matters, time itself is altered."[8] To matter is to have a place in time, and to envision one's life as open toward the future rather than on an inevitable trajectory toward looming death or haunting loss—time suspended.

One of the central questions of this book is thus how we might elaborate a model of time that avoids this kind of structural exclusion, and the repetition-suspension that it effectively brings about. In the context of our present discussion we must ask: How might we articulate a notion of futurity that does not reduce the future to a goal to be achieved by a limited group of privileged people? How might we give an account of futurity that avoids the reduction of singular subjects to a selfsame and unified (colonial-masculine) subject? How to envision a notion of futurity that, precisely, does not depend on the idea of the human, or Dasein, as "neutral"—a neutrality, as we have seen, that in fact is all but neutral, since it tends to cover over an implicitly white, cis-straight, masculine subject? And how, finally, can we avoid the instrumentalization of present, past, and future alike, the effect of which is nothing but the foreclosure of futurity as such?

## Arendt and the Unpredictability of the Future

In order to address these questions, it will be helpful to look at a set of ideas articulated by Arendt in *The Human Condition*. In her discussion of the human capacity for action, she notes that human beings, throughout recorded history, but especially in Western modernity, have attempted to escape "the unpredictability of [action's] outcome" by substituting making for acting (220). Another way of articulating this would be to say that our frustration with the unpredictable nature of the future has led us to "build" or "make" a future in the image of our past and present. This attempt at "domesticating" the future has, as we have already noted, resulted in the foreclosure of futurity. Just like action loses its status as action if it no longer is unpredictable, irreversible, and anonymous (the three characteristics that Arendt ascribes to it—all of which imply that we can never fully control our actions, that we can never be the authors of our own story, and that we are always "doers" and "sufferers" both at once), the future loses its status as future if it is "made" or "fabricated."

Moreover—and I still follow Arendt here—such a substitution or reduction is bound to be violent in nature: "violence, without which no fabrication could ever come to pass, has always played an important role in political schemes and thinking based upon an interpretation of action in terms of making" (HC 228). I spoke to this issue in chapter 3: revolutions driven by utopian ideals or already established goals run the risk of reducing the present and present subjects to mere means for a higher end. The past and the present, as I put it there, become instrumentalized in the name of the future, and the future, as I have just suggested, loses its status as future through the loss of unpredictability that such "making" inevitably entails. Certain kinds of worshipping of the future are therefore bound to violently foreclose the future in their very aspiration for and focus on futurity.

Arendt reminds us that one of the core aspects of the substitution of making for acting is the subsequent distinction between ruler and ruled—a distinction, she notes, that must be seen as pre-political (even anti-political) for any action-based politics, since the public space where action takes place is a realm where, by definition, people are equals (HC 32). While Arendt's discussion of equality and her rigid distinction between the private and the public give rise to a whole range of problems regarding the role of women in political life—problems that I will not be able to address here but that I have tackled elsewhere, and that many feminist critics before me have addressed[9]—we can nevertheless highlight one aspect of this part of her argument that should be helpful for us in the context of our present discussion: Arendt describes the substitution of making for acting as an attempt to escape "the haphazardness and moral irresponsibility inherent in a plurality of agents" (HC 220). It is, in other words, the result of a desire for *mastery*: the actor of deeds becomes a maker of things so as to be able to control the process from beginning till end (i.e., by predicting its outcome, being its sovereign author, and ridding "doing" from "suffering"). But this "solution," Arendt explains, leads to isolation and to the destruction of the public realm as a realm shared by many.[10]

Man, in making women and slaves bear the burden of embodiment and finitude for him, has turned himself into a ruler not just in the sense that he rules over women and slaves (and takes futurity away from them), but also in that he comes to view himself as a master in his own house: a transcendental subject, self-certain and transparent to himself, capable precisely of "building" the future, thus viewing himself as *constituting* rather than as *being constituted* by time. The self-imposed authority of such a subject—his belief that he can be the author both of his own story and of History—precludes, again, the unpredictable status of the future, and thus futurity as such. To have a future is to be vulnerable and unstable, a stranger to oneself. The self-mastering subject, in safeguarding himself against such vulnerability, instability, and strangeness, ends up safeguarding himself against the possibility of having a future, and of future possibilities to come.

If we continue to pursue a reading where we take Arendtian action to be but another way of expressing the unpredictability and open-endedness of the future, we should be able to argue that the unpredictability of the future depends on plurality. Freedom and transcendence (terms that I have articulated in terms of a thrust into the future) can, on Arendt's account, *not* be equated with sovereignty or autonomy, since the latter are meaningless within a web of human relations, and since they would depend on the substitution of making for acting (and therefore rule, violence, isolation and, finally, the disappearance of futurity as well as freedom). If we want to understand freedom as a thrust into the future, we have to define freedom not in terms of sovereignty and autonomy but, rather, as constitutively relational, as depending on the presence of others. If plurality has been seen as a *threat* to our freedom, Arendt views plurality instead as the *sine qua non* for freedom.[11]

At this juncture, I will both depart from Arendt and further elaborate my reading of her. Let me begin by raising a critical point. While Arendt speaks of plurality in neutral terms (a neutrality that, again, proves to be no neutrality at all, since the Greek *polis* of which she speaks is a realm of equals precisely because it is inhabited by free men alone—it thus depends on the expulsion of women and slaves into a private realm driven by necessity, not freedom), I have argued instead that futurity understood in terms of freedom and transcendence (noting the inherent unpredictability of these two) depends not on neutral plurality but on plurality in difference. More specifically, I have argued that such futurity depends on plurality understood in terms of sexuate difference. On my reading, it is through a culture of sexuate difference that plurality can emerge (only in such a culture, I have said, can we depart from the logic of the same). Therefore, the unpredictability of the future depends on sexuate difference. Sexuate difference, in other words, undermines not only the notion of an absolute origin or *archē* (as we have seen in previous chapters), but it simultaneously abolishes any and all notions of a final end or *telos*.

It may come as a surprise that this argument, in a certain sense, is supported even by Arendt. If she is most commonly read—as I have read her here—as someone who articulates human plurality in sexually neutral terms (and this is indeed how her texts read overall), there is a surprising and rarely quoted passage in *The Human Condition* where she, despite herself as it were, seems to ground her account of action and plurality in a difference that looks much like Irigarayan sexuate difference:

> But in its most elementary form, the human condition of
> action is implicit even in Genesis ("Male and female created
> He *them*"), if we understand that this story of man's creation
> is distinguished in principle from the one according to which
> God originally created Man (*adam*), "him" and not "them,"
> so that the multitude of human beings becomes the result
> of multiplication. Action would be an unnecessary luxury, a
> capricious interference with general laws of behavior, if men
> were endlessly reproducible repetitions of the same model,
> whose nature or essence was the same for all and as predict-
> able as the nature or essence of any other thing. Plurality is
> the condition of human action because we are all the same,
> that is, human, in such a way that nobody is ever the same
> as anyone who ever lived, lives, or will live. (8)

Arendt here contrasts two versions of the Hebrew Genesis: in one, man and woman were created at the same time, while the other (a version that, not surprisingly, has left a stronger footprint in Western history) tells the story of how God used Adam's rib in order to create Eve. The latter version provides a solid foundation for the sexual model criticized by Irigaray, where woman is seen as a derivation and deviation of man, a mere copy, or a privative mirror image, of him. Arendt interestingly brings our attention to the fact that such an account lacks creative force: we become "the result of multiplication . . . endlessly reproducible repetitions of the same model," as she puts it. Her formulation should be familiar to us by now—we have seen many variations of it in our encounters with Irigaray. The result of such a formula, Arendt tells us, is *predictability*. If we were all mere copies of a selfsame (male) model, there would be no true plurality, no point in acting, no natality, and hence no futurity.

That Arendt sees the other version of Genesis as providing a better model for plurality and action should indicate to us an implicit assumption underlying her own account, namely that the manifold of human plurality—the condition of possibility for the unpredictability of action—depends on an originary difference. "Male and female created he *them*," Arendt reminds us. It should come as no surprise that she puts the emphasis on "them" rather than on "male and female" here, but her example is nevertheless illustrative and her subsequent comments point to a fact that I have stressed throughout this book, namely that plurality grounded in sexual sameness is no plurality at all. It amounts to nothing but predictable repetition. Plurality grounded in sexuate difference (a difference irreducible to the one) opens a horizon for multiplicity and singularity, and therefore also futurity understood as unpredictability.

Let me reiterate what I have said on several occasions: my stressing sexuate difference in my discussion of time and temporal change is *not* intended to reduce all human experience to a rigid dichotomy. By stressing the irreducibility of two to one, we are, in fact, able to overcome such a dichotomy (the hierarchical difference that is the inevitable result of a model of the same), and this opens up a horizon of possibilities. Sexuate difference is no more a "conclusion" than these concluding remarks are intended to be one. It is a starting point, a beginning, and the condition of possibility for a multiplicity irreducible to the one—an *at-least* two. Like Arendt, I would therefore hesitate to put emphasis on the "male and female" of God's creation, but rather attend to the plurality of an "at least two" that makes a variety of sexuate identities possible. Such a starting point is, as Irigaray so often puts it, as such always *to-come* (*à-venir*). This makes it unpredictable indeed, and it provides an opening that refuses absolute closure. This is why we need sexuate difference to sustain the openness of the future. Without it, we are doomed to repetition, to a linear time that crops up in a circle, and the future becomes closed off, predictable, always-already determined, inhabited by ghosts.

## New Beginnings

In this conclusion that is all but conclusive, I have thus suggested that sexuate difference provides the plurality-singularity that we need in order to think new beginnings. "With the creation of man, the principle of beginning came into the world," Arendt states in a much-quoted passage from her magnum opus (HC 177). In light of what we have said, we must add that this principle of beginning—the miracle that stands at the heart of our human condition—could have never come into the world if man had been created alone. Let us not forget: "Male and female created he *them*." Man alone is not capable of action, nor does he have a future. Beginnings are always at least two in number. We saw this in my reading of Plato, and we have seen it in my readings of both Kristeva and Irigaray. Man needs an *other* in order to enter into time, if by time we understand something other than a predictably straight line.

The principle of beginning is, for Arendt, the principle of freedom, and it is made possible through our capacity to act: "The fact that man is capable of action means that the unexpected can be expected from him," she writes in *The Human Condition*, and she goes on to say: "this again is possible only because each man is unique, so that with each birth something uniquely new comes into the world" (178).[12] The fact of birth—our irreducible singularity—is what inscribes us in a political web marked by unpredictability. Being born, or born-of, grants us freedom and the ability to act. Arendt repeatedly speaks of the *space* of appearance as that which is necessary in order for politics to unfold, but her emphasis on beginnings ultimately gives her political vision a *temporal* framework too. She has been called "the theorist of beginnings,"[13] and while Heidegger explored Dasein's relationship to *death*, she developed a theory of action not only based on the "fact of birth" but also one that describes action as such as a kind of *rebirth*: "With word and deed we insert ourselves into the human world, and this insertion is like a second birth" (HC 176). In the concluding chapter of her trilogy on female genius, Kristeva speaks of an Arendtian meditation "that relies on a different temporality: that of the new beginning, of history as renewal."[14] Such temporality "interrupts linear time," and Kristeva suggests that "the rhythm of the new beginning be a counterweight to the phallic temporality of the desire-to-death, finding its foundation in female fertility."[15] In *This Incredible Need to Believe*, she revisits this Arendtian temporality that "calls for a love of the past and of the future and an extraordinary capacity for rebirth," and she describes this time as "necessarily punctuated by a concern for finitude, but without being haunted by the race to death, and it is calmed by the miracle of birth, a kind of opening out."[16]

The various practices that I have examined in this book—psychoanalysis, poetry, philosophy, art, yoga, love, maternity—have one thing in common: they all, each in their own way, seek to establish new beginnings. Both Kristeva and Irigaray consistently speak of our capacity and need to begin again, to be reborn, to start anew. We have seen that Kristeva labels the transference involved in psychoanalysis a "supreme guarantee for renewal," and that she describes the psychoanalytic cure as "an infinite quest for rebirths."[17] I have explored in various places the capacity of semiotic traces in poetic language to renew and transform the symbolic order, to revolutionize language from within. I examined the breath of yoga and the tension between two subjects in love as instances in which Irigaray elaborates renewal and rebirth. And both Kristeva and Irigaray have written extensively on the maternal body and its capacity for birth, creation, and new beginnings. "*The time* of the mother," Kristeva states in *This Incredible Need to Believe*, "is confronted with this opening, with this beginning—or with beginnings, in the plural."[18]

But how, we must ask, is this emphasis on "the new" different from the idea of progress and development that both Kristeva and Irigaray tend to argue against (i.e., linear time)? Can we think novelty in nonlinear, non-progressive terms? As I have elaborated my notion of revolutionary time, I have stressed that it must be seen as a perpetual movement of return into the past, but that such a movement makes possible renewal and futurity. All the practices mentioned above have been described as involving this movement of return. I have spoken of the need to remember our past, and of the importance of revisiting the body of pre-verbal drives. Following Freud, I have highlighted the need to "access the archaic." How are we to reconcile this movement of return with an emphasis on novelty, unpredictability, and futurity?

Is the prominence we have ascribed to the past not a conservatism of sorts, is it not bound to slow down change, to over-determine the future with the ballast of the past? Can Kristeva and Irigaray truly offer *change*, or are their revolutions merely renovation-restorations of what we already know? Is the turn away from linear time a turn, precisely, to a "non-progressive" notion of time, bound to repeat and reauthorize the very tradition that we, as feminists, should try to challenge and subvert?

To the contrary, and as I have suggested several times already, I see the movement of return as the condition of possibility for a future marked by unpredictability and change. The point, as I made clear in my critique of Butler in chapter 8, is not to *destroy* the symbolic order so as to set in place an entirely *new* law. This would perpetuate the idea that the future can be *made*, and such making, as we have seen, is necessarily grounded in violence. While we need to recognize, as Hartman does in the passage quoted in the epigraph to this chapter, that certain experiences must be left behind so as to make possible a "new order"[19]— and while this is evidently most true precisely for those for whom the past represents violence, trauma, and oppression—it is nevertheless also true that our burying over and repressing such traumatic events will make them repeat themselves in the future—the repressed returns with renewed force. If a "new order" is what we are striving to achieve, we will need to return and return again, so as to make visible and audible what has been rendered invisible and silent. And thus we continue to straddle, precariously, the intersection between present, past, and future. As Hartman goes on to suggest: "Return is as much about the world to which you no longer belong as it is about the one in which you have yet to make a home."[20]

The unpredictability of the future does thus not imply complete erasure of the present or of the past. What it implies, more than anything, is our inherent vulnerability, and the human condition of plurality. To put it in the terminology that I have used hitherto: it implies embodiment and difference. Revolutionary time is a time that can proceed without sacrificing the body, and without erasing sexuate as well as cultural, racial, and other differences. It avoids the sacrificial logic of our current model(s) of time. To say that futurity depends on a movement of return is just another way of saying that change need not depend on violence. Beginnings need not imply the sacrifice and end of that which makes possible new beginnings: the heterogeneous, temporal body. And the end, if there ever is one, is nothing but a new beginning.

# Notes

## Introduction

1. Abby Ohlheiser, "The Woman Behind 'Me Too' Knew the Power of the Phrase When She Created It—10 Years Ago," *Washington Post*, October 19, 2017.

2. Ibid.

3. Ibid.

4. Julia Kristeva, "Women's Time," chap. 14 in *New Maladies of the Soul*, trans. Ross Guberman (New York: Columbia University Press, 1995). I will return to this essay at length in chapter 1. Henceforth, references to this essay will be given parenthetically within the main body of the text, using the abbreviation WT.

5. While Kristeva and Irigaray are often lumped together under the rubric of "French Feminism," alongside thinkers such as Hélène Cixous, Monique Wittig, Michèle le Doeuff, and others, there are actually few books that put them into explicit conversation, or that read their work systematically alongside each other. Elizabeth Grosz's *Sexual Subversions: Three French Feminists* (Crows Nest, AU: Allen & Unwin, 1989) includes careful analysis of the role of sexual difference in the work of Kristeva, Irigaray, and le Doeuff, but they are by and large read separately. Grosz devotes a short section to the relationship between Kristeva and Irigaray, and stresses that "they seem to occupy positions that are the *distorted reflections* or inversions of each other: not identical, but twins nonetheless, similar enough to be mistaken for each other by those who do not know them well" (104). She laments the fact that their positions are assumed to be "compatible if not complementary," and asserts that they, in fact, "are extreme poles apart when judged from a feminist point of view" (104). While Grosz is of course right that there are important differences between these two thinkers—both, as she points out, in their relationship to Sigmund Freud and psychoanalysis, and in their respective treatment of the central question of sexual difference—I nevertheless want to suggest that if we focus on the question of time specifically,

277

a fruitful dialogue between them can be staged, and we can begin to see the contours of important *shared* feminist commitments, despite their differences.

6. For engagements with this particular aspect of their work, see Tina Chanter, "Female Temporality and the Future of Feminism," in *Abjection, Melancholia, and Love: The Work of Julia Kristeva*, ed. John Fletcher and Andrew Benjamin (London: Routledge, 1990); Tina Chanter, *Ethics of Eros: Irigaray's Rewriting of the Philosophers* (New York: Routledge, 1995), 146–51; Ewa Płonowska Ziarek, "Toward a Radical Female Imaginary: Temporality and Embodiment in Irigaray's Ethics," *Diacritics* 28, no. 1 (1998): 59–75; Elizabeth Grosz, "Feminist Futures?," *Tulsa Studies in Women's Literature* 21, no. 1 (2002): 13–20; Elizabeth Grosz, *Time Travels: Feminism, Nature, Power* (Durham, NC: Duke University Press, 2005), 155–83; Cecilia Sjöholm, "The Temporality of Intimacy: Kristeva's Return to the Political," *The Southern Journal of Philosophy* 42 (2004): 73–87; Cecilia Sjöholm, "Revolutions of Our Time," chap. 5 in *Kristeva and the Political* (London: Routledge, 2005); Rebecca Hill, *The Interval: Relation and Becoming in Irigaray, Aristotle, and Bergson* (New York: Fordham University Press, 2012); and Anne van Leeuwen, "Further Speculations: Time and Difference in *Speculum de l'autre femme*," in *Engaging the World: Thinking After Irigaray*, ed. Mary C. Rawlinson (Albany: State University of New York Press, 2016). See also my own work in this regard, much of which comes out of the writing of this book: Fanny Söderbäck, "Motherhood According to Kristeva: On Time and Matter in Plato and Kristeva," *philoSOPHIA: A Journal of Continental Feminism* 1, no. 1 (2011): 65–87; "Revolutionary Time: Revolt as Temporal Return," *Signs: Journal of Women in Culture and Society* 37, no. 2 (2012): 301–24; "Being in the Present: Derrida and Irigaray on the Metaphysics of Presence," *Journal of Speculative Philosophy* 27, no. 3 (2013): 253–64; "Timely Revolutions: On the Timelessness of the Unconscious," *Journal of French and Francophone Philosophy* 22, no. 2 (2014): 46–55; and "In Search for the Mother Through the Looking-Glass: On Time, Origins, and Beginnings in Plato and Irigaray," in *Engaging the World: Thinking after Irigaray*, ed. Mary C. Rawlinson (Albany: State University of New York Press, 2016), 11–37.

7. Irigaray and Kristeva are, indeed, rarely mentioned in overviews of the treatment of the question of time in Western philosophy, even when other twentieth-century thinkers are discussed at length. To give an example, one book that systematically studies philosophical discussions of time and temporality in the last century is David Couzens Hoy, *The Time of Our Lives: A Critical History of Temporality* (Cambridge, MA: MIT Press, 2009). Couzens Hoy, symptomatically, never even once mentions Irigaray, and Kristeva only appears in a footnote (259n1). A welcome exception is Russell West-Pavlov's *Temporalities*, where the chapter devoted to the relationship between gender and temporality includes a reading of Kristeva's essay "Women's Time." See

*Temporalities* (New York: Routledge, 2012), 102ff. That said, Irigaray goes unmentioned in this volume too.

8. Tina Chanter gives similar reasons for why so few scholars have examined the question of time in the work of Emmanuel Levinas. See *Time, Death, and the* Feminine: *Levinas with Heidegger* (Stanford: Stanford University Press, 2001), 1.

9. Indeed, in a recent interview, Kristeva traces in our current cultural and political climate three "anthropological mutations" that, she claims, are in acute need of critical analysis, namely *time, sexual difference*, and *religion*, adding that "never before has time been as paradoxical" as it is in our present. She also describes time as being the "main character" of her most recent novel, *The Enchanted Clock*, suggesting that fiction is perhaps the most appropriate genre for tackling the complex question of time. See Françoise Coblence and Marcela Montes de Oca, "'Une vie psychique est une vie dans le temps': Entretien avec Julia Kristeva," *Revue française de psychanalyse*, no. 2 (2017): 357 (translation mine). See also Julia Kristeva, *The Enchanted Clock*, trans. Armine Kotin Mortimer (New York: Columbia University Press, 2017).

10. In the last few decades a slew of important work has been published where feminist theorists turn to the question of time. The work of Grosz is exemplary in this regard. See *Volatile Bodies: Toward a Corporeal Feminism* (Bloomington: Indiana University Press, 1994); *Space, Time, and Perversion: Essays on the Politics of Bodies* (New York: Routledge, 1995); *Becomings: Explorations in Time, Memory, and Futures* (Ithaca, NY: Cornell University Press, 1999); *The Nick of Time: Politics, Evolution, and the Untimely* (Durham, NC: Duke University Press, 2004); and *Time Travels*. Rosi Braidotti's work is also relevant. See *Nomadic Subjects* (New York: Columbia University Press, 1994); *Metamorphoses: Towards a Materialist Theory of Becoming* (Cambridge, UK: Polity Press, 2002); and *Transpositions: On Nomadic Ethics* (Cambridge, UK: Polity Press, 2006). Additional representative titles are Chanter, *Time, Death, and the Feminine*; Valerie Bryson, *Gender and the Politics of Time: Feminist Theory and Contemporary Debates* (Bristol, UK: The Policy Press, 2007); Victoria Browne, *Feminism, Time, and Nonlinear History* (New York: Palgrave Macmillan, 2014); and Prudence Chamberlain, *The Feminist Fourth Wave: Affective Temporality* (New York: Palgrave Macmillan, 2017). As for edited volumes, see, for example, *Belief, Bodies, and Being: Feminist Reflections on Embodiment*, ed. Deborah Orr, Linda López McAllister, Eileen Kahl, and Kathleen Earle (Lanham, MD: Rowman & Littlefield, 2006); *Feminist Time Against Nation Time: Gender, Politics, and the Nation-State in an Age of Permanent War*, ed. Victoria Hesford and Lisa Diedrich (Lanham, MD: Lexington Books, 2008); *Time in Feminist Phenomenology*, ed. Christina Schües, Dorothea E. Olkowski, and Helen A. Fielding (Bloomington: Indiana University Press, 2011); and *Undutiful Daughters: New Directions*

Gross and
Braidotti
on
time

*in Feminist Thought and Practice*, ed. Henriette Gunkel, Chrysanthi Nigianni, and Fanny Söderbäck (New York: Palgrave Macmillan, 2012). For a less recent example, see *Taking Our Time: Feminist Perspectives on Temporality*, ed. Frieda Johles Forman and Caoran Sowton (Oxford, UK: Pergamon Press, 1989).

11. See Julia Kristeva, *Intimate Revolt*, vol. 2 of *The Powers and Limits of Psychoanalysis*, trans. Jeanine Herman (New York: Columbia University Press, 2002), 29. Henceforth, references to this text will be given parenthetically within the main body of the text, using the abbreviation IR.

12. Needless to say, this "survey" of the history of the concept of time is far too brief and extremely schematic. Exceptions and variations are in abundance. While I will return in more detail to some of the views on time mentioned here, this book does *not* seek to provide a comprehensive account of the rich and complex history of time and temporality. My discussion will be largely limited to the work of Kristeva and Irigaray, and will only occasionally provide keys to other thinkers in cases where I find it fruitful for the sake of clarification or in order to comment on critical concerns raised by Kristeva or Irigaray (I will offer a more lengthy discussion of Simone de Beauvoir in the opening section on revolutionary time, of Jacques Derrida and Sigmund Freud in the section on the present, of Plato in the section on the past, and of Hannah Arendt in my concluding reflections on the future). The secondary literature on time is vast, but for systematic readings of some of the most important figures in this field, see, for example, John F. Callahan, *Four Views of Time in Ancient Philosophy* (Cambridge: Harvard University Press, 1948) [Callahan provides a discussion of the concept of time in Plato, Aristotle, Plotinus, and Saint Augustine]; Roland J. Teske, *Paradoxes of Time in Saint Augustine* (Milwaukee, WI: Marquette University Press, 1996); Françoise Dastur, *Heidegger and the Question of Time*, trans. François Raffoul and David Pettigrew (Atlantic Highlands, NJ: Humanities Press, 1998); Karin de Boer, *Thinking in the Light of Time: Heidegger's Encounter With Hegel* (Albany: State University of New York Press, 2000); Keith Ansell-Pearson, *Philosophy and the Adventure of the Virtual: Bergson and the Time of Life* (New York: Routledge, 2001) [this book focuses on time in Bergson but also includes a discussion on Popper]; Chanter, *Time, Death and the Feminine* [Chanter examines the role of the feminine in the work of Emmanuel Levinas and Martin Heidegger by focusing on their respective discussions of time]; David Wood, *The Deconstruction of Time* (Evanston, IL: Northwestern University Press, 2001) [Wood approaches the question of time through the deconstructive work of Derrida, but his book includes discussions of the concept of time as it appears in Friedrich Nietzsche, Edmund Husserl, and Heidegger]; Martin Hägglund, *Radical Atheism: Derrida and the Time of Life* (Stanford: Stanford University Press, 2008) [apart from an extended discussion of Derrida's views on time, Hägglund discusses the concept of time as it appears in Immanuel Kant, Husserl, and Levinas]; Couzens Hoy, *The Time of Our Lives* [Couzens Hoy first and foremost

examines the treatment of temporality—understood as distinct from time—in twentieth-century continental philosophy. He focuses mostly on the phenomenological tradition, but he also offers careful and illuminating exegesis of the work of Kant and G. W. F. Hegel, Nietzsche, Walter Benjamin, Derrida, and Gilles Deleuze]; Nicolas de Warren, *Husserl and the Promise of Time: Subjectivity in Transcendental Phenomenology* (Cambridge: Cambridge University Press, 2009); West-Pavlov, *Temporalities*; and Felix Ó Murchadha, *The Time of Revolution: Kairos and Chronos in Heidegger* (London: Bloomsbury, 2013).

13. The formulations here are borrowed from Elaine P. Miller, who expressed this set of concerns in a proposal for a panel treating the question of time in French Feminism, held at the 2010 meeting of the Society for Phenomenology and Existentialist Philosophy (SPEP). The panel included presentations by Miller, Sara McNamara, and me.

14. While my analysis by and large is limited to a Western cultural context, it is worth noting that this distinction between cyclical and linear time seems rather universal. While some, like Stephen Gould, have identified it as springing out of a Judeo-Christian tradition, others, like Walter Mignolo, notes that "linear time and cyclical time could be found everywhere, among the ancient Chinese, ancient Mayas, or ancient Indians." See Walter D. Mignolo, "(De)Coloniality at Large: Time and the Colonial Difference," chap. 4 in *The Darker Side of Western Modernity: Global Futures, Decolonial Options* (Durham, NC: Duke University Press, 2011), 171. For a systematic analysis of the linear-cyclical temporal paradigm, see Stephen Jay Gould, *Time's Arrow, Time's Cycle: Myth and Metaphor in the Discovery of Geological Time* (Cambridge, MA: Harvard University Press, 1988).

15. As we will see in what follows, the same can be said about the colonized and their colonizers, and is tied to racist-colonial conceptions about "primitives" and "moderns" just as much as it is tied to sexist-patriarchal presuppositions about women and men.

16. See Simone de Beauvoir, *The Second Sex*, trans. Constance Borde and Sheila Malovany-Chevallier (New York: Alfred A. Knopf, 2010), 73–74. Henceforth, references to this text will be given parenthetically within the main body of the text, using the abbreviation SS.

17. While time and change by no means are the same (the relationship between the two has indeed been disputed among philosophers since Aristotle), I hold that they are interdependent and that we can only conceive of (social and political) change in light of a particular understanding of time. In this regard I follow Grosz, who has argued that a politics of change depends upon a reconsideration of and attention to the question of time: "The more clearly we understand our temporal location as beings who straddle the past and the future without the security of a stable and abiding present, the more mobile our possibilities are, and the more transformation becomes conceivable." See Grosz, *The Nick of Time*, 14.

18. Chanter, *Time, Death, and the* Feminine, 22.

19. Grosz, "Feminist Futures?," 15. See also *Time Travels*, 177. We might add that this task also amounts to imagining a future whose subject not necessarily is white, heterosexual, or cis-gendered. I will return to this issue in what follows.

20. Frantz Fanon, *Black Skin, White Masks*, trans. Richard Philcox (New York: Grove Press, 2008), 200–01.

21. See ibid., 201.

22. As I hope to make clear, this notion is by no means meant to nostalgically uncover an idealized or naturalized foundation or stable ground. Instead, it seeks to establish new horizons and futures-to-come.

23. Irigaray in conversation during a doctoral seminar at Liverpool Hope University, June 2007.

24. Chanter, *Time, Death, and the* Feminine, 23.

25. Moira Gatens, among others, has argued that our current understanding of the relation between sex and gender reproduces the Cartesian mind-body dualism that it was meant to subvert. See "A Critique of the Sex/Gender Distinction," chap. 1 in *Imaginary Bodies: Ethics, Power and Corporeality* (London: Routledge, 1996).

26. Grosz, *The Nick of Time*, 72. Recent feminist debates are to a large extent concerned with questions of materiality and nature. If much feminist theory in the wake of Judith Butler's *Gender Trouble* stressed the importance of gender, culture, and processes of signification, feminist theorists in recent years have attempted to address questions of sexual difference in light of the idea that nature, far from being static, is a dynamic realm marked by change and proliferation. In her later work, Grosz is a big proponent of such views, as are Braidotti and Alison Stone, to mention but a few. Braidotti grounds her work in a sexual ontology of becoming. Stone situates sexual difference in the natural realm, but importantly stresses the fact that nature is "self-differentiating" and thus marked by incessant change. See Alison Stone, *Luce Irigaray and the Philosophy of Sexual Difference* (Cambridge: Cambridge University Press, 2006), 1.

27. While Kristeva and Irigaray more systematically than others have thematized the relationship between time and sexual difference, it is nevertheless worth noting that several other contemporary French thinkers who have pushed the question of time in ethical or political terms (think for example of Levinas, Deleuze, and Derrida) have often done so in light of the question of sexual difference, or of the feminine. In an essay to which I will return in detail, Louise Burchill convincingly argues that French thinkers from Deleuze and Derrida to Jean-François Lyotard, Kristeva, and Irigaray share a common interest in proto-temporalizing processes and that they all use variations of the term "the feminine" as they develop this aspect of their own thinking. These French philosophers, she suggests, deemed it possible "to extract from the attributes associated with 'women' as a psychosocial type a determination of time

or temporality radically at odds with the conception of time shared by both common sense and metaphysics. In other words, the conceptual persona of 'the feminine' was called up, as it were, by the project of contemporary philosophy insofar as it was judged capable of questioning the notion of time as a linear and homogenous succession of present moments." See Louise Burchill, "Re-situating the *Feminine* in Contemporary French Philosophy," in *Belief, Bodies, and Being*, 85. Burchill highlights Deleuze and Felix Guattari's elaboration of "the girl" in *A Thousand Plateaus*, Derrida's early use of the term "hymen," Lyotard's association of the "space-time of the event" with what he calls the "Primordial Mother," and Kristeva and Irigaray's discussion of female *jouissance*. She notes, moreover, that all of these thinkers in one way or another turn to the Platonic *chōra* as they offer a critical engagement with linear models of time. I will give a detailed account of Plato's notion of *chōra*, and its influence especially on Kristeva's thinking, in chapter 8.

28. See Dana Luciano, *Arranging Grief: Sacred Time and the Body in Nineteenth-Century America* (New York: New York University Press, 2007).

29. See Daniel Innerarity, *The Future and Its Enemies: In Defense of Political Hope*, trans. Sandra Kingery (Stanford: Stanford University Press, 2012).

30. See Elizabeth Freeman, *Time Binds: Queer Temporalities, Queer Histories* (Durham, NC: Duke University Press, 2010).

31. Ibid., 3.

32. See Penelope Deutscher, *A Politics of Impossible Difference: The Later Work of Luce Irigaray* (Ithaca, NY: Cornell University Press, 2002); and Gayatri Chakravorty Spivak, "French Feminism in an International Frame," *Yale French Studies*, no. 62 (1981): 154–84.

33. Mignolo, *The Darker Side of Western Modernity*, 168, 171.

34. Ibid., 151.

35. Aníbal Quijano, "Coloniality of Power, Eurocentrism, and Latin America," *Nepantla: Views from South* 1, no. 3 (2009): 553.

36. Ibid., 542.

37. Mignolo, *The Darker Side of Western Modernity*, 151–56.

38. Ibid., 153.

39. María Lugones, "Heterosexualism and the Colonial/Modern Gender System," *Hypatia: A Journal of Feminist Philosophy* 22, no. 1 (2007): 192.

40. Mignolo, *The Darker Side of Western Modernity*, 172.

41. Ibid., 173, 179.

42. Ibid., 162. As Alejandro Vallega puts it, the modern concept of history "is dependent on a specific line of temporality: the past is what has been left behind or what remains to be rewritten by the most advanced Western thought of the present; the future belongs to that Western present, as does the destiny of humanity." See Alejandro Arturo Vallega, *Latin American Philosophy from Identity to Radical Exteriority* (Bloomington: Indiana University Press, 2014), 105.

43. Quijano, "Coloniality of Power, Eurocentrism, and Latin America," 555.

44. Ibid.

45. Decolonial feminist thinkers such as Lugones have pushed these issues further, putting critical pressure on thinkers like Mignolo and Aníbal Quijano, suggesting that their work fails to properly account for the coloniality of gender. See, for example, Lugones, "Heterosexualism and the Colonial/Modern Gender System," 190.

46. Chandra Talpade Mohanty, *Feminism Without Borders: Decolonizing Theory, Practicing Solidarity* (Durham, NC: Duke University Press, 2003), 120. For an example of this kind of temporal multiplicity, see the opening pages of Sara Ahmed's "Close Encounters: Feminism and/in 'The Globe,'" in *Strange Encounters: Embodied Others in Post-Coloniality* (London: Routledge, 2000).

47. Mignolo, *The Darker Side of Western Modernity*, 161.

48. Some have identified a queer "turn" to issues of time as coinciding with the publication of a *GLQ* special issue on queer temporalities in 2007 (see *GLQ: A Journal of Gay and Lesbian Studies* 13, nos. 2–3). But as Sam McBean has pointed out before me, time has in fact been a central question for queer theorists long before the publication of that issue. See Sam McBean, *Feminism's Queer Temporalities* (New York: Routledge, 2016), 10. That said, it is also true that queer theorists, like feminist theorists more broadly construed, historically have focused more on space than on time. For a discussion of this matter, see Freeman, *Time Binds*, 179n5.

49. Simon D. Elin Fisher, Rasheedah Phillips, and Ido H. Katri, "Trans Temporalities," introduction to Special Issue on Trans Temporalities, *Somatechnics* 7, no. 1 (2017): 2.

50. McBean, *Feminism's Queer Temporalities*, 3.

51. Elizabeth Freeman, "Introduction," *GLQ: A Journal of Gay and Lesbian Studies* 13, nos. 2–3 (2007): 162.

52. Ibid.

53. Carolyn Dinshaw, *How Soon Is Now? Medieval Texts, Amateur Readers, and the Queerness of Time* (Durham, NC: Duke University Press, 2012), 4.

54. Ibid., 3–4. See also Atalia Israeli-Nevo, "Taking (My) Time: Temporality in Transition, Queer Delays and Being (in the) Present," *Somatechnics* 7, no. 1 (2017): 34–49.

55. José Esteban Muñoz, *Cruising Utopia: The Then and There of Queer Theory* (New York: New York University Press, 2009), 1.

56. Lee Edelman, *No Future: Queer Theory and the Death Drive* (Durham, NC: Duke University Press, 2004), 3.

57. Jack Halberstam, *In a Queer Time and Place: Transgender Bodies, Subcultural Lives* (New York: New York University Press, 2005), 2.

58. Freeman, "Introduction," 159.

59. Ibid., 164. See also reese simpkins, "Temporal Flesh, Material Becomings," *Somatechnics* 7, no. 1 (2017): 124–41.

60. Kristeva never uses this term in her work. While her notion of sexual difference in many ways is different from that developed by Irigaray, I nevertheless posit a shared commitment to an elaboration of difference that moves beyond the logic of identity so characteristic of our culture. Stone has pointed out that Irigaray uses the term "sexuate" in three main senses: to elaborate a new legal framework; to bespeak a culture that, contrary to our own, recognizes sexual difference in non-hierarchical terms; and to describe our natures qua sexed. It is primarily in the second sense that I will use the term here. See Stone, *Luce Irigaray and the Philosophy of Sexual Difference*, 16n26.

61. I would like to thank the anonymous reviewer who insisted on the potential tension here, and who offered helpful language for clarifying what is at stake in this seemingly paradoxical claim.

62. In *The Ethics of Ambiguity*, Beauvoir asserts that "we are absolutely free today if we choose to will our existence in its finiteness." See Simone de Beauvoir, *The Ethics of Ambiguity*, trans. Bernard Frechtman (New York: Citadel Press, 1976), 159. Henceforth, references to this text will be given parenthetically within the main body of the text, using the abbreviation EoA.

63. Whether or not this is a fair description of the existentialist position in general and Beauvoir's position more particularly is certainly contested. Irigaray describes her own relation to Beauvoir's work in an interview where what I have suggested here comes to the forefront: "Simone de Beauvoir refused to be the Other because she refused to be second in Western culture. In order not to be the Other she said, 'I want to be the equal of man; I want to be the same as man; finally, I want to be a man. I want to be a masculine subject.' And that point of view I find is a very important philosophical and political regression. What I myself say is that there is no true Other in Western culture and that what I want—certainly I don't want to be second—but I want there to be two subjects." See Luce Irigaray, " 'Je—Luce Irigaray': A Meeting with Luce Irigaray," interview conducted by Elizabeth Hirsh and Gary A. Olson, trans. Elizabeth Hirsh and Gaëton Brulotte, *Hypatia: A Journal of Feminist Philosophy* 10, no. 2 (1995): 99. For similar engagements with Beauvoir in Irigaray's work, see "A Personal Note: Equal or Different?," in *Je, Tu, Nous: Toward a Culture of Difference*, trans. Alison Martin (New York: Routledge, 1993), 9–11; "The Other: Woman," in *I Love to You: Sketch for a Felicity Within History*, trans. Alison Martin (New York: Routledge, 1996), 63; and "The Question of the Other," in *Democracy Begins Between Two*, trans. Kirsteen Anderson (New York: Routledge, 2001), 122–26. For important contributions to debates about the relationship between Beauvoir and Irigaray's work, see *Differences: Rereading Beauvoir and Irigaray*, ed. Emily Anne Parker and Anne van Leeuwen (Oxford: Oxford University Press, 2017).

# Chapter 1

1. Stephen Daldry, *The Hours*, 2002. The novel and film are loosely based on the life of Virginia Woolf and on her novel *Mrs. Dalloway*. Woolf famously provided one of the most powerful accounts written on the immediate link between creative work and financial and spatial independence: for a woman to write novels, she contested, she will need a steady income and a room of her own, thus liberating her from household tasks and from sharing a space with the children and other members of the family. This spatial and financial independence, we might add, is also, simultaneously, a temporal independence: To have a steady income and a room of one's own amounts to *having time*. See Virginia Woolf, *A Room of One's Own* (Orlando: Harcourt, 1989).

2. Saidiya Hartman, *Lose Your Mother: A Journey Along the Atlantic Slave Route* (New York: Farrar, Straus and Giroux, 2007), 194–95.

3. That woman, as a maternal figure, has been confined not only to childbearing but also to household tasks is one central reason for why she might experience time to go "round and round." Beauvoir writes: "Because housework alone is compatible with the duties of motherhood, she is condemned to domestic labor, which locks her into repetition and immanence; day after day it repeats itself in identical form from century to century; it produces nothing new" (SS 73). It is interesting to note that Julianne Moore's character in *The Hours* is capable of going on living—of inserting herself in the forward-bound trajectory of linear time—if and only if she leaves her family and children behind (like Nora had done before her in Henrik Ibsen's *A Doll's House*).

4. Elizabeth Freeman, "Time Binds; or, Erotohistoriography," *Social Text* 84–85, nos. 3–4 (2005): 62.

5. For a paradigmatic analysis of how the categories developed by Beauvoir can be used to provide an analysis of the *spatial* limitations of woman and her bodily comportment, see Iris Marion Young, "Throwing Like a Girl: A Phenomenology of Feminine Body Comportment, Motility, and Spatiality," chap. 2 in *On Female Body Experience: "Throwing Like a Girl" and Other Essays* (Oxford: Oxford University Press, 2005). See also Sherry B. Ortner, "Is Female to Male as Nature Is to Culture?," in *Feminism, the Public and the Private*, ed. Joan B. Landes (Oxford: Oxford University Press, 1998), 20–22.

6. Beauvoir discusses this at length in the opening passages of *The Second Sex*: "immobile, the ovum waits; by contrast, the open sperm, tiny and agile, embodies the impatience and worry of existence" (28). While Beauvoir herself warns us of pushing such allegories too far, she gives us a convincing account of how such "facts" of biology nevertheless have been formative for the way in which we have come to characterize women as passive-spatial and men as active-temporal. For further elaboration of this theme, see Emily Martin, "The Egg and the Sperm: How Science Has Constructed a Romance Based on

Stereotypical Male-Female Roles," in *Feminist Theory and the Body*, ed. Janet Price and Margrit Shildrick (New York: Routledge, 1999), 179–89. See also Lisa Campo-Engelstein and Nadia L. Johnson, "Revisiting 'The Fertilization Fairytale': An Analysis of Gendered Language Used to Describe Fertilization in Science Textbooks from Middle School to Medical School," *Cultural Studies of Science Education* 9 (2014): 201–20.

7. Think only of Kant, who famously claimed that "the entire fairer sex" gladly would "remain immature for life." See Immanuel Kant, "An Answer to the Question: What Is Enlightenment?," in *What Is Enlightenment? Eighteenth-Century Answers and Twentieth-Century Questions*, trans. and ed. James Schmidt (Berkeley: University of California Press, 1996), 58.

8. See, for example, *The Ethics of Ambiguity*, 37–38 and 141–42.

9. This is also reflected in the quite common view that women are incapable of developing moral character. Think, for example, of Freud's contention that women—due to the specific nature of their psychosexual development—fail to fully develop a superego: "In the absence of fear of castration the chief motive is lacking which leads boys to surmount the Oedipus complex. Girls remain in it for an indeterminate length of time; they demolish it late and, even so, incompletely. In these circumstances the formation of the super-ego must suffer; it cannot attain the strength and independence which give it its cultural significance, and feminists are not pleased when we point out to them the effects of this factor upon the average feminine character." See Sigmund Freud, "Femininity," in *Freud on Women: A Reader*, trans. James Strachey, ed. Elisabeth Young-Bruehl (New York: W. W. Norton & Company, 1990), 357. Elsewhere, Freud examines how the dissolution of the Oedipus complex differs in boys and girls, and how this relates to temporal projection. In "Some Psychical Consequences of the Anatomical Distinction Between the Sexes," he concludes that boys leave the Oedipal phase in a sudden and disclosed manner ("in boys . . . it is literally smashed to pieces by the shock of threatened castration"), while girls develop in a more gradual way, characterized by process rather than rupture ("In girls . . . the Oedipus complex escapes the fate which it meets with in boys: it may be slowly abandoned or dealt with by repression, or its effects may persist far into women's normal mental life"), thus inscribing girls in a different temporal relationship to development. See Sigmund Freud, "Some Psychical Consequences of the Anatomical Distinction Between the Sexes," in vol. 19 of *The Standard Edition of the Complete Psychological Works of Sigmund Freud*, ed. and trans. James Strachey (London: Hogarth Press, 1953–1974), 257. Kristeva has written extensively on the developmental difference between boys and girls with regard to the Oedipus complex, and she connects it to the question of temporality: "That temporality, whether or not it is based on the experience of menstrual cycles and motherhood, which interrupts linear time and the course of desire-to-death, also seems to resonate with female psychosexuality.

From *Oedipus prime* to *Oedipus double prime* . . . a woman completes a complex journey, changing positions and objects: passivation, receptivity, aggression, possession. She goes from the mother to the father, from the sensory to the signifiable, from the cloacal and the vaginal to the phallic, from the internal object to the external object, and back to that perpetual Oedipus, which never seems completed in the female subject, never closed, but that is appeased when love is stripped of its passion in motherhood, friendships, cosmic relationships. Could the two-faced Oedipus, interminable, always beginning again, be the source of this insistence on the rhythm of renewal, against the linear time of fated completion?" See Julia Kristeva, *Colette*, vol. 3 of *Female Genius: Life, Madness, Words—Hannah Arendt, Melanie Klein, Colette*, trans. Jane Marie Todd (New York: Columbia University Press, 2004), 424.

10. Judith Butler, "Variations on Sex and Gender: Beauvoir, Wittig and Foucault," in *Feminism as Critique: On the Politics of Gender*, ed. Seyla Benhabib and Drucilla Cornell (Minneapolis: University of Minnesota Press, 1987), 133.

11. Ibid.

12. Later in *The Ethics of Ambiguity*, Beauvoir stresses again that our reducing the other to immanence amounts to reducing them to a thing: "Reduced to pure facticity, congealed in his immanence, cut off from his future, deprived of his transcendence and of the world which that transcendence discloses, a man no longer appears as anything more than a thing among things" (100).

13. See Elizabeth V. Spelman, "Woman as Body: Ancient and Contemporary Views," *Feminist Studies* 8, no. 1 (1982): 109–31.

14. Fanon, *Black Skin, White Masks*, xvi.

15. Deutscher, *A Politics of Impossible Difference*, 119.

16. bell hooks explains her use of the term: "I often use the phrase 'imperialist white-supremacist capitalist patriarchy' to describe the interlocking political systems that are the foundation of our nation's politics." See *The Will to Change: Men, Masculinity, and Love* (New York: Atria Books, 2004), 17.

17. See the epigraph of this chapter. As we shall see in the course of what follows, I will argue that both women and men, in fact, have had their wings cut. If men are unaware of this mutilation (they live under the illusion that they are creatures of progress and futurity), women are more immediately and acutely aware of their having been robbed of time. Using the terminology employed by Beauvoir in *The Ethics of Ambiguity*, we might say that "the genuinely free man" in fact is nothing but an "adventurer." The former, on her own account, is "conscious of the real requirements of his own freedom, which can will itself only by destining itself to an open future, by seeking to extend itself by means of the freedom of others" (60), while the latter, on the contrary, "thinks he can assert his own existence without taking into account that of others" (61). Contra Beauvoir, I want to argue that what she calls "the genuinely free man" in fact is bound to be an oppressor, since the very notion of freedom upon which

he—and Beauvoir—operate is one that ascribes the possibility for freedom and transcendence exclusively to a linear model of time. Both men and women, on my account, are therefore prisoners of a rigid temporal model that forecloses transcendence and freedom altogether (women because they are imprisoned in cyclical time; men because they are imprisoned in a model of time that depends upon the repression-oppression of cyclical time—namely the linear model of time that Beauvoir herself associates with freedom).

18. "Because she herself is also an existent, because transcendence also inhabits her and her project is not repetition but surpassing herself toward another future; she finds the confirmation of masculine claims in the core of her being," Beauvoir asserts (SS 74).

19. To be sure, the distinction made here between "equality" and "difference" feminisms—and the characterization of each—is extremely schematic and reductive. I bring it up here mostly because it offers a way of entering into Kristeva's discussion of the different waves of feminism in her classic essay "Women's Time," which will be the focus of my attention in what follows.

20. Such a strategy runs the risk of reproducing other forms of oppression. As Chanter has noted in the opening chapter of *Gender: Key Concepts in Philosophy*: "There are . . . a number of reasons to be wary of defining feminism as a movement to achieve equality. If we assume that feminism aims to accomplish the equality of women with men, the question arises, which men? With whom do women want equality? Presumably feminists are not striving to be the equals of oppressed, disenfranchised, or disadvantaged men. It becomes clear then that an inexplicit assumption built into the idea that feminists should strive for equality with men is that women seek equality with privileged men. Since privilege plays itself out in ways that typically benefit white, middle class, and heterosexual identities, to define feminism in terms of equality is in effect to build into the definition of feminism privileged assumptions that bias it from the start." See Tina Chanter, "Formative Movements and Concepts in the History of Feminism," chap. 1 in *Gender: Key Concepts in Philosophy* (London: Continuum, 2006), 8. For similar concerns, see also bell hooks, "Feminism: A Movement to End Sexist Oppression," in *Feminist Theory: From Margin to Center* (New York: South End Press, 1985), 17–18. To privilege linear time over cyclical time in other words amounts to privileging not only a male outlook on the world, but it also serves to reproduce the privilege of white people over people of color, rational thought over manual labor, and heterosexual over homosexual identity. The white heterosexual man is, precisely, associated with progress and futurity, while women, people of color, the working class, and gay folks are seen as bound by (cyclical) repetition.

21. See *The Second Sex*, 764–66. It should be noted that I am giving a very schematic account of Beauvoir's project here—I merely use her text as a point of departure in order to organize my argument. Needless to say, her work is

complex, and a more generous reading would unearth several instances in which Beauvoir's text would allow us to imagine alternative modes of, for example, female embodiment. For a strong critique of the kind of reading of Beauvoir that I am pursuing here, see Sara Heinämaa, "What Is a Woman? Butler and Beauvoir on the Foundations of the Sexual Difference," *Hypatia: A Journal of Feminist Philosophy* 12, no. 1 (1997): 20–39. Heinämaa argues that *The Second Sex* is a phenomenological study of sexual difference rather than an ideological definition or sociological explanation. See also many of the contributions to the recent edited volume *Differences: Rereading Beauvoir and Irigaray*, edited by Emily Anne Parker and Anne van Leeuwen.

22. Kathryn Sophia Belle (formerly known as Kathryn Gines), has noted that "Beauvoir conceals the whiteness of the woman/women she is most often describing as Other while also dismissing the gendered aspects of anti-Black racism, antisemitism, colonialism, and class oppression to which she compares white women's oppression." See Kathryn T. Gines, "Comparative and Competing Frameworks of Oppression in Simone de Beauvoir's *The Second Sex*," *Graduate Faculty Philosophy Journal* 33, nos. 1–2 (2014): 251. It is worth noting that this critique by and large applies to the work of Kristeva and Irigaray too.

23. In Beauvoir's defense, however, we should note that what she might fail to do conceptually, she achieves performatively. While she expressed skepticism about cyclical time, her own project in a certain sense follows the movement of return that I seek to elaborate here: it is, precisely, only by *returning* to the set of historical and fictive myths that have exiled women from transcendence and self-realization that she is able to envision liberation and a transformation of female subjectivity. Our liberation—the possibility of a different future—thus depends on anamnesis, on coming to grips with our past.

24. I should note, as decolonial thinkers like Mignolo and Quijano have done before me, that the dualism between linear and cyclical time reaches its most radical manifestation under conditions of modernity. The modern age—or *Neuzeit* in German—can quite literally be described both as a new time, as a time with a novel conception of time, and as a time that views time in terms of, precisely, novelty. Modernity is marked by a series of "new beginnings" (think only of the philosophical projects of René Descartes, Kant, and Hegel; or the French Revolution, secularism, the nuclear bomb, or our first trip to the moon). Linear time, and the emphasis on futurity that it implies, is the utmost manifestation of Western modern ideality and our thoroughgoing escape from the body. But such *escape* from the body, paradoxically, results in the reduction of (some) human beings to *mere bodies*: the diminution, in chattel slavery or concentration camps, or in the prison industrial complex of our own times, of human life to "bare life" (to borrow a term from Giorgio Agamben), or "superfluousness" (borrowing instead from Arendt), only reflects a political project

following a linear logic—a logic where life is a means to the lowliest of ends, and where singular lives are reduced to an indistinguishable and anonymous mass.

25. Dean Spade, "Resisting Medicine, Re/modeling Gender," *Berkeley Women's Law Journal* 15 (2003): 28.

26. For a critique of these kinds of "forward-moving truer identity" models, see Mariana Ortega, *In-Between: Latina Feminist Phenomenology, Multiplicity, and the Self* (Albany: State University of New York Press, 2016), 180–83. Here, Ortega draws from Latina thinkers such as Gloria Anzaldúa and Lugones to argue in favor of a complex multiplicitous self that refuses assimilationist linearity and instead embraces "ambiguity, liminality, multiplicity, and even contradiction," since, as she argues, "one's identification with a particular identity does not necessarily move linearly in a forward manner toward a truer identity" (180).

27. Julia Kristeva, *Strangers to Ourselves*, trans. Leon S. Roudiez (New York: Columbia University Press, 1991), 3, 7. Henceforth, references to this text will be given parenthetically within the main body of the text, using the abbreviation SO.

28. Albert Memmi, *Colonizer and Colonized*, trans. Howard Greenfeld (Boston: Beacon Press, 1991), 122.

29. Dean Spade's critique of the social regulation of trans narratives echoes that of Ortega: "the scripted transsexual childhood narrative must be performed . . . maintaining an idea of two discrete gender categories that normally contain everyone but occasionally are wrongly assigned, requiring correction to reestablish the norm." See Spade, "Resisting Medicine, Re/modeling Gender," 26. He goes on to note that "such a standard naturalizes and depoliticizes gender and gender role distress. It creates a fictional transsexual who just knows in *hir gut* what man is and what woman is, and knows that *sie* is trapped in the wrong body" (25). What's more, and here Spade is explicitly drawing from personal experience: "*in order to be deemed real I need to be willing to make the commitment to 'full-time' maleness, or they can't be sure that I won't regret my surgery*" (21). There can be no looking back, no in-between, no simultaneity or ambiguity or fluctuation. The linear narrative requires static and self-assured identity categories, gaze fixed forward, dichotomies left unchallenged and untouched.

30. Fisher, Phillips, and Katri, "Trans Temporalities," 9.

31. Marie Draz, "Born This Way? Time and the Coloniality of Gender," *Journal of Speculative Philosophy* 31, no. 3 (2017): 376.

32. Fisher, Phillips, and Katri, "Trans Temporalities," 4, 2.

33. Yirmiyahu Yovel has argued that Kant's philosophy of history in effect is a rewriting of his philosophy of religion. We might say that "history" comes to replace "religion" as a placeholder for the realization of future ideals. See Yirmiyahu Yovel, *Kant and the Philosophy of History* (Princeton, NJ: Princeton University Press, 1980).

34. Julia Kristeva, "Julia Kristeva Reads *The Second Sex* Sixty Years Later," trans. Timothy Hackett, *philoSOPHIA: A Journal of Continental Feminism* 1, no. 2 (2011): 141.

35. Of course it matters who we include in the "we" here. We are not all lacking a past in the same way, which is also to say that the "return" to the past that I am advocating for in this book will not have the same implications for everyone. Power dynamics matter, as do our epistemic standpoints, and there is a huge difference between appeals to the past made by dominant groups ("Make America Great Again!") and those made by marginalized groups seeking to reclaim a past that was stolen from them. As Albert Memmi has noted about the lived conditions of the colonized: "He has been torn away from his past and cut off from his future, his traditions are dying and he loses the hope of acquiring a new culture." See Memmi, *The Colonizer and the Colonized*, 127–28.

36. Julia Kristeva, "In Times Like These, Who Needs Psychoanalysts?," chap. 2 in *New Maladies of the Soul*, 30.

37. Julia Kristeva, *The Sense and Non-Sense of Revolt*, vol. 1 of *The Powers and Limits of Psychoanalysis*, trans. Jeanine Herman (New York: Columbia University Press, 2000), 9. Henceforth, references to this text will be given parenthetically within the main body of the text, using the abbreviation SNS.

38. Grosz shares this view, noting that "the very questions of subjectivity, matter, power, and knowledge—the most central concepts of contemporary politics—face reconsideration once their temporal underpinnings are made explicit." And she claims—correctly I think—that this is what is at stake in the work of Irigaray too: "A reconfiguration of the subject will, sooner or later, require that our understanding of space and time themselves undergo dramatic metamorphoses." Grosz, "Feminist Futures?," 15, 13. To provide women with a subject position would, on Irigaray's account, "presuppose a change in the whole economy of space-time." Luce Irigaray, "Sexual Difference," chap. 1 in *An Ethics of Sexual Difference*, trans. Carolyn Burke and Gillian C. Gill (Ithaca, NY: Cornell University Press, 1993), 11. Henceforth, references to this essay will be given parenthetically within the main body of the text, using the abbreviation SD.

39. I will say more about the relationship between semiotic and symbolic later on. For now, let me simply note that the semiotic, for Kristeva, alludes to affective aspects of signification, while the symbolic represents syntactic organization. As we shall see, however, the point of Kristeva's work is precisely to challenge the idea that there would be a rigid dualism between two such realms, and to show instead that they necessarily are co-implicated and co-dependent (that both, to be more precise, have an organizing function, and that no coherent meaning can be produced unless both aspects of signification are present).

40. Luce Irigaray, *The Forgetting of Air in Martin Heidegger*, trans. Mary Beth Mader (Austin: University of Texas Press, 1999), 151. Henceforth, references to this text will be given parenthetically within the main body of the text, using the abbreviation FAMH.

41. When I say that the body has been "de-sexualized," I obviously do not mean to deny the intense sexualization of (especially female) bodies in our culture. I am simply arguing that the particularity and singularity of female sexuality have been overshadowed by a model of sexuality crafted on male psychosexual development alone (remember that Freud describes the little girl as a castrated boy). The body, in other words, has been made to be *sexual* rather than *sexuate*. Put differently, we might say that our culture makes room for *male* bodies and *non-male* bodies, but that no discourse exists as of yet for making sense of the singularly *female* body. Or, to be sure, of any and all bodies that can be categorized neither as male nor female, but that fall in-between or beyond such categories.

42. "Theoretically there would be no such thing as woman. She would not exist. The best that can be said is that she does *not exist yet*." See Luce Irigaray, "How to Conceive (of) a Girl," in *Speculum of the Other Woman*, trans. Gillian C. Gill (Ithaca, NY: Cornell University Press, 1985), 166.

43. Deutscher, *A Politics of Impossible Difference*, 121. Drawing from the work of John Caputo, Deutscher suggests that we view Irigaray's notion of sexuate difference as "messianic" (103–06).

44. Grosz, "Feminist Futures?," 14.

45. Luce Irigaray, "The Female Gender," chap. 7 in *Sexes and Genealogies*, trans. Gillian C. Gill (New York: Columbia University Press, 1993), 108. Henceforth, references to this essay will be given parenthetically within the main body of the text, using the abbreviation FG.

46. Luce Irigaray, "A Chance for Life: Limits to the Concept of the Neuter and the Universal in Science and Other Disciplines," chap. 11 in *Sexes and Genealogies*, 200.

47. Ibid., 200–01.

48. That said, it is clearly the case that Irigaray by and large envisions sexuate difference in dual terms, and that her discussion is haunted by cis- and heteronormative assumptions throughout. This is a problem that has been addressed in the secondary literature, and that we need to continue to address even as we draw from and find resources in her thinking on these matters. I hope that my engagement with her work in this book will convince the reader that we need not throw the baby out with the bath water—that Irigaray's work on sexuate difference can be salvaged and that it offers some very valuable resources, despite its obvious limitations and blind spots.

49. The issue of essentialism has always been central in debates about French Feminism, especially in discussions of Irigaray's philosophy. Naomi Schor gives a clear account of the various ways in which the very notion of "essentialism" has been interpreted. See "This Essentialism Which Is Not One: Coming to Grips with Irigaray," in *Engaging with Irigaray: Feminist Philosophy and Modern European Thought*, ed. Carolyn Burke, Naomi Schor, and Margaret Whitford (New York: Columbia University Press, 1994), 57–78. Quoting the *Dictionary of Philosophy*

*and Religion*, Schor explains that "essentialism is the belief that things have an essence," and goes on to specify the meaning of the term in the context of feminism: it "consists in the belief that woman has an essence, that woman can be specified by one or a number of inborn attributes that define across cultures and throughout history her unchanging being" (59). Essentialism in the context of feminism is, in other words, typically associated with biological determinism. The question that some feminist thinkers have asked, however, is whether or not "biologism" (a return to biology and nature) necessarily implies essentialism. As I noted in the introduction—and as I will stress in my discussion of Irigaray in what follows—nature and biology are realms that, while traditionally described as driven by the repetitive movement of cyclical time, in fact are marked by differentiation and continual change. To say that sexuate difference is "natural," or even "real," would thus not necessarily amount to saying that it is static, that it does not change, or that it would be fully independent from culture and history. Making a distinction between "strategic" and "realist" essentialism, Stone embraces the latter in her own interpretation of Irigaray's later work. She stresses that the former (strategic essentialism) "aims to revalue female identity and bodies only as imagined and symbolised," and that it therefore reinforces "the conceptual hierarchy of culture over nature." The latter (realist essentialism) allows us instead to ascribe natural characteristics to sexual difference without for that matter viewing it as static or absolute, since nature precisely is "fluid and everchanging." See Stone, *Luce Irigaray and the Philosophy of Sexual Difference*, 13, 45. Stone thus redefines the very notion of essentialism to mean, in the context of feminist philosophy, that sexual difference is *real*, but that its reality (a reality that, precisely, exceeds the *merely* cultural realm of signification) by no means renders it static or unchanging. It is also worth noting, here, that the reality of sexual difference need not (indeed *ought* not) be framed in dichotomous terms, since the prevalence of intersex folks is an important reminder of the biological variability of sex. For further reflections on this issue, see Anne Fausto-Sterling, *Sexing the Body: Gender Politics and the Construction of Sexuality* (New York: Basic Books, 2000). In short, an appeal to the reality of sex need not amount to assuming that it is static, unchanging, or dichotomous.

## Chapter 2

1. Luce Irigaray, "On the Maternal Order," chap. 4 in *Je, Tu Nous: Toward a Culture of Difference*, trans. Alison Martin (New York: Routledge, 1993), 37, emphasis mine.

2. It is, in my mind, no coincidence that Irigaray's philosophy of sexuate difference is marked by a concern with environmental issues. Her work as a whole could be described as seeking to establish a sustainable future. The very

culture of sameness against which she turns is manifestly a self-destructive one. If we understand her emphasis on the cultivation of difference not only as an outcry against the subjugation of women (and the simultaneous reduction of female subjects to the negative mirror image of man) but also as a protest against our systematic subjugation of nature (and the reduction of our living earth to a reservoir of resources to be [ab]used for higher ends) we begin to see that her worries about the future are more than empty rhetoric or hyperbolism. The current fragility of our future (in the wake of global warming and nuclear threats) is indeed an immediate reflection of the dangers inherent in a culture of sameness. It is interesting to note that the long poetic prologue to her book *To Be Two*—a meditation on the urgent need to cultivate a world of sexuate difference—is a mournful celebration of the earth that birthed us and that we are well under way to bury in ashes. See Luce Irigaray, *To Be Two*, trans. Monique M. Rhodes and Marco F. Cocito-Monoc (New York: Routledge, 2001), 1–16. In conversation, Irigaray has revealed that this prologue was written on an airplane between Montréal and Paris, and that it instigated her environmentally motivated decision to never again fly (that trip was, indeed, her last airborne journey to this day). Her most recent book, co-authored with Michael Marder, is an exploration into the vegetal world and its potential to rescue our planet and our species. If Irigaray has argued that living and coexisting are deficient unless we recognize sexuate difference as a crucial dimension of our existence, Marder believes the same is true for vegetal difference. See Luce Irigaray and Michael Marder, *Through Vegetal Being: Two Philosophical Perspectives* (New York: Columbia University Press, 2016).

3. Luce Irigaray, *Between East and West: From Singularity to Community*, trans. Stephen Pluháček (New York: Columbia University Press, 2002), 46. Henceforth, references to this text will be given parenthetically within the main body of the text, using the abbreviation BEW.

4. Ziarek, "Toward a Radical Female Imaginary," 64.

5. Ewa Płonowska Ziarek sees Irigaray's own philosophy as an attempt to disrupt this division: "By emphasizing the temporality and intensity of bodily becomings, Irigaray contests the confinement of time to the interiority of the male subject and the corresponding association of the female body with the exteriority of space—a set of distinctions, as her work on Aristotle and Plato shows, deeply entrenched in the Western philosophical tradition" (68).

6. The maternal dimensions of this critical discussion of time will be thoroughly examined in the chapters that treat the past. Our task, Irigaray seems to suggest, is to bring the mother back to life again, to, as it were, give time back to the figure who gave us the gift of time (life) in the first place. To return is to reclaim a lost maternal continent.

7. Luce Irigaray, "The Difference Between the Sexes," interview with Roger-Pol Droit (originally published in *Le Monde*, June 7, 1985), in *Why*

*Different? A Culture of Two Subjects*, trans. Camille Collins, ed. Luce Irigaray
and Sylvère Lotringer (New York: Semiotext(e), 2000), 45.

8. Luce Irigaray, "The Neglect of Female Genealogies," chap. 1 in *Je, Tu
Nous*, 15. It is of course this kind of argument that has made queer theorists
suspicious of the future. As I pointed out in the introduction, either they have
tried to articulate novelty and futurity in terms that avoid conventional views
about family relations and child rearing (such as in the work of Jack Halberstam), or they have rejected the value of futurity altogether since it is seen as
problematically embedded in a heteronormative overvaluation of reproduction
(such as in the work of Edelman). While I think it is safe to say that Irigaray's
work is plagued by heteronormative presuppositions throughout, I nevertheless
hope to be able to show, in what follows, that the insistence that change/futurity
be tied to sexuate difference need not assume that heterosexual procreation is a
vehicle for change. To the contrary, by insisting on *sexuate* rather than sexual
difference, and on a *culture* of sexuate difference rather than biological discourse
about procreation and the survival of the species, I argue that we gain the ability
to move from a mono-sexual culture to one that allows for sexual proliferation
and variation. I will return to this issue later in this chapter.

9. Luce Irigaray, preface to *Key Writings*, trans. Laine Harrington (London:
Continuum, 2004), ix.

10. Luce Irigaray, "Flesh Colors," chap. 9 in *Sexes and Genealogies*, 163.

11. To these two must be added yet another meaning that Irigaray attributes
to sexuate difference: it is to be understood as that which has always already
been excluded from philosophical discourse, and yet that around which such a
discourse necessarily revolves.

12. We should note that Irigaray is careful to stress the irreducibility of
sexuate difference merely to its reproductive or biological function. Her reading
of Diotima's speech in Plato's *Symposium* attests to this. Here, she emphasizes
that Diotima's mistake is to reduce the encounter between two (the act of
love) to the production of a third (the child). Such a reduction diminishes the
indeterminacy of love and turns it into a teleological project, thus reducing
sexuate difference to a means for reproduction only. Irigaray describes this as
a "failure of love," and ties it to the question of time: "Something becomes
frozen in space-time, with the loss of a vital intermediary and of an accessible
transcendental that remains alive. A sort of teleological triangle is put into
place instead of a perpetual journey, a perpetual transvaluation, a permanent
becoming. For this, love was the vehicle. But, if procreation becomes its goal,
it risks losing its internal motivation, its 'inner' fecundity, its slow and constant
generation, regeneration." See Luce Irigaray, "Sorcerer Love: A Reading of
Plato, *Symposium*, 'Diotima's Speech,'" chap. 2 in *An Ethics of Sexual Difference*,
27. I will return to the question of love and its central place in what Irigaray

has called her "ethics of sexual difference" (and what I will call an "ethics of temporal difference") in chapter 6.

13. For a more systematic attempt to highlight the heterogeneity and self-differentiation that marks the natural-biological realm, see Grosz, *The Nick of Time*. See also Stone, "Nature, Sexual Duality, and Bodily Multiplicity," chap. 3 in *Luce Irigaray and the Philosophy of Sexual Difference*.

14. Patricia Huntington has argued that the very way in which metaphysicians have conceptualized questions of being and origins in principle is modeled on male morphology: "Metaphysical depictions that reify Being as transcendent principle, first cause, absolute spirit, or powerful God evince a consistent privileging of phallic attributes." See *Ecstatic Subjects, Utopia, and Recognition* (Albany: State University of New York Press, 1998), 48. Quoted in Stone, *Luce Irigaray and the Philosophy of Sexual Difference*, 34. Stone explains that "the 'first cause' is symbolised as male in that it is assumed to share the form of the male body imagined as solid, phallic, erect, and unified" (34).

15. Hannah Arendt, *The Human Condition* (Chicago: University of Chicago Press, 1998), 96. Henceforth, references to this text will be given parenthetically within the main body of the text, using the abbreviation HC.

16. Barbara Duden, *The Woman Beneath the Skin* (Cambridge, MA: Harvard University Press, 1991), vi.

17. Irigaray, "A Chance for Life," in *Sexes and Genealogies*, 198.

18. Luce Irigaray, "When Our Lips Speak Together," chap. 11 in *This Sex Which Is Not One*, trans. Catherine Porter (Ithaca, NY: Cornell University Press, 1985), 205. The ellipses are in the original text; nothing has been omitted here.

19. Luce Irigaray, "An Ethics of Sexual Difference," chap. 8 in *An Ethics of Sexual Difference*, 128.

20. Irigaray, "How to Conceive (of) a Girl," in *Speculum of the Other Woman*, 164.

21. Ibid.

22. Luce Irigaray, "Plato's *Hystera*," in ibid., 267. Henceforth, references to this essay will be given parenthetically within the main body of the text, using the abbreviation PH.

23. Fausto-Sterling, *Sexing the Body*, 21–22.

24. Ibid., 26.

25. As Talia Mae Bettcher puts it: "The wrong-body narrative outlines a standard telos (genital reconstruction surgery), and any identity that fails to desire that telos is ruled ineligible." See "Trapped in the Wrong Theory: Rethinking Trans Oppression and Resistance," *Signs: Journal of Women in Culture and Society* 39, no. 2 (2014): 402. See also Fisher, Phillips, and Katri, who describe the essays in their special issue of *Somatechnics* on trans temporalities as demonstrating "how

the linearity of this normative trope—the traumatic past, the intervening present and the hopeful future—informs, shapes, shadows and haunts trans lifeforms and discourses." Fisher, Phillips, and Katri, "Trans Temporalities," 3.

26. Spade, "Resisting Medicine, Re/modeling Gender," 28. The literature on the effects of medical gatekeeping and its tendency to streamline diverse trans experiences through strict enforcement of binary gender norms is vast. For a paradigmatic example, see Sandy Stone, "The *Empire* Strikes Back: A Posttranssexual Manifesto," in *Body Guards: The Cultural Politics of Gender Ambiguity*, ed. Julia Epstein and Kristina Straub (New York: Routledge, 1991).

27. Bettcher, "Trapped in the Wrong Theory," 392.

28. Spade, "Resisting Medicine, Re/modeling Gender," 25.

29. For an analysis of how Irigaray's philosophy of sexuate difference can be used to think through trans identity, see Danielle Poe, "Can Luce Irigaray's Notion of Sexual Difference Be Applied to Transsexual and Transgender Narratives?," in *Thinking with Irigaray*, ed. Mary C. Rawlinson, Sabrina L. Hom, and Serene J. Khader (Albany: State University of New York Press, 2011).

30. Luce Irigaray, "Feminine Identity: Biology or Social Conditioning?," chap. 2 in *Democracy Begins Between Two*, trans. Kirsteen Anderson (New York: Routledge, 2001), 37.

31. It is obviously not *actually* disembodied, but it is articulated as such in much of modern philosophy. The body, we might say, becomes a *problem* for any philosophical project that seeks to establish a foundational notion of truth. For a classic feminist analysis of this aspect of Western thought, see Genevieve Lloyd, *The Man of Reason: "Male" and "Female" in Western Philosophy* (Minneapolis: University of Minnesota Press, 1984).

32. As for Irigaray's emphasis on *two*, a generous reading would allow us to say that this aspect of her thought, rather than foreclosing plurality and reducing human subjects to two genders alone, in fact is meant to make plurality possible in the first place. Throughout her work, she consistently argues that all attempts to think plurality or heterogeneity are bound to fail if they do not follow from an initial challenge of the paradigm of the one (the only paradigm hitherto known to us). The construction of a world of two is, in other words, not necessarily a reductive project, but one that at least potentially challenges the paradigm of the one so as to make possible multiple subjectivities and sexual variation (this is, we might guess, why Irigaray time and again speaks of "at least two" and "two" interchangeably).

33. Irigaray, "The Three Genders," chap. 10 in *Sexes and Genealogies*, 172. Elsewhere, Irigaray expresses a similar thought: Within a Freudian paradigm, she complains, "sexuality is linked to the laws of physics and thus has no freedom and a future that involves only repetition and explosion, never evolution. The only way to escape this sad fate would be procreation. . . . Becoming man or

woman would merely mean becoming reproductive units, with no energy to spare for thinking, sharing, growing with the other sex." See Irigaray, "A Chance for Life," in ibid., 197.

34. I use the term transcendence here not to describe a movement into a world beyond or above the one we know, but rather as temporal projection within this world. I will say more about this in what follows.

35. Luce Irigaray, *Sharing the World* (London: Continuum, 2008), ix–x.

36. In an interview, Irigaray stresses her own interest in transcendence: "I think Simone de Beauvoir said that woman remains always within the dimension of immanence and that she's incapable of transcendence. But—by I don't know what mystery!—transcendence is something that interests me very much. Often the way in which I'm read and interpreted is too immanent, too much tied to contiguity, and the source and reference of my work is misunderstood. It's true that a woman who has a relationship to transcendence and to the transcendental in a real rather than a formal way is something all too rare. But I'd say there's been a little of that in my life." See Irigaray, " 'Je—Luce Irigaray,' " 113.

37. As Ghanaian-British artist John Akomfrah puts it, with reference to his own artistic practice: "the great shifts in human progress that are made possible by technology can also cause the profoundest destruction and suffering." See Sean O'Hagan, "John Akomfrah: 'Progress Can Cause Profound Suffering,' " interview in *The Guardian*, October 1, 2017, accessed at https://www.theguardian.com/artanddesign/2017/oct/01/john-akomfrah-purple-climate-change.

38. See Jean-Paul Sartre, *Being and Nothingness: An Essay on Phenomenological Ontology*, trans. Hazel E. Barnes (London: Routledge, 2009), 141. It would of course be unfair and inaccurate to say that the existentialists call for an unconditional repression of the body or the past. Consider, for example, this passage from Beauvoir's *The Ethics of Ambiguity*: "the fact of having a past is part of the human condition; if the world behind us were bare, we would hardly be able to see anything before us but a gloomy desert. . . . One does not love the past in its living truth if he insists on preserving its hardened and mummified forms. The past is an appeal; it is an appeal toward the future which sometimes can save it only by destroying it. Even though this destruction may be a sacrifice, it would be a lie to deny it: since man wants there to be being, he can not renounce any form of being without regret. *But a genuine ethics does not teach us either to sacrifice it or deny it: we must assume it*" (93, 95, emphasis mine). For an elaboration of Beauvoir's *positive* treatment of embodiment (and hence a defense of Beauvoir in light of the many critiques raised against her on this point), see Heinämaa, "What Is a Woman?"

39. See Wood, *The Deconstruction of Time*, 375–76.

40. For a discussion of this meaning of the term, see Paul Woodruff,

"Aristotle on *Mimesis*," in *Essays on Aristotle's* Poetics, ed. Amélie Oksenberg Rorty (Princeton, NJ: Princeton University Press, 1992), 73.

41. Plato speaks of *mimesis* already in book 3 of this text, but his most thorough (and most controversial) discussion of this topic appears in book 10, where he examines the relationship between the ideal forms, the sensible beings in the world, and the reproduction of sensible things and beings in works of art. See Plato, *Republic*, trans. Allan Bloom (New York: Basic Books, 1991), especially 595a–602b.

42. As always with Plato, this is a comment that needs qualification. There are several places where he speaks in more positive terms about *mimesis*. For references and examples, see Woodruff, "Aristotle on *Mimesis*," 77. Needless to say, Plato's own philosophy is mimetic in nature, not only because of the fact that it is presented in the form of dialogues, but also because Plato makes heavy use of images and metaphors throughout. I will return to the question of metaphor in Plato in my discussion of the cave allegory in chapter 9 of this book.

43. See Aristotle, *Poetics*, trans. Richard Janko (Indianapolis: Hackett, 1987).

44. For a discussion of the development of Greek mimesis in modern aesthetics, see Stephen Halliwell, *The Aesthetics of Mimesis: Ancient Texts and Modern Problems* (Princeton, NJ: Princeton University Press, 2002).

45. See, for example, Walter Benjamin, "The Work of Art in the Age of Its Technological Reproducibility," in vol. 3 of *Selected Writings 1935–1938*, trans. Edmund Jephcott and Harry Zohn, ed. Howard Eiland and Michael W. Jennings (Cambridge, MA: The Belknap Press of Harvard University Press, 2002), 101–33. For an original and nuanced discussion of the relationship between art and "truth-only cognition" in modernity and in "post-aesthetic" theories of art, see J. M. Bernstein, *The Fate of Art: Aesthetic Alienation from Kant to Derrida and Adorno* (University Park: Pennsylvania State University Press, 1992).

46. An interesting challenge to this view of machines as lacking rhythm can be found in Lars von Trier's film *Dancer in the Dark*, where the character played by Björk, Selma (who is blind), finds the most powerful music precisely in the "noise" of the machines in the factory where she works.

47. Luce Irigaray, "The Power of Discourse and the Subordination of the Feminine," chap. 4 in *This Sex Which Is Not One*, 76.

48. Gwendolyn DuBois Shaw, *Seeing the Unspeakable: The Art of Kara Walker* (Durham, NC: Duke University Press, 2004). Miller, in her book on Kristeva, describes sublimation as making present "that which is by nature unrepresentable." See Elaine P. Miller, *Head Cases: Julia Kristeva on Philosophy and Art in Depressed Times* (New York: Columbia University Press, 2014), 131.

49. I would like to thank María del Rosario Acosta López for suggesting that I engage the work of Kara Walker in this context.

50. Shaw, *Seeing the Unspeakable*, 5.

51. Ibid., 40. Walker capitalizes on this effect by "adding projectors to her installations so that the viewer's body is actually cast into the shadow play in works like *Insurrection*" (40).

52. See Amy Ray Stewart, "Extimate Trauma, Intimate Ethics: Kristevan Revolt in the Artwork of Kara Walker," in *New Forms of Revolt: Essays on Kristeva's Intimate Politics*, ed. Sarah K. Hansen and Rebecca Tuvel (Albany: State University of New York Press, 2017), 85–106.

53. Ibid., 98.

54. Ibid., 99.

55. Miller, *Head Cases*, 130–31.

56. Ibid., 130.

57. Shaw, *Seeing the Unspeakable*, 39.

58. Robert Storr, "Spooked," in *Kara Walker: My Complement, My Enemy, My Oppressor, My Love*, catalog published on the occasion of an exhibition at the Walker Art Center, curated by Philippe Vergne (Minneapolis: Walker Art Center, 2007), 65.

59. Hélène Cixous, "The Laugh of the Medusa," trans. Keith Cohen and Paula Cohen, *Signs: Journal of Women in Culture and Society* 1, no. 4 (1976): 875–93.

60. Storr, "Spooked," 65.

61. Cixous, "The Laugh of the Medusa," 875–76.

62. Quoted in Thomas McEvilley, "Primitivism in the Works of an Emancipated Negress," in *Kara Walker: My Complement, My Enemy, My Oppressor, My Love*, 53.

63. Storr, "Spooked," 65.

64. Kevin Young, "Triangular Trade: Coloring, Remarking, and Narrative in the Writings of Kara Walker," in *Kara Walker: My Complement, My Enemy, My Oppressor, My Love*, 37.

65. See, especially, Judith Butler, "Imitation and Gender Insubordination," in *The Second Wave: A Reader in Feminist Theory*, ed. Linda Nicholson (New York: Routledge, 1997), 301–15; and "Subversive Bodily Acts," chap. 3 in *Gender Trouble: Feminism and the Subversion of Identity*, tenth anniversary edition (New York: Routledge, 1999). Henceforth, references to this edition of *Gender Trouble* will be given parenthetically within the main body of the text, using the abbreviation GT. See also Butler's more recent *Notes Toward a Performative Theory of Assembly* (Cambridge, MA: Harvard University Press, 2015).

66. It should be noted that while some parallels can be drawn between Irigaray's use of mimesis and Butler's emphasis on performativity, my characterization of mimesis as a movement of return to our maternal-material beginnings also establishes a sharp difference between these two thinkers. As will become evident in my discussion of the past in this book, both Irigaray and Kristeva offer a thoroughgoing challenge to Butler's strong emphasis on language and

discursivity in her elaboration of materiality and embodiment. For a careful comparative analysis of the stakes involved in Irigaray and Butler's respective treatment of the role and status of sexual difference, see Stone, "Judith Butler's Challenge to Irigaray," chap. 2 in *Luce Irigaray and the Philosophy of Sexual Difference*. See also Annemie Halsema, "Reconsidering the Notion of the Body in Anti-essentialism, with the Help of Luce Irigaray and Judith Butler," in *Belief, Bodies, and Being*, 152–84.

67. Irigaray, "When Our Lips Speak Together," in *This Sex Which Is Not One*, 216. Her statement here might be read both as challenging the notion that woman would be a copy of man, and the notion that each subject is reducible to one. It is, of course, worth noting that her analysis in this text and elsewhere is cis-normative. Not all women have lips, and not all women want lips. That said, the logic of multiplicity explored here is nevertheless a helpful resource for thinking sexed embodiment beyond a phallic logic of the one and the same. And the very language in the passage cited here seems particularly fruitful for challenging the cis-normative, indeed transphobic, reality enforcement, which, among other things, relies on "the appearance-reality contrast" and the "deceiver-pretender double-bind." See Bettcher, "Trapped in the Wrong Theory," 392.

68. Kristeva, too, has been preoccupied with exploring that which transgresses clear boundaries and divisions. In her work, this is most often articulated in terms of *abjection*—the term that has received perhaps the most attention by feminist readers of her work. For her most extended elaboration of this term, see Julia Kristeva, *Powers of Horror: An Essay on Abjection*, trans. Leon S. Roudiez (New York: Columbia University Press, 1982). For an overview of its transgressive potential, see my essay on Kristeva in *Fifty-One Key Feminist Thinkers*, ed. Lori J. Marso (New York: Routledge, 2016), 129–34.

69. Irigaray, "When Our Lips Speak Together," in *This Sex Which Is Not One*, 212. The ellipsis is in the original text; nothing has been omitted here.

70. Ibid., 209.

71. Ibid., 210. Not all imitation is deliberate though. Irigaray argues that women have been doomed to mimicry and repetition, and she expresses concern about the time that has been lost through such unintentional mimicry: "The ebb and flow of our lives spent in the exhausting labor of copying, miming. Dedicated to reproducing—that sameness in which we have remained for centuries, as the other" (207).

72. Irigaray, "The Power of Discourse," in *This Sex Which Is Not One*, 76.

73. One of the best-known legacies of French Feminism is its emphasis on a "feminine" style of writing, what has been called *écriture féminine*. Perhaps the most central aspect of this writing style is its challenge to the traditional linearity of the narrative or plot.

74. Julia Kristeva, *Revolution in Poetic Language*, trans. Margaret Waller (New York: Columbia University Press, 1984), 57. Henceforth, references to

this text will be given parenthetically within the main body of the text, using the abbreviation RPL. Kristeva's notion of *chōra* will be explicated in detail in chapter 8.

75. The *thetic* is first introduced in *Revolution in Poetic Language* and is described as a "break" that produces the positing of signification. It in other words marks the entry into the symbolic order (43–45). In the next chapter, and even more so in chapter 8, I will further elucidate the relationship between the semiotic and the symbolic.

# Chapter 3

1. In her discussion of Charles Darwin, Grosz is careful to point out that an analysis of the temporality of organic life in central ways informs our views on political life: "While presenting an ontology of life, Darwin also provokes a concern with the possibilities of becoming, and becoming-other, inherent in culture, which are also the basic concerns of feminist and other political and social activists." See Grosz, *The Nick of Time*, 19–20.

2. See Sara Beardsworth, "From Revolution to Revolt Culture," in *Revolt, Affect, Collectivity: The Unstable Boundaries of Kristeva's Polis*, ed. Tina Chanter and Ewa Płonowska Ziarek (Albany: State University of New York Press, 2005).

3. Sjöholm, *Kristeva and the Political*, 1. Henceforth, references to this text will be given parenthetically within the main body of the text, using the abbreviation KP. Sjöholm has accurately noted that there is continuity between Kristeva's early work on *chōra* and her later work on the displacing movement of repetition (123). In what follows, I will primarily focus on the notion of revolt as a movement of return that appears in some of her later books. I will turn to the temporal aspects of *chōra* in detail in chapter 8.

4. Julia Kristeva, "What's Left of 1968?," interview conducted by Philippe Petit, in *Revolt, She Said*, trans. Brian O'Keeffe, ed. Sylvère Lotringer (New York: Semiotext(e), 2002), 42. Henceforth, references to this interview will be given parenthetically within the main body of the text, using the abbreviation WL.

5. Jean-Paul Sartre too has suggested a temporal modification of the *cogito*, although a different one. In *Being and Nothingness*, he notes that it ought to be formulated as "I think; therefore I was," since the human subject, on his account, *is* its past: "whatever I can be said to be in the sense of being-in-itself with a full, compact density . . . is always *my past*." The type of being of the for-itself is, he argues, the *was*. See Sartre, *Being and Nothingness*, 131–43.

6. While Irigaray emphasizes the calculative character of what has been broadly construed as "Western metaphysics," Kristeva's critique is not first and foremost aimed at the Western philosophical tradition as such (although the latter, too, evidently holds significance for her). She focuses more specifically

on the aesthetic and political culture of Western modernity. Sara Beardsworth has provided the most systematic reading of Kristeva within the context of secular modernity. See *Julia Kristeva: Psychoanalysis and Modernity* (Albany: State University of New York Press, 2004).

7. For a discussion of how recent the political usage of this term is, see Hannah Arendt, *On Revolution* (London: Penguin Books, 1990), 35–41.

8. Julia Kristeva, "It Is Right to Rebel . . . ," interview conducted by Philippe Petit, in *Revolt, She Said*, 85.

9. That Freud attaches no moral or political meaning to revolt should by no means mean that revolt is *apolitical* on Kristeva's own account. Sjöholm explains that revolt "gains its political power in the displacement produced through such a repetitive return" (KP 120). Kristeva herself alludes quite clearly to what she herself sees as the political potential of her work: "this cultural revolt intrinsically concerns public life and consequently has profoundly political implications" (IR 11).

10. Butler, "Variations on Sex and Gender," 133.

11. Noëlle McAfee, *Julia Kristeva* (New York: Routledge, 2005), 17.

12. I emphasize this because those who have accused Kristeva of being a biological essentialist—a common critique among especially Anglo-American feminists—have usually done so precisely because they fail to see this *coimplication* of the two modes: they think that Kristeva posits the semiotic as somehow *prior to* and neatly *demarcated from* the symbolic, which she simply never does. I will address some of these criticisms in detail in chapter 8.

13. The disappearance of the body in much scientific-philosophical discourse is one of the central concerns for feminist philosophy—a concern that both Kristeva and Irigaray seek to address throughout their writing (both conceptually and performatively). Sjöholm's analysis of revolt and revolution in Kristeva is colored throughout by the notion that the polymorphous and heterogeneous body is that to which and from which we return: "The question of how we are to regard Kristeva's notion of the political cannot be detached from the corporeal determination of what she calls the fourth term of the dialectic: the drives of the embodied subject, which determines its temporal quality of signification. . . . If the revolt has a temporality of its own, it is precisely in terms of corporeal frailty that it must be thought. The dialectics of such a revolt moves through pleasure, decapitation, displacement and return. Return to where, return from where? Perhaps to and from that through which we have found ourselves capable of the greatest pleasure: the polymorphous, sensuous body that still has so many secrets to be uncovered" (KP 119, 127).

14. While many feminist critics point to Kristeva as a "sacrificial" thinker, Sjöholm has, before me, highlighted Kristeva's own skepticism of the sacrificial logic that underpins Western culture and that eliminates singularity in the

name of universality, and embodiment in the name of disembodied thought and language (KP 60).

15. Paulo Freire, *Pedagogy of the Oppressed*, 30th Anniversary Edition, trans. Myra Bergman Ramos (New York: Bloomsbury Academic, 2016), 44. I would like to thank James Walker for bringing my attention not only to this quote, but to the central concerns of power, privilege, and positionality when we explore the movement of return at play in revolutionary time.

16. Cecilia Sjöholm, "The Temporality of Intimacy: Kristeva's Return to the Political," *The Southern Journal of Philosophy*, special issue on Kristeva's ethical and political thought, proceedings from the Spindel Conference, 42 (2004): 86.

17. McAfee, *Julia Kristeva*, 105–06.

18. Kristeva, "It Is Right to Rebel . . . ," in *Revolt, She Said*, 85.

19. Kristeva, *New Maladies of the Soul*, 3.

20. Ibid., 10.

21. Ibid., 8.

22. Ibid., 6.

23. McAfee, *Julia Kristeva*, 110.

24. For a rich analysis of the repetitive character of the discourse of depressed subjects, see Julia Kristeva, "Life and Death of Speech," chap. 2 in *Black Sun: Depression and Melancholia*, trans. Leon S. Roudiez (New York: Columbia University Press, 1989). Here, Kristeva characterizes the speech of the depressed as "repetitive and monotonous," as a "repetitive rhythm" and a "monotonous melody," which eventually will deteriorate into complete "asymbolia" (33).

25. Julia Kristeva, "The Soul and the Image," chap. 1 in *New Maladies of the Soul*, 5. Kristeva often asserts that psychoanalysis is founded on the conviction that sexuality and thought are co-present. See, for example, *Intimate Revolt*, 144.

26. Freud famously drew attention to the analysand's compulsion to repeat. I will address this issue in more detail in my discussion of the timelessness of the unconscious in chapter 6.

27. Kelly Oliver, "Revolt and Forgiveness," in *Revolt, Affect, Collectivity*, 79.

28. Julia Kristeva, *Tales of Love*, trans. Leon S. Roudiez (New York: Columbia University Press, 1987), 1, 16.

29. Freud acknowledged that this is a risk inherent in the psychoanalytic cure as well. Despite its explicit aim to replace repression-repetition with memory, and despite its transformative potential, the analytic cure could be undone precisely by the compulsion to repeat that, according to Freud, overrides the pleasure principle not only in neurotics, but in all of us. See Sigmund Freud, *Beyond the Pleasure Principle*, trans. and ed. James Strachey (New York: W. W. Norton & Company, 1989).

30. Kristeva, "It Is Right to Rebel . . . ," in *Revolt, She Said*, 92. Grosz has expressed a similar concern—pointing to the fact that the most progressive forms of politics in fact fear the open-endedness of the future. Her own thinking promotes what we might call a politics of radical renewal, but she points to the risks that such a project entails: "This is a most disconcerting and dangerous idea: politics seems to revel in the idea of progress, development, movement, but the very political discourses that seem to advocate it most vehemently (Marxism, feminism, postcolonial and anticolonial discourses, the discourses of antiracism) seem terrified by the idea of a transformation somehow beyond the control of the very revolutionaries who seek it, of a kind of 'anarchization' of the future. If the revolution can carry no guarantee that it will *improve* the current situation or provide something *preferable* to what exists now, what makes it a sought-for ideal? What prevents it from blurring into fascism or conservatism?" See Elizabeth Grosz, "Thinking the New: Of Futures Yet Unthought," in *Becomings: Explorations in Time, Memory, and Futures*, 17, emphasis mine. In *The Human Condition*, Arendt emphasizes the unpredictable and irreversible character of human action, and points to the fact that this very unpredictability has led to the political substitution of making for acting (220–30). I will address this set of issues in more depth in the conclusion to this book.

31. Julia Kristeva, "Revolt and Revolution," interview conducted by Rainer Ganahl, in *Revolt, She Said*, 102.

32. René Descartes, "Meditation One: Concerning Those Things That Can Be Called into Doubt," in *Meditations on First Philosophy*, trans. Donald A. Cress (Indianapolis: Hackett, 1993), 17. This gesture, we might add, can be illustrated by the invention of the French Republican calendar, which would begin in 1792 (when the French First Republic was proclaimed), as if no history prior to that year had existed—a gesture, again, similar to the Cartesian attempt to establish a "first philosophy." This custom of instituting a "new beginning" originates in Christianity (our own time beginning, crucially, with the birth of Christ) and is, in my view, symptomatic of a linear-temporal worldview.

33. We might add, parenthetically, that decapitated women appear in several of Kristeva's novels. These murdered women have, quite literally, been reduced to mere bodies. See, for example, Julia Kristeva, *Possessions*, trans. Barbara Brey (New York: Columbia University Press, 1996), 3. For a discussion of decapitation in art, see also Julia Kristeva, *The Severed Head: Capital Visions*, trans. Jody Gladding (New York: Columbia University Press, 2011), as well as Miller, *Head Cases*.

34. Freire, *Pedagogy of the Oppressed*, 45.

35. Ibid., 84.

36. Echoing the language of Irigaray, she goes on to explain that life must be understood as "growth" and "becoming" (WL 26).

37. Sjöholm makes this claim in contrast with Arendt who, in her view, was concerned with novelty in more straightforward ways.

38. And neither, we should add, is Arendt.

39. Arendt explains that the term "permanent revolution" was coined in the middle of the nineteenth century, by Pierre-Joseph Proudhon. The notion that she refers to, however, implies that "there never has been such a thing as several revolutions, that there is only one revolution, selfsame and perpetual." See Arendt, *On Revolution*, 51. Kristeva's point, as I see it, is not that there would be one revolution only, but rather that revolution, understood as an ongoing critical engagement with the past (our individual pasts and the collective past of history) has no clear beginning or end, but depends on a process that must be kept alive. Once we stop pursuing the movement of return—in other words, once we stop the process of perpetual interrogation—life and culture lose their aliveness and risk the thoughtlessness of totalitarianism or the numbness of the spectacle. We might compare this to the Arendtian idea that *power* is something that can be neither stored nor owned. Instead, it comes into existence if and only if human beings come together and act in concert. It is in the dynamic interactions between members of a community that power emerges—this is why power, on Arendt's account, is fundamentally different from both strength and violence. It is both more powerful and more vulnerable than those latter categories (HC 199–207).

40. See Hannah Arendt, *Eichmann in Jerusalem: A Report on the Banality of Evil* (New York: Penguin Books, 1994).

41. Grosz, "Feminist Futures?," 18–19.

42. Oliver, "Revolt and Forgiveness," 79.

43. We have already seen that Christ's first arrival marked the beginning of our time. Adding that his second arrival will put an end to all time provides us with some further philosophical ground for what I have already said in the introduction: that linear time is organized around the idea of a stable *archē* (origin) and a final *telos* (end). I will return to this issue at length in the section on the present. Derrida has rejected what he sees as a utopian tendency in the work of Benjamin, whose parable of the *Angelus Novus*, as Couzens Hoy has noted, displays the hope for "the redemption of past injustices to others through memorialization." Couzens Hoy, *The Time of Our Lives*, 163. Couzens Hoy explains that Derrida calls for a messianicity "without messianism," by which he means that the Messiah is bound to never actually come: the essence of the Messiah is, in fact, to be always *about to come* (*à venir*). For Derrida, what is at stake is the unpredictability of the future. Couzens Hoy explains: "Messianicity is thus the eschatological possibility of an unpredictable, unexpected event that could break into the present at any instant. Derrida thinks that there is still some value in this vestigial bit of eschatology. What he rejects is messianism, which

is based on the teleological draw of some remote future ideal" (164). He adds a thought that should be familiar to us by now, as it has been pressed by Kristeva time and again, namely that "such future ideals are often only projections of current cultural paradigms" (164).

44. Julia Kristeva, "Can There Be Revolt without Representation?," interview conducted by Rubén Gallo, in *Revolt, She Said*, 120. In *The Ethics of Ambiguity*, Beauvoir notes that "morality resides in the painfulness of an indefinite questioning" (133). For a relevant discussion on the unpredictable nature of democratic politics, see Jacques Derrida, "Call It a Day for Democracy," chap. 3 in *The Other Heading: Reflections on Today's Europe*, trans. Pascale-Anne Brault and Michael B. Naas (Bloomington: Indiana University Press, 1992). See also the final chapter of Hägglund, *Radical Atheism*.

45. Much of what follows draws from my review of Miller's book. See Fanny Söderbäck, "Forging A Head and Forging Ahead—Miller's *Head Cases*," *Theory and Event* 20, no. 1 (2017): 274–79.

46. Miller, *Head Cases*, 7.

47. Ibid.

48. Ibid., 8.

49. See Kristeva, *The Severed Head*, vii.

50. Miller, *Head Cases*, 14.

51. Ibid., 73. See also 79–80.

52. Ibid., 16.

53. Ibid.

54. Frederick Douglass, "What to the Slave Is the Fourth of July?," speech delivered on July 5, 1852, accessed at http://teachingamericanhistory.org/library/document/what-to-the-slave-is-the-fourth-of-july/ on August 27, 2018.

55. Miller, *Head Cases*, 199n142.

56. Campbell Robertson, "A Lynching Memorial Is Opening. The Country Has Never Seen Anything Like It," *New York Times*, April 25, 2018, accessed at https://www.nytimes.com/2018/04/25/us/lynching-memorial-alabama.html on August 28, 2018.

57. Ibid.

58. Ibid.

59. Miller, *Head Cases*, 7.

60. Nicholas Mirzoeff, "Below the Water: Black Lives Matter and Revolutionary Time," *e-flux*, no. 79 (February 2017).

61. David Roediger, *Seizing Freedom: Slave Emancipation and Liberty for All* (New York: Verso, 2015), 18.

62. Robertson, "A Lynching Memorial Is Opening."

63. Kara Walker in video directed by Jay Buim, accessed on Creative Time's website at http://creativetime.org/projects/karawalker/ on August 28, 2018.

64. Subtleties, as the curator Nato Thompson explains, were "sugar sculptures that adorned aristocratic banquets in England and France [in] the Middle Ages, when sugar was strictly a luxury commodity." Nato Thompson, Curatorial Statement for Kara Walker's A *Subtlety*, accessed on Creative Time's website at http://creativetime.org/projects/karawalker/curatorial-statement/ on June 14, 2016.

65. Walker in video directed by Jay Buim.

66. Miller, *Head Cases*, 48.

67. Thompson, Curatorial Statement. Amber Jamilla Musser juxtaposes Walker's decision to show the sphinx's vulva with Judy Chicago's omission of the vulva on her Sojourner Truth plate in the classic feminist installation piece *The Dinner Party*. Truth is the only Black woman present at the table in this piece, and her plate is one of the few that does not feature vaginal imagery. Her body is racialized, insofar as the plate offers references to slavery and Black suffering, but it lacks explicit reference to desire, in juxtaposition to the many plates on the table that center sexuality through, exactly, vaginal imagery. Following Hortense Spillers, Musser problematizes the omission in Chicago's piece, and suggests that it is symptomatic of our incapacity and unwillingness to think Black female sexuality. Walker's sphinx-size vulva, on the other hand, represents a rare exhibition of Black female genitalia that allows for the appearance of Black female sexuality and desire—a desire that Musser reads as queer. As such, it opens an important space for thinking, in conjunction, female sexuality and race: "If Chicago's ceramic vulvas are celebrated for unifying women and illustrating the power and potential pleasures of the female body, let us imagine reading the sphinx and her sugarcoated vulva as providing a way to incorporate black women into this lineage and to consider vulnerability anew. . . . Not only is it a corrective to a tradition of art that has focused on the phallus while ignoring the vagina, it also incorporates black female bodies into a lineage of feminism where they are not usually found." See Amber Jamilla Musser, "Queering Sugar: Kara Walker's Sugar Sphinx and the Intractability of Black Female Sexuality," *Signs: Journal of Women in Culture and Society* 42, no. 1 (2016): 168. Interestingly, Musser highlights that the presence of the vulva situates us squarely within Irigaray's language of the two lips touching, which I examined in the previous chapter in my discussion of mimesis in Irigaray.

68. *White Out*, exhibition on Swedish and Sami identity, Museum of National Antiquities, Sweden, 2002.

69. Jacques Rancière, "The Work of the Image," 1. See www.shalev-gerz. net/DE/index_de.html.

70. Esther Shalev-Gerz, "Reflecting Spaces/Deflecting Spaces," 4. See www. shalev-gerz.net/DE/index_de.html.

71. Julia Kristeva, *Hannah Arendt*, vol. 1 of *Female Genius: Life, Madness, Words*, trans. Ross Guberman (New York: Columbia University Press, 2001), 96.

# Chapter 4

1. Freire, *Pedagogy of the Oppressed*, 85.

2. Adriana Cavarero, who has devoted her entire body of work to a systematic critique of universalizing notions such as "Man," "the subject," or "the individual"—insisting precisely on singularity and uniqueness—tends to formulate such a critique with reference to the present. In *For More than One Voice*, for example, she explores the vocal ontology of uniqueness (the expression of uniqueness through *voice* rather than *logos*) through temporal language: "In the uniqueness that makes itself heard as voice, there is an embodied existent, or rather, a 'being-there' [*esserci*] in its radical finitude, *here and now*." See Adriana Cavarero, *For More than One Voice: Toward a Philosophy of Vocal Expression*, trans. Paul A. Kottman (Stanford: Stanford University Press, 2005), 173, emphasis mine.

3. Irigaray, *Sharing the World*, back matter, emphasis mine. Interestingly, Irigaray here *does* use the language of "humans" rather than, as Freire did, "men and women"—despite her own insistence on sexuate difference.

4. Freire, *Pedagogy of the Oppressed*, 85.

5. For a detailed discussion of this issue, as it is taken up by Arendt and Cavarero, see my essay "Natality or Birth? Arendt and Cavarero on the Human Condition of Being Born," *Hypatia: A Journal of Feminist Philosophy* 33, no. 2 (2018): 273–88.

6. Hägglund, *Radical Atheism*, 52. Hägglund's book on Derrida offers a rich analysis of how the logic of deconstruction is defined by reflections on time. Turning to figures such as Kant, Husserl, Levinas, Augustine, and Ernesto Laclau (alongside a wide range of interpreters of Derrida), Hägglund argues for the irreducibility of time. My own engagement with Derrida is influenced by Hägglund's reading, but while he repeatedly emphasizes that no ethics can be drawn from the deconstructive insights about time and finitude, I argue instead that an ethics in fact can be teased out of the idea that life is constitutively temporal.

7. See Mignolo, *The Darker Side of Western Modernity*, 168.

8. Jacques Derrida, "Différance," in *Margins of Philosophy*, trans. Alan Bass (Chicago: University of Chicago Press, 1982), 16. Henceforth, references to this essay will be given parenthetically within the main body of the text, using the abbreviation Df.

9. Jacques Derrida, "*Ousia* and *Grammē*: Note on a Note from *Being and Time*," in *Margins of Philosophy*, 38, 34. Henceforth, references to this essay will be given parenthetically within the main body of the text, using the abbreviation OG.

10. Chanter, *Time, Death, and the* Feminine, 26.

11. G. W. F. Hegel, *Hegel's Philosophy of Nature*, vol. 1, trans. M. J. Petry (London: George Allen & Unwin, 1970), §258.

12. Aristotle, *Physics*, trans. Philip H. Wicksteed and Francis M. Cornford (Cambridge, MA: Harvard University Press/Loeb Classical Library, 1993), book 4, chapter 11, 217b–218a. Aristotle famously defines time as follows: "this is just what time is, the calculable measure or dimension of motion with respect to before-and-afterness." See Aristotle, *Physics*, book 4, chapter 11, 219b. In a long footnote in *Being and Time*, Heidegger argues that Hegel's account of time is nothing but a rehearsal of Aristotelian insights: "The priority which Hegel has given to the 'now' which has been levelled off, makes it plain that in defining the concept of time he is under the sway of the manner in which time is *ordinarily* understood; and this means that he is likewise under the sway of the *traditional* conception of it. It can even be shown that his conception of time has been drawn *directly* from the 'physics' of Aristotle." See Martin Heidegger, *Being and Time*, trans. John Macquarrie and Edward Robinson (San Francisco: Harper & Row, 1962), 500nxxx. It is this footnote that is the center of attention for Derrida in his essay "*Ousia* and *Grammē*."

13. Augustine, *Confessions*, trans. R. S. Pine-Coffin (New York: Penguin Books, 1986), book 11, §14. These quotes should bring our attention to the perplexing way in which time in a certain sense escapes the logic of non-contradiction, which is one of the reasons that the question of the present gives rise to an antinomy at the heart of all philosophical thinking about Being.

14. In *The Ethics of Ambiguity*, Beauvoir notes that the very activity of philosophical contemplation often aspires to overcome the instability of our temporal condition: "Some men, instead of building their existence upon the indefinite unfolding of time, propose to assert it in its eternal aspect and to achieve it as an absolute. They hope, thereby, to surmount the ambiguity of their condition" (68).

15. Hägglund, *Radical Atheism*, 16.

16. Cavarero describes the metaphysical distinction between abstract-eternal universal Being and concrete-temporal particular beings beautifully: "According to Plato, empirical vision is always illusory, tricky, and imprecise, not so much because the eyes of the body see badly, but because the things of the ordinary world are mutable and contingent. For Plato, what makes the gray dog (seen at profile at three-fifteen in the afternoon) an object that always plays tricks on the eyes is the fact that the dog is alive—and thus particular, subject to change, in the process of becoming. . . . Plato . . . eternalizes the instantaneity of vision, transferring and fixing it into an immobile duration that withdraws from the contingency of this world. Thus frozen in the eternal present of an immobile contemplation, the idea of the dog radiates a universal and fixed dog-ness. It is always the same, admitting no spatial or temporal change." See Cavarero, *For More than One Voice*, 50–51.

17. Augustine, *Confessions*, book 11, §11.

18. Ibid.

19. When I speak of "the metaphysical tradition" here, what I mean is quite simply a tradition that distinguishes selfsame presence and Being from the

temporal movement of beings, and that grants privilege to the former. Such a tradition (exemplified most commonly by the Platonic distinction between ideal forms and the shadowy realm of becoming) is grounded in the positing of oppositional dualisms and the notion of a singular foundational origin (*archē*). Needless to say, this "tradition" is taken up in a variety of ways by different thinkers within it, and the comments provided here are thus bound to be simplifying. I am aware that seeing this tradition as *one* in fact repeats the very gesture of repetition of sameness that I have tried to challenge in the opening chapters of this book. I do not have time here to provide a detailed reading of each and every figure within this tradition—such an endeavor would be huge, and would most certainly force us to revise some of the claims inherent in most critiques of it. My treatment of Plato in several of the chapters in this book should provide an example of how a more careful reading necessarily leads to revisions. For my purposes here, however, and for the sake of brevity and clarity, I will assume a rather standard characterization of this tradition, as articulated by Irigaray in her critique of it.

20. For a rich and explicit discussion of the impossibility of the present (through an analysis of the concept of the gift—*present* in German), see Derrida's "The Time of the King," in *Given Time: I. Counterfeit Money*, trans. Peggy Kamuf (Chicago: University of Chicago Press, 1992), 1–33. While this is an especially fruitful text to turn to, it is by no means the only one from Derrida's corpus that addresses these issues. The impossibility of selfsame presence guides most of Derrida's work, and underpins the very logic of deconstruction.

21. For a lucid and rich account of Heidegger's articulation of the question of time and his critique of the metaphysics of presence, see Chanter, "Heidegger's Critique of Metaphysical Presence," chap. 3 in *Time, Death and the* Feminine.

22. Derrida moreover shows that the entire tradition—stretching from Aristotle via Kant and Hegel to Heidegger himself—depends on a conceptualization of time as "the condition for the possibility of the appearance of beings in (finite) experience [time understood as the pure form of sensibility]," and that, therefore, the Heideggerian "destruction of metaphysics remains within metaphysics, only making explicit its principles" (OG 48).

23. While Derrida, in the passage quoted above, maintains that time belongs and necessarily will belong to metaphysical conceptuality, Wood has argued that he nevertheless attempts to think time beyond metaphysics. He points to a claim made by Derrida in his essay "Grammatology as a Positive Science," where he speaks of his own search for a "pluri-dimensional and delinearised temporality." See Wood, *The Deconstruction of Time*, 372.

24. While we presumably stop growing after we die, the moment of death by no means marks the end of the decay of the body: we continue to "change" even in death.

25. We should make a distinction between the simple past and the imperfect, the former being over and done with, while the latter is still effective in

the present. It is of the former that I speak here. In his discussion of the past, Heidegger makes a distinction between *Vergangenheit* (which is expressed by the simple past in that it reifies the past into present-to-hand objects) and *Gewesenheit* (which is captured in the imperfect tense and involves the future). For a lucid explication of the relationship between the two, see Couzens Hoy, *The Time of Our Lives*, 105–09. While the past in a certain sense is "absent" in that it is not "here and now," it nevertheless signals a sense of completion and self-identity. In *Being and Nothingness*, Sartre equates the past with being-in-itself, precisely for this reason: "the past which I *was* is what it is; it is an in-itself like the things in the world. The relation of being which I have to sustain with the past is a relation of the type of the in-itself—that is, an identification with itself." See Sartre, *Being and Nothingness*, 139. Sartre is of course aware that the *meaning* of the past might change, but *as such* it remains stable: "we continually preserve the possibility of changing the *meaning* of the past in so far as this is an ex-present *which has had a future*. But from the content of the past as such I can remove nothing, and I can add nothing to it," he asserts (139).

26. Couzens Hoy, *The Time of Our Lives*, 156.

27. Wood, *The Deconstruction of Time*, 369.

28. Ibid.

29. For an analogous analysis articulated in spatial rather than temporal terms, see Cavarero's critique of the upright posture in *Inclinations: A Critique of Rectitude*, trans. Amanda Minervini and Adam Sitze (Stanford: Stanford University Press, 2016). If the moral ideal of autonomy finds its geometrical shape in the paternal-vertical line, and if democratic ideals of equality are embodied in a fraternal-horizontal geometrical figure, Cavarero seeks to trouble this Cartesian plane of existence by offering a disruptive geometrical model grounded in relational ontology, here exemplified by the maternal-inclined line: a geometrical figure that bends over and leans out of and beyond itself.

30. I make a similar claim in chapter 8, in my reading of Kristeva's essay "Stabat Mater," when I argue that we must give a three-dimensional account of the maternal in order to avoid the idealized image represented by the Virgin Mary. As I hope to make clear in that chapter, such a three-dimensional account depends on our ability and willingness to think the necessary co-implication of time and space. The need to think the two together is articulated both by Derrida and Irigaray, and it is only insofar as we take this thought seriously that we can begin to understand their respective accounts of the irreducibility of time. For Derrida, this is most explicitly articulated as a "spacing of time" (exemplified by the "trace" or by "arche-writing" in his work). I will look at some of the passages in which this thought appears in the work of Irigaray in the chapters that follow.

31. This is in many ways similar to Heidegger's attempt to think the unity of the three ecstases of time. Chanter explains: "Heidegger interprets the past

and the future not as derivative versions of the present—not as a past that once was present, nor as a future that is yet to become present. Rather, each ecstasis has its own dynamic, and each ecstasis is also a dimension of each of the other ecstases. The present is not a simple now, adequately represented as an isolated point but capable of being joined up with other now-points to form a linear, graphical, and abstract conception of time as continuous. The present bends under the weight of the past, and has significance because of the impending future. In this sense, the now as present includes within itself a relation to the past and a relation to the future." See Chanter, *Time, Death, and the* Feminine, 126. A crucial difference, however (and one which I will develop in further detail), is that while Heidegger nevertheless gives priority to the future insofar as it is the ecstasis that corresponds to our being-towards-death, Irigaray, as we will see, puts less emphasis on death and focuses instead on the role of birth as it pertains to the question of time. Birth, interestingly, sustains a relation both to the past and to the future: our own birth, on the one hand, lies in the past, but birth simultaneously always marks new beginnings and futurity. Death, conversely, lies in the future yet marks the limit of futurity: it is an end rather than a beginning. That death would be an end is, of course, only true in cultures that do not believe in reincarnation. The Dogon in Mali, for example (a predominantly animist culture that believes in reincarnation), shave the heads of their dead before burying them, and up until recently they buried their dead in fetal position. For them, death is viewed as the beginning of a new life, which is why they try to approximate the appearance of a fetus when preparing the dead for their last journey. End and beginning, in such cultures, coincide.

32. Jacques Derrida, *Of Grammatology*, trans. Gayatri Chakravorty Spivak (Baltimore: Johns Hopkins University Press, 1974), 155.

33. Hägglund, *Radical Atheism*, 28–29. Hägglund explains: "what I call radical atheism not only denies the existence of God and immortality but also takes issue with the assumption that God and immortality are desirable" (48). The inherently violent and annihilating nature of pure presence is discussed in chapter 3 of his book ("Arche-Violence: Derrida and Levinas"). The parallel between selfsame presence and a sort of numb or disinterested "indifference" runs through Irigaray's work on the question of sexual difference.

34. Adriana Cavarero, *Relating Narratives: Storytelling and Selfhood*, trans. Paul A. Kottman (New York: Routledge, 2000), 87.

35. Judith Butler, *Frames of War: When Is Life Grievable?* (London: Verso, 2010), 18.

36. Jacques-Yves Cousteau, *The Ocean World* (New York: Abradale Press, 1985), 17.

37. Hägglund, *Radical Atheism*, 30.

38. Ibid., 32–33.

39. Jacques Derrida, *Specters of Marx*, trans. Peggy Kamuf (London: Rout-ledge, 1994), 175.

40. See Nathaniel Hawthorne, "The Birthmark," in *Hawthorne's Short Stories*, ed. Newton Arvin (New York: Alfred A. Knopf, 1975), 177–93.

41. At the sight of the crystal clear liquid, his wife Georgiana exclaims: "It is so beautiful to the eye that I could imagine it the elixir of life." Her husband explains: "In one sense it is . . . or, rather, the elixir of immortality. It is the most precious poison that ever was concocted in this world. By its aid I could apportion the lifetime of any mortal at whom you might point your finger." But the elixir is similar to the *pharmakon* that Derrida traces in the Platonic text—the gift of life and the poison [*gift*] that puts an end to all life: "The strength of the dose would determine whether he were to linger out years, or drop dead in the midst of a breath," Aylmer remarks. See Hawthorne, "The Birthmark," 186. See also Jacques Derrida, "Plato's Pharmacy," in *Dissemination*, trans. Barbara Johnson (Chicago: University of Chicago Press, 1981), 61–171.

42. Hawthorne, "The Birthmark," 190ff.

43. Ibid., 181.

44. Ibid., 193.

45. Ibid. Aylmer is a good example of the male rational subject who has fled the burden of embodiment, by letting his assistant, Aminadab, carry that burden for him: "With his vast strength, his shaggy hair, his smoky aspect, and the indescribable earthiness that incrusted him, [Aminadab] seemed to represent man's physical nature; while Aylmer's slender figure, and pale, intellectual face, were no less apt a type of the spiritual element," Hawthorne writes. Aylmer is described as someone who "redeemed himself from materialism by his strong and eager aspiration towards the infinite. In his grasp the veriest clod of earth assumed a soul." As the story comes to an end, Aminadab cannot but laugh at the naïveté of his master. To seek spirit without matter is to seek death, and it is to lose all that matters in life. See ibid., 183, 187, and 192.

46. The latter fact (our being engendered) is covered over by the very language that we use. The German *endlich* or the English and French *finitude* bring full attention to the *end*, not the *beginning*.

47. While it is true that Heidegger, throughout his work, characterizes the existence of Dasein as a being-towards-death, it should be noted that he, too, acknowledges the fact of birth (albeit far too briefly). In the chapter on temporality and historicality in *Being and Time*, he pauses to reflect on the constitutive nature of birth: "But death is only the 'end' of Dasein; and, taken formally, it is just *one* of the ends by which Dasein's totality is closed around. The other 'end,' however, is the 'beginning,' the 'birth.' Only that entity which is 'between' birth and death presents the whole which we have been seeking. Accordingly the orientation of the analytic has so far remained 'one-sided,' in spite of all its tendencies towards a consideration of *existent* Being-a-whole

and in spite of the genuineness with which authentic and inauthentic Being-towards-death have been explicated. Dasein has been our theme only in the way in which it exists 'facing forward,' as it were, leaving 'behind it' all that has been. Not only has Being-towards-the-beginning remained unnoticed; but so too, and above all, has the way in which Dasein *stretches along between* birth and death. The 'connectedness of life,' in which Dasein somehow maintains itself constantly, is precisely what we have overlooked in our analysis of Being-a-whole." See Heidegger, *Being and Time*, part 2, chap. 5, 425. For rich readings of this passage, which focus on the meaning of birth in Heidegger, see Ó Murchadha, *The Time of Revolution*, 28–38; Lisa Guenther, "Being-from-Others: Reading Heidegger After Cavarero," *Hypatia: A Journal of Feminist Philosophy* 23, no. 1 (2008): 99–118; and Anne O'Byrne, *Natality and Finitude* (Bloomington: Indiana University Press, 2010), 15–45. Levinas, who has written extensively on the role of death, is one of a few male thinkers who has put great emphasis on what he calls fecundity. He does so, however, primarily by focusing on the *father* and the *son*, thus repeating the gesture of covering over the maternal function. For a discussion of this, see Luce Irigaray, "The Fecundity of the Caress: A Reading of Levinas, *Totality and Infinity*, 'Phenomenology of Eros,'" chap. 11 in *An Ethics of Sexual Difference*. See also Lisa Guenther, "Fathers and Daughters: Levinas, Irigaray, and the Transformation of Maternity," chap. 4 in *The Gift of the Other: Levinas and the Politics of Reproduction* (Albany: State University of New York Press, 2006), 75–94.

48. Luce Irigaray, *To Be Born: Genesis of a New Human Being* (New York: Palgrave Macmillan, 2017), 7.

49. We might say that Irigaray's own work, in a certain sense, is metaphysical in nature (inasmuch as she speaks of the ontological status of sexuate difference, or the irreducibility of two worlds separated by an abyss prompted by this very difference). But if traditional metaphysics has been concerned with things that do not change—with the everlasting beyond, with Being, and with the first cause of things—Irigaray's thinking is a metaphysics of the *living* and of *life*. And it does, importantly, not posit itself as *above* or *beyond* nature, but rather *with* and *alongside* it. Irigaray's ontological-metaphysical teaching is a teaching of *metabolē* (the Greek term for *change*) insofar as it inscribes the flux of time into the very structure of existence, and, as we have seen, inasmuch as it collapses the distinction between immanence and transcendence.

50. It is, of course, only because we are embodied that we are mortal (at least within a tradition that views the soul as immortal and the body as that which causes us to decay). But death as such is, nevertheless, most often seen as an *escape* from the body.

51. Irigaray, *To Be Born*, 38.

52. Ibid.

53. Ibid.

54. Luce Irigaray, *The Way of Love*, trans. Heidi Bostic and Stephen Pluháček (London: Continuum, 2002), 3, emphasis mine. Henceforth, references to this text will be given parenthetically within the main body of the text, using the abbreviation WOL.

55. Rachel Jones, *Irigaray: Towards a Sexuate Philosophy* (Cambridge, UK: Polity Press, 2011), 49.

56. It is no coincidence that Augustine points out that eternity must be understood not only as everlasting but also as non-engendered. An eternal God will never cease to be *and* has, importantly, never come into being. In God, nothing can ever pass away, nor can anything come into being. This is in part why the question of God's creativity is a complicated one: How can a perfect being transcend itself, how can it be creative? How, moreover, can it move from a state of non-creativity to the "decision" to create a world (such a decision would, after all, imply that God himself was subject to change)? See Augustine, *Confessions*, book 11, especially the questions raised in §10 onward, where it becomes clear that insofar as God is a creator, his existence prior to creation must be viewed as having taken place *outside* of time, or, as it were, *before* time. I will address this issue more carefully in part 4, in my discussion of the maternal body and its creative powers, but let me simply note, for now, that Jesus is an interesting divinity in the monotheistic Western context insofar as he not only *dies* on the cross, but also is *engendered* and *born*. For a discussion of how this complicates the story of time and eternity, see chapter 8, note 45. Irigaray's most extended discussion of the self-engendered nature of God (God as an ultimate cause, a *casa sui*) is developed in dialogue with Baruch Spinoza. See Luce Irigaray, "The Envelope: A Reading of Spinoza, *Ethics*, 'Of God,'" chap. 6 in *An Ethics of Sexual Difference*.

57. Grosz, *The Nick of Time*, 18.

58. It is interesting to note that Sartre, in his discussion of temporality in *Being and Nothingness*, provides an elaborate discussion of our condition of being born, but he does so without even once mentioning that we are *of woman born*. The existential condition for any consciousness is, according to Sartre, "*to be born*," and it is thanks to our birth that we even have access to time or to a notion of pastness (and thus to a notion of a preceding In-itself): "There is not *first* one universal time where a For-itself suddenly appears not yet having a Past. Rather it is in terms of *birth* as the original and *a priori* law of being for the For-itself that there is revealed a world with a universal time in which we can designate a moment when the For-itself was not yet and a moment when it appeared. . . . Through birth a Past appears in the world." See Sartre, *Being and Nothingness*, 162–63. Sartre's critique of metaphysics is similar to the one that I am trying to elaborate here and that I will develop in the next section, except—and this is crucial—that he elaborates it without any mention of the maternal body, or the fact that we are born *from* someone. According to Sartre (and with this

I agree), it is because we are *born* that we cannot speak of an ultimate origin or beginning. Sartre warns us of trying to posit a "before" that would escape the condition of birth: "one should not next raise *metaphysical* questions concerning the In-itself from which the For-itself was born, questions such as: 'How was there an In-itself *before* the birth of the For-itself? How was the For-itself born from *this* In-itself rather than from another?' *Etc.* All these questions fail to take into account the fact that it is through the For-itself that the Past in general can exist. If there is a *Before*, it is because the For-itself has arisen in the world, and it is from the standpoint of the For-itself that the past can be established" (162). We have already seen that the In-itself (understood as timeless being) lacks time and, for this very reason, not only is untenable but also undesirable. The difference between Sartre's account and the one that I will elaborate here is that he, again, posits a solitary and seemingly self-sufficient consciousness who (at worst) will ask metaphysical questions about an origin that would lie outside of time (the In-itself that, for the metaphysician, would precede the For-itself), and who (at best) will acknowledge and accept the fact that any notion of a "before" only arises *with* consciousness, and that no selfsame In-itself therefore can be thought outside of it. My own account is meant to make the case that to be born is equivalent to being born *of*, and that no consciousness therefore can be thought outside of a *relation*. It is *this* insight, I argue, that makes impossible any notion of a selfsame being preceding temporal consciousness. This insight, moreover, undermines any notion of a completed or selfsame past, since there is no such thing as a past that is mine alone. Another way of putting this would be to say that any *For-itself* always already is a *With-an-other* (not to be confused with the Sartrean inauthentic *Being-for-Others!*). It is, moreover, interesting to note that if God most often has been characterized as an immobile and self-perfected In-itself (and Sartre rightly suggests that such an In-itself in fact is undesirable and that our striving toward it is nothing but a consequence of bad faith), the mother, too, has been depicted as an In-itself (albeit not in terms of perfected divinity but rather as an immanent thing or a passive material ground). The point of my own argument is precisely to undermine the privilege granted to a divine selfsame In-itself by highlighting that our beginnings are material-maternal (hence the centrality of birth), and that the mother, contrary to what is commonly assumed, is a *For-itself* in her own right. There is thus no ultimate In-itself to which existence can be reduced or traced back, which is to say that there is no timeless stable ground or origin to which we should return. All this will be discussed in further detail in my discussion of the maternal body in part 4 of this book (although I will leave Sartre behind at this juncture).

59. Irigaray, "Feminine Identity: Biology or Social Conditioning?," in *Democracy Begins Between Two*, 37.

60. In her book on Kristeva, Sjöholm touches on these matters: "only in the face of the alterity present in the mother/child dyad is the affirmation of life

and thus of creation and thought made possible" (KP 58). Kristeva consistently characterizes human life as constitutively intersubjective, and she does so precisely by pointing out that each subject—through the fact of birth—is faced with otherness from the outset. In her article "Natality and Mortality: Rethinking Death with Cavarero," Stone argues that an understanding of natality as intrinsically embodied and relational might also make possible an interpretation of death as corporeal and relational. Her article goes on to show that the feminist insistence on acknowledging birth as constitutive of the human condition—something that she attributes first and foremost to Cavarero's feminist reading of Arendt—opens up for different modes of approaching the question of death and mortality, such that we might undo the common view that death is a solitary affair. See Alison Stone, "Natality and Mortality: Rethinking Death with Cavarero," *Continental Philosophy Review* 43 (2010): 353–72.

61. Irigaray, *To Be Born*, 7.

62. For an interesting discussion of cloning in relation to natality and finitude, see O'Byrne, "What Will the Clone Make of Us?," afterword to *Natality and Finitude*. O'Byrne asks, "Would the human clone not offer a pointed challenge to Arendt's claim that our natality lies in the fact that we share the quality of uniqueness so that when we each are born, the world has never seen anyone quite like us before? When the clone is born, the world *will* have seen someone rather like her before. Does this mean that the clone will be *innatal*?" (149).

63. Of course this is a complex issue, and I am in no way suggesting that the event of birth depends on heterosexual intercourse, nor that we are all gestated by people who identify as mothers. While Irigaray might make such assumptions, we should certainly be careful not to reproduce them. But while we should clearly complicate the heteronormative assumptions built into her analysis in this regard, I would nevertheless insist that our beginnings are plural, and that the gestating body is marked by sex, even when the birth parent does not identify as a woman or a mother. And this, it seems to me, matters for challenging traditional-metaphysical accounts of origins as selfsame and sexually neutral.

64. Guenther, *The Gift of the Other*, 10, 30.

65. Irigaray develops this thought further: "If Being resolves into two that are radically different, how can the unified whole be reconstructed? What if, in the place of entry into presence, two—at least—stayed always mysteriously adjoined?" (FAMH 127). Note that both here and in the passage quoted in the body of the text Irigaray speaks of "at least" two. I take these moments in her work to be interesting in terms of allowing us to move beyond the paradigm of the two that many have criticized. The two—or *at least two*—offers us a horizon for thinking plurality and multiplicity.

66. Chanter, *Time, Death, and the* Feminine, 134.

67. Although it is worth noting, yet again, that while Kristeva and Irigaray are attentive to the power relations that posit a hierarchical relationship

between the sexes, they offer no critical analysis of the coloniality of presence, and tend to overlook the intersection between issues of sexual difference and racial/colonial difference.

# Chapter 5

1. In the epigraph of his book *Time Driven: Metapsychology and the Splitting of the Drive*, Adrian Johnston quotes a passage from Blaise Pascal that speaks powerfully to the issues addressed here: "We never keep to the present. We recall the past; we anticipate the future as if we found it too slow in coming and were trying to hurry it up, or we recall the past as if to stay its too rapid flight. We are so unwise that we wander about in times that do not belong to us, and do not think of the only one that does; so vain that we dream of times that are not and blindly flee the one that is. The fact is that the present usually hurts. We thrust it out of sight because it distresses us, and if we find it enjoyable, we are sorry to see it slip away. We try to give it the support of the future, and think how we are going to arrange things over which we have no control for a time we can never be sure of reaching. Let each of us examine his thoughts; he will find them wholly concerned with the past or the future. We almost never think of the present, and if we do think of it, it is only to see what light it throws on our plans for the future. The present is never our end. The past and the present are our means, the future alone our end. Thus we never actually live, but hope to live, and since we are always planning to be happy, we should never be so." See Adrian Johnston, *Time Driven: Metapsychology and the Splitting of the Drive* (Evanston, IL: Northwestern University Press, 2005), ix.

2. See, for example, Morny Joy, *Divine Love: Luce Irigaray, Women, Gender, and Religion* (Manchester: Manchester University Press, 2007). Joy's work has become increasingly critical of Irigaray's treatment of Eastern spirituality since the publication of this book. See also Deutscher, *A Politics of Impossible Difference*.

3. Similar critiques have been raised—and remain a concern—in response to Kristeva's early *About Chinese Women*, a text that also sets out to celebrate "Eastern culture" but that arguably does so in a manner that is both orientalist and homogenizing. For a pointed critique of this text, see Spivak, "French Feminism in an International Frame." See also Julia Kristeva, *About Chinese Women*, trans. Anita Barrows (London: Marion Boyars, 1977).

4. Breath is a central category in Irigaray's thought. For engagements with this dimension of her work, see *Breathing with Luce Irigaray*, ed. Emily A. Holmes and Lenart Škof (London: Bloomsbury, 2013). See also Sara Beardsworth, "Psychoanalysis and Yoga," in *Engaging the World: Thinking After Luce Irigaray*, ed. Mary C. Rawlinson (Albany: State University of New York Press, 2016), 288–89.

5. Beardsworth, "Psychoanalysis and Yoga," 281.

6. Gail Schwab describes yoga as "the most perfect living expression of the sensible transcendental," referring to the concept developed by Irigaray to challenge and overcome metaphysical dualisms. She goes on to portray yoga as "the transformational union of body and mind, emotion and tranquility, intellect and senses, carnality and spirituality, humanity and divinity," thus giving "form and content to the sensible transcendental." See Gail M. Schwab, "Beyond the Vertical and the Horizontal: Spirituality, Space, and Alterity in the Work of Luce Irigaray," in *Thinking with Irigaray*, ed. Mary C. Rawlinson, Sabrina L. Hom, and Serene J. Khader (Albany: State University of New York Press, 2011), 84. For a detailed discussion of the way in which Eastern non-duality has influenced and can further inform Irigaray's own work, see Jean Byrne's PhD dissertation, "Enlightenment Between Two: Luce Irigaray, Sexual Difference and Nondual Oneness," University of Queensland, 2008.

7. Beardsworth, "Psychoanalysis and Yoga," 281.

8. Needless to say, most "aerobified" or "gymified" yoga as it is practiced in the West neglects these central aspects of the spiritual practice.

9. Elisha Foust, "Breathing the Political: A Meditation on the Preservation of Life in the Midst of War," in *Breathing with Luce Irigaray*, 186.

10. See Laura Stampler, "Project Air: Yoga Helps HIV-Positive Rape Victims in Rwanda," *Huffington Post*, September 30, 2011, accessed at https://www.huffingtonpost.com/2011/07/31/project-air-yoga-rwanda-hiv-women_n_914521.html on November 19, 2018.

11. See Beth S. Catlett and Mary Bunn, "Yoga as Embodied Feminist Praxis: Trauma, Healing, and Community-Based Responses to Violence," in *Yoga, the Body, and Embodied Social Change: An Intersectional Feminist Analysis*, ed. Beth Berila, Melanie Klein, and Chelsea Jackson Roberts (Lanham, MD: Lexington Books, 2016), 263–64.

12. Beardsworth, "Psychoanalysis and Yoga," 284. Interestingly, Beardsworth will go on to describe yoga as a practice that aims at a movement of return to subtle bodily registers (288–93).

13. Ibid., 282.

14. It should be noted that this notion of a "living present" cannot be reduced to a Husserlian thinking of time. I will not be able to develop the differences between Husserl and Irigaray here, but let me simply say that his emphasis on the internal (in his discussion of time-consciousness) would be hard to reconcile with Irigaray's philosophy of sexuate difference. Later in this chapter, I will say more about why Irigaray's philosophy of sexuate difference provides a thorough critique of any modern understanding of transcendental consciousness.

15. In this sense we might say that Irigaray, just like Heidegger and other phenomenological thinkers, privileges (lived) temporality over (objective) time. She differs from the early phenomenologists, however, through her consistent

emphasis on sexuate difference. It should also be noted that Heidegger, throughout his life, remained interested in asking the question of Being as such. While
he himself thought he had failed to properly address this question in *Being and
Time* (he was, on his own account, only able to properly examine Dasein and
not the "is" of the "there is" [*es gibt*]), his ambition was nevertheless to raise
the allegedly unthematized question of Being. Irigaray is not interested in such
abstract notions such as "Being." Her analysis is colored, throughout, by a return
to the ontic-singular (i.e., sexed *beings*).

16. Luce Irigaray, *To Speak Is Never Neutral*, trans. Gail Schwab (New
York: Routledge, 2002), 56.

17. Ibid., 57–58.

18. Ibid., 55. When, in an interview, Irigaray is asked to differentiate
"utterances" from "enunciations," she explains that the former "refer to mes-
sages that have already been produced, finished, *that are like dead*, if you put
aside the meaning they retain in their final form," while the latter "designates
speech as it unfolds, *its live, actual engendering, not yet stabilized*." See Irigaray,
"The Difference Between the Sexes," interview with Roger-Pol Droit, in *Why
Different? A Culture of Two Subjects*, 42, emphasis mine. This interview was
originally published in *Le Monde* on June 7, 1985.

19. Irigaray, *To Speak Is Never Neutral*, 5.

20. Think, for example, of the astonishment expressed by Woolf in *A Room
of One's Own*, when she, in doing her research at the British Museum, realizes
how much ink has been spilled on the "problem" of woman and how *little* of said
ink has been spilled by women themselves: "Have you any notion of how many
books are written about women in the course of one year? Have you any notion
how many are written by men? Are you aware that you are, perhaps, the most
discussed animal in the universe?" See Woolf, *A Room of One's Own*, 26. This
is echoed by Freud, who, four years after Woolf had given the two lectures that
were compiled in her now classic book, in a lecture on female sexuality, noted
that people, throughout history, "have knocked their heads against the riddle of
the nature of femininity," and then added: "Nor will *you* have escaped worrying
over this problem—those of you who are men; to those of you who are women
this will not apply—you are yourselves the problem." See Freud, "Femininity," in
*Freud on Women*, 342–43. But what, Irigaray asks, would happen if "the 'object'
started to speak," what if women were to articulate their own language? See
Irigaray, "Any Theory of the 'Subject' Has Always Been Appropriated by the
'Masculine,'" in *Speculum of the Other Woman*, 135. This is, of course, in large
part the task of her own philosophy, and of the *parler femme* or *écriture féminine*
for which she is widely known and celebrated.

21. For an interesting analysis of the difficulty for women to speak
themselves—given the historical reduction of women to symbolic alienation or
absence—see Adriana Cavarero, "Towards a Theory of Sexual Difference," in

*The Lonely Mirror*, ed. Sandra Kemp and Paola Bono (New York: Routledge, 1993), 189–221.

22. For a systematic analysis of the way in which Western logos has served to repress the *vocal* register of human expression—and the corporeal uniqueness that it represents—see Cavarero, *For More than One Voice*. Cavarero quotes Walter Ong's *The Presence of the Word*: "Since sound indicates an activity that takes place 'here and in this moment,' speech as sound establishes a personal presence 'here and in this moment.'" See Cavarero, *For More than One Voice*, 173. Cavarero herself stresses both this temporal horizon of the "here and now" and the constitutive relationality of a vocal ontology of uniqueness (indeed, she argues that there is a necessary bond between relationality and temporality understood in this way): "The thinker . . . knows his own thoughts beforehand. The time required for the questioning and answering thus ends up being an obstacle or a delay with regards to the speed of thought. Speaking, on the contrary, is always bound to time. It does not know in advance where it is going, and it entrusts itself to the unpredictable nature of what the interlocutors say. In short, thought is as solitary as speech is relational" (174).

23. Luce Irigaray, *Everyday prayers / Prières quotidiennes*, trans. Luce Irigaray with Timothy Mathews (Paris: Maisonneuve & Larose and University of Nottingham Press, 2004), 30–31. In a culture that reduces nature to an object, Irigaray suggests, "we lose a coexistence with nature, a sharing in its life and becoming" (44).

24. Ibid., 29, 35. The fusion of form and matter in Irigaray's work is articulated, elsewhere, through the term "sensible transcendental."

25. Ibid., 34. In my discussion of Kristeva and motherhood in chapter 8, I will look more closely at what was already broached earlier in this book, namely Kristeva's characterization of poetic language as, similarly, a discourse that marries form with matter, and that, insofar as it does, differs from more straightforwardly conceptual philosophical-scientific language.

26. Ibid.

27. Ibid., 44.

28. Wood, among others, has emphasized the way in which pluralism might work as an antidote to the metaphysics of presence. He points out that a pluralist notion of history undercuts any attempt to universalize history: "*The very plurality* of these histories, histories that do not require, and would almost certainly resist appropriation by History, is for that very reason a threat to History," he explains. Pluralism more generally undercuts and puts into question any notion of unity: "the pluralism in question is radical in the sense that there is no enveloping unity by which this multiplicity can be contained, and no theoretical place for such a unity." See Wood, *The Deconstruction of Time*, 373–74. What makes Irigaray's work distinct from that of others who have stressed the primacy of difference and plurality is her emphasis, precisely, on *sexuate* difference. The

latter is, for her, the condition of possibility for all other differences, since it is the condition of possibility for alteration and fecundity. Unless we establish a culture of sexuate difference, all other differences are, on her account, bound to be, precisely, enveloped and contained by unity or sameness. For Irigaray, the notion of plurality embraced by Wood (in the wake of Derrida) would thus run the risk of being appropriated by the metaphysics of presence. Needless to say, this is a controversial aspect of her thought—both among feminists and non-feminists—and it has given rise to manifold debates. In recent years, several attempts have been made to think beyond Irigaray's notion of sexuate difference in order to tie it to questions of, for example, cultural and racial difference. For the most sustained attempt of this kind, see Deutscher, A *Politics of Impossible Difference*. While I will treat the question of sexuate difference in its relation to the question of time in what follows, I will not be able to give appropriate attention to the broader implications of the primacy of sexuate difference within the scope of this book, although let me simply flag here that I too find it problematic. For an analysis of the ontological stakes in granting it such primacy, see Stone, *Luce Irigaray and the Philosophy of Sexual Difference*. In chapter 3 of that book, Stone treats the question of the relationship between sexual duality and sexual multiplicity with great care.

29. Irigaray, "The Power of Discourse," in *This Sex Which Is Not One*, 78. Irigaray also notes that "the feminine is defined as the necessary complement to the operation of male sexuality, and, more often, as a negative image that provides male sexuality with an unfailingly phallic self-representation" (70).

30. See, especially, Irigaray's readings of Freud: "The Blind Spot of an Old Dream of Symmetry," in *Speculum of the Other Woman*, 13–129; and "Psychoanalytic Theory: Another Look," chap. 3 in *This Sex Which Is Not One*. Irigaray here develops a thoroughgoing critique of the paradigmatic psychoanalytic equation of woman with lack (woman as a castrated man), and the fact that Freud's psychosexual theory is based on what she describes as a mono-sexual model (the idea that the girl, at first, is a "little man"). This critique runs through her entire corpus, but is perhaps most explicitly articulated in these texts.

31. Derrida makes a similar connection between consciousness and the problem of presence (although he does not stress the *male* character of consciousness as strongly as Irigaray does). Addressing the question "what is consciousness?," he asserts that "the subject as consciousness has never manifested itself except as self-presence. The privilege granted to consciousness therefore signifies the privilege granted to the present" (Df 16). For a lucid and convincing argument against the notion of a transcendental ego (understood as exempt from time), see the first two chapters of Hägglund's *Radical Atheism*. In "Autoimmunity of Time: Derrida and Kant," Hägglund argues that the transcendental unity of apperception in Kant is the primary example of the attempt to "solve" the problem of time by positing an entity exempt from it (the "I think" that saves

Kant from the problem of infinite regress, and that helps him explain the synthesis of time: since time never is *as such*, it needs something other than itself
to synthesize it, or else it won't appear). What is at stake for Derrida, according
to Hägglund, is to explain synthesis *without* resorting to a self-present subject
exempt from time, which is to say that synthesis must be achieved "*without
grounding it in an indivisible presence*" (18, emphasis mine). The Derridean answer
to this problem is his notion of the "trace," which means that the answer is
grounded in an insight that space and time must be thought together: "If the
spatialization of time makes the synthesis *possible*, the temporalization of space
makes it *impossible* for the synthesis to be grounded in an indivisible presence"
(18). Infinite regress is, importantly, only a "problem" to be "solved" within a
logic of identity and presence—it is only a problem if we assume an absolute
origin or end (67–68). In the chapter "Arche-Writing: Derrida and Husserl,"
Hägglund deepens his critique of Kant in light of Derrida's term "arche-writing,"
which he sees not only as "a transcendental condition for the experience of a
finite consciousness," but more importantly as "an 'ultratranscendental' condition
for life in general" (73). The originary status of writing undermines the very
notion of originary presence, just like the trace did: "arche-writing allows us to
think the necessary synthesis of time without grounding it in a nontemporal
unity" (71), and writing, just like the trace, "*spatializes time*" and "*temporalizes
space*" (72). While Hägglund sees Husserl as a thinker to whom Derrida turns
exactly because he can *not* be reduced to a metaphysician of presence, he nevertheless goes on to criticize (following Derrida) Husserl's notion of a "living
presence" or "absolute flow," and his concept of "prereflexivity," viewing these
as shortcuts to safeguard originary presence: "In spite of his ambition to provide
a description of consciousness that is purged from metaphysical presuppositions,
it remains axiomatic for Husserl that the subject must essentially be present to
itself. . . . Phenomenology is not a traditional ontotheology or idealism, but
Husserl nevertheless pledges to a version of the philosophical logic of identity"
(57). The Derridean insight is that the subject is in no position to *constitute*
time: "The subject does not constitute but is rather *constituted by* the movement
of temporalization" (70). This is a thought that I will touch upon and develop
in my discussion of Irigaray and Kristeva in what follows. The emphasis on
thinking time and space together is something to which I will return in detail
in part 4 of this book, when I discuss the maternal body as a temporal principle.

32. It is perhaps no coincidence that those religions that view God as
a timeless and perfect being also rely on the idea(l) of *one* solitary God. Such
a divinity, we might say, is "full of himself," both literally (insofar as God is
selfsame) and in the sense implied by the expression (a selfsame God cannot,
strictly speaking, be with an other or care about this other). Polytheistic religions
tend to view their divinities as embodied and changing beings, exempt neither
from time nor from difference, and Irigaray often notes that these traditions

conceive of their gods as *couples*, introducing male and female counterparts and thus inscribing sexual difference into the very concept of the divine.

33. See, for example, Irigaray, " 'Je—Luce Irigaray,' " 110.

34. It may seem, here, that by conflating the two levels through an emphasis on how we must understand the ontological level as one marked by time and difference, I am no longer speaking of ontology but rather epistemology (how we *understand* the relationship between the ontological and the ontic, not what that relationship actually *is*). I want to be clear, however, that ontology never has been and never can be some "untouched truth" about the nature of Being. It is, and has always been, a (philosophical) expression of how we *conceptualize* the basic structures of our existence. Our characterization of this structure will, inevitably, be colored not only by our view of ourselves as beings who "inhabit" such a structure, but also by our most fundamental ways of articulating something like subjectivity. Ontology, put simply, attempts to bespeak Being beyond history, but as such it is always articulated from *within* a particular historical horizon. Plato's ontological cosmology was inevitably colored by the ancient worldview, and the Cartesian subject was born at a time when subjectivity in the realm of politics began to be articulated exactly in terms of sovereignty and autonomy. Any ontology that fails to acknowledge this is bound to exclude certain kinds of experience. Frantz Fanon makes the following remark in his discussion of the lived experience of the Black man: "Ontology does not allow us to understand the being of the black man, since it ignores the lived experience. . . . From one day to the next, the Blacks have had to deal with two systems of reference. Their metaphysics, or less pretentiously their customs and the agencies to which they refer, were abolished because they were in contradiction with a new civilization which imposed its own." See Fanon, *Black Skin, White Masks*, 90. If our views of ontology are colored by the historical context in which they emerge (whether we acknowledge this or not), the reverse is equally true: our ontological understanding of the world and of "Being" inevitably colors our intersubjective comportments and commitments. If Heidegger insisted on the priority of ontology over ethics, and Levinas reversed the logic, I would argue that we must think ontology and ethics together. When I say, at different points throughout this book, that time is *ontological*, I am not merely pointing out and acknowledging an ontological *fact*, but I am, in so doing, preparing the ground for a particular kind of ethos—one grounded in the acknowledgment of our finitude and the temporal structure of Being.

35. Luce Irigaray, *I Love to You: Sketch of a Possible Felicity in History*, trans. Alison Martin (New York: Routledge, 1996), 111.

36. This is one reason why Irigaray so often emphasizes that the relation is *horizontal*, not *vertical*.

37. Irigaray, *Sharing the World*, 8.

38. Irigaray, *To Speak Is Never Neutral*, 3.

39. bell hooks, "Toward a Worldwide Culture of Love," *Shambhala Sun*, July 2006. Reprinted on PBS's blog *The Buddha*, June 2010, accessed at http://www.pbs.org/thebuddha/blog/2010/jun/3/toward-worldwide-culture-love-bell-hooks/ on November 5, 2018.

40. Ibid.

41. Irigaray, *I Love to You*, 150.

42. Ibid., 111.

43. Beauvoir expresses a similar thought in *The Ethics of Ambiguity*: "It is only as something strange, forbidden, as something free, that the other is revealed as an other. And to love him genuinely is to love him in his otherness and in that freedom by which he escapes. Love is then renunciation of all possession, of all confusion" (67).

44. Plato, "Symposium," in *The* Symposium *and the* Phaedrus: *Plato's Erotic Dialogues*, trans. William S. Cobb (Albany: State University of New York Press, 1993), 189a–193e.

45. Stanley Rosen, *Plato's* Symposium (New Haven, CT: Yale University Press, 1968), 150.

# Chapter 6

1. Irigaray, *Sharing the World*, 3, 7. Her poetry is, as we have seen, characterized by similar language.

2. As Hägglund puts it: "The structural uncertainty in the relation to the other has nothing to do with a cognitive limitation that would prevent us from having access to the true nature of the other. *There is no true nature of the other, since the other is temporal and cannot know what it will become.* The reason why the other cannot finally be identified or recognized is not because it is an ineffable Other that belongs to another realm, but because it is inherently mutable and may come to contradict any given identification or recognition." See Hägglund, *Radical Atheism*, 125, emphasis mine. He goes on to note that "every one is wholly other because the alterity of time cannot be overcome. Every one is wholly other because every one is a temporal singularity that always can be lost and never be reappropriated by anyone else" (145).

3. Augustine, *Confessions*, book 10, §33.

4. The distinction between the ignorant and the wise, for Socrates, is precisely that the former thinks that they know, while the latter is aware of the limitations of their knowledge.

5. While Irigaray ascribes enormous value to the relation between two, her shortcoming in this matter nevertheless brings her close to Heidegger's characterization of *Mitsein* (being-with) as *inauthentic* (insofar as the only truly "authentic" moment for her would be the return to self). Authenticity, for

Heidegger, means exactly propriety. The authentic, *eigentlich* in German, is that which belongs to oneself, the proper, the *mine*. The most authentic is our solitary encounter with death for Heidegger, but insofar as it is authentic ("proper") we might say that this is the *least* temporal of all human experiences.

6. Irigaray, "This Sex Which Is Not One," in *This Sex Which Is Not One*, 28, 31, 24.

7. Irigaray, "Any Theory of the 'Subject' Has Always Been Appropriated by the 'Masculine,'" in *Speculum of the Other Woman*, 134.

8. See Irigaray, "Divine Women," chap. 4 in *Sexes and Genealogies*, 63.

9. Julia Kristeva, *Time and Sense: Proust and the Experience of Literature*, trans. Ross Guberman (New York: Columbia University Press, 1996), vii.

10. See Plato, *Symposium*, 189a–193e.

11. Kristeva, *Tales of Love*, 70, emphasis mine.

12. Ibid., 71, emphasis mine.

13. What Kristeva fails to acknowledge, however, is that the androgyne (who, importantly, is both male and female) carries otherness within—a mode of existence that comes very close to her own account of human subjectivity as being marked by internal strangeness (an account that will be examined in what follows). The Aristophanic androgyne may be self-sufficient and a narcissist, but it is, in my mind, nevertheless a being marked by strangeness, otherness, and difference.

14. Sjöholm characterizes the cosmopolitanism developed in this book as a "hollow universalism." See Sjöholm, "Love and the Question of Identity," chap. 3 in *Kristeva and the Political*. Some of the thoughts developed in *Strangers to Ourselves* have been further explored in Julia Kristeva, *Nations Without Nationalism*, trans. Leon S. Roudiez (New York: Columbia University Press, 1993).

15. Julia Kristeva, "The Impenetrable Power of the Phallic Matron," *Libération*, September 25, 2008, accessed at http://kristeva.fr/palin_en.html. This article is a commentary on what Kristeva herself calls the "Sarah Palin syndrome."

16. Both Plato and Aristotle repeatedly stress the manifold structure of the soul, and view ethical life as a balancing act between the different parts of the soul—one that could be achieved through moderation (which is not to say repression of any one part). In this regard, their view of the human soul could be described as proto-psychoanalytical. See Plato, *Republic*; and Aristotle, *On the Soul* (*De Anima*), trans. Hippocrates G. Apostle (Grinnell, IA: The Peripatetic Press, 1981).

17. In book 4 of the *Republic*, Plato develops an analogy between the threefold structure of the human soul (calculative, spirited, and desirous) and the three classes of the city (deliberative, auxiliary, and money-making). If a just individual is one that has established balance between the three parts of the soul (if each part, as Socrates puts it, minds its own business), the same can be said about a just city. A just city is thus a city in which rulers are allowed to rule,

where guardians guard the city, and where its inhabitants (the money-makers) perform the tasks allotted to them: "this city was just because each of the classes in it minds its own business," Socrates remarks. See Plato, *Republic*, 441d. The analogy between city and soul is established at 441a.

18. Freud, too, was careful to point out that the relationship between the different parts of the human psyche must be one marked by harmony and balance. The aim of psychoanalysis is, however, *not* to "erase" unconscious instincts altogether or bring complete unity to the mind. The point—and this was so already for Plato—is to establish a *balanced* relationship between the different levels of consciousness without repressing one or privileging the other. As Alan Bass has noted in a commentary on Freud: "In 'Analysis Terminable and Interminable,' one of his last papers, Freud states that when there is a conflict between the ego and an instinctual demand, the aim of analysis is not to make the instinct disappear. In this typical situation, the aim of analysis can be described only roughly as a 'taming' of the instinct; or, to use a more psychological language, the aim is to bring the instinct into harmony of the ego, thereby making it accessible to all the influences of the other ego trends so that it does not seek independent satisfaction." See Alan Bass, "Time and the Witch: Femininity, Metapsychology and the Temporality of the Unconscious," *Modern Language Notes* 91, no. 5 (1976): 871.

19. As Arendt has noted: "how one rules himself, he will rule others" (HC 238).

20. Kristeva, "Revolt and Revolution," interview conducted by Rainer Ganahl, in *Revolt, She Said*, 100.

21. The idea of the unconscious stands at the heart of the Copernican revolution that Freud instigated through his challenge of modern subjectivity (if the latter is understood as providing a stable, unified, and fully conscious ground à la Descartes's *cogito* or Kant's transcendental unity of apperception). In his essay "The Unconscious," Freud writes: "Our right to postulate an unconscious in the psyche, and to use this postulation in scientific work, is contested from many sides. In response, we can state that it is both *necessary* and *legitimate* to postulate the unconscious, and that we have a great deal of *evidence* for its existence. . . . it is nothing less than an *untenable presumption* to insist that everything occurring in the psyche must also be known to consciousness." See Sigmund Freud, *The Unconscious*, trans. Graham Frankland (London: Penguin Books, 2005), 50.

22. Kristeva, "The Impenetrable Power of the Phallic Matron."

23. Sigmund Freud, "The Uncanny," in vol. 17 of *The Standard Edition of the Complete Psychological Works of Sigmund Freud*, trans. and ed. James Strachey (London: Hogarth Press, 1953–1974), 220. The German term *unheimlich* is derived from *heimlich*, which means both "secret" and "homely." The term as such thus implies the strange and the familiar both at once. Freud gives a detailed etymological analysis of the term on 220–26 of the essay.

24. Ibid., 240–41, 245.

25. It is interesting to note that Freud stresses the fact that *aesthetic experience* is what triggers this uncanny feeling. He opens the essay by stating that psychoanalysts rarely feel "impelled to investigate the subject of aesthetics" (219), but that the topic that he is about to broach calls for such an investigation. The belief that poetic language has the capacity to bring forth the most archaic aspects of early subject formation and individual development is, as we have already seen, central in the work of Kristeva.

26. See also ibid., 245. While woman is the Other of our culture, one could thus claim that she is so precisely because of her ultimate *familiarity*, albeit a familiarity that we repress, in an attempt to deny our own original otherness and dependency on the other—our mother. Peter J. Euben has noted the etymological connection between hostess (*xene*) and stranger (*xenos*), thus drawing our attention to the age-long association of the strange and the intimate or familiar. See Peter J. Euben, *The Tragedy of Political Theory: The Road Not Taken* (Princeton, NJ: Princeton University Press, 1990), 80. In part 4 of this book, I will examine the fact that it is precisely *as mother* that woman has been reduced to an *other*.

27. Arendt, who has noted that "the most general condition of human existence" is our finitude—"birth and death, natality and morality" (she importantly includes birth, just like Kristeva and Irigaray)—argues that plurality (the fact that we are born into a world with others) is the central condition for human action, "because we are all the same, that is, human, in such a way that nobody is ever the same as anyone else who ever lived, lives, or will live" (HC 8). It is precisely through the fact of birth and finitude that singularity appears. I will return to this aspect of Arendt's thought in the conclusion of this book.

28. The real challenge here is of course to establish a bond between the self and the *radically* other, without caving in to gestures of assimilation and appropriation. Here the Greeks cannot serve as our model. As is well known, in the *Republic* Plato argues that balance must be established between individuals *within* a given community (justice is sought within the city proper), whereas he simply assumes the exclusion of and enmity toward foreigners (barbarians). The just city, on Plato's account, must avoid *internal* fraction (civil war), but it will inevitably go to war with other cities. For a rich analysis of the role of war in Plato's *Republic*, see chapter 9 of Claudia Baracchi's *Of Myth, Life, and War in Plato's* Republic (Bloomington: Indiana University Press, 2002).

29. The political consequences of the ethical model developed here have been examined at length by Sjöholm in *Kristeva and the Political*. For an interesting analysis of how Kristeva's cosmopolitanism is foregrounded by Aristotelian ethical thought, see Claudia Baracchi's discussion of friendship in the concluding chapter of *Aristotle's Ethics as First Philosophy* (Cambridge: Cambridge University Press, 2008).

30. Kristeva typically insists on the dangers of assimilation or appropriation, and stresses the importance of not leveling off differences. The moments where she herself nevertheless tends toward assimilationist politics happen almost exclusively whenever she speaks of Muslims in France (and in particular when she broaches the question of veiling). I think, especially, of her remarks in *Nations Without Nationalism*, where she speaks of "an influx of humiliated and demanding Arabian masses" (38), wonders why French citizens should "accept [that daughters of Maghrebin immigrants wear] the Muslim scarf [to school]," or why the French should feel compelled to "change spelling" (36). And she proposes that "the 'abstract' advantages of French universalism may prove to be superior to the 'concrete' benefits of a Muslim scarf" (47). These are for me extremely troubling moments in her work, and ones that require critical attention.

31. See Butler, *Notes Toward a Performative Theory of Assembly*, 67. For Butler's helpful distinction between precariousness and precarity, see her introduction to *Frames of War*: "Precariousness and precarity are intersecting concepts. Lives are by definition precarious: they can be expunged at will or by accident; their persistence is in no sense guaranteed. In some sense, this is a feature of all life, and there is no thinking of life that is not precarious—except, of course, in fantasy, and in military fantasies in particular. . . . Precarity designates that politically induced condition in which certain populations suffer from failing social and economic networks of support and become differentially exposed to injury, violence, and death" (25). This kind of distinction is missing in Kristeva's discussion. She does not offer a conceptual toolbox that would allow us to differentiate between our shared and constitutive strangeness (what Butler, in the context of vulnerability, refers to as precariousness), and the politically induced condition in which certain populations suffer from being marked as strangers because they depart from normative conceptions of selfhood (the assumption that the self is white, male, middle class, straight, Western, able-bodied, and so on). The lack of such a distinction in Kristeva's work is symptomatic, and ultimately limits her capacity to tend to power dynamics in her analysis of foreignness.

32. Sara Ahmed, "The Skin of the Community: Affect and Boundary Formation," in *Revolt, Affect, Collectivity*, 96.

33. In her book *Strange Encounters*, we find a similar formulation: "*some others are designated as stranger than other others.*" See Ahmed, *Strange Encounters*, 6.

34. Ibid., 109, emphasis mine. Kristeva's references to Muslims in *Nations Without Nationalism* are paradigmatic in this regard.

35. When describing analysis as an emancipation from the "symptom of 'being conscious,'" Kristeva is quoting Freud from his essay "The Unconscious."

36. Freud, *The Unconscious*, 69–70.

37. Ibid., 78.

38. Freud, *Beyond the Pleasure Principle*, 31–32.

39. Ibid., 32.

40. "The Unconscious" was published in his *Papers on Metapsychology*. Metapsychology is an attempt to establish the fundamental concepts used to represent and describe the operation of the mental apparatus. We might say that it is meant to establish the conditions of possibility for all subsequent clinical work, it sets up the *scene* for analysis. Freud himself gives the following definition of the term: "When we succeed in describing a psychic process in its *dynamic*, *topographical* and *economic* aspects, I propose we call this a *metapsychological* account." See Freud, *The Unconscious*, 64. Freud's *Beyond the Pleasure Principle* is usually seen as marking a second phase in his metapsychological thinking. If in his essay from 1915 he had divided the psychic apparatus into conscious (*cs*), preconscious (*pcs*), and unconscious (*ucs*), in his later work he introduces the structural model of ego, superego, and id. It is significant to note that Freud remains faithful to his idea of the timelessness of the unconscious even as he transitions into the second topography. In his *New Introductory Lectures on Psycho-Analysis* (1933), he again revisits the topic of the timeless, now using the terminology of the id rather than the unconscious: "There is nothing in the id that corresponds to the idea of time; there is no recognition of the passage of time, and—a thing that is most remarkable and awaits consideration in philosophical thought—no alteration in its mental processes is produced by the passage of time. Wishful impulses which have never passed beyond the id, but impressions, too, which have been sunk into the id by repression, are virtually immortal; after the passage of decades they behave as though they had just occurred. They can only be recognized as belonging to the past, can only lose their importance and be deprived of their cathexis of energy, when they have been made conscious by the work of analysis, and it is on this that the therapeutic effect of analytic treatment rests to no small extent." See Sigmund Freud, "The Dissection of the Psychical Personality," Lecture XXXI in *New Introductory Lectures on Psycho-Analysis*, trans. and ed. James Strachey (New York: W. W. Norton & Company, 1989), 92. It is interesting to note that Freud here defines the task of psychoanalysis as *making temporal* the atemporal content of the id. To bring repressed memories to consciousness would precisely amount to giving them a proper place in linear time—to acknowledge them as belonging to the past.

41. Johnston, *Time Driven*, 11.

42. In her more recent essay "New Forms of Revolt," Kristeva again describes psychoanalysis as the " 'Copernican revolution' that Freud introduced in the twentieth century and that we increasingly perceive to be one of the only ones that does not turn away from either affliction or the revolts of modernity." See Julia Kristeva, "New Forms of Revolt," *Journal of French and Francophone Philosophy* 22, no. 2 (2014): 10.

43. In "New Forms of Revolt" she again underlines the originality of the concept, as she speaks of the "*unprecedented* timelessness" that "*no philosophy had identified before [Freud]*" (10, emphasis mine).

44. Johnston, *Time Driven*, 5.

45. Ibid., 5.

46. Freud, *The Unconscious*, 69–70.

47. Freud, *Beyond the Pleasure Principle*, 31–32.

48. Kristeva, "New Forms of Revolt," 10, emphasis mine.

49. Jacques Derrida, "Freud and the Scene of Writing," chap. 7 in *Writing and Difference*, trans. Alan Bass (Chicago: University of Chicago Press, 1978), 215.

50. More specifically, it appears as a parenthetical remark within a discussion about our means for protecting ourselves against various external stimuli, and Freud in fact suggests that the abstract idea of time (linear time)—an idea that belongs wholly to the conscious system—might "constitute another way of providing a shield against stimuli." See Freud, *Beyond the Pleasure Principle*, 32. Linear time would thus be a secondary structure and a *defense mechanism* set in place in order to protect the human organism from the intensity of the external world. I will not have time to further explore this issue here, but let me simply note that it would be interesting to examine this aspect of the Freudian analysis in light of the account that I provided in the opening chapters of this book, where linear time appeared precisely as a kind of patriarchal defense against our embodied and sexed condition.

51. Freud notes that "what appears to be reality is in fact only a reflection of a forgotten past" (19).

52. Ibid., 23.

53. "If we take into account observations such as these, based upon behaviour in the transference and upon the life-histories of men and women, we shall find courage to assume that there really does exist in the mind a compulsion to repeat which overrides the pleasure principle" (24).

54. Kristeva, "New Forms of Revolt," 10–11.

55. Freud, *Beyond the Pleasure Principle*, 23. As Bass has pointed out before me, Freud makes similar use of the Nietzschean notion of eternal return in "The Uncanny" (also written in 1920). In that essay, the reference appears in a list of those situations that provoke feelings of uncanny strangeness: "And finally there is the constant recurrence of the same thing—the repetition of the same features or character-traits or vicissitudes, of the same crimes, or even the same names through several consecutive generations." See Freud, "The Uncanny," 234. The question of repetition is central in both essays. See also Bass, "Time and the Witch," 905.

56. Johnston, *Time Driven*, 9.

57. Ibid., 7–8. Kristeva presents a case study that illustrates this temporal structure. Danièle has been in analysis for four years and speaks rarely of her

mother: "She had always maintained outside of time the painful memory of this mother" (IR 37). But when she finds out through friends that her analyst (Kristeva) is traveling to Jerusalem, Danièle has a dream about her mother, who had gone to Jerusalem as a little girl while her own parents (Danièle's grandparents) were deported to the camps. The news about Kristeva's present trip to Jerusalem is what triggers the repressed memories of an earlier trip to Jerusalem, and this present event marks the beginning of a possible working-through. Kristeva highlights the temporality at play for this patient: "Danièle had suffered, in the fullest sense of the term, an intersection between linear time, on the one hand, accentuated by my trip, which we were able to discuss, and, on the other hand, the timelessness of the mother-daughter symbiosis, in this case, opening onto a traumatic generational history" (38).

58. There is no standard English translation of this term. James Strachey usually translates it as "deferred action" or "secondary revision." Jean Laplanche prefers the term "afterwardsness." The French term (that is used by Kristeva and Irigaray alike) is l'après-coup.

59. Jean Laplanche and Jean-Bertrand Pontalis, The Language of Psycho-Analysis, trans. Donald Nicholson-Smith (New York: W. W. Norton & Company, 1973), 112.

60. Alison Stone, Feminism, Psychoanalysis, and Maternal Subjectivity (New York: Routledge, 2012), 143.

61. See Jacques Lacan, The Seminar of Jacques Lacan, Book I: Freud's Papers on Technique 1953–1954, trans. John Forrester (New York: W. W. Norton & Company, 1988), 274–75.

62. Irigaray, Speculum of the Other Woman, 28. Irigaray revisits Nachträglichkeit in an interview published in This Sex Which Is Not One, using an almost identical formulation: "Freud undermines a certain way of conceptualizing the 'present,' 'presence,' by stressing deferred action [l'après-coup], overdetermination, the repetition compulsion, the death drive, and so on." See Irigaray, "The Power of Discourse," in This Sex Which Is Not One, 72. I would like to thank Sara McNamara for drawing my attention to these passages in Irigaray. My brief comments on Nachträglichkeit are deeply indebted to her work on this topic. See Sara McNamara, "In the Beginning Was the End of Her Story: Irigaray and Freud on Nachträglichkeit and Feminine Temporality," paper presented at the Society for Phenomenology and Existentialist Philosophy (SPEP), Montreal, 2010.

63. Bass, "Time and the Witch," 904.

64. Ibid., 907–08.

65. Stone, Feminism, Psychoanalysis, and Maternal Subjectivity, 144.

66. Sigmund Freud, "Remembering, Repeating and Working-Through (Further Recommendations on the Technique of Psycho-Analysis II)," in vol. 12 of The Standard Edition of the Complete Psychological Works of Sigmund Freud, ed. and trans. James Strachey (London: Hogarth Press, 1958), 147, emphasis

mine. Later in this essay, Freud again stresses the temporal structure of analysis: "We have learnt that the patient repeats instead of remembering, and repeats under the condition of resistance. . . . we must treat his illness, not as an event of the past, but as a *present-day force*" (151, emphasis mine). It is worth noting that this essay contains the first explicit instance of the concept of the compulsion to repeat: "the patient does not *remember* anything of what he has forgotten and repressed, but *acts* it out. He reproduces it not as a memory but as an action; he *repeats* it, without, of course, knowing that he is repeating it. . . . As long as the patient is in the treatment he cannot escape from this *compulsion to repeat*; and in the end we understand that this is his way of remembering" (150, last emphasis mine). Strachey points out that while this is the first instance of the concept of compulsory repetition, the ideas presented herein had been developed much earlier: "This had been made plain by Freud very much earlier, in his postscript to his analysis of 'Dora,' where the topic of transference is under discussion" (150n1). In the present essay, Freud again ties the question of compulsive repetition to that of transference, viewing the latter as the means through which the former can be interrupted: "The main instrument . . . for curbing the patient's compulsion to repeat and for turning it into a motive for remembering lies in the handling of the transference. We render the compulsion harmless, and indeed useful, by giving it the right to assert itself in a definite field" (154).

67. Stone, *Feminism, Psychoanalysis, and Maternal Subjectivity*, 146–47.

68. Bass, "Time and the Witch," 910.

# Chapter 7

1. Mary O'Brien, *The Politics of Reproduction* (Boston: Routledge & Kegan Paul, 1981), 8.

2. Imogen Tyler, "Introduction: Birth," *Feminist Review* 93 (2009): 2.

3. See Reyes Lázaro, "Feminism and Motherhood: O'Brien vs Beauvoir," *Hypatia: A Journal of Feminist Philosophy* 1, no. 2 (1986): 87. See also Kelly Oliver, "Motherhood, Sexuality, and Pregnant Embodiment: Twenty-Five Years of Gestation," *Hypatia: A Journal of Feminist Philosophy* 25, no. 4 (2010): 761.

4. Oliver, "Motherhood, Sexuality, and Pregnant Embodiment," 762.

5. See also Alison Stone, "Beauvoir and the Ambiguities of Motherhood," in *A Companion to Simone de Beauvoir*, ed. Laura Hengehold and Nancy Bauer (Hoboken, NJ: Wiley-Blackwell, 2017), 123.

6. See, for example, Sarah LaChance Adams, *Mad Mothers, Bad Mothers, and What a "Good" Mother Would Do: The Ethics of Ambivalence* (New York: Columbia University Press, 2014). See also Stone, "Beauvoir and the Ambiguities of Motherhood." In an interview from 1982, Beauvoir herself clarifies that

"motherhood in itself is not something negative or something inhuman," but rather that it is motherhood as a patriarchal reality, what she calls "enslaved motherhood," that is a problem. See Simone de Beauvoir, Margaret A. Simons, and Jane Marie Todd, "Two Interviews with Simone de Beauvoir," *Hypatia: A Journal of Feminist Philosophy* 3, no. 3 (1989): 18.

7. Christine Battersby, *The Phenomenal Woman: Feminist Metaphysics and the Patterns of Identity* (New York: Routledge, 1998), 16.

8. Donna J. Haraway, *Simians, Cyborgs, and Women: The Reinvention of Nature* (New York: Routledge, 1991), 253n8.

9. The latter might apply to surrogates, birth mothers who give their child(ren) up for adoption, or gestating and birthing transmen who identify as fathers.

10. For a particularly rich critical engagement, which focuses on the nostalgia for a lost maternal continent and offers a critique of the notion of the lost mother as a ground for thinking about sexual difference, see Lynne Huffer, *Maternal Pasts, Feminist Futures: Nostalgia, Ethics, and the Question of Difference* (Stanford: Stanford University Press, 1998). This books treats both Kristeva and Irigaray's work in detail, as well as that of Maurice Blanchot and Nicole Brossard.

11. Julia Kristeva, "The Meaning of Parity," in *The Kristeva Critical Reader*, trans. John Lechte, ed. John Lechte and Mary Zournazi (Edinburgh: Edinburgh University Press, 2003), 207.

12. One might ask whether Kristeva and Irigaray situate themselves within such female genealogies. To what extent do they include other women in their texts? How willing are they to enter into dialogue with their "mothers," or, for that matter, with their "sisters" or "daughters"? Kristeva's early work almost fully excludes women (she engages with plenty of male artists and writers, but really only with one woman, Marguerite Duras, in any substantial way). In her later work, however, she has turned to several female figures, most prominently in her trilogy *Female Genius: Life, Madness, Words* (on Arendt, Melanie Klein, and Colette), and in her more recent work on Saint Teresa of Avila (see *Teresa, My Love: An Imagined Life of the Saint of Avila*, trans. Lorna Scott Fox [New York: Columbia University Press, 2014]). She has also initiated the Prix Simone de Beauvoir pour la liberté des femmes (Simone de Beauvoir Prize for Women's Liberation), the first of which was shared in 2008 between Bangladeshi gynecologist and author Taslima Nasreen and Ethiopian politician and writer Ayaan Hirsi Ali, and the tenth of which was offered in 2017 to the Polish women's rights group Save the Women. Irigaray has often emphasized the importance of female genealogy: "If we are not to be accomplices in the murder of the mother we also need to assert that there is a genealogy of women. Each of us has a female family tree: we have a mother, a maternal grandmother and great-grandmothers, we have daughters. Because we have been exiled into the house of our husbands, it is easy to forget the special quality of the female genealogy; we

might even come to deny it. Let us try to situate ourselves within that female genealogy so that we can win and hold on to our identity. Let us not forget, moreover, that we already have a history, that certain women, despite all the cultural obstacles, have made their mark upon history and all too often have been forgotten by us." See Luce Irigaray, "Body Against Body: In Relation to the Mother," chap. 2 in *Sexes and Genealogies*, 19. Henceforth, references to this text will be given parenthetically within the main body of the text, using the abbreviation BAB. This quote might seem strange, however, given Irigaray's de facto silence—indeed forgetting—of female thinkers and authors in her own work. In her early "critical" period, she engages exclusively with the male philosophical tradition and never gives any female counterexamples. In her later "affirmative" period, women continue to be absent. She does of course speak a great deal of relationships between women (especially mothers and daughters) and the importance thereof, as well as female mythical figures and goddesses, but she rarely mentions any specific female artists, thinkers, activists, or historical figures. One exception is her interview with the French biology teacher Hélène Rouch in "On the Maternal Order" (*Je, Tu, Nous*, 37–44), and her subsequent use of the commentary offered by Rouch there to develop her thoughts on the so-called placental economy (more on this in chapter 9). There are also a few references to Beauvoir in her work, largely critical. See, for example, "A Personal Note: Equal or Different?" (*Je, Tu, Nous*, 9–14); "The Other: Woman" (*I Love to You*, 59–68); and "The Question of the Other" (*Democracy Begins Between Two*, 121–41). In an interview from 1995, Irigaray comments on the charge that she has failed to properly acknowledge the influence of Beauvoir on her own work: "Another error occurs when filiations are imputed on me that are not mine: for example, it's said that I'm a daughter of Simone de Beauvoir and that I haven't acknowledged enough the source of my thinking in relation to her. But that's because I'm not a daughter of Simone de Beauvoir. I don't know her work well. I read her novels when I was an adolescent. Two years ago I tried, for the sake of my students, to take another look at *The Second Sex*; in fact, I read it in 1952 and read only the Introduction and a little of the first chapter, but this is not at all the source of my work." She goes on to explain that her "theoretical filiation . . . is much more to the tradition of Western philosophy," by which she means, judging from her work, thinkers like Plato, Aristotle, Descartes, Kant, Hegel, Nietzsche, Heidegger, Maurice Merleau-Ponty, and Levinas—in short, the male canon. See Irigaray, " 'Je—Luce Irigaray,' " 113. When asked during a seminar at Liverpool Hope University to mention any women by whom her work has been inspired, she refused to do so, emphasizing the singularity of her own work, which, again, seems strange in the context of her own very consistent insistence on female genealogies. For a discussion of the role of female genealogy in Irigaray's work, and particularly the role of female mythological figures, see Gail M. Schwab, "Mothers, Sisters, and Daughters:

Luce Irigaray and the Female Genealogical Line in the Stories of the Greeks," in *Rewriting Difference: Luce Irigaray and "the Greeks,"* ed. Elena Tzelepis and Athena Athanasiou (Albany: State University of New York Press, 2008).

13. Quoting several prominent women, Miglena Nikolchina addresses the issue of the absence of foremothers: " 'I am the first of a new genus' (Mary Wollstonecraft). 'When I looked around, I saw and heard of none like me' (Mary Shelley). 'I look everywhere for grandmothers and find none' (Elizabeth Barrett Browning). 'Why isn't there a tradition of the mothers?' (Virginia Woolf). Women have 'no past, no history' (Simone de Beauvoir). 'I look for myself throughout the centuries and I don't see myself anywhere' (Hélène Cixous)." And she goes on to emphasize that "the conditions that produced the 'strange spaces of silence' [Woolf] and made the repetitive generic loneliness from Wollstone-craft to Cixous possible are still operative." See Miglena Nikolchina, *Matricide in Language: Writing Theory in Kristeva and Woolf* (New York: Other Press, 2002), 2.

14. Nancy Tuana, *The Less Noble Sex: Scientific, Religious, and Philosophical Conceptions of Woman's Nature* (Bloomington: Indiana University Press, 1993), 111–52.

15. Luce Irigaray, "And the One Doesn't Stir without the Other," trans. Hélène Vivienne Wenzel, *Signs: Journal of Women in Culture and Society* 7, no. 1 (1981): 67.

16. Ibid., 66.

17. Irigaray, *I Love to You*, 46, 131.

18. Julia Kristeva, " 'unes femmes': The Woman Effect," interview with Julia Kristeva conducted by Elaine Boucquey, in *Julia Kristeva: Interviews*, ed. Ross Mitchell Guberman (New York: Columbia University Press, 1996), 108.

19. Irigaray, "And the One Doesn't Stir without the Other," 63.

20. See Maria Margaroni, " 'The Lost Foundation': Kristeva's Semiotic *Chora* and Its Ambiguous Legacy," *Hypatia: A Journal of Feminist Philosophy* 20, no. 1 (2005): 78–98.

21. Kristeva herself notes that the poet—who is characterized as someone who refuses to forget the maternal figure, who returns to her time and again in search for affective-semiotic elements in language—is able to "produce what is *new* in 'culture'" through this very movement of return: "The innovator, then, would be that child that doesn't forget." See Julia Kristeva, "The Novel as Polylogue," in *Desire in Language: A Semiotic Approach to Literature and Art*, trans. Thomas Gora, Alice Jardine, and Leon S. Roudiez, ed. Leon S. Roudiez (New York: Columbia University Press, 1980), 196.

22. I use "materialism" here to label an interest for, and an emphasis on, the materiality of the body. As I will try to show, however, this by no means amounts to essentialism, precisely because of the temporal dimensions that will be the focus of my attention here.

23. Stone, *Feminism, Psychoanalysis, and Maternal Subjectivity*, 147. Stone stresses that her own past-centered analysis in no way situates the experience of motherhood exclusively in the past. She views lived maternal time as containing an "organic unity" of past, present, and future, such that we can "see maternal time as past-centered *and* see the mother as open to the future" (146).

24. Lisa Baraitser, *Maternal Encounters: An Ethic of Interruption* (New York: Routledge, 2009), see especially 74–87.

25. Both Kristeva and Irigaray tend to return to the Greeks in their work. For the most sustained attempt to gather essays that speak to Irigaray's relation to Greek philosophy and literature, see *Rewriting Difference: Luce Irigaray and "the Greeks."* See also Paul Allen Miller, *Diotima at the Barricades: French Feminists Read Plato* (Oxford: Oxford University Press, 2016).

26. Chanter explains: "If Kristeva's elaboration of the semiotic is regarded as collapsing onto essentialism, she fares no better in her attempts to acknowledge that, with the subject's entry into language, there is always already present the influence of culture. She is accused of committing the equally grave sin of phallocentrism by accepting the rule of the symbolic." See Tina Chanter, "Kristeva's Politics of Change: Tracking Essentialism with the Help of a Sex/ Gender Map," in *Ethics, Politics, and Difference in Julia Kristeva's Writing*, ed. Kelly Oliver (New York: Routledge, 1993), 184.

27. Kristeva, *Black Sun*, 27–28.

28. Kristeva, "'unes femmes': The Woman Effect," 109.

29. We might want to add that the necessary separation from the mother is a consequence of maternal agency: it is because the *mother* turns *her* desire elsewhere that the child begins to separate and acknowledge its own subjectivity as distinct from that of the mother. I say this, here, to avoid a certain kind of "victimization" of a mother construed as mere passivity—a characterization that simply does not correspond to the account that Kristeva offers, but one which has nevertheless often been ascribed to her.

30. Luce Irigaray, *In the Beginning, She Was* (London: Bloomsbury, 2013), 81.

31. Jones has noted that Kristeva and Irigaray share a commitment to drawing "attention to the constitutive repression of the maternal body and the feminine in western thought and culture," but she goes on to stress that "the ways in which they seek to reclaim this repressed otherness are very different." See Jones, *Irigaray*, 30. While she is of course right that there are deep differences between how these two thinkers treat the question of the maternal, I will nevertheless try to show that if we focus on how the maternal relates to issues of temporality, we will see more overlap between the two than we might have otherwise.

32. Kristeva, *Tales of Love*, 357.

33. See Sigmund Freud, *Totem and Taboo: Some Points of Agreement between the Mental Lives of Savages and Neurotics*, trans. and ed. James Strachey (New York: W. W. Norton & Company, 1989).

34. Luce Irigaray, "So When Are We to Become Women?," chap. 16 in *Je, Tu, Nous*, 133.

35. Irigaray, preface to *Key Writings*, vii.

36. Irigaray, *In the Beginning, She Was*, 38, 111.

37. Aeschylus, *The Oresteia*, trans. Robert Fagles (New York: Viking Press, 1979), 260–61.

38. For a different approach, see Erich Neumann, *The Fear of the Feminine and Other Essays on Feminine Psychology*, trans. Boris Matthews, Esther Doughty, Eugene Rolfe, and Michael Cullingworth (Princeton, NJ: Princeton University Press, 1994). The landmark text on this issue is, of course, Adrienne Rich, *Of Woman Born: Motherhood as Experience and Institution* (New York: W. W. Norton & Company, 1976). Tuana's *The Less Noble Sex* is also a useful reference.

39. For a clear discussion of the mechanisms behind such association, see Ortner, "Is Female to Male as Nature Is to Culture?," 21–44. For a critique of the traditional association of woman (and the maternal) with nature, and man (and the paternal) with culture, see Kelly Oliver, *Family Values: Subjects Between Nature and Culture* (New York: Routledge, 1997). See also Tuana, "The Weaker Seed," chap. 7 of *The Less Noble Sex*, 130–52.

40. Ortner makes an attempt to explain this kind of contradiction. Having argued that woman is an intermediate between culture and nature, she explains that such an intermediate "is located on the continuous periphery of culture's clearing; and though it may thus appear to stand both above and below (and beside) culture, it is simply outside and around it. We can begin to understand then how a single system of cultural thought can often assign to woman completely polarized and apparently contradictory meanings, since extremes, as we say, meet." See Ortner, "Is Female to Male as Nature Is to Culture?," 40.

41. Nikolchina, *Matricide in Language*, 5.

42. Art, according to Kristeva, is the "semiotization of the symbolic," and "represents the flow of jouissance into language" (RPL 79).

43. Julia Kristeva, "From One Identity to Another," in *Desire in Language*, 136.

44. Irigaray shares this view on language, but while she agrees with Kristeva that art (or poetic language) has the potential to bring forth forgotten or lost territory, she is far more skeptical about the role of psychoanalysis, and even argues that it is one of the repressive discourses par excellence. This is a standpoint that runs throughout her entire work, but it is maybe most explicitly articulated in her essay "The Blind Spot of an Old Dream of Symmetry," in *Speculum of the Other Woman*, 13–129.

45. Irigaray, *To Be Two*, 7.

46. Irigaray, "How to Conceive (of) a Girl," in *Speculum of the Other Woman*, 166.

47. Think, also, of our genesis as told by Aristophanes in Plato's *Symposium*, where the navel is described as a trace of the punishment placed on us by Zeus, the god of gods, who, in his anger at human hubris had decided to cut the then spherical human beings in half, to weaken their strength. It was thus that we became the two-legged (and desiring) figures that we are today, and the navel is there to remind us of our original wholeness. On this account the navel comes to represent a mark of divine (male) agency rather than being a reminder of our maternal origins. Human genesis as narrated by Aristophanes is one devoid of maternal origins. See Plato, *Symposium*, 191a.

48. Irigaray, "The Blind Spot of an Old Dream of Symmetry," in *Speculum of the Other Woman*, 68. On this account, Irigaray seems to suggest not that we lack memories of such a loss full stop but rather that we lack the tools to put such memories into representation. We would, in other words, sense the loss, but we are often unable to articulate it. What is at stake is a kind of retention or repression below the threshold of consciousness and representation, but by no means ignorance unqualified. This would imply that the task, more than anything else, is to reinscribe the maternal function in our genealogical narratives and in the symbolization of our own beginnings.

49. Beardsworth understands Kristeva's psychoanalytical approach to first and foremost address what she calls the "loss of loss," associating it with modern nihilism. She argues that Kristeva, just like Butler, "finds that Western cultures are afflicted by melancholia," which for Kristeva would mean something like "the loss of the capacity to lose." See Beardsworth, *Julia Kristeva*, 20, 96. For a rich analysis of Kristeva's thought on melancholia, see also Miller, *Head Cases*.

50. Kaila Adia Story, *Patricia Hill Collins: Reconceiving Motherhood* (Bradford, ON: Demeter Press, 2014), 1.

51. Sophie Lewis, "Defending Intimacy Against What? Limits of Anti-surrogacy Feminisms," *Signs: Journal of Women in Culture and Society* 43, no. 1 (2017): 103.

52. Indeed, the autobiography of Thomas Beatie—one of the first transmen to go public about his pregnancy and birthing experience—fundamentally challenged ingrained social expectations about who mothers, and how. See Thomas Beatie, *Labor of Love: The Story of One Man's Extraordinary Pregnancy* (Berkeley: Seal Press, 2009). Not all gender-queer folk saw the publication of Beatie's autobiography as a step forward, however. Halberstam, for example, wonders "what price was paid, and by whom," in "this riot of visibility," wherein the image of Beatie's pregnant belly sensationalized trans parenthood: "He was far from being, in his own words, the 'first pregnant transman,' he was simply the first posttransition transgender male to go public with his decision to keep his female reproductive organs and then to use them." Halberstam further worries that "rather than promoting a queer narrative about difference and gender shifts,

his story ultimately came to rest upon an all too familiar narrative of humanity and universality—it is universal to want a child, it is only human to want to give birth." See Jack Halberstam, "The Pregnant Man," *The Velvet Trap Light* 65 (2010): 77–78.

53. Dorothy Roberts, *Killing the Black Body: Race, Reproduction, and the Meaning of Liberty* (New York: Vintage Books, 1999), 5.

54. Patricia Hill Collins, *Black Feminist Thought: Knowledge, Consciousness, and the Politics of Empowerment* (New York: Routledge, 2009), 188, 211.

55. Ibid., 214–15.

56. Nikolchina, *Matricide in Language*, 43. Lisa Walsh raises a similar concern: "And if, for all this, we were to begin at the beginning. With the mother. Her uniqueness and her femininity. Her womanhood and her desire. And the enormity of our debt to her. If we were to refuse the Lacanian supposition that the mother qua mother exists only in the psyche of her (male) child, as the criminal origin of his interminable suffering, and instead were to assume that she is and always has been a much richer presence to herself, to her son or daughter, and to the many others in her life, her unique role as forbidden Thing would cease to function as an unconscious black hole and would render the supremacy of the Phallus theoretically invalid." See Lisa Walsh, "Her Mother Her Self: The Ethics of the Antigone Family Romance," *Hypatia: A Journal of Feminist Philosophy* 14, no. 3 (1999): 120.

# Chapter 8

1. Part of the text was translated into English in 1984, but it has yet to be translated in its entirety.

2. I transcribe *chōra* with the Greek spelling throughout, even though Kristeva herself does not.

3. I am indebted to Claudia Baracchi for much of my understanding of Plato's *Timaeus*. Her lecture course on this dialogue, offered at The New School for Social Research in 2008, has had a great impact on how I have come to read and understand it. I want to express my gratitude to her for introducing me to this text, and for bringing my attention to the profound care with which one must approach the question of *chōra* as it is treated by Plato. While I do not give direct references to her lectures here, let me simply acknowledge that my reading of the *Timaeus* is colored by her insights throughout.

4. Following Derrida, I refer to *chōra* without using the definite article (except when I speak specifically of the *semiotic chōra*). For a discussion on the reasons for doing so, see Jacques Derrida, "Khōra," in *On the Name*, trans. Ian McLeod, ed. Thomas Dutoit (Stanford: Stanford University Press, 1995), 96.

5. Chanter notes that, "to the extent that Kristeva seeks to focus upon the maternal experience as a dimension whose significance patriarchal society

has tended to overlook, and to the extent that the semiotic is associated with maternity, it is inferred that in embracing the semiotic, Kristeva endorses essentialism." See Chanter, "Kristeva's Politics of Change," 183. Jacqueline Rose describes the "essentialism and primacy of the semiotic" as "one of the most problematic aspects" of Kristeva's work. See Jacqueline Rose, "Julia Kristeva— Take Two," in *Ethics, Politics, and Difference*, 53. Gerardine Meaney speaks of a "quasi-mystical realm" that "looks suspiciously like the eternal feminine." See Gerardine Meaney, *(Un)Like Subjects: Women, Theory, Fiction* (New York: Routledge, 1993), 84. Jennifer Stone dismisses *chōra* as a regression to ahistorical perceptions of femininity. See Jennifer Stone, "The Horrors of Power: A Critique of Kristeva," in *The Politics of Theory*, ed. Francis Barker, Peter Hulme, Margaret Iversen, and Diana Loxley (Colchester, UK: University of Essex Press, 1983), 42. Butler argues that Kristeva "delimits maternity as an essentially precultural reality," and complains that her "naturalistic descriptions of the maternal body effectively reify motherhood and preclude an analysis of its cultural construction and variability" (GT 103). Finally, in an interview, Spivak admits to being "repelled by Kristeva's politics," accusing her of a "long-standing implicit sort of positivism: naturalizing of the chora, naturalizing of the pre-semiotic." See Spivak, "In a Word," interview conducted by Ellen Rooney, *Differences* 1, no. 2 (1989): 145. These are only a few examples that shed light on the controversial status of the maternal in feminist philosophy in general, and in Kristeva's work in particular. Sjöholm is among the thinkers who object to this criticism: "The maternal, in Kristeva, must be considered to undo accusations of essentialism or Oedipal dogmatism, given its capacity to give way to the possibility not only of dissent, revolt or revolution, but to thought as such" (KP 58). Sjöholm does, interestingly, ground her argument against an essentialist reading of the maternal in Kristeva in the question of time, but she does not do so as systematically as I intend to do in what follows.

     6. F. E. Peters translates the Greek term into "land," "area," and "space." See F. E. Peters, *Greek Philosophical Terms: A Historical Lexicon* (New York: New York University Press, 1967), 30.

     7. Sjöholm defines it in the following way: "In Kristeva's theory, the *chora* is the economy of drives of a corporeal subject, representing a notion of embodiment transgressing the problematic restrictions of the social contract" (KP 89). McAfee speaks of an "early psychic space," where "the infant experiences a wealth of drives," and she reminds us that it is "the space in which the meaning that is produced is semiotic: the echolalis, glossolalias, rhythms, and intonations of an infant who does not yet know how to use language to refer to objects, or of a psychotic who has lost the ability to use language in a properly meaningful way." See McAfee, *Julia Kristeva*, 19.

     8. Kristeva, *Powers of Horror*, 14.

     9. Plato, *Timaeus*, trans. Peter Kalkavage (Newburyport, MA: Focus, 2001), 49B, 50D. Henceforth, references to this text will be given parenthetically

within in the main body of the text, using the abbreviation Tm followed by the Greek line number. For a discussion of Plato's own difficulties in associating *chōra* with maternity, see Derrida's discussion in "Khōra," 97ff.

10. See, for example, Rose, who notes that Kristeva borrows the term *chōra* from Plato exactly because he associated it with the maternal: "But if Plato did so, it was because the mother was seen as playing no part in the act of procreation, a receptacle or empty vessel *merely* for the gestation of the unborn child." See Rose, "Julia Kristeva—Take Two," 50. See also Grosz, who offers a critique of Plato based on the assumption that *chōra* is reduced to mere passivity and neutrality: "Its function is a neutral, traceless production that leaves no traces of its contributions, and thus allows the product to speak indirectly of its creator without need for acknowledging its incubator." See Grosz, "Women, Chora, Dwelling," in *Space, Time, and Perversion*, 115. Derrida refers to *chōra* as "passive and virgin matter," which he in turn associates with "the feminine element" in Greek culture. See Derrida, "Khōra," 97.

11. Kristeva uses similar terminology when describing the semiotic activity of *chōra*, noting that it "introduces *wandering* or fuzziness into language." See Kristeva, "From One Identity to Another," in *Desire in Language*, 136, emphasis mine. In his influential reading of the *Timaeus*, John Sallis stresses that the "necessity" represented by *chōra* must be understood as, precisely, *indeterminacy*. See John Sallis, *Chorology: On Beginning in Plato's* Timaeus (Bloomington: Indiana University Press, 1999), 93.

12. Plato, *Timaeus*, 80n70.

13. Derrida, "Khōra," 125.

14. *Chōra*, in other words, represents nonlinear time. With reference to the movement of *chōra*, Sallis notes that "nothing here will be simple or linear," and describes the discourse on *chōra* as "a more complex, if not aporetic, movement with respect to the beginning." See Sallis, *Chorology*, 95.

15. "Language as symbolic function constitutes itself at the cost of repressing instinctual drive and continuous relation to the mother. On the contrary, the unsettled and questionable subject of poetic language (for whom the word is never uniquely a sign) maintains itself at the cost of reactivating this repressed instinctual, maternal element." See Kristeva, "From One Identity to an Other," in *Desire in Language*, 136. Irigaray, similarly, points to the repression at stake in philosophical-logical discourse, here in terms of the repression of the imaginary of the cave in Plato's famous allegory from the *Republic*: "Do you think he can remember his 'old habitation' and 'the wisdom of the cave'? Does the logos set up a space in which fantasies, phantoms, hallucinations, can re-emerge? Where even the babbling and stuttering of childhood can revive? Or does the coherence of the logos demand that these be named, or even connoted—as poor copies, for example—thus eliminating any value they may have as truth? Such clear-cut distinctions conjure away realities that are a little too expansive, set them

in frames of definition, and thus prevent their antecedents from overflowing. From now on, relationships with those antecedents can only be reconstructed, raised in a dialectic that is always already a descendant. The place (of) dream is occupied by representations of its topos, which is thus irrevocably metamerized. . . . Excess of logos, which one no longer reaches by returning into the mother, but by trusting in the ex-sistence of the father" (PH 346). In her essay on Aristotle, Irigaray again points to the way in which language will cover over and repress the maternal: "Every utterance, every statement, will thus be developed and affirmed by covering over the fact that being's unseverable relation to mother-matter has been buried." See Irigaray, "How to Conceive (of) a Girl," in *Speculum of the Other Woman*, 162.

16. I will return in detail to the implications of this statement in my reading of Butler's critique of Kristeva.

17. Louise Burchill, in contrast, points out that "some commentators have argued 'chora' to yield the meaning of the chain of preceding names . . . such that Plato's use of the term in the *Timaeus* would constitute 'the first occurrence in Greek literature of the word *chora* in the sense of space in general, as distinct from the space occupied by any particular thing.' Even Heidegger subscribes, in a certain sense, to such an interpretation . . . when he situates 'chora' as preparing the way for the later metaphysical conception of space as defined by extension." See Burchill, "Re-situating the *Feminine*," 89. I agree with Derrida who, contra Heidegger, suggests that "the ordered polysemy of the word [*khōra*] always includes the sense of political place or, more generally, of *invested* place, by opposition to abstract space. *Khōra* 'means': place occupied by someone, country, inhabited place, marked place, rank, post, assigned position, territory, or region. And in fact, *khōra* will always already be occupied, invested, even as general place, and even when it is distinguished from everything that takes place in it. Whence the difficulty . . . of treating it as an empty or geometric space, or even, and this is what Heidegger will say of it, as that which 'prepares' the Cartesian space, the *extensio* of the *res extensa*." See Derrida, "Khōra," 109. We see, thus, that *chōra* must be understood not only in terms of materialized space, but also as a space that is always already invested, inhabited, even politicized. How could such a place or space possibly be neutral, passive, or amorphous?

18. Kristeva similarly emphasizes the intermediary aspect of poetic language: "it posits its own process as an undecidable process between sense and nonsense, between *language* and *rhythm* . . . between the symbolic and semiotic." See Kristeva, "From One Identity to an Other," in *Desire in Language*, 135.

19. In the preface to *Desire in Language*, Kristeva suggests that her own gender too might have mattered as she set out to delimit male rationality: "It was perhaps also necessary to be a *woman* to attempt to take up that exorbitant wager of carrying the rational project to the outer borders of the signifying ventures of men." See Kristeva, *Desire in Language*, x.

20. I am, of course, aware that this statement challenges the founding principle of the entire metaphysical-theological tradition, and this is exactly what it is meant to do. In granting creative powers solely to a paternal God, this tradition not only forgets its maternal roots (thus erasing difference in favor of selfsameness), but it also denies the inherently temporal nature of Being (relying on the fantasmatic idea[l] of an eternal creator, one without beginning or end). Throughout this book I argue, instead, for the constitutive status of time and difference alike, which means that no ultimate, perfected, and selfsame beginning can be assumed. In conversation, Irigaray has noted that the very openness of the female body is what makes it threatening to man, and that our culture has found two ways of responding to the aporia that this openness creates (an aporia that, in fact, makes futurity possible): the theological model introduces God as a function of closure, while the Lacanian-psychoanalytic path has been to reduce woman to lack or negativity. Both models are based on the repression of time and difference (Irigaray in conversation during a doctoral seminar at Liverpool Hope University, June 2007).

21. The difference, however, is crucial. As we saw in part 3, male thinkers such as Heidegger or Derrida tend to view death as the necessary horizon upon which finitude must be understood. Female philosophers such as Arendt, Kristeva, Irigaray, and Cavarero speak instead of human finitude first and foremost in terms of birth and natality. The point, as I argued there, is that any account of finitude that wants to challenge the notion of everlasting divine presence (an Augustinian God that always has and always will be), must acknowledge that temporal life is engendered *and* finite, not just the latter.

22. Grosz overlooks this aspect in her reading of Plato. She claims that *chōra* is understood as that which must not "procreate or produce—this is the function of the father, the creator, god, the Forms," but that the function of *chōra* is rather "to nurse, to support, surround, protect, incubate, to sort, or engender the worldly offspring of the Forms." See Grosz, "Women, *Chora*, Dwelling," in *Space, Time, and Perversion*, 115. It seems to me that *chōra* does more than simply "nurse," and to the extent that she "sorts," she is no less creative than the demiurge, who after all also "creates" exactly by way of sorting and ordering.

23. Burchill, "Re-situating the *Feminine*," 93.

24. Ibid.

25. Ibid.

26. For a discussion of the musical education of the guardians, see book 3 of Plato's *Republic*. Socrates speaks at length about the importance of the right kind of music in the city since it would allow its inhabitants to grow and to become law-abiding citizens. In book 4, he asserts that "never are the ways of music moved without the greatest political laws being moved." See Plato, *Republic*, 424c.

27. Kristeva, *Powers of Horror*, 14.

28. "Only in *dream logic*," Kristeva explains, have the primary processes of the semiotic *chōra* "attracted attention, and only in certain signifying practices, such as the *text*, do they dominate the signifying process." She goes on to state that her "positing of the semiotic is obviously inseparable from a theory of the subject that takes into account the Freudian positing of the unconscious" (RPL 29–30).

29. Grosz, "Women, *Chora*, Dwelling," in *Space, Time, and Perversion*, 114.

30. Margaroni, "The Lost Foundation," 79.

31. Ibid., 87.

32. Kristeva, *Powers of Horror*, 14.

33. This is, in fact, exactly what Timaeus urges us to do on 88D–E.

34. Heidegger's 1962 lecture *Zeit und Sein* introduces the term *Zeit-Raum* (time-space) to refer to the "spacing of time." Heidegger here modifies the 1927 text (*Sein und Zeit*) by recognizing the property of space in the event. We see traces, in Kristeva's thinking, of this Heideggerian attempt to think time and space together, but Heidegger certainly never did so in light of motherhood or natality. Kristeva makes reference to this aspect of Heidegger's thought in *Intimate Revolt*, 32. See also Martin Heidegger, "Time and Being," in *On Time and Being*, trans. Joan Stambaugh (Chicago: University of Chicago Press, 1972), 14–15.

35. Margaroni, "The Lost Foundation," 85.

36. Judith Butler, *Bodies That Matter: On the Discursive Limits of "Sex"* (New York: Routledge, 1993), 31.

37. Ibid.

38. Kristeva herself has described this essay as her "favorite chapter" in *Tales of Love*. See Julia Kristeva, *This Incredible Need to Believe*, trans. Beverley Bie Brahic (New York: Columbia University Press, 2009), 42.

39. Julia Kristeva, "Stabat Mater," chap. 12 in *Tales of Love*, 234. Henceforth, references to this text will be given parenthetically in the main body of the text, using the abbreviation SM. The rejection of motherhood in the name of feminism is an issue often noted by Kristeva. In an interview from 1977, she raises the concern that some feminists "are relying too much on an existentialist concept of woman, a concept that attaches a guilt complex to the maternal function. Either one has children, but that means one is not good for anything else, or one does not, and then it becomes possible to devote oneself to serious undertakings." See Julia Kristeva, "Julia Kristeva: à quoi servent les intellectuels?," interview conducted by Jean-Paul Enthoven, *Le Nouvel Observateur* (1977): 106, quoted in Leon S. Roudiez, introduction to *Desire in Language*, 10. The wink to Beauvoir is obvious. The latter, of course, speaks less of the need to *return* to the mother, and more of the importance of being able to choose *not* to be a mother (her account of motherhood in *The Second Sex* importantly begins with the question of abortion).

40. As is well known, Socrates describes his philosophical method as a form of midwifery, giving credit to his mother, Phaenarete, who was a midwife: "My art of midwifery is in general like theirs [real midwives]; the only difference is that my patients are men, not women, and my concern is not with the body but with the soul that is in travail of birth." See Plato, "Theaetetus," in *Plato's Theory of Knowledge: The Theaetetus and the Sophist*, trans. Francis M. Cornford (Mineola, NY: Dover, 2003), 150b. There is a plethora of feminist critiques of the male appropriation of birth in Plato's dialogues. Cavarero offers the perhaps most sustained such critical engagement in her now classic *In Spite of Plato: A Feminist Rewriting of Ancient Philosophy*, trans. Serena Anderlini-D'Onofrio and Áine O'Healy (New York: Routledge, 1995). See also Page duBois, who notes that "philosophical reproduction is ascribed exclusively to men who will inseminate each other with ideas in a sexual act in which women are excluded" ("The Platonic Appropriation of Reproduction," in *Feminist Interpretations of Plato*, ed. Nancy Tuana [University Park: Pennsylvania State University Press, 1994], 152). Cynthia D. Coe's essay "Plato, Maternity, and Power: Can We Get a Different Midwife?" (in *Coming to Life: Philosophies of Pregnancy, Childbirth, and Mothering*, ed. Sarah LaChance Adams and Caroline R. Lundquist [New York: Fordham University Press, 2013]), looks at how Plato's appropriation of maternal powers has come to shape the dominant construction of maternity in contemporary America. And Stella Sandford devotes a chapter of her book *Plato and Sex* to the issue of Plato's appropriation of pregnancy ("'I, a Man, am Pregnant and Give Birth' (*Symposium*)," chap. 4 in *Plato and Sex* [Cambridge, UK: Polity Press, 2010]). Sandford offers a brief overview of some of the central literature on this topic on 109–15.

41. Kristeva, *Tales of Love*, 75.

42. Kristeva, *This Incredible Need to Believe*, 44.

43. Kristeva, *Powers of Horror*, 8–9.

44. This is of course too simplistic a reading of Hegel, and one that would need qualification, but it is basically the critique implied in Kristeva's argument at this juncture. The focus of my attention is, in any event, not Hegel here, but rather the way in which Kristeva characterizes maternal time.

45. While the column that treats the figure of Mary in part does so in order to show how Christianity actually has carved out a space for the maternal in religious terms (Christ is, after all, in some sense *engendered*, he is a divinity with a mother), it is also meant to illustrate how the very introduction of a maternal figure within religious discourse immediately raised temporal concerns that had to be solved in order to save Christianity from sin and the corporeal aspects of life. If temporal life is engendered and finite (Kristeva describes it as "the intertwining of sex and death" [SM 239]), and if Jesus as a divine being in some sense is to escape finitude (insofar as he is resurrected), the Fathers of the Church had to solve the problem of Mary, his mother, by turning her

into a figure of eternal virginity. It is these "problematics of *time*, similar to that of cause," that interest Kristeva the most as she reports the development of a Christian cult of the Mother (240). Mary stands out as a complex and paradoxical figure: she at once introduces semiotic heterogeneity into culture, and at the same time comes to represent an "ideal totality that no individual woman could possibly embody" (246). And her own immortality is a strange one indeed: her life follows the very cyclicality of maternity—through transposition she is born and re-born, offering continuity to the species and making possible new beginnings. Mothers *do* provide us with a sense of immortality (as long as regeneration takes place we will live on in our children and grandchildren and so on: mothers provide "stability . . . so that our speaking species, which knows it is mortal, might withstand death" [262–63]), but at the same time they function as reminders that we are engendered and hence *will die*, whether we want it or not (Kristeva notes that Freud, who in her view "offers only a massive *nothing*" regarding the experience of motherhood, nevertheless, in facing his own mother, is reminded "that his own body is anything but immortal and will crumble away like dough" [255]). We begin to see the contours of how important a locus the maternal body is for thinking through the question of time, and for helping us orient ourselves within our own existence as finite beings who wish to overcome our finitude. The maternal "overcoming" of finitude is fundamentally different from the traditional-metaphysical one. It seeks (a qualified kind of) infinity *through* regeneration, not as an attempt to *overcome* or *put an end* to the latter.

46. Kristeva, *This Incredible Need to Believe*, 47.

47. Ibid., 44.

48. Beardsworth, *Julia Kristeva*, 110.

49. In *Time Driven*, Johnston, despite his criticisms of Kristeva, confirms this view: "Kristeva's central thesis is that signifying practices are always a combination, although not always a smooth synthesis, of the semiotic and the symbolic, the affective and the structural. Put differently, any text is simultaneously constituted by both a 'genotext' (the infusion of libido, drives, and/or affects into a signifying medium) and a 'phenotext' (the strictly formal, linguistic dimension of the explicit medium of signification)" (363).

50. Rose, "Julia Kristeva—Take Two," 45, 49, 50.

51. Ibid., 49.

52. Julia Kristeva, "Il n'y a pas de maitre à language," *Nouvelle Revue de Psychanalyse: Regards sur la psychanalyse en France* 20 (1979): 130–31, emphasis mine; quoted on 49.

53. Emphasizing the interdependence between the two realms in Kristeva, Chanter stresses this temporal relation: "What has not been sufficiently appreciated is the extent to which the semiotic is a realm that only acquires meaning—or indeed existence—within the realm of the symbolic. The semiotic/symbolic distinction is not offered as a mutually exclusive one. Semiotic meaning can

only emerge *retroactively*, and can only be expressed within the terms of the symbolic." See Chanter, "Kristeva's Politics of Change," 184, emphasis mine. Johnston too has highlighted this point: "Kristeva's semiotic is a non-Symbolic category that, while seemingly a hypostatized 'energy' or 'force' outside of given linguistic networks, is nonetheless a phenomenon internal to this very network itself. . . . *Its chronological anteriority is a retroactive positing* effectuated from within the closure of signifying matrices." See Johnston, *Time Driven*, 366, emphasis mine.

54. Chanter, "Kristeva's Politics of Change," 183.

55. Distinguishing Kristeva from Lacan, Sjöholm asserts that the symbolic "is intertwined with the semiotic, and cannot be understood as its opposite" (KP 17). Later, she responds to feminist critics who have charged Kristeva with placing the semiotic "beyond" or "above" the symbolic: "The semiotic is not a transgressive, aggressive discourse, hidden underneath the symbolic. It is a dialectical construction, or theoretical supposition, neither preceding the symbolic nor holding a privileged place in relation to it. . . . Representing subjectivity, affectivity and embodiment, the semiotic is not presymbolic or presocial, it is *already an aspect of society and culture*" (22). Addressing Butler directly, Sjöholm goes on to stress, in line with what I have argued here, that there is no "outside" in Kristeva's thought: "Both Butler and de Lauretis read Kristeva as arguing that the homosexual is outside of culture. But this view can only be upheld if one assumes the maternal, the pre-Oedipal, the pre-discursive, the semiotic, etc. to be outside of culture as well, and as we have persistently argued there is no such 'outside' in Kristeva's work" (54).

56. Sjöholm emphasizes the political implications of the fact that Kristeva is careful to sustain the tension and oscillation between the two realms, and that her thinking never is teleological in nature: "the revolution of the semiotic does not challenge or change norms for any given reasons, or with any given goals in mind. It takes pleasure in challenging them, going through the motions of displacement and destabilisation. But it is precisely its unwillingness to simply replace one norm instead of another, or to erect a stronger law in the place of a weak one, which makes the semiotic into such a powerful political concept. It lives in ambiguity, rather than deteriorates into fixations" (KP 32). This characterization should bring to mind my own discussion of revolt as return, and my emphasis on the need for perpetual revolt rather than revolt that seeks to achieve an ultimate and final goal.

57. Oliver raises similar concerns in "Julia Kristeva's Feminist Revolutions," *Hypatia: A Journal of Feminist Philosophy* 8, no. 2 (1993): 100.

58. Kristeva asserts that "only the subject, for whom the thetic is not a repression of the semiotic *chora* but instead a position either taken on or undergone, can call into question the thetic so that a new disposition may be articulated" (RPL 51). Again, what is at stake here is *renewal*, not absolute destruction. Later

in *Revolution in Poetic Language*, she reminds us that while the thetic is "absolutely necessary," it is nevertheless "not exclusive: the semiotic . . . constantly tears it open, and this transgression brings about all the various transformations of the signifying practice that are called 'creation' . . . what remodels the symbolic order is always the influx of the semiotic" (62).

59. Kristeva notes: "In the extreme, negativity aims to foreclose the thetic phase, which, after a period of explosive semiotic motility, may result in the loss of the symbolic function, as seen in schizophrenia" (RPL 69).

60. Chanter signals that the difficulties we encounter when attempting to subvert the symbolic order in no way means "that we should give up trying to change things. It means that we should remain aware of the limits of such attempts. These limits are due to the tendency of the logic of metaphysics to recuperate whatever transgressions it sustains." See Chanter, "Kristeva's Politics of Change," 185.

61. Ibid., 186.

62. Ibid., 189.

63. See Judith Butler, *Undoing Gender* (New York: Routledge, 2004).

64. For relevant discussions on this topic, see Grosz, *Volatile Bodies* and *The Nick of Time*, 72; Braidotti, *Metamorphoses*; and Chanter, "Tracking Essentialism with the Help of a Sex/Gender Map," chap. 1 in *Ethics of Eros*.

65. See Halsema, "Reconsidering the Notion of the Body in Anti-essentialism," 155.

66. Luce Irigaray, "Flesh Colors," chap. 9 in *Sexes and Genealogies*, 159. This essay was originally delivered at a seminar on psychoanalysis in 1986. It was reprinted in *Key Writings*, 112–22 (the quoted passage appears on 117 in that collection).

67. We might moreover suggest that the maternal body is the clearest evidence or example of such a non-binary structure available to us. How can we speak of "inside" and "outside" when approaching a person who carries another human being within their own body? Where does one begin and the other end? What constitutes a boundary in this relationship? Oliver speaks to this in her essay "Julia Kristeva's Feminist Revolutions": "Kristeva does not delimit maternity as an essentially precultural reality. In fact, she argues that maternity calls into question the boundary between culture and nature. She chooses maternity as a prototype precisely because it breaks down the borders between culture and nature and between subject and other." See Oliver, "Julia Kristeva's Feminist Revolutions," 100. To speak of a "before" and an "after" also proves problematic: the maternal body is generally seen as the locus where life begins, but it remains contested *when* exactly we should speak of "life" (which is painstakingly evident in debates about abortion).

68. One could perhaps argue that we are faced with something similar to Heidegger's distinction between primordial and vulgar/fallen temporality here.

69. Sjöholm, again, pursues a similar line of argument in response to Butler, who she argues "implicitly criticizes the body as 'pre-political' or 'pre-discursive' as a form of naturalization. What is natural is, however, always already given and Kristeva's body is never given, but produced negatively in relation to the sign. A Freudian rather than a socially instituted negation makes possible a play of the semiotic in the symbolic, challenging any kind of fixation as well as any illusion of a natural past. . . . The definition of the body as pre-Oedipal, pre-linguistic and so on does not exclude it [from] having a distinct cultural and political quality" (KP 88).

70. Julia Kristeva, "Place Names," in *Desire in Language*, 286.

71. Burchill, "Re-situating the *Feminine*," 87.

72. Ibid.

73. Kristeva, "The Novel as Polylogue," in *Desire in Language*, 205.

74. Ibid.

# Chapter 9

1. The idea of a placental economy is developed in an interview that Irigaray conducted with Hélène Rouch entitled "On the Maternal Order," chap. 4 in *Je, Tu, Nous*, 37–44.

2. Hélène Rouch in ibid., 42, emphasis mine.

3. Irigaray in ibid., 41.

4. We saw, in Kristeva's comments on the Aristophanic myth from the *Symposium*, that such fusion or wholeness for her necessarily is *atemporal*. On her account, the Aristophanic androgynes were beings who, precisely because of their lack of an *other*, also were lacking *time*.

5. Kristeva, *This Incredible Need to Believe*, 42.

6. In *Powers of Horror*, Kristeva stresses this point: While primary narcissism may appear to be "a return to a self-contemplative, conservative, self-sufficient haven," it is in fact never "the wrinkleless image of the Greek youth in a quiet fountain. The conflicts of drives muddle its bed, cloud its water, and bring forth everything that, by not becoming integrated with a given system of signs, is abjection for it." See Kristeva, *Powers of Horror*, 14.

7. The thinker who perhaps most systematically has developed a psychoanalytically grounded theory of subjectivity that rejects primary fusion and the sacrificial logic underpinning traditional accounts is Bracha L. Ettinger, who has articulated the concept of a "matrixial borderspace" to describe this condition. For further elaboration, see Bracha L. Ettinger, *The Matrixial Borderspace* (Minneapolis: University of Minnesota Press, 2006), especially the very clarifying introduction by Griselda Pollock.

8. Jones, *Irigaray*, 38.

9. Both books were their doctoral dissertations, and both were published in France in 1974. *Revolution in Poetic Language* first appeared in English in 1984 (albeit in an abridged version—it has never been translated in its entirety), and *Speculum of the Other Woman* was translated into English the following year.

10. Irigaray, *Speculum of the Other Woman*, 243–364. The cave allegory in Plato's *Republic* appears on 514a–520a.

11. Jones comments on the non-linear structure of the book: "By refusing to work through the tradition in a linear fashion—either wholly forwards or backwards—Irigaray displaces two tempting but dangerous models for feminist thought: on the one hand, an autonomous female identity is not to be found by moving beyond the tradition into a utopian future; on the other, neither is it to be recovered as a lost origin buried in the pre-patriarchal past." See Jones, *Irigaray*, 42.

12. Plato, *Republic*, 514a.

13. Ibid., 515a.

14. Margaret Whitford states that it "is obvious, even banal, that the cavern represents a womb; this is not a reflex, stereotypical Freudian reading—in the Platonic dialogues themselves Socrates is described as a midwife, his method as a maieutic method, and his role to assist the birth into knowledge of the truth." See Margaret Whitford, *Luce Irigaray: Philosophy in the Feminine* (New York: Routledge, 1991), 106. Consider, also, the reference to the "waves" of paradox, which involve the role of women and women's bodies in the polis in book 5 of the *Republic*. Holly Moore has brought my attention to the fact that the term there, *kuma*, while translated as "wave," is also heard as "fetus," as well as the swollen womb of pregnancy.

15. To be fair to Plato, however, we should at least note that the journey out of the cave by no means is depicted as easy or smooth. His account is, in fact, full of pain, aching eyes, physical force, and other characteristics that make evident that those leaving the cave in fact have bodies and are burdened by gravity. The journey is corporeal indeed, even though it is perhaps meant to lead to disembodied contemplation. Again, this is a place where Irigaray seems to engage more with "Platonism" as it has been developed in later texts than with Plato himself.

16. Rich, "Hands of Flesh, Hands of Iron," in *Of Woman Born*, especially 145–47.

17. Plato, *Theaetetus*, 150b.

18. We should note that Irigaray's usage of the term "receptacle" here brings to mind the role of *chōra* in the *Timaeus*. And while the essay from *Speculum* first and foremost engages with the cave allegory of the *Republic*, it does also contain several references to the *Timaeus*. I would, in fact, suggest that the essay implicitly is a reading of that dialogue throughout. I say so, partially, because the cave allegory gives us an epistemology, while Timaeus provides us with a

cosmological ontology. Irigaray's essay, as I see it, blurs the line between the two, as she simultaneously addresses the question of philosophy and the production of knowledge, on the one hand, and questions of human genesis and origins, on the other. That said, I do not agree with Irigaray that the father, on Timaeus's account, alone would be capable of producing the real, while *chōra* generates nothing but copies. As should be clear from my analysis in the previous chapter, my reading suggests that Plato in fact points to the *interdependence* of the two causes for any engendering to take place. Irigaray's critique of *chōra* tends to assume the passivity and amorphousness of the term, and she often equates it with Aristotelian *hyle*. In fact, one of the middle essays of *Speculum*, entitled "Une Mère de Glace," consists of several extracts from Plotinus's Sixth Tractate, "The Impassivity of the Unembodied," where Plotinus indeed collapses *chōra* and *hyle*, and equates the two with a kind of maternal passivity. Irigaray, problematically, seems to have appropriated this type of reading, which I think is a misrendering of the Platonic text. Later in this chapter (and implicitly in what has already been said in my reading of Kristeva), I argue that *chōra*, in fact, offers an alternative and challenge to the dualistic logic that Irigaray ascribes to the cave allegory. See Luce Irigaray, "Une Mère de Glace," in *Speculum of the Other Woman*, 168–79.

19. To be more precise, the sensible for Plato is temporal while the intelligible is all-temporal (it does not *lack* time but is rather the *full presence of all time*). This, as we saw in my analysis of metaphysical presence, is nevertheless equivalent to non-time, since time, crucially, never can be fully present. I will develop this further in what follows.

20. Perversion, here, should be understood in its most literal sense, as a turn toward the father—a *père-version*—a denial of the specificity and fecundity of the maternal body.

21. "The *womb*, unformed, 'amorphous' origin of all morphology, is transmuted by/for analogy into a circus and a projection screen, a theater of/for fantasies" (PH 265).

22. Irigaray, "The Power of Discourse," in *This Sex Which Is Not One*, 74–75.

23. Whitford, *Luce Irigaray: Philosophy in the Feminine*, 108.

24. Ibid., 106.

25. Butler, *Bodies That Matter*, 47.

26. Ibid. Butler also refers to Derrida, who, she claims, "suggests as well that matter must be redoubled, at once as a pole within a binary opposition, and as that which exceeds that binary coupling, as a figure for its nonsystematizability" (38). "For both Derrida and Irigaray," Butler continues, "what is excluded from this binary is also *produced* by it in the mode of exclusion and has no separable or fully independent existence as an absolute outside. A constitutive or relative outside is, of course, composed of a set of exclusions that are nevertheless *internal* to that system as incoherence, disruption, a threat to its own systematicity" (39). As should become clear, my own understanding of Irigaray is that while

she thinks that this has been the function of the "feminine" hitherto, she does in fact believe in the possibility of an altogether different logic, one that would escape these binaries and hence not be founded on constitutive exclusion. This possibility, as I understand it, is what is at stake for her when she speaks of a logic or world of (at least) *two*.

27. Ibid., 37. Butler goes on to explain that "Irigaray insists that this exclusion that mobilizes the form/matter binary is the differentiating relation between masculine and feminine, where the masculine occupies both terms of a binary opposition, and the feminine cannot be said to be an intelligible term at all. We might understand the feminine figured within the binary as the *specular* feminine and the feminine which is erased and excluded from that binary as the *excessive* feminine. And yet, such nominations cannot work, for in the latter mode, the feminine, strictly speaking, cannot be named at all and, indeed, is not a mode" (39).

28. Whitford, *Luce Irigaray: Philosophy in the Feminine*, 110.

29. Plato, *Republic*, 327a.

30. Ibid., 515a.

31. Jones, *Irigaray*, 50.

32. For an interesting and thought-provoking discussion of the relationship between metaphoricity and philosophy, and how this relates to the question of origins, see Jacques Derrida, "White Mythology: *La métaphysique—relève de la métaphore*," in *Margins of Philosophy*, 258–71. Derrida notes that metaphor "is included by metaphysics as that which must finish by rediscovering the origin of its truth" (268). Later, he states that metaphor "always carries its death within itself" (271). Irigaray notes that metaphor is "reinscribed in a matrix of resemblance, family likeness" (PH 247).

33. Butler, *Bodies That Matter*, 45. For a discussion of the political implications of this logic, especially as it pertains to gender identity and sexuality, see Butler, *Gender Trouble* and "Imitation and Gender Insubordination." Butler's own theory of performativity is based precisely on such a displacement of the traditional relation between original and copy. If compulsory heterosexuality has set itself up as the original, and if this results in the common view that homosexuality is a mere copying or imitating of this norm, Butler sets out to show that gender, in fact, "is a kind of imitation that produces the very notion of the original as an *effect* and consequence of the imitation itself." She goes on to note that "the entire framework of copy and origin proves radically unstable as each position inverts into the other and confounds the possibility of any stable way to locate the temporal or logical priority of either term." See Butler, "Imitation and Gender Insubordination," 306–07.

34. Butler, *Bodies That Matter*, 45.

35. Irigaray in conversation during a doctoral seminar at Liverpool Hope University, June 2007.

36. In *The Forgetting of Air in Martin Heidegger*, she makes a similar claim. For the production of Being to take place, she writes, "a being already has lent its 'matter,' a being that subsists beneath presence and assists it, always staying covered over and forgotten by it" (91).

37. Irigaray, preface to *Key Writings*, ix, emphasis mine.

38. Irigaray, *In the Beginning, She Was*, 106.

39. Grosz suggests that the denial of our debt to the maternal body has deprived not only women, but all human beings, of a home: "Men have conceived of themselves as self-made, and in disavowing this maternal debt, have left themselves, and women, in dereliction, homelessness." See Grosz, "Women, Chora, Dwelling," in *Space, Time, and Perversion*, 121. This resonates with a comment made by Nikolchina, regarding Kristeva's account of symbolic and linguistic existence: "The speaking being dwells in language as an exile," Nikolchina writes. Echoing (by perverting) Heidegger, she continues: "With Kristeva, language is the homelessness of being." See Nikolchina, *Matricide in Language*, 49.

40. See Irigaray, "'Je—Luce Irigaray,'" 98.

41. John Swan, *Speculum Mundi*, available at http://digital.library.adelaide.edu.au/coll/special/swan/index.html.

42. Irigaray often recalls the sadness and disappointment that she experienced when she, having sent a copy of her book to Beauvoir, was met with silence on the part of her female colleague. See, especially, "A Personal Note: Equal or Different?," in *Je, Tu, Nous*, 9–14; "The Other: Woman," in *I Love to You*, 59–68; "The Question of the Other," in *Democracy Begins Between Two*, 121–41; and "'Je—Luce Irigaray.'"

43. For assistance in understanding the details of the various meanings of this term, I would like to thank Dan Restrepo and Holly Moore. In "'Je—Luce Irigaray,'" Irigaray also comments on the subtitle, especially the word "Other." She points to this very term as one that distinguishes her work from Beauvoir: "It was there, that moment, that marked the counterpoint to Simone de Beauvoir. That is, Simone de Beauvoir refused to be the Other because she refused to be second in Western culture. In order not to be the Other she said, 'I want to be the equal of man; I want to be the same as man; finally, I want to be a man. I want to be a masculine subject.' And that point of view I find is a very important philosophical and political regression. What I myself say is that there is no true Other in Western culture and that what I want—certainly I don't want to be second—but I want there to be two subjects." See Irigaray, "'Je—Luce Irigaray,'" 99. On this account, the title suggests what I have stressed throughout this book, namely that the task of elaborating an alternative model of time (the task, to put it in the terms explored in this chapter, of bringing light to our dual beginnings) depends on the elaboration of a model of difference that defies a logic that juxtaposes the other with the same. If this indeed is what Irigaray intended when she formulated the title, we begin to see that

there is more continuity than we have tended to admit between her early and late work. While *Speculum* indeed is *critical* and *mimetic* in its scope, Irigaray is already attempting to establish a culture of two, not merely deconstructing the logic of the same. Irigaray herself confirms this view: "it's been thought that in the second part of my work I turn my back on the first, that I renounce the first part. This error follows, among other things, from errors of translation in the title and subtitle of *Speculum*" (99).

44. Irigaray, "The Blind Spot of an Old Dream of Symmetry," in *Speculum of the Other Woman*, 60. See also the French original, "La tache aveugle d'un vieux rêve de symétrie," in *Speculum de l'autre femme* (Paris: Les Éditions de Minuit, 1974), 70.

45. Ibid., 33/35.

46. Whitford makes no distinction between origins and beginnings. She speaks of "the entry into language and the symbolic, and thus the definitive loss . . . of the original symbiotic relation with the mother" as a "loss of origin," while I argue that such a move is what *introduces* origins in the first place. See Whitford, *Luce Irigaray*, 84. Edward Said, conversely, *does* distinguish between origins and beginnings, but he completely reverses the logic of Irigaray's account, viewing beginnings as culturally established while origins are more archaic. See Edward W. Said, *Beginnings: Intention and Method* (New York: Columbia University Press, 1975).

47. Irigaray in conversation during a doctoral seminar at Liverpool Hope University, June 2007.

48. Irigaray, *I Love to You*, 46, 131.

49. Irigaray, "So When Are We to Become Women?," in *Je, Tu, Nous*, 135.

50. Irigaray, "The Blind Spot of an Old Dream of Symmetry," in *Speculum of the Other Woman*, 41; "La tache aveugle d'un vieux rêve de symétrie," in *Speculum de l'autre femme*, 45.

51. Irigaray, "La tache aveugle d'un vieux rêve de symétrie," in *Speculum de l'autre femme*, 45.

52. Irigaray notes: "Obviously, neither the coming together of two entities in copulation, nor its product, can be counted into two halves. . . . Copulation cannot be divided in this way. Unless control is already being wielded by the fixed idea of the same" (PH 275). It seems important to add that copulation is not necessary for birth and reproduction, and while all human conception depends on sexually different cells, certainly the parental functions need not be heterosexually determined or cis-gendered.

53. In *I Love to You*, Irigaray notes that man "has imagined that spiritual becoming can be realized on the basis of *one* and not *two*" and objects that "we do not come from *one*: we are engendered by *two* and Man as a man is born of another." She associates this reduction with the appearance of cultural origins, suggesting that "in patriarchal mythologies becoming on the basis of *one* has

been inscribed as origin, the *two* continuing to thrive socially in female cultures."
See Irigaray, *I Love to You*, 40.

54. Derrida, "Khōra," 126.

55. Ibid., 125–26. We might read Derrida's reference to a "normal couple"
as a reference to sexual difference in oppositional terms. It is exactly the reduction
of sexual difference to a dual-oppositional relation that has reduced woman to a
mirror-screen on which man can reproduce himself through reflection-repetition.

56. Irigaray, *I Love to You*, 40.

57. For a similar claim, although with reference to a different passage from
the same essay than the one I am about to unpack, see Jones, *Irigaray*, 51–52.
Jones notes that Irigaray's text speaks in a "double voice."

58. The following passage is similarly ambiguous in this regard: "But suddenly, in the name of truth, the prisoner is unchained, disenchanted, turned away
from what he had considered true, from what he, and the others, had designated
by the name of truth, and he is required to say what these things are that had
always been behind him and of which he had previously seen only the shadows.
How could he obey, given that for these new 'beings'—if beings they be for
him, coming as they do almost from another world—he has no appropriate term,
no agreed upon or suitable denomination, since he looks upon them all on his
own and has lost his point of view of the true, on being, as a result of being
forced to turn around? Outside of language, outside of convention and communal
recognition, outside of identical perception that can be identified within a set of
procedures for conversation with others who share his view, these things *are* for
him *nothing*. Or they are *strange*. Strangeness, the *stranger*. In any case he does
not have the means to distinguish them—*apokrinesthai*. They are nothing he is
in a position to delineate or define adequately in words" (PH 272).

59. Irigaray has ventured to compare herself with the figure of Antigone,
who suffered a similar fate of exclusion. See "Between Myth and History: The
Tragedy of Antigone," in *In the Beginning, She Was*, 114–19. She has returned
to Antigone throughout her work. See "The Eternal Irony of the Community,"
in *Speculum of the Other Woman*; "An Ethics of Sexual Difference," in *An Ethics
of Sexual Difference*; and "She before the King," in *To Be Two*.

60. We see here yet another similarity between Irigaray and Kristeva, namely
their understanding of regeneration not only as procreation but, perhaps more
importantly still, as creativity or the injection of life and aliveness into discourse.

61. Grosz, *Space, Time, and Perversion*, 121.

62. Whitford, *Luce Irigaray: Philosophy in the Feminine*, 112.

63. Irigaray, *In the Beginning She Was*, 84–85.

64. Plato, *Republic*, 509d–511e.

65. Kristeva pursues a similar argument. She notes that a symbolic order
that fails to acknowledge the semiotic process that produces it inevitably is
tautological in nature: "the path thus programmed is circular and merely returns

to its thetic point of departure" (RPL 59). Poetic language offers an alternative to such a tautological discourse in that it introduces alteration and change. It is able to do so "by introducing into the thetic position the stream of semiotic drives" (RPL 60). The concrete "processes" that bring about this change are three in number: *displacement* (metonymy), *condensation* (metaphor), and *inter-textuality* (transposition of one sign system into another).

66. This view began to change with Aristotle, whose account of time in the *Physics* marks a break with the temporal meditations of his teacher, and introduced the understanding of time as a series of now-points. For a thoroughgoing account of the different ancients' views on time (Plato, Aristotle, Plotinus, and Augustine), see Callahan, *Four Views of Time in Ancient Philosophy*.

67. The "original" matrix or womb would, on such a reading, be an eternal Idea.

68. Irigaray is careful, in these passages and elsewhere, to sustain and draw our attention to the intimate relationship between space and time: "For *hysteron*, defined as what is behind, is also the last, the hereafter, the ultimate. *Proteron*, defined as what is in front, is also the earlier, the previous" (PH 244).

69. The "Other" woman in the title is, as we have seen, precisely *not* merely secondary (as in Beauvoir) but radically and ontologically Other. As Irigaray puts it in her concluding remarks in the interview I have quoted above: Beauvoir "refuses to be Other and I demand to be radically Other." See Irigaray, "'Je—Luce Irigaray,'" 114.

70. Plato, *Symposium*, 206c.

71. Butler, *Bodies That Matter*, 39.

## Conclusion

1. See Irigaray, "Plato's *Hystera*" and "The Blind Spot of an Old Dream of Symmetry," in *Speculum of the Other Woman*, 243, 34.

2. hooks, "Feminism: A Movement to End Sexist Oppression," 17–18.

3. Fanon, *Black Skin, White Masks*, xvi.

4. To be sure, Fanon does not hold that the solution to the problem would be to take off the "white mask" so as to uncover the "authentically black skin" hiding underneath. The point is, precisely, that the Black skin is a product of white culture, just like "woman" (viewed as the negative mirror image of man) is a product of patriarchal culture. The task, in other words, is to think "Black" or "female" as *irreducible* to "white" and "male" (which ultimately also means, of course, to think beyond the very categories of "Black" and "female").

5. Audre Lorde, "The Master's Tools Will Never Dismantle the Master's House," in *Sister Outsider: Essays and Speeches* (New York: Crossing Press, 2007), 112.

6. Denise Ferreira da Silva, *Toward a Global Idea of Race* (Minneapolis: University of Minnesota Press, 2007), xi (ellipses in original, nothing has been omitted here).

7. Claudia Rankine, " 'The Condition of Black Life Is One of Mourning,' " *New York Times Magazine*, June 22, 2015.

8. Mirzoeff, "Below the Water."

9. See Fanny Söderbäck, "Impossible Mourning: Sophocles Reversed," in *Feminist Readings of Antigone*, ed. Fanny Söderbäck (Albany: State University of New York Press, 2010), and "Natality or Birth?" For other examples of feminist critiques of this aspect of Arendt's work, see Adrienne Rich, *On Lies, Secrets and Silence: Selected Prose, 1966–1978* (New York: Norton, 1979); O'Brien, *The Politics of Reproduction*; Anne Philips, *Engendering Democracy* (Cambridge, UK: Polity Press, 1991); Joan B. Landes, "Jürgen Habermas, *The Structural Transformation of the Public Sphere*: A Feminist Inquiry," *Praxis International* 12, no. 1 (April 1992): 106–27; Seyla Benhabib, "Feminist Theory and Hannah Arendt's Concept of Public Space," *History of the Human Sciences* 6, no. 2 (1993): 97–114; Seyla Benhabib, "Models of Public Space: Hannah Arendt, the Liberal Tradition, and Jürgen Habermas," in *Feminism: The Public and the Private Realm*, ed. Joan B. Landes (Oxford: Oxford University Press, 1998); and Butler, *Notes Toward a Performative Theory of Assembly*. There are several interesting essays as well as an annotated bibliography of feminist engagements with Arendt in Bonnie Honig, ed., *Feminist Interpretations of Hannah Arendt* (University Park: Pennsylvania State University Press, 1995).

10. If the Greek "solution" to the precarious nature of action was the *polis*, modern man turned instead to isolation, which resulted in the disappearance of the public realm (HC 192, 220).

11. For further elaboration of Arendt's conception of freedom along these lines, see Hannah Arendt, "What Is Freedom?," in *Between Past and Future* (New York: Penguin Books, 1993).

12. Kristeva, too, elaborates freedom in terms of new beginnings: "Philosophers teach us that freedom's logic does not reside in a transgression, as one might easily think, but in the capacity to begin." She goes on to associate such a notion of freedom with the *maternal* capacity to begin: "Freedom means having the courage to start over: such is the philosophy of maternity." See Kristeva, *This Incredible Need to Believe*, 44.

13. Margaret Canovan, introduction to *The Human Condition*, vii.

14. Julia Kristeva, *Colette*, vol. 3 of *Female Genius: Life, Madness, Words—Hannah Arendt, Melanie Klein, Colette*, trans. Jane Marie Todd (New York: Columbia University Press, 2004), 423.

15. Ibid., 424ff.

16. Kristeva, *This Incredible Need to Believe*, 75, 39.

17. Kristeva, *Tales of Love*, 16, 1.

18. Kristeva, *This Incredible Need to Believe*, 44.
19. Hartman, *Lose Your Mother*, 100.
20. Ibid.

# Bibliography

Adams, Sarah LaChance. *Mad Mothers, Bad Mothers, and What a "Good" Mother Would Do: The Ethics of Ambivalence*. New York: Columbia University Press, 2014.

Aeschylus. *The Oresteia*. Translated by Robert Fagles. New York: Viking Press, 1979.

Ahmed, Sara. *Strange Encounters: Embodied Others in Post-Coloniality*. London: Routledge, 2000.

———. "The Skin of the Community: Affect and Boundary Formation." In *Revolt, Affect, Collectivity: The Unstable Boundaries of Kristeva's Polis*, edited by Tina Chanter and Ewa Płonowska Ziarek, 95–111. Albany: State University of New York Press, 2005.

Ansell-Pearson, Keith. *Philosophy and the Adventure of the Virtual: Bergson and the Time of Life*. New York: Routledge, 2001.

Arendt, Hannah. *On Revolution*. London: Penguin Books, 1990.

———. "What Is Freedom?" Chap. 4 in *Between Past and Future*. New York: Penguin Books, 1993.

———. *Eichmann in Jerusalem: A Report on the Banality of Evil*. New York: Penguin Books, 1994.

———. *The Human Condition*. Chicago: University of Chicago Press, 1998.

Aristotle. *On the Soul (De Anima)*. Translated by Hippocrates G. Apostle. Grinnell, IA: The Peripatetic Press, 1981.

———. *Poetics*. Translated by Richard Janko. Indianapolis: Hackett, 1987.

———. *Physics*. Translated by Philip H. Wicksteed and Francis M. Cornford. Cambridge, MA: Harvard University Press/Loeb Classical Library, 1993.

Augustine. *Confessions*. Translated by R. S. Pine-Coffin. New York: Penguin Books, 1986.

Baracchi, Claudia. *Of Myth, Life, and War in Plato's* Republic. Bloomington: Indiana University Press, 2002.

———. *Aristotle's Ethics as First Philosophy*. Cambridge: Cambridge University Press, 2008.

Baraitser, Lisa. *Maternal Encounters: The Ethics of Interruption.* New York: Routledge, 2009.

Bass, Alan. "Time and the Witch: Femininity, Metapsychology and the Temporality of the Unconscious." *Modern Language Notes* 91, no. 5 (1976): 871–912.

Battersby, Christine. *The Phenomenal Woman: Feminist Metaphysics and the Patterns of Identity.* New York: Routledge, 1998.

Beardsworth, Sara. *Julia Kristeva: Psychoanalysis and Modernity.* Albany: State University of New York Press, 2004.

———. "From Revolution to Revolt Culture." In *Revolt, Affect, Collectivity: The Unstable Boundaries of Kristeva's Polis,* edited by Tina Chanter and Ewa Płonowska Ziarek, 37–56. Albany: State University of New York Press, 2005.

———. "Psychoanalysis and Yoga." In *Engaging the World: Thinking After Irigaray,* edited by Mary C. Rawlinson, 281–95. Albany: State University of New York Press, 2016.

Beauvoir, Simone de. *The Ethics of Ambiguity.* Translated by Bernard Frechtman. New York: Citadel Press, 1976.

———. *The Second Sex.* Translated by Constance Borde and Sheila Malovany-Chevallier. New York: Alfred A. Knopf, 2010.

Beauvoir, Simone de, Margaret A. Simons, and Jane Marie Todd. "Two Interviews with Simone de Beauvoir." *Hypatia: A Journal of Feminist Philosophy* 3, no. 3 (1989): 11–27.

Benhabib, Seyla. "Feminist Theory and Hannah Arendt's Concept of Public Space." *History of the Human Sciences* 6, no. 2 (1993): 97–114.

———. "Models of Public Space: Hannah Arendt, the Liberal Tradition, and Jürgen Habermas." In *Feminism: The Public and the Private Realm,* edited by Joan B. Landes, 65–99. Oxford: Oxford University Press, 1998.

Benjamin, Walter. "The Work of Art in the Age of Its Technological Reproducibility." In vol. 3 of *Selected Writings 1935–1938,* edited by Howard Eiland and Michael W. Jennings, translated by Edmund Jephcott and Harry Zohn, 101–33. Cambridge, MA: The Belknap Press of Harvard University Press, 2002.

Bernstein, J. M. *The Fate of Art: Aesthetic Alienation from Kant to Derrida and Adorno.* University Park: Pennsylvania State University Press, 1992.

Bettcher, Talia Mae. "Trapped in the Wrong Theory: Rethinking Trans Oppression and Resistance." *Signs: Journal of Women in Culture and Society* 39, no. 2 (2014): 383–406.

de Boer, Karin. *Thinking in the Light of Time: Heidegger's Encounter with Hegel.* Albany: State University of New York Press, 2000.

Braidotti, Rosi. *Nomadic Subjects.* New York: Columbia University Press, 1994.

———. *Metamorphoses: Towards a Materialist Theory of Becoming.* Cambridge, UK: Polity Press, 2002.

———. *Transpositions: On Nomadic Ethics.* Cambridge, UK: Polity Press, 2006.

Browne, Victoria. *Feminism, Time, and Nonlinear History*. New York: Palgrave Macmillan, 2014.

Bryson, Valerie. *Gender and the Politics of Time: Feminist Theory and Contemporary Debates*. Bristol, UK: The Policy Press, 2007.

Burchill, Louise. "Re-situating the *Feminine* in Contemporary French Philosophy." In *Belief, Bodies, and Being: Feminist Reflections on Embodiment*, edited by Deborah Orr, Linda López McAllister, Eileen Kahl, and Kathleen Earle, 81–102. Lanham, MD: Rowman & Littlefield, 2006.

Butler, Judith. "Variations on Sex and Gender: Beauvoir, Wittig and Foucault." In *Feminism as Critique: On the Politics of Gender*, edited by Seyla Benhabib and Drucilla Cornell, 128–42. Minneapolis: University of Minnesota Press, 1987.

———. *Bodies That Matter: On the Discursive Limits of "Sex."* New York: Routledge, 1993.

———. "Imitation and Gender Insubordination." In *The Second Wave: A Reader in Feminist Theory*, edited by Linda Nicholson, 300–15. New York: Routledge, 1997.

———. *Gender Trouble: Feminism and the Subversion of Identity*. 10th Anniversary Edition. New York: Routledge, 1999.

———. *Undoing Gender*. New York: Routledge, 2004.

———. *Frames of War: When Is Life Grievable?* London: Verso, 2010.

———. *Notes Toward a Performative Theory of Assembly*. Cambridge, MA: Harvard University Press, 2018.

Callahan, John F. *Four Views of Time in Ancient Philosophy*. Cambridge, MA: Harvard University Press, 1948.

Campo-Engelstein, Lisa, and Nadia L. Johnson. "Revisiting 'The Fertilization Fairytale': An Analysis of Gendered Language Used to Describe Fertilization in Science Textbooks from Middle School to Medical School." *Cultural Studies of Science Education* 9 (2014): 201–20.

Catlett, Beth S., and Mary Bunn. "Yoga as Embodied Feminist Praxis: Trauma, Healing, and Community-Based Responses to Violence." In *Yoga, the Body, and Embodied Social Change: An Intersectional Feminist Analysis*, edited by Beth Berila, Melanie Klein, and Chelsea Jackson Roberts, 259–75. Lanham, MD: Lexington Books, 2016.

Cavarero, Adriana. "Towards a Theory of Sexual Difference." In *The Lonely Mirror*, edited by Sandra Kemp and Paola Bono, 189–221. New York: Routledge, 1993.

———. *In Spite of Plato: A Feminist Rewriting of Ancient Philosophy*. Translated by Serena Anderlini-D'Onofrio and Áine O'Healy. New York: Routledge, 1995.

———. *Relating Narratives: Storytelling and Selfhood*. Translated by Paul A. Kottman. New York: Routledge, 2000.

―――. *For More than One Voice: Towards a Philosophy of Vocal Expression*. Translated by Paul A. Kottman. Stanford: Stanford University Press, 2005.

―――. *Inclinations: A Critique of Rectitude*. Translated by Amanda Minervini and Adam Sitze. Stanford: Stanford University Press, 2016.

Chamberlain, Prudence. *The Feminist Fourth Wave: Affective Temporality*. New York: Palgrave Macmillan, 2017.

Chanter, Tina. "Female Temporality and the Future of Feminism." In *Abjection, Melancholia, and Love: The Work of Julia Kristeva*, edited by John Fletcher and Andrew Benjamin, 63–79. London: Routledge, 1990.

―――. "Kristeva's Politics of Change: Tracking Essentialism with the Help of a Sex/Gender Map." In *Ethics, Politics, and Difference in Julia Kristeva's Writing*, edited by Kelly Oliver, 179–95. New York: Routledge, 1993.

―――. *Ethics of Eros: Irigaray's Rewriting of the Philosophers*. New York: Routledge, 1995.

―――. *Time, Death, and the Feminine: Levinas with Heidegger*. Stanford: Stanford University Press, 2001.

―――. *Gender: Key Concepts in Philosophy*. London: Continuum, 2006.

Cixous, Hélène. "The Laugh of the Medusa." Translated by Keith Cohen and Paula Cohen. *Signs: Journal of Women in Culture and Society* 1, no. 4 (1976): 875–93.

Coblence, Françoise, and Marcela Montes de Oca. "'Une vie psychique est une vie dans le temps': Entretien avec Julia Kristeva." *Revue française de psychanalyse* 2 (2017): 351–67.

Coe, Cynthia D. "Plato, Maternity, and Power: Can We Get a Different Midwife?" In *Coming to Life: Philosophies of Pregnancy, Childbirth, and Mothering*, edited by Sarah LaChance Adams and Caroline R. Lundquist, 31–46. New York: Fordham University Press, 2013.

Collins, Patricia Hill. *Black Feminist Thought: Knowledge, Consciousness, and the Politics of Empowerment*. New York: Routledge, 2009.

Cousteau, Jacques-Yves. *The Ocean World*. New York: Abradale Press, 1985.

Couzens Hoy, David. *The Time of Our Lives: A Critical History of Temporality*. Cambridge, MA: MIT Press, 2009.

Dastur, Françoise. *Heidegger and the Question of Time*. Translated by François Raffoul and David Pettigrew. Atlantic Highlands, NJ: Humanities Press, 1998.

Derrida, Jacques. *Of Grammatology*. Translated by Gayatri Chakravorty Spivak. Baltimore: Johns Hopkins University Press, 1974.

―――. "Freud and the Scene of Writing." Chap. 7 in *Writing and Difference*, translated by Alan Bass. Chicago: University of Chicago Press, 1978.

―――. "Plato's Pharmacy." Chap. 1 in *Disseminations*, translated by Barbara Johnson. Chicago: University of Chicago Press, 1981.

―――. "*Ousia* and *Grammē*: Note on a Note from *Being and Time*." Chap. 2 in *Margins of Philosophy*, translated by Alan Bass. Chicago: University of Chicago Press, 1982.

———. "Différance." Chap. 1 in *Margins of Philosophy*, translated by Alan Bass. Chicago: University of Chicago Press, 1982.

———. "White Mythology: Metaphor in the Text of Philosophy." Chap. 8 in *Margins of Philosophy*, translated by Alan Bass. Chicago: University of Chicago Press, 1982.

———. "Call It a Day for Democracy." Chap. 2 in *The Other Heading: Reflections on Today's Europe*, translated by Pascale-Anne Brault and Michael B. Naas. Bloomington: Indiana University Press, 1992.

———. "The Time of the King." Chap. 1 in *Given Time: I. Counterfeit Money*, translated by Peggy Kamuf. Chicago: University of Chicago Press, 1992.

———. "Apparition of the Inapparent." Chap. 5 in *Specters of Marx*, translated by Peggy Kamuf. London: Routledge, 1994.

———. "Khōra." Chap. 3 in *On the Name*, translated by Ian McLeod and edited by Thomas Dutoit. Stanford: Stanford University Press, 1995.

Descartes, René. *Meditations on First Philosophy*. Translated by Donald A. Cress. Indianapolis: Hackett, 1993.

Deutscher, Penelope. *A Politics of Impossible Difference: The Later Work of Luce Irigaray*. Ithaca, NY: Cornell University Press, 2002.

Dinshaw, Carolyn. *How Soon Is Now? Medieval Texts, Amateur Readers, and the Queerness of Time*. Durham, NC: Duke University Press, 2012.

Douglass, Frederick. "What to the Slave Is the Fourth of July?" Speech delivered on July 5, 1852. Accessed at http://teachingamericanhistory.org/library/document/what-to-the-slave-is-the-fourth-of-july/ on August 27, 2018.

Draz, Marie. "Born This Way? Time and the Coloniality of Gender." *Journal of Speculative Philosophy* 31, no. 3 (2017): 372–84.

duBois, Page. "The Platonic Appropriation of Reproduction." In *Feminist Interpretations of Plato*, edited by Nancy Tuana, 139–56. University Park: Pennsylvania State University Press, 1994.

Duden, Barbara. *The Woman Beneath the Skin*. Cambridge, MA: Harvard University Press, 1991.

Edelman, Lee. *No Future: Queer Theory and the Death Drive*. Durham, NC: Duke University Press, 2004.

Ettinger, Bracha L. *The Matrixial Borderspace*. Minneapolis: University of Minnesota Press, 2006.

Euben, Peter J. *The Tragedy of Political Theory: The Road Not Taken*. Princeton, NJ: Princeton University Press, 1990.

Fanon, Frantz. *Black Skin, White Masks*. Translated by Richard Philcox. New York: Grove Press, 2008.

Fausto-Sterling, Anne. *Sexing the Body: Gender Politics and the Construction of Sexuality*. New York: Basic Books, 2000.

Fisher, Simon D. Elin, Rasheedah Phillips, and Ido H. Katri. "Trans Temporalities." Introduction to Special Issue on Trans Temporalities, *Somatechnics* 7, no. 1 (2017): 1–15.

Forman, Frieda Johles, and Caoran Sowton, eds. *Taking Our Time: Feminist Perspectives on Temporality*. Oxford, UK: Pergamon Press, 1989.

Foust, Elisha. "Breathing the Political: A Meditation on the Preservation of Life in the Midst of War." In *Breathing with Luce Irigaray*, edited by Emily A. Holmes and Lenart Škof, 186–202. London: Bloomsbury, 2013.

Freeman, Elizabeth. "Packing History, Count(er)ing Generations." *New Literary History* 31, no. 4 (2000): 727–44.

———. "Time Binds; or, Erotohistoriography." *Social Text* 84–85, nos. 3–4 (2005): 57–68.

———. "Introduction." Special issue on queer temporalities of *GLQ: A Journal of Gay and Lesbian Studies* 13, nos. 2–3 (2007): 159–76.

———. *Time Binds: Queer Temporalities, Queer Histories*. Durham, NC: Duke University Press, 2010.

Freire, Paulo. *Pedagogy of the Oppressed*. 30th Anniversary Edition. Translated by Myra Bergman Ramos. New York: Bloomsbury Academic, 2016.

Freud, Sigmund. "Remembering, Repeating and Working-Through (Further Recommendations on the Technique of Psycho-Analysis II)." In vol. 12 of *The Standard Edition of the Complete Psychological Works of Sigmund Freud*, edited and translated by James Strachey, 145–56. London: Hogarth Press, 1958.

———. "The Uncanny." In vol. 17 of *The Standard Edition of the Complete Psychological Works of Sigmund Freud*, edited and translated by James Strachey, 219–52. London: Hogarth Press, 1953–1974.

———. "Some Psychical Consequences of the Anatomical Distinction Between the Sexes." In vol. 19 of *The Standard Edition of the Complete Psychological Works of Sigmund Freud*, edited and translated by James Strachey, 248–58. London: Hogarth Press, 1953–1974.

———. *New Introductory Lectures on Psycho-Analysis*. Edited and translated by James Strachey. New York: W. W. Norton & Company, 1989.

———. *Beyond the Pleasure Principle*. Edited and translated by James Strachey. New York: W. W. Norton & Company, 1989.

———. *Totem and Taboo: Some Points of Agreement between the Mental Lives of Savages and Neurotics*. Edited and translated by James Strachey. New York: W. W. Norton & Company, 1989.

———. "Femininity." In *Freud on Women: A Reader*, edited by Elisabeth Young-Bruehl and translated by James Strachey, 342–62. New York: W. W. Norton & Company, 1990.

———. *The Unconscious*. Translated by Graham Frankland. London: Penguin Books, 2005.

Gatens, Moira. *Imaginary Bodies: Ethics, Power and Corporeality*. London: Routledge, 1996.

Gines, Kathryn T. "Comparative and Competing Frameworks of Oppression in Simone de Beauvoir's *The Second Sex*." *Graduate Faculty Philosophy Journal* 33, nos. 1–2 (2014): 251–73.

Gould, Stephen Jay. *Time's Arrow, Time's Cycle: Myth and Metaphor in the Discovery of Geological Time.* Cambridge, MA: Harvard University Press, 1988.

Grosz, Elizabeth. *Sexual Subversions: Three French Feminists.* Crows Nest, AU: Allen & Unwin, 1989.

———. *Volatile Bodies: Toward a Corporeal Feminism.* Bloomington: Indiana University Press, 1994.

———. *Space, Time, and Perversion: Essays on the Politics of Bodies.* New York: Routledge, 1995.

———. *Becomings: Explorations in Time, Memory, and Futures.* Ithaca, NY: Cornell University Press, 1999.

———. "Feminist Futures?" *Tulsa Studies in Women's Literature* 21, no. 1 (2002): 13–20.

———. *The Nick of Time: Politics, Evolution, and the Untimely.* Durham, NC: Duke University Press, 2004.

———. *Time Travels: Feminism, Nature, Power.* Durham, NC: Duke University Press, 2005.

Guenther, Lisa. *The Gift of the Other: Levinas and the Politics of Reproduction.* Albany: State University of New York Press, 2006.

———. "Being-from-Others: Reading Heidegger After Cavarero." *Hypatia: A Journal of Feminist Philosophy* 23, no. 1 (2008): 99–118.

Gunkel, Henriette, Chrysanthi Nigianni, and Fanny Söderbäck, eds. *Undutiful Daughters: New Directions in Feminist Thought and Practice.* New York: Palgrave Macmillan, 2012.

Hägglund, Martin. *Radical Atheism: Derrida and the Time of Life.* Stanford: Stanford University Press, 2008.

Halberstam, Jack. *In a Queer Time and Place: Transgender Bodies, Subcultural Lives.* New York: New York University Press, 2005.

———. "The Pregnant Man." *The Velvet Trap Light* 65 (2010): 77–78.

Halliwell, Stephen. *The Aesthetics of Mimesis: Ancient Texts and Modern Problems.* Princeton, NJ: Princeton University Press, 2002.

Halsema, Annemie. "Reconsidering the Notion of the Body in Anti-essentialism, with the Help of Luce Irigaray and Judith Butler." In *Belief, Bodies, and Being: Feminist Reflections on Embodiment,* edited by Deborah Orr, Linda López McAllister, Eileen Kahl, and Kathleen Earle, 152–84. Lanham, MD: Rowman & Littlefield, 2006.

Haraway, Donna J. *Simians, Cyborgs, and Women: The Reinvention of Nature.* New York: Routledge, 1991.

Hartman, Saidiya. *Lose Your Mother: A Journey Along the Atlantic Slave Route.* New York: Farrar, Straus and Giroux, 2007.

Hawthorne, Nathaniel. "The Birthmark." In *Hawthorne's Short Stories,* edited by Newton Arvin, 177–93. New York: Alfred A. Knopf, 1975.

Hegel, G. W. F. *Hegel's Philosophy of Nature.* Vol 1. Translated by M. J. Petry. London: George Allen & Unwin, 1970.

Heidegger, Martin. *Being and Time*. Translated by John Macquarrie and Edward
    Robinson. San Francisco: Harper & Row, 1962.
———. "Time and Being." In *On Time and Being*, translated by Joan Stambaugh.
    Chicago: University of Chicago Press, 1972.
Heinämaa, Sara. "What Is a Woman? Butler and Beauvoir on the Foundations
    of the Sexual Difference." *Hypatia: A Journal of Feminist Philosophy* 12,
    no. 1 (1997): 20–39.
Hesford, Victoria, and Lisa Diedrich, eds. *Feminist Time Against Nation Time:
    Gender, Politics, and the Nation-State in an Age of Permanent War*. Lanham,
    MD: Lexington Books, 2008.
Hill, Rebecca. *The Interval: Relation and Becoming in Irigaray, Aristotle, and
    Bergson*. New York: Fordham University Press, 2012.
Holmes, Emily A., and Lenart Škof, eds. *Breathing with Luce Irigaray*. London:
    Bloomsbury, 2013.
Honig, Bonnie, ed. *Feminist Interpretations of Hannah Arendt*. University Park:
    Pennsylvania State University Press, 1995.
hooks, bell. "Feminism: A Movement to End Sexist Oppression." In *Feminist
    Theory: From Margin to Center*, 18–33. New York: South End Press, 1985.
———. *The Will to Change: Men, Masculinity, and Love*. New York: Atria
    Books, 2004.
———. "Toward a Worldwide Culture of Love." *Shambhala Sun*, July 2006.
    Reprinted on PBS's blog *The Buddha*, June 2010. Accessed at http://www.
    pbs.org/thebuddha/blog/2010/jun/3/toward-worldwide-culture-love-bell-
    hooks/ on November 5, 2018.
Huffer, Lynne. *Maternal Pasts, Feminist Futures: Nostalgia, Ethics, and the Question
    of Difference*. Stanford: Stanford University Press, 1998.
Huntington, Patricia. *Ecstatic Subjects, Utopia, and Recognition*. Albany: State
    University of New York Press, 1998.
Innerarity, Daniel. *The Future and Its Enemies: In Defense of Political Hope*.
    Translated by Sandra Kingery. Stanford: Stanford University Press, 2012.
Irigaray, Luce. *Speculum de l'autre femme*. Paris: Les Éditions de Minuit, 1974.
———. "And the One Doesn't Stir without the Other." Translated by Hélène
    Vivienne Wenzel. *Signs: Journal of Women in Culture and Society* 7, no.
    1 (1981): 60–77.
———. *Speculum of the Other Woman*. Translated by Gillian C. Gill. Ithaca,
    NY: Cornell University Press, 1985.
———. *This Sex Which Is Not One*. Translated by Catherine Porter. Ithaca, NY:
    Cornell University Press, 1985.
———. *Marine Lover of Friedrich Nietzsche*. Translated by Gillian C. Gill. New
    York: Columbia University Press, 1991.
———. *An Ethics of Sexual Difference*. Translated by Carolyn Burke and Gillian
    C. Gill. Ithaca, NY: Cornell University Press, 1993.

———. *Je, Tu, Nous: Toward a Culture of Difference*. Translated by Alison Martin. New York: Routledge, 1993.

———. *Sexes and Genealogies*. Translated by Gillian C. Gill. New York: Columbia University Press, 1993.

———. "'Je—Luce Irigaray': A Meeting with Luce Irigaray." Interview with Luce Irigaray conducted by Elizabeth Hirsh and Gary A. Olson. Translated by Elizabeth Hirsh and Gaëton Brulotte. *Hypatia: A Journal of Feminist Philosophy* 10, no. 2 (1995): 93–114.

———. *I Love to You: Sketch of a Possible Felicity in History*. Translated by Alison Martin. New York: Routledge, 1996.

———. *The Forgetting of Air in Martin Heidegger*. Translated by Mary Beth Mader. Austin: University of Texas Press, 1999.

———. *Why Different? A Culture of Two Subjects*. Edited by Luce Irigaray and Sylvère Lotringer. Translated by Camille Collins. New York: Semiotext(e), 2000.

———. *Democracy Begins Between Two*. Translated by Kirsteen Anderson. New York: Routledge, 2001.

———. *To Be Two*. Translated by Monique M. Rhodes and Marco F. Cocito-Monoc. New York: Routledge, 2001.

———. *Between East and West: From Singularity to Community*. Translated by Stephen Pluháček. New York: Columbia University Press, 2002.

———. *The Way of Love*. Translated by Heidi Bostic and Stephen Pluháček. London: Continuum, 2002.

———. *To Speak Is Never Neutral*. Translated by Gail Schwab. New York: Routledge, 2002.

———. *Everyday prayers / Prières quotidiennes*. Translated by Luce Irigaray with Timothy Mathews. Paris: Maisonneuve & Larose and University of Nottingham Press, 2004.

———. *Key Writings*. Edited by Luce Irigaray. Translated by Laine Harrington. London: Continuum, 2004.

———. *Sharing the World*. London: Continuum, 2008.

———. *In the Beginning, She Was*. London: Bloomsbury, 2013.

———. *To Be Born: Genesis of a New Human Being*. New York: Palgrave Macmillan, 2017.

Irigaray, Luce, and Michael Marder. *Through Vegetal Being: Two Philosophical Perspectives*. New York: Columbia University Press, 2016.

Israeli-Nevo, Atalia. "Taking (My) Time: Temporality in Transition, Queer Delays and Being (in the) Present." *Somatechnics* 7, no. 1 (2017): 34–49.

Johnston, Adrian. *Time Driven: Metapsychology and the Splitting of the Drive*. Evanston, IL: Northwestern University Press, 2005.

Jones, Rachel. *Irigaray: Towards a Sexuate Philosophy*. Cambridge, UK: Polity Press, 2011.

Joy, Morny. *Divine Love: Luce Irigaray, Women, Gender, and Religion*. Manchester, UK: Manchester University Press, 2007.

Kant, Immanuel. "An Answer to the Question: What Is Enlightenment?" In *What Is Enlightenment? Eighteenth-Century Answers and Twentieth-Century Questions*, edited and translated by James Schmidt, 58–64. Berkeley: University of California Press, 1996.

Kristeva, Julia. *About Chinese Women*. Translated by Anita Barrows. London: Marion Boyars, 1977.

———. "Julia Kristeva: à quoi servent les intellectuels?" Interview conducted by Jean-Paul Enthoven. *Le Nouvel Observateur* (1977): 98–134.

———. "Il n'y a pas de maitre à language." *Nouvelle Revue de Psychanalyse: Regards sur la psychanalyse en France* 20 (1979): 119–40.

———. *Desire in Language: A Semiotic Approach to Literature and Art*. Edited by Leon S. Roudiez. Translated by Thomas Gora, Alice Jardine, and Leon S. Roudiez. New York: Columbia University Press, 1980.

———. *Powers of Horror: An Essay on Abjection*. Translated by Leon S. Roudiez. New York: Columbia University Press, 1982.

———. *Revolution in Poetic Language*. Translated by Margaret Waller. New York: Columbia University Press, 1984.

———. *Tales of Love*. Translated by Leon S. Roudiez. New York: Columbia University Press, 1987.

———. *Black Sun: Depression and Melancholia*. Translated by Leon S. Roudiez. New York: Columbia University Press, 1989.

———. *Strangers to Ourselves*. Translated by Leon S. Roudiez. New York: Columbia University Press, 1991.

———. *Nations Without Nationalism*. Translated by Leon S. Roudiez. New York: Columbia University Press, 1993.

———. *New Maladies of the Soul*. Translated by Ross Guberman. New York: Columbia University Press, 1995.

———. *Possessions*. Translated by Barbara Brey. New York: Columbia University Press, 1996.

———. *Time and Sense: Proust and the Experience of Literature*. Translated by Ross Guberman. New York: Columbia University Press, 1996.

———. "'unes femmes': The Woman Effect." Interview with Julia Kristeva conducted by Elaine Boucquey. In *Julia Kristeva: Interviews*, edited by Ross Mitchell Guberman, 103–21. New York: Columbia University Press, 1996.

———. *The Sense and Non-Sense of Revolt*. Translated by Jeanine Herman. Vol. 1 of *The Powers and Limits of Psychoanalysis*. New York: Columbia University Press, 2000.

———. *Hannah Arendt*. Translated by Ross Guberman. Vol. 1 of *Female Genius: Life, Madness, Words*. New York: Columbia University Press, 2001.

———. *Intimate Revolt*. Translated by Jeanine Herman. Vol. 2 of *The Powers and Limits of Psychoanalysis*. New York: Columbia University Press, 2002.

———. *Revolt, She Said*. Edited by Sylvère Lotringer. Translated by Brian O'Keeffe. New York: Semiotext(e), 2002.

———. "The Meaning of Parity." In *The Kristeva Critical Reader*, edited by John Lechte and Mary Zournazi, and translated by John Lechte, 202–09. Edinburgh: Edinburgh University Press, 2003.

———. *Colette*. Translated by Jane Marie Todd. Vol. 3 of *Female Genius: Life, Madness, Words*. New York: Columbia University Press, 2004.

———. "The Impenetrable Power of the Phallic Matron." Accessed at http://kristeva.fr/palin_en.html on August 23, 2017. Originally published in French in *Libération*, September 25, 2008.

———. *This Incredible Need to Believe*. Translated by Beverley Bie Brahic. New York: Columbia University Press, 2009.

———. "Julia Kristeva Reads *The Second Sex* Sixty Years Later." Translated by Timothy Hackett. *philoSOPHIA: A Journal of Continental Feminism* 1, no. 2 (2011): 137–49.

———. *The Severed Head: Capital Visions*. Translated by Jody Gladding. New York: Columbia University Press, 2011.

———. "New Forms of Revolt." *Journal of French and Francophone Philosophy* 22, no. 2 (2014): 1–19.

———. *Teresa, My Love: An Imagined Life of the Saint of Avila*. Translated by Lorna Scott Fox. New York: Columbia University Press, 2014.

———. *The Enchanted Clock*. Translated by Armine Kotin Mortimer. New York: Columbia University Press, 2017.

Lacan, Jacques. *The Seminar of Jacques Lacan, Book I: Freud's Papers on Technique 1953–1954*. Edited by Jacque Alain-Miller. Translated by John Forrester. New York: W. W. Norton & Company, 1988.

Landes, Joan B. "Jürgen Habermas, *The Structural Transformation of the Public Sphere*: A Feminist Inquiry." *Praxis International* 12, no. 1 (April 1992): 106–27.

Laplanche, Jean, and Jean-Bertrand Pontalis. *The Language of Psycho-Analysis*. Translated by Donald Nicholson-Smith. New York: W. W. Norton & Company, 1973.

Lázaro, Reyes. "Feminism and Motherhood: O'Brien vs Beauvoir." *Hypatia: A Journal of Feminist Philosophy* 1, no. 2 (1986): 87–102.

Lewis, Sophie. "Defending Intimacy Against What? Limits of Antisurrogacy Feminisms." *Signs: Journal of Women in Culture and Society* 43, no. 1 (2017): 97–125.

Lloyd, Genevieve. *The Man of Reason: "Male" and "Female" in Western Philosophy*. Minneapolis: University of Minnesota Press, 1984.

Lorde, Audre. "The Master's Tools Will Never Dismantle the Master's House." In *Sister Outsider: Essays and Speeches*, 110–13. New York: Crossing Press, 2007.

Luciano, Dana. *Arranging Grief: Sacred Time and the Body in Nineteenth-Century America*. New York: New York University Press, 2007.

Lugones, María. "Heterosexualism and the Colonial/Modern Gender System." *Hypatia: A Journal of Feminist Philosophy* 22, no. 1 (2007): 186–209.

Margaroni, Maria. "'The Lost Foundation': Kristeva's Semiotic *Chora* and Its Ambiguous Legacy." *Hypatia: A Journal of Feminist Philosophy* 20, no. 1 (2005): 78–98.

Martin, Emily. "The Egg and the Sperm: How Science Has Constructed a Romance Based on Stereotypical Male-Female Roles." In *Feminist Theory and the Body*, edited by Janet Price and Margrit Shildrick, 179–89. New York: Routledge, 1999.

McAfee, Noëlle. *Julia Kristeva*. New York: Routledge, 2005.

McBean, Sam. *Feminism's Queer Temporalities*. New York: Routledge, 2016.

McEvilley, Thomas. "Primitivism in the Works of an Emancipated Negress." In *Kara Walker: My Complement, My Enemy, My Oppressor, My Love*, catalog published on the occasion of an exhibition at the Walker Art Center, curated by Philippe Vergne, 52–61. Minneapolis: Walker Art Center, 2007.

Meaney, Gerardine. *(Un)Like Subjects: Women, Theory, Fiction*. New York: Routledge, 1993.

Memmi, Albert. *Colonizer and Colonized*. Translated by Howard Greenfeld. Boston: Beacon Press, 1991.

Mignolo, Walter D. *The Darker Side of Western Modernity: Global Futures, Decolonial Options*. Durham, NC: Duke University Press, 2011.

Miller, Elaine P. *Head Cases: Julia Kristeva on Philosophy and Art in Depressed Times*. New York: Columbia University Press, 2014.

Miller, Paul Allen. *Diotima at the Barricades: French Feminists Read Plato*. Oxford: Oxford University Press, 2016.

Mirzoeff, Nicholas. "Below the Water: Black Lives Matter and Revolutionary Time." *e-flux*, no. 79 (February 2017). Accessed at http://www.e-flux.com/journal/79/94164/below-the-water-black-lives-matter-and-revolutionary-time/ on August 28, 2018.

Mohanty, Chandra Talpade. *Feminism Without Borders: Decolonizing Theory, Practicing Solidarity*. Durham, NC: Duke University Press, 2003.

Muñoz, José Esteban. *Cruising Utopia: The Then and There of Queer Theory*. New York: New York University Press, 2009.

Musser, Amber Jamilla. "Queering Sugar: Kara Walker's Sugar Sphinx and the Intractability of Black Female Sexuality." *Signs: Journal of Women in Culture and Society* 42, no. 1 (2016): 153–74.

Neumann, Erich. *The Fear of the Feminine and Other Essays on Feminine Psychology.* Translated by Boris Matthews, Ester Doughty, Eugene Rolfe, and Michael Cullingworth. Princeton, NJ: Princeton University Press, 1994.

Nikolchina, Miglena. *Matricide in Language: Writing Theory in Kristeva and Woolf.* New York: Other Press, 2002.

Ó Murchadha, Felix. *The Time of Revolution: Kairos and Chronos in Heidegger.* London: Bloomsbury, 2013.

O'Brien, Mary. *The Politics of Reproduction.* Boston: Routledge and Kegan Paul, 1981.

O'Byrne, Anne. *Natality and Finitude.* Bloomington: Indiana University Press, 2010.

O'Hagan, Sean. "John Akomfrah: 'Progress Can Cause Profound Suffering.'" *The Guardian*, October 1, 2017. Accessed at https://www.theguardian.com/artanddesign/2017/oct/01/john-akomfrah-purple-climate-change on July 9, 2018.

Ohlheiser, Abby. "The Woman Behind 'Me Too' Knew the Power of the Phrase When She Created It—10 Years Ago." *Washington Post*, October 19, 2017. Accessed at https://www.washingtonpost.com/news/the-intersect/wp/2017/10/19/the-woman-behind-me-too-knew-the-power-of-the-phrase-when-she-created-it-10-years-ago/?noredirect=on&utm_term=.49f36e6b2a3a on August 29, 2018.

Oliver, Kelly. "Julia Kristeva's Feminist Revolutions" *Hypatia: A Journal of Feminist Philosophy* 8, no. 2 (1993): 94–114.

———. *Family Values: Subjects Between Nature and Culture.* New York: Routledge, 1997.

———. "Revolt and Forgiveness." In *Revolt, Affect, Collectivity: The Unstable Boundaries of Kristeva's Polis*, edited by Tina Chanter and Ewa Płonowska Ziarek, 77–92. Albany: State University of New York Press, 2005.

———. "Motherhood, Sexuality, and Pregnant Embodiment: Twenty-Five Years of Gestation." *Hypatia: A Journal of Feminist Philosophy* 25, no. 4 (2010): 760–77.

Orr, Deborah, Linda López McAllister, Eileen Kahl, and Kathleen Earle, eds. *Belief, Bodies, and Being: Feminist Reflections on Embodiment.* Lanham, MD: Rowman & Littlefield, 2006.

Ortega, Mariana. *In-Between: Latina Feminist Phenomenology, Multiplicity, and the Self.* Albany: State University of New York Press, 2016.

Ortner, Sherry B. "Is Female to Male as Nature Is to Culture?" In *Feminism, the Public and the Private*, edited by Joan B. Landes, 21–44. Oxford: Oxford University Press, 1998.

Parker, Emily Anne, and Anne van Leeuwen, eds. *Differences: Rereading Beauvoir and Irigaray.* Oxford: Oxford University Press, 2017.

Peters, F. E. *Greek Philosophical Terms: A Historical Lexicon.* New York: New York University Press, 1967.

Philips, Anne. *Engendering Democracy*. Cambridge, UK: Polity Press, 1991.

Plato. *Republic*. Translated by Allan Bloom. New York: Basic Books, 1991.

———. *The* Symposium *and the* Phaedrus: *Plato's Erotic Dialogues*. Translated by William S. Cobb. Albany: State University of New York Press, 1993.

———. *Timaeus*. Translated by Peter Kalkavage. Newburyport, MA: Focus, 2001.

———. "Theaetetus." In *Plato's Theory of Knowledge: The Theaetetus and the Sophist*, translated by Francis M. Cornford, 15–164. Mineola, NY: Dover, 2003.

Poe, Danielle. "Can Luce Irigaray's Notion of Sexual Difference Be Applied to Transsexual and Transgender Narratives?" In *Thinking with Irigaray*, edited by Mary C. Rawlinson, Sabrina L. Hom, and Serene J. Khader, 111–28. Albany: State University of New York Press, 2011.

Quijano, Aníbal. "Coloniality of Power, Eurocentrism, and Latin America." *Nepantia: Views from South* 1, no. 3 (2009): 533–80.

Rancière, Jacques. "The Work of the Image." Accessed at http://www.shalev-gerz.net/?page_id=215 on August 27, 2018.

Rankine, Claudia. "'The Condition of Black Life Is One of Mourning.'" *New York Times Magazine*, June 22, 2015. Accessed at https://www.nytimes.com/2015/06/22/magazine/the-condition-of-black-life-is-one-of-mourning.html on August 29, 2018.

Rich, Adrienne. *Of Woman Born: Motherhood as Experience and Institution*. New York: W. W. Norton & Company, 1976.

———. *On Lies, Secrets and Silence: Selected Prose, 1966–1978*. New York: Norton, 1979.

Roberts, Dorothy. *Killing the Black Body: Race, Reproduction, and the Meaning of Liberty*. New York: Vintage Books, 1999.

Robertson, Campbell. "A Lynching Memorial Is Opening. The Country Has Never Seen Anything Like It." *New York Times*, April 25, 2018. Accessed at https://www.nytimes.com/2018/04/25/us/lynching-memorial-alabama.html on August 28, 2018.

Roediger, David. *Seizing Freedom: Slave Emancipation and Liberty for All*. New York: Verso, 2015.

Rose, Jacqueline. "Julia Kristeva—Take Two." In *Ethics, Politics, and Difference in Julia Kristeva's Writing*, edited by Kelly Oliver, 41–61. New York: Routledge, 1993.

Rosen, Stanley. *Plato's* Symposium. New Haven, CT: Yale University Press, 1968.

Said, Edward W. *Beginnings: Intention and Method*. New York: Columbia University Press, 1975.

Sallis, John. *Chorology: On Beginning in Plato's* Timaeus. Bloomington: Indiana University Press, 1999.

Sandford, Stella. *Plato and Sex*. Cambridge, UK: Polity Press, 2010.

Sartre, Jean-Paul. *Being and Nothingness: An Essay on Phenomenological Ontology*. Translated by Hazel E. Barnes. London: Routledge, 2009.

Schor, Naomi. "This Essentialism Which Is Not One: Coming to Grips with Irigaray." In *Engaging with Irigaray: Feminist Philosophy and Modern European Thought*, edited by Carolyn Burke, Naomi Schor, and Margaret Whitford, 57–78. New York: Columbia University Press, 1994.

Schües, Christina, Dorothea E. Olkowski, and Helen A. Fielding, eds. *Time in Feminist Phenomenology*. Bloomington: Indiana University Press, 2011.

Schwab, Gail M. "Mothers, Sisters, and Daughters: Luce Irigaray and the Female Genealogical Line in the Stories of the Greeks." In *Rewriting Difference: Luce Irigaray and "the Greeks*," edited by Elena Tzelepis and Athena Athanasiou, 79–92. Albany: State University of New York Press, 2008.

———. "Beyond the Vertical and the Horizontal: Spirituality, Space, and Alterity in the Work of Luce Irigaray." In *Thinking with Irigaray*, edited by Mary C. Rawlinson, Sabrina L. Hom, and Serene J. Khader, 77–97. Albany: State University of New York Press, 2011.

Shalev-Gerz, Esther. "Reflecting Spaces/Deflecting Spaces." Accessed at www. shalev-gerz.net/DE/index_de.html on October 16, 2010.

Shaw, Gwendolyn DuBois. *Seeing the Unspeakable: The Art of Kara Walker*. Durham, NC: Duke University Press, 2004.

Silva, Denise Ferreira da. *Toward a Global Idea of Race*. Minneapolis: University of Minnesota Press, 2007.

simpkins, reese. "Temporal Flesh, Material Becomings." *Somatechnics* 7, no. 1 (2017): 124–41.

Sjöholm, Cecilia. "The Temporality of Intimacy: Kristeva's Return to the Political." *The Southern Journal of Philosophy*, special issue on Kristeva's ethical and political thought, proceedings from the Spindel Conference, 42 (2004): 73–87.

———. *Kristeva and the Political*. London: Routledge, 2005.

Söderbäck, Fanny. "Impossible Mourning: Sophocles Reversed." In *Feminist Readings of Antigone*, edited by Fanny Söderbäck, 65–82. Albany: State University of New York Press, 2010.

———. "Motherhood According to Kristeva: On Time and Matter in Plato and Kristeva." *philoSOPHIA: A Journal of Continental Feminism* 1, no. 1 (2011): 65–87.

———. "Revolutionary Time: Revolt as Temporal Return." *Signs: Journal of Women in Culture and Society* 37, no. 2 (2012): 301–24.

———. "Being in the Present: Derrida and Irigaray on the Metaphysics of Presence." *Journal of Speculative Philosophy* 27, no. 3 (2013): 253–64.

———. "Timely Revolutions: On the Timelessness of the Unconscious." *Journal of French and Francophone Philosophy* 22, no. 2 (2014): 46–55.

———. "In Search for the Mother Through the Looking-Glass: On Time, Origins, and Beginnings in Plato and Irigaray." In *Engaging the World:*

*Thinking after Irigaray*, edited by Mary C. Rawlinson, 11–37. Albany: State University of New York Press, 2016.

———. "Kristeva." In *Fifty-One Key Feminist Thinkers*, edited by Lori J. Marso, 129–34. New York: Routledge, 2016.

———. "Forging A Head and Forging Ahead—Miller's *Head Cases*," review of Elaine P. Miller's *Head Cases: Julia Kristeva on Philosophy and Art in Depressed Times*. *Theory and Event* 20, no. 1 (2017): 274–79.

———. "Natality or Birth? Arendt and Cavarero on the Human Condition of Being Born." *Hypatia: A Journal of Feminist Philosophy* 33, no. 2 (2018): 273–88.

Spade, Dean. "Resisting Medicine, Re/modeling Gender." *Berkeley Women's Law Journal* 15 (2003): 15–37.

Spelman, Elizabeth V. "Woman as Body: Ancient and Contemporary Views." *Feminist Studies* 8, no. 1 (1982): 109–31.

Spivak, Gayatri Chakravorty. "French Feminism in an International Frame." *Yale French Studies*, no. 62 (1981): 154–84.

———. "In a Word." Interview conducted by Ellen Rooney. *Differences* 1, no. 2 (1989): 124–56.

Stampler, Laura. "Project Air: Yoga Helps HIV-Positive Rape Victims in Rwanda." *Huffington Post*, September 30, 2011. Accessed at https://www.huffington-post.com/2011/07/31/project-air-yoga-rwanda-hiv-women_n_914521.html on November 19, 2018.

Stewart, Amy Ray. "Extimate Trauma, Intimate Ethics: Kristevan Revolt in the Artwork of Kara Walker." In *New Forms of Revolt: Essays on Kristeva's Intimate Politics*, edited by Sarah K. Hansen and Rebecca Tuvel, 85–106. Albany: State University of New York Press, 2017.

Stone, Alison. *Luce Irigaray and the Philosophy of Sexual Difference*. Cambridge: Cambridge University Press, 2006.

———. "Natality and Mortality: Rethinking Death with Cavarero." *Continental Philosophy Review* 43 (2010): 353–72.

———. *Feminism, Psychoanalysis, and Maternal Subjectivity*. New York: Routledge, 2012.

———. "Beauvoir and the Ambiguities of Motherhood." In *A Companion to Simone de Beauvoir*, edited by Laura Hengehold and Nancy Bauer, 122–33. Hoboken, NJ: Wiley-Blackwell, 2017.

Stone, Jennifer. "The Horrors of Power: A Critique of Kristeva." In *The Politics of Theory*, edited by Francis Barker, Peter Hulme, Margaret Iversen, and Diana Loxley, 38–48. Colchester, UK: University of Essex Press, 1983.

Stone, Sandy. "The *Empire* Strikes Back: A Posttranssexual Manifesto." In *Body Guards: The Cultural Politics of Gender Ambiguity*, edited by Julia Epstein and Kristina Straub, 280–304. New York: Routledge, 1991.

Storr, Robert. "Spooked." In *Kara Walker: My Complement, My Enemy, My Oppressor, My Love*, catalog published on the occasion of an exhibition at the Walker Art Center, curated by Philippe Vergne, 62–73. Minneapolis: Walker Art Center, 2007.

Story, Kaila Adia, ed. *Patricia Hill Collins: Reconceiving Motherhood*. Bradford, ON: Demeter Press, 2014.

Swan, John. *Speculum Mundi*. Accessed at http://digital.library.adelaide.edu.au/coll/special/swan/index.html on May 16, 2009. Originally published by Cambridge University Press, 1635.

Teske, Roland J. *Paradoxes of Time in Saint Augustine*. Milwaukee, WI: Marquette University Press, 1996.

Thompson, Nato. Curatorial statement for Kara Walker's *A Subtlety*. Accessed at Creative Time's website http://creativetime.org/projects/karawalker/curatorial-statement/ on June 14, 2016.

Tuana, Nancy. *The Less Noble Sex: Scientific, Religious, and Philosophical Conceptions of Woman's Nature*. Bloomington: Indiana University Press, 1993.

Tyler, Imogen. "Introduction: Birth." *Feminist Review* 93 (2009): 1–7.

Tzelepis, Elena, and Athena Athanasiou, eds. *Rewriting Difference: Luce Irigaray and "the Greeks."* Albany: State University of New York Press, 2008.

Vallega, Alejandro Arturo. *Latin American Philosophy from Identity to Radical Exteriority*. Bloomington: Indiana University Press, 2014.

Van Leeuwen, Anne. "Further Speculations: Time and Difference in *Speculum de l'autre femme*." In *Engaging the World: Thinking After Irigaray*, edited by Mary C. Rawlinson, 51–63. Albany: State University of New York Press, 2016.

Walsh, Lisa. "Her Mother Her Self: The Ethics of the Antigone Family Romance." *Hypatia: A Journal of Feminist Philosophy* 14, no. 3 (1999): 96–125.

Warren, Nicolas de. *Husserl and the Promise of Time: Subjectivity in Transcendental Phenomenology*. Cambridge: Cambridge University Press, 2009.

West-Pavlov, Russell. *Temporalities*. New York: Routledge, 2012.

Whitford, Margaret. *Luce Irigaray: Philosophy in the Feminine*. New York: Routledge, 1991.

Wittgenstein, Ludwig. *Tractatus Logico-Philosophicus*. Translated by C. K. Ogden. New York: Cosimo Classics, 2007.

Wood, David. *The Deconstruction of Time*. Evanston, IL: Northwestern University Press, 2001.

Woodruff, Paul. "Aristotle on *Mimesis*." In *Essays on Aristotle's Poetics*, edited by Amélie Oksenberg Rorty, 73–95. Princeton, NJ: Princeton University Press, 1992.

Woolf, Virginia. *A Room of One's Own*. Orlando: Harcourt, 1989.

Young, Iris Marion. "Throwing Like a Girl: A Phenomenology of Feminine Body Comportment, Motility, and Spatiality." Chap. 2 in *On Female*

*Body Experience: "Throwing Like a Girl" and Other Essays.* Oxford: Oxford University Press, 2005.

Young, Kevin. "Triangular Trade: Coloring, Remarking, and Narrative in the Writings of Kara Walker." In *Kara Walker: My Complement, My Enemy, My Oppressor, My Love,* catalog published on the occasion of an exhibition at the Walker Art Center, curated by Philippe Vergne, 36–51. Minneapolis: Walker Art Center, 2007.

Yovel, Yirmiyahu. *Kant and the Philosophy of History.* Princeton, NJ: Princeton University Press, 1980.

Ziarek, Ewa Płonowska. "Toward a Radical Female Imaginary: Temporality and Embodiment in Irigaray's Ethics." *Diacritics* 28, no. 1 (1998): 59–75.

## Lectures and Unpublished Work

Byrne, Jean. "Enlightenment Between Two: Luce Irigaray, Sexual Difference and Nondual Oneness." PhD Diss., University of Queensland, 2008.

McNamara, Sara. "In the Beginning Was the End of Her Story: Irigaray and Freud on *Nachträglichkeit* and Feminine Temporality." Paper presented at the Society for Phenomenology and Existentialist Philosophy, 2010.

Miller, Elaine P. "French Feminists on the Question of Time." Proposal for the 2010 meeting of the Society for Phenomenology and Existentialist Philosophy.

# Index

abjection, 45, 201, 302n68, 352n6
  time of, 217
absence
  absolute, 120, 124
  metaphysics of, 115–25, 132, 159
  of time, 155
  woman as, 55, 148–52, 322n21
action
  Arendt's conception of, 266,
    269–73, 306n30, 330n27
  collective, 4
  deferred, 175, 334n62, 335n66. See
    also *Nachträglichkeit*
  Enlightenment idea of, 38
  life and, 141–42
activity
  creative, 193
  mental, 167
  of *chōra*, 259, 344n11
  of contemplation, 311n14
  of life, 141–44
  of nature, 146
  of Platonic divine intellect, 204
  of temporal process, 43
  sexual difference and, 29–33,
    55–59, 195, 203
  sound and, 323n22
affect, 88–94, 169
  Platonic mimesis and, 75
  semiotic, 88, 201
Ahmed, Sara, 169, 331n33

air, 128, 136–41, 237
  Project Air, 139
  *See also* breath
aliveness, 82, 121–25, 166, 188
  birth and, 125
  destruction of, 123, 307n39
  in the *Timaeus*, 207, 212
  of discourse, 222
  of temporality, 45–46, 114, 121
alteration, 45, 238, 254, 258
  alterity and, 53–84, 135–36,
    148–50, 151, 153, 157, 222
  cyclicality of revolt and, 37–38,
    49, 51, 87–88
  fecundity and, 324n28
  mimicry and, 75, 359n65
  of *chōra*, 207, 213
  *See also* differentiation
alterity
  alteration and, 53–84, 135–36,
    148–50, 151, 153, 157, 222
  immanent, 165
  in the *Timaeus*, 207
  of mother/child dyad, 318n60
  *See also* otherness; strangeness
ambiguity, 291n26
  prohibition of, 39–40, 291n29
amnesia, 109
  anamnesis as, 252
  the maternal and, 195, 199
  *See also* forgetfulness; oblivion

anamnesis, 11, 76, 83, 128, 195,
290n23
in psychoanalytic praxis, 83, 95,
166, 176
Plato's conception of, 252
See also memory; recollection
ananke, 206
See also chōra; necessity
Antigone, 358n59
Anzaldúa, Gloria, 291n26
aporia, 101, 161, 346n20
in Derrida's conception of life,
129, 344n14
of chōra, 211
of ethical life, 165
appearance
political space of, 273
vs. reality, 302n67
worldly, 60, 312n22
appropriation
alterity and, 152, 160
ironic, 78
of beginning, 4
of motherhood, 216, 235, 348n40
of objects, 154
See also instrumentalization;
objectification
archaic, 87, 91, 95, 166, 178, 274
in the Timaeus, 208, 227
motherhood and, 191–93, 215–16
See also anamnesis; beginning
archē, 80, 90–91, 125, 128–29, 271
linear time and, 58, 120, 307n43
maternal conception of, 229
metaphysical tradition and, 186,
312n19
of nature, 146
writing and, 325n31
See also archaic; origin
Arendt, Hannah, 108, 266, 306n30,
330n27, 360n9
on action, 269–72

on evil, 100, 307n39
on freedom, 273
on future, 269–72
on life, 59–60
on nature, 63
Aristophanes, 155, 163, 328n13,
352n4
Aristotle, 328n16
Irigaray's critique of, 61–62, 196,
345n15
on mimesis, 75
on time, 6, 117–18, 172, 281n17,
311n12, 359n66
art
film, 30, 139, 286n1, 300n46
Kristeva on anamnesis and, 195,
206, 338n21
memorial, 101–09
mimesis and, 75–81
poetic composition as, 141–07
See also poetry
ascent
Platonic conception of, 237–38, 253
assimilation, 40, 330n28
audibility, 108, 275
Augustine, 6, 100, 117, 172, 317n56
auto-eroticism, 177
autonomy
moral idea of, 313n29
of the subject, 166, 326n34
vs. freedom, 270

Battersby, Christine, 187
Beardsworth, Sara, 138–40, 219,
341n49
Beauvoir, Simone de, 28, 59–73,
225–26, 266–67
on becoming woman, 47, 226,
298n33
on biological discourse, 286n6
on feminine immanence, 51, 56,
59, 69–72, 288n12

on freedom, 288n17
on motherhood, 186–87, 286n3,
 336n6
on time/temporality, 29–38. *See
 also* sexual division of temporal
 labor
becoming, 141–47, 204, 212–13, 258,
 260
 of *chōra*, 207
 of the mother, 189, 194
 other, 170, 303n1
 Platonic conception of, 311n16,
  312n19
 sexual ontology of, 282n26
 with, 153–56, 161–62, 166, 179
 woman, 47, 162, 226, 298n33
beginning, 246–59, 273–75
 absolute, 91
 action and, 270
 *chōra* and, 204–14
 feminist, 4
 new, 98, 216
 plurality of, 80, 125–28
 return to, 189, 191
 temporal, 58–62
 vs. origin, 244–46
 *See also under* maternal
being
 fullness of, 124
 in the Western metaphysical
  tradition, 12, 117–19, 122, 130,
  138, 225–27, 297n14, 322n15,
  326n34, 356n36
 maternal, 260
 Parmenidean, 148
 present, 116, 153, 257
 static, 144, 149, 210
 there, 71, 266. *See also* Dasein
 two, 80, 150, 154–56, 163, 295n2
 with, 166, 170, 327n5
Benjamin, Walter, 119–20, 307n43
Bergson, Henri, 172

Bettcher, Talia Mae, 64, 297n25
between, 291n26
 birth and death, 316n47
 in-between, 81, 122, 147, 212
 time as, 71, 165
 two, 142, 150–55, 159, 163–70
 world as, 114
 *See also* indeterminacy
binary
 sexual, 22, 24, 39, 64, 226. *See also
  under* sexual difference
 *See also* dualism
biology
 as drive, 43
 Beauvoir's critique of, 29–32,
  286n6
 death and, 178
 determinism and, 294n49
 motherhood and, 192, 198
 sexual difference and, 57, 64, 66.
  *See also under* sex
*bios*
 Arendtian conception of, 60
 *See also* life
biothanatology, 178
birth, 123–33, 176–81, 215–18
 death and, 60, 141
 in Plato, 237–38
 in the *Timaeus*, 204–05, 208
 motherhood and, 185–88
 women as birth-givers, 30–31
 *See also* natality
body, 20–25, 60–65, 70–72, 88–94
 *chōra* and, 202–14
 maternal, 185–99, 225–33
 sexual difference and, 31–33, 54,
  58, 60, 81
 time and the, 40–50
 yoga and the, 136–40
 *See also* corporeality; embodiment;
  soma
 *See also under* dualism: mind/body

Braidotti, Rosi, 282n26, 351n64
breath
    Irigaray's conception of, 128–29,
        320n4
    speech and, 162
    yogic (*pranayama*), 136–41
    *See also* air
Burchill, Louise, 208–09, 229,
    282n27, 345n17
Burke, Tarana, 3–4
Butler, Judith, 79–80, 89, 169, 187,
    228, 242, 244
    *Gender Trouble*, 80, 189, 218, 223,
        231
    on Irigaray, 242, 244, 260, 302n66,
        354n26
    on Kristeva, 189–90, 218–28
    on performativity, 79–80, 301n66,
        355n33
    on vulnerability. *See* vulnerability
    on woman, 32

causality
    insufficiency of, 215, 220–22
    principle of, 214
    unconscious processes and, 173
Cavarero, Adriana, 123, 195, 310n2,
    311n16, 313n29, 322n21,
    323n22, 346n21, 348n40
cave
    air in, 137
    Plato's allegory of, 191, 236–61,
        344n15, 353n18
    See also *hystera*
celestial body
    and time, 6, 87, 213
change, 10–15, 55–59, 223–27
    culture of, 235, 239
    *See also* alteration
Chanter, Tina, 11, 13, 221, 224,
    289n20, 313n31, 339n26, 342n5,
    349n53, 351n60

chaos, 208, 211
Chicago, Judy, 309n67
*chōra*, 201–14, 343n5, 345n17
    Butler's critique of, 189–90
    Derrida on, 205, 251, 342n4,
        344n10, 345n17
    Kristeva on, 81, 202–14, 229,
        343n5, 344n10
    maternal, 247
    Plato on, 201–14, 345n17
    semiotic, 81, 148, 191, 201,
        350n58
chronobiopolitics, 15
chronology
    anteriority and, 220, 350n53
    geography as, 17
    historical progress as, 16–17, 40–41
    unconscious and, 171–73
chrononormativity, 15
chronopolitics, 15
Cixous, Hélène, 78–79
clone, 129, 319n62
closure
    cyclicality's lack of, 49
    of finitude, 68, 346n20
    refusal of, 273
cogito
    Camusian, 86, 96
    Cartesian, 329n21
    illusion of, 149
    Sartrean, 303n5
Collins, Patricia Hill, 198
colonial difference, 110, 121, 132,
    281n14
coloniality
    of academia, 100
    of Beauvoir, 36, 290n22
    of gender, 284n45
    of Irigaray, 196–99, 320n2,
        319–20n67
    of Kristeva, 169–70, 196–99,
        320n3, 319–20n67

of motherhood, 196–99
of time, 15–18, 33, 40, 51, 59, 63,
    91, 116, 268, 281n14
patriarchal regime of, 11, 12, 37,
    59, 63, 91
violence of, 62
See also decolonial theory
constructivism, 13
continuity
in history, 120
of time and matter, 229
temporality and, 142
transcendental ego and, 161
wave as a figure for, 45
Copernican revolution
psychoanalysis as, 172, 329n21
copy
Butler's conception of, 355n33
Irigaray's conception of, 75, 80,
    226, 240, 243–44
Plato's cave and the idea of, 246
woman as, 80, 243, 272, 302n67
See also mimesis
corporeality. See body; embodiment
cosmopolitanism
Kristeva's conception of, 168, 330n39
Couzens Hoy, David, 120, 307n43,
    313n24
creation
artistic, 57, 222
ex nihilo, 204
of cosmos in the Timaeus, 203–14
procreation and, 186, 193–95, 245
time and the capacity for, 127
See also genesis
creation myths, 271–74
Greek, 188
Judeo-Christian, 247. See also
    genesis
cultural difference, 275
sexuate and, 54, 57, 59
See also colonial difference

cyclicality. See under time: cyclical
    time

Dasein
ecstatic character of, 70
Heidegger's conception of, 131,
    266, 268, 273, 314n47,
    322n15
death, 65–66, 119–33, 154–56
being-towards, 130, 273–74,
    314n31, 315n47
birth and, 60, 137–38
culture of, 66, 88–90, 105
life and, 92
time of, 178, 258
death-bearing, 167–68
death drive, 174–75, 178–79, 274,
    334n62
debt
to the maternal, 130–31, 254,
    342n56, 356n39
decolonial theory, 15–20, 33, 116,
    290n24, 306n30
See also coloniality
deconstruction
Derridean, 115–16, 312n20
method and, 74
of host/stranger opposition, 169
of metaphysics of presence, 148
Deleuze, Gilles, 281n12, 282n27,
    283n27
demiurge, 203–10, 346n22
Derrida, Jacques, 9, 114–33, 141,
    143, 205, 251, 307n43, 313n30
on death, 115, 123–27
on différance. See différance
on metaphoricity, 355n32
on presence, 116–19, 324–25n31
on time, 115–19, 122–23, 173–74,
    312n20, 312n22, 312n23
Descartes, René, 6, 74, 98, 290n24,
    306n32, 337n12

descent
  birth as, 237
  into cave (Plato), 242, 255
desire, 155, 167–68
  Black, 309n67
  feminine, 248
  for presence, 119, 123
  in the *Timaeus*, 212
  psychoanalysis and, 250
  queer, 121
Deutscher, Penelope, 33, 47, 293n43
dichotomy. *See* binary; dualism
*différance*, 117–18, 131, 143
  woman as, 242
differentiation, 13, 58–59
  and becoming, 58
  ethical stakes of, 147–56
  pregnancy and, 234
  revolt and, 109
  *See also* alteration
Diotima, 259, 296n12
disappearance
  appearance and, 60, 94
  in memorial art, 106–08
  of embodiment in scientific
    discourse, 304n13
  of public realm, 360n10
  of time, 255, 294n49
disembodiment, 32, 81–82, 91, 238,
    298n31
  thought as, 93–95, 149, 304n14,
    353n15
  time and, 55, 65
dismemberment
  Cixous' conception of, 78–79
displacement, 73–82, 359n65
  *chōra* and, 213
  colonialism and, 40
  cyclicality and, 48–51
  in psychoanalysis, 95–96
  of temporal origin, 244, 258

of the political, 85
  revolt as, 87, 99–100
Douglass, Frederick, 103
dream, 211
  in psychoanalysis, 170, 173
  time and, 216
drive, 83, 88–94, 176, 320n1
  *chōra* and, 202–03
  semiotic, 195, 223
  time and, 43
  unconsciousness of, 164–69
  *See also* death drive
dualism, 122, 138
  form/matter, 242
  mind/body, 18, 139, 190, 225,
    282n25
  sex/gender, 64
  symbolic/semiotic, 232
  temporal, 34, 37
  *See also* binary
duration
  Bergsonian, 142
  Kristeva's conception of, 216, 230
dwelling, 54, 145, 166

*écriture féminine*, 81, 302n73,
    322n20
Edelman, Lee, 20, 296n8
*eidos. See* idea
emancipation, 36, 222, 266
  *See also* liberation
embodiment, 24–25, 225–30
  burden of, 15, 29, 56, 59, 91, 270,
    315n45
  female, 15, 31, 44, 59–60, 91, 149,
    290n21
  sexed, 63, 80, 168, 302n67
  trans, 64
  *See also* body; soma
encounter, 144, 153, 155, 159–70
end. *See* telos

engendering, 66, 80, 125, 128–32,
238–40, 245–46, 317n56,
346n21, 348n45
Enlightenment, 42, 164
idea of progress, 38–39, 265
epistemology, 116, 224, 326n34
erasure, 199
of beginning, 245
of mother, 197, 254
of sexuate difference, 39, 46
eschatology, 266, 307n43
essence
of woman, 50, 55
static, 50, 225
essentialism, 14, 293–94n49
in Irigaray, 50, 79, 160, 162
in Kristeva, 202, 231, 339n26,
343n5
eternal return, 60–61, 126–27
of the repressed, 89, 93–98, 206, 213
eternity, 117–22, 173, 179, 259,
317n56
yogic praxis and, 137–41
ethics
in Beauvoir, 29, 47, 71
in Levinas, 326n34
of temporal difference, 159–81
sexual difference and, 53–54, 69
Ettinger, Bracha L., 352n7
Eurocentrism, 16, 78, 82, 266
exclusion, 354n26
in Plato, 234
of the feminine, 76–77
of the other, 169
exile
from maternal body, 196
of poetry from Plato's city in
speech, 223
excess
femininity as, 260, 355n27
of logos, 354n15

Fanon, Frantz, 2, 11–12, 33, 267,
326n34, 359n4
Fausto-Sterling, Anne, 64, 294n49
fecundity, 54, 57, 66, 316n47
female embodiment. See embodiment
female subjectivity. See subjectivity
femininity, 55, 177–80, 265
maternity and, 187, 215, 217
finitude, 115, 123–33
embodied life as, 92, 238, 258,
270, 330n27, 346n21
infinite, 143
sensibility as, 23
flash, 214–30
flesh
flesh flash, 214–30
historiographical conception of, 20
word and, 230
fluid, 147
in Kristeva, 45
vs. solid, 81
flux
becoming as, 210
Heraclitean, 148
temporal, 141, 153, 207
foreigner
Kristeva's conception of, 40,
163–68
See also stranger
foreignness, 164–70
unequal distribution of, 169
forgetfulness, 11, 126, 150, 195–96
See also amnesia; oblivion
freedom, 24–25, 29–39, 71–72,
119–20, 266–73
Freeman, Elizabeth, 15, 19–20, 28,
31
Freire, Paulo, 91, 99, 112, 113–14,
124, 125, 129, 168
French feminism, 5–10, 277n5,
293n49

Freud, Sigmund, 167–81, 194, 258,
    265, 304n9, 322n20, 329n21
  Irigaray on, 236, 298n33, 324n30
  Kristeva on, 201–02, 287n9,
    347n28, 349n45
  on repetition compulsion, 335n66
  on the uncanny, 167–68, 178,
    330n25
  on time, 87, 94–95, 98, 167–80,
    332n40, 335n66. See also *Zeitlos*
fusion
  erotic love and, 153, 155, 352n4
  of mother and child, 233–35
future, 263–75
  anticipation of, 79, 130
  foreclosure of, 266–69
  linear time and, 31–38, 71–72,
    95–98, 273–75
  messianism and, 308n43
  unpredictability of, 45–46, 99–100,
    178, 269–73
  *See also* telos

Garner, Eric, 140
Gatens, Moira, 282n25
gender
  cis-, 18, 63, 167–68, 293n48,
    302n67
  roles, 23, 66, 189
  sex and, 10, 13–14, 63–64, 224,
    266, 282n25
  trouble, 64
  *See also* embodiment; sexual
    difference
genealogy
  female, 188–90, 249, 336n12
genesis (biblical), 188, 218, 246,
    271–72
  *See also* creation; creation myths
gestation, 197, 319n63, 344n10
god, 119–20, 317n56, 325n32
  disembodied, 90

Greek, 341n47
  Judeo-Christian, 128–29, 218,
    271–72
  *See also* demiurge
goddess, 194
gravity, 237–38, 353n15
Grosz, Elizabeth, 11, 14, 48, 57, 100,
    127, 212, 264, 277n5, 279n10,
    281n17, 292n38, 303n1, 304n10,
    346n22, 356n39
Guenther, Lisa, 129

Halberstam, Jack, 20, 296n8, 341n52
Hartman, Saidiya, 30, 264, 275
Hawthorne, Nathaniel, 124–25,
    315n41, 315n45
Hegel, G. W. F., 12, 32, 68, 74,
    116–17, 119, 172
  Heidegger's critique of, 311n12
Heidegger, Martin, 67–68, 114–19,
    130–33, 137, 145–46
heterogeneity, 45–50, 298n32
  loss of, 65
  originary status of, 235
  restoration of, 82, 92, 166
  Virgin Mary and, 349n45
heteronormativity
  in Irigaray, 66, 293n48, 296n8,
    319n63
  of motherhood, 196–97
  of time, 15–16, 18–20
history, 119–20
  alternate, 79
  American, 104–07
  deprivation of, 219–21
  time and/of, 30–44, 56–60
Hoffmann, E. T. A., 167
Holocaust memorial, 103, 108–09
hooks, bell, 33, 112, 153–54, 267,
    288n16
horizon, 119, 122
  of possibilities, 47–49, 56–57

of two, 150–51
of worlds, 67–69
Husserl, Edmund, 116, 321n14,
     325n31
*hystera*
     Plato's cave as, 191, 236–47, 256–57
     *See also* placental economy; womb

ideology, 47, 49
     feminism as, 42
     of presence, 120
     of whiteness, 83, 198
     socialist, 39
     teleology as, 47, 97
illusion
     art as, 75
     in Plato's cave, 78
     of natural past, 352n69
     of transcendence, 60, 149
immanence, 29–33, 59–73
     reduction to, 267, 288n12
     *See also under* time: cyclical time
immortality, 123–25, 137–40, 259,
     349n45
impropriety, 81, 164, 167, 169
indigenous, 13, 15, 16, 37, 62
individuation, 192–93
indeterminacy, 61, 176, 344n11
     *See also* between
infinity, 143
     negative, 143
     of finitude, 138
     positive, 124, 132, 149, 159
instrumentalization, 41, 43, 100,
     268–69
     *See also* appropriation; objectification
integration
     psychic, 96, 98, 176
     religious, 168
intelligible, 117, 239
     sensible vs., 206, 225, 242, 255,
     258–59

intersex, 64, 294n49
intersubjectivity, 93, 147–56, 160–70,
     319n60
     freedom and, 71
     revolt and, 86
     time and, 255
intimacy, 85–88, 94–101, 155, 163
     in difference, 69
     revolt and, 170, 173, 176, 180. *See
     also under* revolt: intimate
invisibility, 76–79
     of feminine origin, 127–28, 177,
     228
     of monument, 107
     of semiotic content, 219
     Plato's cave and, 243, 251
irony, 74
     in Butler, 124
     in Cixous, 78
     in Irigaray, 74, 78
irreducibility
     of difference, 12, 68, 71, 149, 163,
     146
     of female experience, 53
     of sexuate difference, 58, 160,
     296n12
     of time, 117, 213
     of twoness, 272

Jesus, 101, 317n56, 348n45
Jones, Rachel, 127, 236, 243, 39n31,
     353n11, 358n57
Joyce, James, 44

Kant, Immanuel, 171, 212, 219,
     287n7
     on teleology, 119
     on time, 6, 324n31
Klee, Paul, 120

Lacan, Jacques, 175, 201, 346n20

language, 20–25, 201–32
  Irigaray's critique of, 141–47
  See also *écriture féminine*
  See also *under* poetry: poetic
    language
Laplanche, Jean, 175, 334n58
laughter
  in Hawthorne, 315
  mimesis as, 74
  of the medusa, 78–79
Levinas, Emmanuel, 151, 315n47,
  326n34
liberation
  from *samsara*, 141
  in Beauvoir, 35–36, 186–87, 267
  of Auschwitz, 108
  refusal of, 231
  women's, 90
  See also emancipation; freedom
life
  biological, 60
  finite, 129, 132, 138, 172
  time of, 128, 137–40, 150, 152,
  154
  See also biological; *bios*; *zoē*
limit
  body as, 226
  finitude and, 124–25, 129, 168,
  314n31
  in the *Timaeus*, 207, 211
  of human life, 60
  of the thinkable, 101, 212
  space as, 286n5
  woman as, 56
linearity
  cyclicality and, 23, 87
  disruption of, 18
  logic of, 255–58
  male, 176
  of Hegelian synthesis, 217
  of language, 82, 143

progress and, 95, 97–101
  See also *under* time: linear time
lips
  duality of (in Irigaray), 80–81
  speech and, 162
logocentrism. See phallogocentrism
logos
  as origin, 244–45
  in the *Republic*, 240, 344n15
  in the *Timaeus*, 211
  masculine, 233
  phallus and, 200
  *phusis* and, 65
  the vocal and, 310n2, 323n22
Lorde, Audre, 267–68
loss
  for words, 253
  memorial art and, 103–05
  of symbolic function, 351n59
  of the body, 65
  of the mother, 180, 190–06,
  228, 235–36, 245–46, 341n48,
  357n45
  of time, 254
love, 147–56, 163, 274
  of wisdom, 100
Lugones, María, 17, 284n45

masculinity
  cogito and, 149
  of the subject, 268
  perspective, 32
  time and, 18, 34, 41, 56
materialism, 190, 214, 314n45,
  338n22
materiality, 60, 87, 128, 185, 190,
  196, 214–15
maternal, 55–58, 185–260
  beginnings, 126, 128, 206–14, 229,
  233, 236–46
  body. See *under* body

origins, 191–93, 215–16, 246–54.
See also under *archē*; origin
subjectivity. *See under* subjectivity
matricide, 45, 190, 192–96
in Plato, 235, 239, 252
Irigaray on, 190–96, 235, 239, 252,
260
Kristeva on, 190–96, 228, 235,
356n39
matter, 196, 203–06, 208–09, 214,
228, 239–42
Aristotelian, 354n18
form and, 145, 212, 254
McAfee, Noëlle, 92–93, 343n7
mechanical
culture, 65
reproduction, 61, 75
melancholia, 102, 341n49
Memmi, Albert, 40, 292n35
memory, 40, 107–08, 167, 196
repressed, 174
work of, 54, 95
See also anamnesis; recollection
Messianism, 101, 307n43
metaphysics
critique of, 115–06, 121
of presence, 120–32, 148–54, 173
See also absence
metapsychology, 171, 177–78,
332n40
midwifery, 216, 237–38, 348n40
Mignolo, Walter, 16–17, 281n14,
290n24
mimesis, 37, 73–82, 302n71
in Aristotle, 300n75
in Irigaray, 74–83, 238, 301n66
in Plato, 300n41, 300n42
technological, 238
mind, 148, 180, 225, 229
body and, 89, 139, 156, 190, 198,
225, 32n6

life of the, 86, 92
See also psyche; soul
See also under dualism: mind/body
Miller, Elaine P., 7, 77, 103–04, 106,
281n13
mirror, 70–71, 246–48
in Plato, 241, 243
stage, 220
See also speculum
*Mitsein*. See under being: with
modernity, 11–12, 16–18, 55, 59,
61–62, 98, 269
Mohanty, Chandra Talpade, 18
morphology, 354n21
of gender, 81, 297n14
mortality. See death; finitude
motherhood
Black, 198
coloniality and, 196–99
feminism and, 186–92, 215
in Plato, 202–14, 236–46
Irigaray on, 233–61
Kristeva on, 201–31
matricide and, 192–96
mother earth, 148, 196
origin and, 185–99
temporality and, 126, 128, 206–14,
229, 233, 236–46
See also maternal; matricide
See also under Beauvoir: motherhood
mourning, 196
Blackness and, 168
for the mother, 191
movement
of *chōra*, 202–14
of return, 53–82
See also activity; progress
multiplicity, 121, 226, 272
Muñoz, José Esteban, 19
mystery, 90
of the other, 154, 161

mystery (*continued*)
  sexual difference and, 69, 72

*Nachträglichkeit*, 102, 175, 205,
    334n58, 334n62
  *See also under* action: deferred
narcissism
  primary, 177, 215, 216
  secondary, 177
narrative
  Holocaust and, 108
  linearity of, 302n73
  logic and, 173
  of the body, 40–41, 297n25
  queer, 19
  trans, 291n29
natality, 115, 132, 129–32, 272. *See*
    *also* birth
nature, 61–67, 72–76
  time and, 29–51
  culture and, 64, 67, 76, 138, 224,
    226
  See also *phusis*
navel, 196, 341n47
necessity, 204, 206–07, 271, 344n11
  women as bearers of, 29, 59–60
negativity
  death and, 115, 127, 132
  death drive and, 179
  function of, 99
  Hegelian, 178
  Kristeva's conception of, 221, 222,
    351n59
  moment of, 129
  reduction of woman to, 346n20
Nietzsche, Friedrich, 12, 174
Nikolchina, Miglena, 195, 200,
    338n13, 356n39
non-binary, 110, 197, 351n67
nostalgia, 198–99, 336n10
not-yet, 9, 46–47, 93, 117
noun, 144

novelty, 31, 46–51, 98, 193, 265–75
  change and, 21, 66

object, 142–46, 149–56
  sensible, 75
objectification, 29, 38, 55–56
  *See also* appropriation;
    instrumentalization
oblivion, 144, 194, 217
  *See also* amnesia; forgetfulness
Oliver, Kelly, 96, 101, 350n57, 351n67
oneness, 150, 155, 235
  *See also* sameness
ontology, 12, 117–18, 210, 260
  of becoming, 148–50, 282n26
  of difference, 148
  of time, 116–21, 148–50
  relational, 121, 234
opening
  *chōra* as, 207
  of Plato's cave, 239
  sexual difference as, 168, 273
  woman as, 81
oppression, 24–25, 33, 38, 31, 91,
    289n20
  racial, 104
origin, 246–54
  linear time and, 126–29
  loss of, 192–96
  singular, 58–59, 221, 250
  See also *archē*; beginning
  *See also under* maternal: origins
Ortega, Mariana, 291n26
oscillation, 154–55, 213, 227–28
  *See also* rhythm; vibration
otherness, 68, 78, 147–48, 164–65,
    234, 328n15, 330n26, 339n31
  *See also* alterity; strangeness

passivity
  maternal, 354n18
  of matter, 214

of woman, 29–32, 55, 195
See also *chōra*
past, 183–261
as beginning and/or origin, 246–54
as dynamic process, 43, 51, 90–91,
332n40
birth and, 274, 314n31, 317n58.
See also birth; maternal
beginnings; natality
*chōra* and, 202–14
maternal body and, 185–99
memory/memorialization and,
101–09
motherhood and, 201–30, 254–60,
339n23
prime mover and, 61
repetition of, 76, 108–09, 312n19,
335n66. See also repetition;
sameness
repression of, 126, 177, 193–95,
240–42, 248–55
See also anamnesis; birth; matricide;
return
paternal
god, 346n20
in the *Timaeus*, 202–14
law, 35, 211, 213, 222–23
symbolic, 192
performativity, 79–80, 355n33
See also under Butler:
performativity
permanence, 40, 60
perversion, 240, 354n20
phallic, 19, 250, 255, 257
power, 216
temporality, 274
phallogocentrism, 156, 242, 244
*phusis*, 65, 68, 146
See also nature
placental economy, 233–35, 259,
337n12
See also *hystera*; womb

Plato
Irigaray on, 75, 78, 80, 127, 155,
191, 235–61, 312n19, 353n15,
354n18
Kristeva on, 163–64, 191, 202–14,
344n10
midwifery in. See under Socrates:
midwifery
mimesis in, 75, 147, 300n41,
300n42. See also mimesis
*Republic*, 235–46, 328n17, 330n28,
353n14, 353n15
soul, conception of, 328n16
*Symposium*, 155, 163, 259, 296n12,
341n27
*Timaeus*, 191, 202–14, 229–32,
259, 342n3, 344n11, 345n17,
354n18
Platonism, 210, 236, 353n15
pleasure principle, 171, 174, 305n29
plurality. See multiplicity
poetry, 141–47
Irigaray on, 57, 81, 145–47,
340n44
Kristeva on, 81–82, 88–90, 94,
146–47, 192, 195, 205–06,
220–23, 274, 338n21, 344n15
Plato on, 75, 212, 223
poetic language, 76, 88–90, 192,
195, 205–06, 222–23, 251
poetic strategy, 75
poetic style, 75
See also under art: poetic
composition
*polis*, 165, 271, 353n14
See also public
power, 42, 91, 188, 201
dynamics of, 3, 99, 179, 292n35
maternal, 216–17
See also creation; engendering
praxis
artistic, 101–09

praxis *(continued)*
  love as, 147–56
  of breath, 136–41
  poetic, 141–47
  yogic, 136–41
precariousness, 331n31
  *See also* vulnerability
precarity, 169, 331n31
presence
  co-presence, 71, 147–51, 153–57,
    166, 169, 179
  eternal/everlasting, 123, 258–59
  metaphysics of. *See under*
    metaphysics
  selfsame, 132, 125, 127, 130,
    148–49
present, 111–57
  as present, 118, 174, 314n31
  in its unfolding, 96, 119, 136,
    142–44, 153, 311n14
  living, 8–9, 43, 65, 136, 140–44,
    150–52, 216
  metaphysical/static, 116–23
  practices of the, 135–57
  relationality and the, 147–56,
    160–70
prime mover, 61
private, 31, 254, 269, 271
privilege
  of the present, 116, 118
  of the semiotic, 219
  of whiteness, 11, 15, 36, 91, 197,
    168, 289n20
progress, 16–17, 38–42, 95, 97–101,
    265
propriety, 144–47, 160–64, 167, 169
Proust, Marcel, 87, 163, 216, 248
  on memory, 102
psyche, 165, 10, 172, 329n18, 342n56
  female, 35
  psychic life, 92–95, 109
  psychic space, 100, 203

vs. soma, 43, 46, 169
  *See also* mind; soul
psychoanalysis, 85–101, 162–66,
    171–80, 234, 274
  ethics of, 166–68
  Irigaray's critique of, 94, 277n5,
    340n44, 351n66
public, 31, 85, 269–70
  See also *polis*

queer, 15–16, 18–20, 62–66, 91, 197,
    267
  desire, 121
  theory, 9, 15, 19, 33
Quijano, Aníbal, 16–18

race, 15–18, 33, 79, 82, 170, 266–68,
    309n67
racial difference, 15–18, 110, 121,
    132, 137, 275, 320n67
racism, 78–79, 106, 170, 198, 290n22
Rancière, Jacques, 107
rebirth, 95–98, 101, 139–41, 176, 274
  love as, 153
  *See also* renewal
receptacle
  *chōra* as, 202–14, 231
  mother as, 238, 244, 251, 254
reciprocity, 144, 153–54, 168
recollection, 86, 252
  *See also* anamnesis; memory
recovery, 11, 190
reincarnation, 256, 314n31
re-membering, 76–78, 82, 101–09
renewal, 57, 61, 64–66, 74–75, 77,
    87, 101, 103, 176, 186, 217, 274
  psychoanalysis and, 95–97
  *See also* rebirth
repetition
  as fate of woman, 31, 36–38, 76–78
  compulsion to, 175, 334n62
  nature and, 36–38, 60–63, 76

of the past, 76, 108–09. *See also* past
of the same, 51, 56, 140, 155, 246
representation, 215, 241–46, 248–49,
    255–57
  mimetic, 75
repression
  of beginning, 126, 177, 193–95,
    240–42, 248–55
  of corporeal registers, 32–36
  of memory, 167
  psychoanalysis and, 77–79, 89–93
reproduction, 214–15, 224
  production and, 244, 157
  racial dimensions of, 198
  realm of, 186–87
  women as upholders of, 31–32, 59
  *See also* copy; mimesis
retroactive, 175
return
  movement of, 53–82
  of the repressed, 76–79, 89, 93–98,
    103–05, 206, 213. *See also*
    eternal return
  revolt as, 88–94. *See also* revolt
  to beginnings, 189, 191. *See also*
    beginnings
  to the body, 22, 88–94. *See also*
    body
  to the maternal, 185–99. *See also*
    maternal; motherhood
revolt
  culture of, 100–01, 105
  cyclicality and, 38, 49, 87
  intimate, 85–101
  Kristeva on, 77, 85–88, 94–101
  revolution and, 86–88, 97–102
rhythm
  cyclical, 55, 139
  natural, 61, 145–46, 257
  of breath, 136–41
  temporal, 45
  *See also* oscillation; vibration

Rich, Adrienne, 184, 238
Rose, Jacqueline, 219, 344n10

sacrifice, 44, 62
  foundational, 88–90
  of the body, 136–37
  of the earth's fertility, 217
  of the future, 120
Said, Edward, 357n46
sameness, 147–56, 224
  culture of, 50, 53–54, 59, 66,
    73–74, 80, 130, 147–48, 153,
    295n2
  logic of, 37, 54, 62, 80, 116, 129,
    137, 144, 148–50
  *See also* oneness
Sartre, Jean-Paul, 72, 303n5, 313n25,
    317n58
  on transcendence, 16
selfhood, 160–63, 331n31
  fragmented, 108
  relational, 151–56, 160–63
  sexed, 63–67
  unified, 162, 165
  *See also* subjectivity
semiotic, 46–47, 89–92, 108–09,
    218–30
  *chōra*, 190, 201–32
sensible
  in Plato, 75, 80, 239, 258–59,
    300n41, 354n19
  objects, 75
  realm of the, 23, 68, 75, 117, 239
  transcendental, 139, 147
  vs. intelligible, 206, 225, 242, 255,
    258–59
sex
  biological, 54, 57, 64, 66, 286n6,
    294n49. *See also under* biology:
    sexual difference
  legal, 40, 285n60
  vs. gender. *See* gender

sex (continued)
  See also embodiment; gender;
    intersex; sexual difference
sexual difference
  beyond the binary, 22, 69, 226,
    298n29. See also intersex; trans
  binary, 24
  biology and. See under biology:
    sexual difference; and sex:
    biological
  embodiment and. See under body
  essentialism and, 50, 294n49. See
    also essentialism
  futurity and, 273
  in Irigaray, 39, 46–48, 63–73,
    127–28, 150–52, 168, 293n48,
    295n2, 323n28
  in Kristeva, 47–49, 88, 91, 164,
    285n60
  reproduction and, 296n12
  time/temporal change and, 45–50,
    55–59, 74–76, 80–83, 141,
    148–52, 321n14
  vs. sexuate difference, 22–23,
    293n41, 296n8
sexual division of temporal labor,
    33–38, 51, 54, 5, 59, 73, 90,
    131, 149
sexuality, 39, 55, 266, 193n41
sexuate difference. See sexual
    difference
shadow
  in Kara Walker's art, 77–78
  in Plato, 237
  woman as, 253
Shalev-Gerz, Esther, 106–09
silence, 75, 108, 210, 338n13
  silencing of woman, 5, 11, 128,
    338n13
singularity, 35, 42–43, 91–92, 139
  love and, 153
  of origin, 172–73

  of the body, 22–23
  See also uniqueness
social media, 3–5
Socrates, 207, 212, 242, 253–56, 259
  as midwife, 216, 238, 348n40,
    353n14
  on self-knowledge, 161, 165
  See also Plato
soma, 88–90, 94, 98, 169
  vs. semiotic, 43, 46
  See also body; embodiment
soul, 88–94, 125, 127, 165, 225
  maladies of the, 93–94, 102
  See also mind; psyche
sovereignty, 121, 130, 160–62,
    165–66, 226, 270
spatiotemporal, 54, 209, 229
Spade, Dean, 39, 64, 291n29
spatiality, 34, 206, 208
speculum, 240, 246–48, 253
speech, 92–94, 141–45
  city in, 207
  Diotima's, 259, 296n12
Spinoza, Baruch, 73
Spivak, Gayatri Chakravorti, 16, 343n5
stability, 40
  fantasy of, 260
  of the mother, 349n45
stasis, 7, 90, 153
Stone, Alison, 175, 180, 191, 285n60,
    294n49, 319n60, 339n23
strangeness, 163–70
  internal, 328n13
  See also alterity; otherness
stranger, 163–70
  to oneself, 270
  See also foreigner
subjectivity
  female, 11, 34, 35–37, 51, 62, 187,
    248–49, 288n9, 290n23
  male, 44, 55–56, 69–70, 143,
    148–49, 253

subject formation, 13, 90, 192–93, 234–35, 330n25
subject-in-process (*sujet en procès*), 44, 166, 226
transcendental, 6, 81, 149, 154, 161, 324n31
*See also* selfhood
sublimation, 77–78, 300n48
as sublation/appropriation, 215–16, 237
subversion, 206, 222
surrogacy, 197
survival, 222
of the social, 90
of the species, 30–31, 50, 57, 92, 296n8
suspension, 98, 266–68
symbolic, 144, 192–95, 201–03, 206, 211–30, 303n75, 304n12, 339n26
symbolic order, 76–77, 88–90, 192, 195, 233–35, 250, 274–75

teleology
disruption of, 178
linear time and, 48, 89, 191
progress and, 38–42, 100–01
*telos*, 58, 62
of history, 109, 120, 307n43
trans bodies and, 297n25
temporality. *See* time
TERF, 197
thanatology, 178
thetic, 82, 195, 220–21, 234, 303n75, 350n58, 359n65
Timaeus (character), 211–12, 229, 347n33
*See also* Plato
time
authentic, 118
cyclical, 29–51, 59–63, 73, 93, 104, 109, 136

linear, 29–51, 55–76, 87–89, 104, 109, 113–20, 127–30, 173–80, 265–75
lost, 87, 172–73, 218, 254
of life, 128, 137–40, 150, 152, 154
ontology of, 116–21, 148–50
regimes of, 15–17, 64, 231
revolutionary, 12–18, 27–110, 51, 58, 88–94, 99, 104, 258–59, 266–73
spacing of, 154, 313n30
the body and, 185–99
time-space, 206, 347n34
vulgar, 118, 174
timelessness, 170–80, 146, 246, 254–58, 318n58, 332n40
of woman, 55–56
See also *Zeitlos*
to-come (*à-venir*), 53, 86, 93, 273
totalitarianism, 39, 42, 97–98, 100
trace, 205, 313n30, 325n31
*différance* as, 118, 128, 132
maternal, 192
semiotic, 274
woman as, 242
tragedy, 164, 358n59
trans, 39–41, 64, 69, 226, 267, 341n52
temporalities, 19, 40
transcendence, 23–25, 29–38, 59–73, 148–53, 288n12
freedom and, 94, 187, 267, 270–71
transference, 95, 274, 333n53, 335n66
transformation. *See* alteration; change
transgression, 95, 220–21
trauma, 102, 139–40, 275
in psychoanalysis, 95–96
Truth, Sojourner, 309n67

uncanny, 167–69, 178–80
*See also under* Freud: on the uncanny
unconscious, 164–68, 170–80, 210–11, 258

universality, 138
  of foreignness, 168–69
uniqueness, 310n2, 319n62, 323n22
  of Black motherhood, 198
  of the mother, 342n56
  See also singularity
unpredictability, 269–73
unspeakability, 77, 212, 219

variation. See alteration; change;
  heterogeneity
vegetal, 138, 295n2
verb, 141–45
vibration, 209
  See also oscillation; rhythm
violence, 92, 127, 269–70, 275
  colonial, 62
  cycle of, 42, 98
  sexual, 3
  white supremacist, 106, 198
virginity, 349
Virgin Mary, 198, 215, 218, 231, 313n30
  See also mother; maternity
visibility
  as feminist praxis, 77–79
  in the Timaeus, 203
  making-visible, 128, 275
  monumentality and, 106–07
  of affect, 83
vulnerability
  human condition of, 123, 131, 275
  in Arendt, 307n39
  in Butler, 124, 331n31
  temporal determination and, 124,
    270
  See also precariousness

Walker, Kara, 77–79, 82–83, 105–
  106, 309n64, 309n67
waves
  feminist, 44–45
  in Kristeva's "Womens Time,"
    34–43, 49

of paradox (in Plato), 353n14
Whitford, Margaret, 241–42, 254,
  353n14, 357n46
wholeness
  Aristophanic conception of,
    341n47, 352n4
  originary conception of, 150,
    155
  vs. difference, 235
woman
  as passive, 55, 70, 195
  Beauvoir's conception of, 29–34
  definition of, 290n21
  feminist conceptions of, 41–42
  historical conception of, 7
  reduction of, 23, 46, 55, 69,
    109, 189, 215, 249, 322n20,
    358n55
  See also maternal; motherhood
  See also under embodiment: female
womb, 196, 233–44, 247–52, 255–
  60
  as tomb, 193, 238, 240
  See also hystera; placental economy
Woolf, Virginia, 286n1, 322n20,
  338n13
word
  as beginning, 213–14
  as symbol, 195
  author's use of, 20–25
  flesh and, 216–18, 230
  silence between, 108–09
  vs. act, 140, 143

yoga, 136–41

Zeitlos, 170–81
  Derrida on the, 173, 177
  scandal of the, 170
  See also timelessness
Zeus, 163, 341n47
Ziarek, Ewa Płonowska, 55, 295n5
zoē, 60